VISIONS

A Faith Inspired Journey of The Human Spirit

Janie P. Bess

Oct 7, 2020

Happy Reading!

Janie P. Bess

urlink
PRINT & MEDIA

URLink Print and Media
Cheyenne, Wyoming

First originally published by URLink Print and Media. 2018

ISBN 978-1-64367-020-1 (Paperback)
ISBN 978-1-64367-022-5 (Digital)

Printed in the United States of America

DEDICATION

I n memory of "Mother"(Johnnie Partee Lightfoot Prather) who taught me so much through her undying love for God, her family and friends.

Thank you to my late father, Reverend Calvin Lightfoot Sr., and his late wife, Louise for the love and guidance you gave me down through the years. And dedicated to my big sister, Sydney, who taught me about life through her own experiences, and who was my constant angel advising and protecting me. And to my other sister Earlie, who taught me the joys of being a true entrepreneur.

I dedicate this story to my dearest husband, David. Thanks for believing in me. I truly thank God for you. You are my hero! With patience and perseverance you supported my writing career financially as well as spiritually, allowing me to write freely. Thank you for all your love and support. You are my" Honey Do". Thanks for the time you spent cooking meals, running errands, being a mother and a father when I was away at writers conferences and meetings. You made sure I didn't have to work and I appreciate the many times you spent alone while I worked on my manuscript. For this I am truly grateful for your understanding and faithfulness.

To my children and loved ones. I hope this book will help you understand and really know your family. I want to thank my oldest son, David Jr. who unknowingly taught me to never give up. Through his own determination and stamina for life itself I learned persistence does pay.

I want to personally acknowledge my only daughter, Terri, who supported me, made lunches for my writers' group meetings, ran errands, assisted me at the Writers Resource Center conference, and chauffeuring me when I needed to see an agent 150 miles away. You have been my secretary, chef, promoter, and supporter.

To Tony who so patiently listened during many reading sessions.

Heartfelt appreciation to Arline Chase, my first writing teacher from Writers Digest.

Special thanks to Betty Cozart. Lula Mathis and Virginia Bryant for their encouragement and support. I just have to thank my dear friends, Gloria Coleman and her daughter, Amy for working with me on my chapter revisions. George Cager, Bobby Watts, Jarvis Grays, and the whole Travis retiree bunch for helping me learn how to use the internet and website.

Also to Catherine Armstrong, Ruth McClanahan, Maria Burrrows, Willa Dean Ingram, Ruth Cager and Charlene Stevens, who took the time to read my manuscripts.

Thanks also to Eileen Mills, The "Clean Up Woman" for keeping my home neat and orderly so I could concentrate. You're my angel!

To all the members of the Writers Resource Center for their love and support.

Thanks for having faith in me.

I am running out of space so to all those family members and friends I didn't mention, thank you for your faith and support.

CHAPTER ONE

We came from Batesville, Miss., shortly after my grandmother died. I believe it was late 1945 when the Southern Pacific train on which we traveled stopped in West Oakland, Calif. Mother, my sisters Flordnette, Sydney and Earlie, and I, Janie, had traveled through the Deep South westward for two days and I was tired, but my face lit up when I saw my daddy again. Daddy had left us a week earlier. With our mother's brother and her brother-in-law, Daddy had scouted out a place for us to live in our new hometown. I imagine we made quite a sight walking, sometimes single file, as he led us to a big, old, brown, wooden tenement house nearby.

I was fascinated by everything I saw in the clean, well-lit city but nothing peaked my curiosity as much as the beautiful young women who seemed to be everywhere. With the gap-mouthed stare of a little country girl, I marveled at the bright red, blue and yellow dresses, the jewelry and shiny Marcelled-waved hair in colors I never seen on black women. They were the ladies of the night in their glittery sexy dresses parading up and down Seventh Street. I stared at them admiring their flirty, smiling faces and they returned my smile.

"Them women are Jezebels," Daddy said. "Don't look at them!" Daddy grabbed my croaker sack and threw it over his shoulder. He then picked me up and carried me down the long block with Mother, Flordnette, Sydney and Earlie in tow.

We walked right by the town drunks loitering near their favorite spots. A small liquor store stood on the corner of Seventh and Wood streets. We stopped in front of a large Victorian-style home.

"This is it," Daddy said, your new home in California."

My first impression was of stairs, lots of stairs. We traveled up one flight to reach a landing and then went up another flight. With all the colorful Victorian homes in the Bay Area, our new home was a natural wood stain, but from the outside it gave a nice impression.

Inside we had one large room. My father had stocked the communal kitchen with cereal and milk and other foods in anticipation of our arrival. The food was gone before we arrived.

The first night was frighteningly noisy. The streetwalkers were constantly fighting, battling for their territory. I remember sailors in their wide bell-bottom pants and soldiers in green uniforms frequenting the rooms at all hours of the night. One time a soldier attacked a tall beautiful woman. She beat him senseless. Sisters didn't take any smack from them.

After only seven days, we moved. Our dad woke us up in the middle of the night. He said he couldn't have "his chil'ren listening to those winos cussing." He "didn't want his girls watching the Jezebels with their bright red painted lips parading round all night with no clothes on." They were constantly fighting one another battling for their territory on the streets. Mother grabbed up our meager belongings and dumped them into her old family trunk with her big holy Bible and family portraits. Daddy and Mother rushed us across the street to another place with several rooms in it.

We passed the white police officers with their night sticks beating up on the winos. The women who loudly protested were hustled right along with the town drunks into a big black van with flashing lights.

The proprietress of our new home was a big, dark-skinned Negro woman. A long deep slash on her cheek was the mark of an abused woman. Her husband cut her with a butcher knife when she caught him with another woman in their bed, according to rumors. I heard them gossiping that she looked good compared to what she did to him in retaliation. A neighbor said he stayed drunk and limped when he walked from that beating.

She started preaching after that. I saw her on Sunday mornings in her black robe carrying her Bible preaching as she walked the streets.

She talked to the sinners, backsliders, hypocrites, and whoremongers who hung out on the corner of Seventh and Wood streets. She waved her Bible in the air as she called all sinners to Christ.

"You should be in the house of the Lord praising His name," she yelled.

Her sermons were loud and clear.

I was confused because just the night before, the cops broke into her apartment to arrest her. She had beaten her husband so badly with his own wine bottle he couldn't see. The blood was running all down into his eyes. She cussed like a sailor one minute and preached about God the next. Her tall, skinny husband stumbled out the door, slumping over the staircase on the second-story landing in the hallway. He was clutching a blood-soaked handkerchief to his forehead. Boy, I was scared of that woman. I was so happy when we moved.

We moved several times in the next few years. At this one house, the landlord's German shepherd was in the backyard where I always played. He was friendly with me. It was my fourth birthday. I had a new dress and my hair was so pretty. Mother was having a party for me. Mother put the cake in the oven to bake. Then she made the frosting. While waiting for the cake, she hung clothes on the old line upstairs on the back porch as I played alone in the grass within view. The giant dog approached me slowly with his head down and his fur standing on end. He looked like a mean wolf as he leaped on me, pinning me down to the ground. I screamed loudly. I heard my mother's piercing cries over my own pleas for help. On the way back from the store with birthday candles, my daddy heard my mother's cries and the dog's mauling. Daddy, a short, stout man, jumped a tall fence, grabbed the dog from behind and pulled it off me. He pummeled that dog with his fists before slamming him down on the ground. Daddy twisted that dog's neck until his growling changed into a mere whimper.

The old fat Negro proprietress came out just in time.

"What you doing to Shep?" she yelled.

"Hey, woman, can't you see your dog Shep just attacked my daughter! Look at her!"

Quickly grabbing me up from the ground, he cradled me in his big, strong arms. He ran around the corner to a doctor's office nearby. The doctor stitched the wounds under my left eye and lip. She was mighty lucky, he just missed her eye," the doctor said. "An inch more, she would have lost it."

My daddy got down on his knees right there in that doctor's office.

"Thank you, Lord," he said. Unashamed, Daddy cried out, "Lord, please have mercy! I brought my children from Mississippi for a better life. Lord, we need you now. I don't have no money right now to pay this doctor but you said, whatever you ask, and it shall be given unto you. I'm asking you to help us, Lord."

I hugged my father.

"Don't cry Daddy. God hears you."

Daddy shook his head as he looked at the thick, blue thread that held my wounds closed.

"Mr. Lightfoot, I know you are a Christian," the doctor said. "You can pay me whenever you can. Don't you worry about it now." He hugged my daddy, gave him instructions on how to care for me, and then escorted us out the front door.

As we walked home, we passed the street people who stared curiously at us. My dress was bloody and torn. My face was swollen and slightly disfigured. Daddy told them as he made his way, "That dog bit my baby." Fresh tears streamed down his face as he carried me back down that long block home.

"Don't cry, Daddy. I'm all right."

When Daddy and I returned home, Mother removed my bloody clothing and gave me a hot bath. She applied her homemade salve on my wounds. It smelled like chocolate. She told me it was cocoa butter.

"I mixed it with some roots I brought with me from Mississippi."

Daddy went out for a long walk. When he came back, he was determined.

"I found a new place," he said. "We are moving tomorrow. That landlady was furious 'cause her dog is in quarantine at the pound now." We moved the next day.

It was 1949. We moved to Berkeley after living in West Oakland for three long years. It was a mixed neighborhood with different economic backgrounds. Our property owners were Negro. They lived at 1316 Harmon in a big two-story house with a real basement. The back steps from their three-bedroom house were right in the front of our door. They even had a garage for their shiny new car. They had one daughter who was about five years younger than I.

I went upstairs to play and read books to her daily. I sang the latest Gospel hymns we sang at church to her. Our families grew very close. We lived in a small two-bedroom flat in the rear. Daddy parked our car in a gravel driveway right up close to our door. About five steps led up to the wooden porch. The kitchen was smack inside the door with a worn-out hardwood floor my mother scrubbed and waxed until it sparkled clean.

To the left of the open door of my parents' small bedroom, stood an old-fashioned Wedgewood gas stove with the black cast-iron top and lift-out burners. It was truly an art to light it. Mother took the burners out with an old black handle that fit into a groove. She then lit the stove by twisting a piece of a newspaper with a lit match. She promptly replaced the round lid covering the burners to avoid injury. In the center of the room was an old large wooden table with six mix-match ladder-back chairs. To the right was my parents' bedroom where I usually ended up sleeping during the middle of the night. Their double bed filled up the master bedroom. My parents gave us the largest bedroom for obvious reasons. It was conveniently close to the bathroom. I shared a small twin bed with my sister, Earlie.

I had nightly "accidents" without fail. My mother would get up, give me a spanking then a quick bath, and change our sheets. It was worth it, because I always ended up sleeping between my parents. Earlie slept so hard she would sleep right through it. The only thing that would wake her was when I peed on her. My daddy said it served her right for scaring me. I was afraid to go to the bathroom. Sydney and Earlie had me so scared of the dark I was afraid to get out the bed at night. They told me, "That Boogie Man's gonna' get you." At 2 a.m., that small 9-by-12, darkened bedroom seemed at least a mile away from the bathroom. When you are a scared 6-year-old, you have only two choices: Take your chances with the Boogie Man or try to hold it until morning. I took my chance. I tried to hold it. Very few times did I make it. The problem was, I slept so hard I only woke up after my chronic "toilet" dream. In my dream, I was always sitting on the toilet seat relieving myself. I felt comforting warmth and then suddenly it would turn cold! Earlie always woke up wet and mad, too.

"Daddy, Janie peed on me again," she'd yell.

We lived in that little house from the first grade at Lincoln Elementary School until I finished eighth grade at Burbank Junior High. That was when we could finally afford to rent a nice house. When we moved to Burnett Street, I thought we had a mansion. We had a large living room, three bedrooms, a decent kitchen with a real stove and a nice big bathroom. I thought we had struck gold or something!

My father was raised by his grandmother, a holy roller of the Pentecostal Faith. That was why he was so strict with us.

My father would sit us on his knee and tell us Bible stories. My favorite was about David and Goliath. I also liked the one about Joseph and his 12 brothers. Of course, he would always have stories to tell about his life in the South. He told the same stories, repeatedly.

He told his stories in bits and pieces because my Mother always interrupted. He never had a chance to finish them.

"Lightfoot, oh, Lightfoot," she'd say. "Don't nobody want to hear that again!"

Sometimes he would say, "OK, Johnnie, all right, Mother." I felt his disappointment even though he tried his best to hide the hurt. But the sad look in his eyes gave him away.

One time I helped my father. He actually got a chance to finish telling his story. My sisters were busy in the kitchen helping Mother cook dinner. Daddy was attempting to tell me the story about his sad life as a young boy. He had attempted several other times to tell us why he was an orphan. Mother started in on him again. I saw that hurt look on his face. I was sitting on his knee.

"Excuse me," I interrupted her. "Daddy, finish telling me about your life as a boy." I was so anxious to know about my family. I was the only one.

Earlie and Sydney rolled their eyes at me. Earlie looked so mean to me, as if to say, "We will tend to you later."

Daddy was so engrossed in his story he didn't have a clue what was happening. He dove into his story about his life, ignoring Mother's disdainful looks. For the first time, I learned why I didn't have any grandparents like my friends. I always felt left out when they talked about their summer vacation with their grandparents.

"What happened to my grandparents? Why don't we have grandparents like all of our friends?"

"Baby, they didn't live long enough. My father, he died when I was just a boy." He wiped his eyes with his handkerchief. It was once white but now was stained with sweat and tears.

"His name was James Lightfoot. He was a dark-skinned, good-lookin' man. Now, he was a tall, heavy built man. He was over six feet tall. You see, I got my color from my mother; she was very short and light and I am short like she was, too! Now, Henry was my grandfather. He was my father's father. He was half Cherokee and half Mandingo—that's African blood— Mandingo and Cherokee. He was a dark red-skinned man, tall and handsome, too. They say I smile just like him!" Daddy's mischievous eyes shined like black marbles. He talked excitedly while he explained his bloodline.

"Henry's wife, Mary Louise, was full-blooded Cherokee. My mother, Parthenia, was full-bloodied Cherokee. Her black hair was straight and silky. It was so long until she could actually sit on it! When she stood up, it touched the floor!" Daddy had gotten out of his seat and was standing up now. "Now Parthenia's mother was Creole. That's French, Spanish, Cherokee Indian, and Negro blood all in one. Full-blooded Creole."

Mother interrupted again.

"Oh, Lightfoot, Calvin Lightfoot, nobody wants to hear you talk about your family."

His eyes were so expressive as he smiled, but he didn't say a word.

"You get all emotional, then you start that crying and, and…"

I cut in.

"Daddy, I do! I want to hear about your family. Please go ahead."

My sisters rolled their eyes at one another and then gave me another dirty look. Daddy continued.

"My mother was Creole! She was light-skinned with long wavy hair. Ooh, whee, she was pretty! She was a quarter Crete Indian, half French, and a quarter Cherokee. James met Parthenia. That was my mother, Parthenia Kaiser. She was from New Orleans. He kidnapped her from the French Quarter and took her to Mississippi. She married him as soon as they got there.

"He brought her back to Mississippi, to Batesville, that's where I was born. Yes, sir! I was their only child. She never had any more children. I was an orphan at 8 years old.

"That's when God called me! I knew I was going to preach! My grandmother on my daddy's side raised me because my mother was fatally stabbed by a jealous female. It was a case of mistaken identity. She was trying to hide her friend from this crazy woman. Her friend had been sneakin' around with this married man. And his wife found out about it! The woman chased her. She managed to lose her for a minute. She came running into my mother's house. 'Help me, this woman is trying to kill me. She got a knife! Hide me please!' My mother hid her under the bed. I ran under the kitchen table. I saw the whole thing! That jealous woman burst through he door. She was crazy. I still can see her bloodshot eyes. She chased Parthenia around the house with a knife calling her out her name. She mistook her for the adulteress."

Daddy started running, demonstrating how his mother ran from the woman. I saw the woman chasing Parthenia and I could hear her screaming for help.

"Before she could escape, my mother, well, she tripped and fell. That's when that woman caught up wit' her and stabbed her! Ump, ump, Lord have mercy. Killed her dead right in front of me." Tears started down my father's face.

Mother was rinsing a bunch of Collard greens in the kitchen sink for dinner. Without looking up, she said, "Calvin, stop that crying, I don't want to hear that mess. There you go, filling these children's head with all that junk. Everybody got Indian blood in them. Don't matter none to the white man what you got. If you got a speck of Negro blood in you then you are still a Nigga'. You know I ain't lying."

She turned around and gave him a look of disgust.

"Stop filling that girl's head up with all that mess. I get tired of hearing how our parents died. Talk about something else now. You done ran out."

Dad looked at Mother with pleading eyes.

"Okay. I just wants my children to know who they are. Anyway, my baby asked me to tell her. I'm almost finished now." Daddy again pulled out his handkerchief and wiped his tears away.

"It wasn't but two weeks later, I'll never forget that, my father died— killed, while gambling. Oh, Lord, I was only 8 years old. He had a dispute.

That gambler shot and killed my father at the craps table. My father and my mother, they were both very young. I was only 8 years old at the time they left me. My parents died because they didn't live right. They were drinking, gambling, and listening to the Devil's music. It was their lifestyle. They hardly ever went to church. My father was a heavy gambler. From that time forward, I promised the Lord that if he let me live, I would serve him until I die. I never drank any liquor, or gambled. I knew I was going to be a preacher. God called me at an early age."

Daddy dried his eyes and stuffed his handkerchief into the back pocket of his overalls. He looked at Mother, who stood over him with a disgusted look on her face. She put her hands on her wide hips.

"Lightfoot, there you go, you start flapping your lips. I need you to go to the store now, bring me a package of yeast. I am baking hot rolls for dinner."

"Oh, okay, Mother."

I said, "Daddy, can I go with you?" I had to go with him. I knew my sisters were waiting for him to leave. I wasn't staying. Oh, no.

"Oh, sure, you can go. Come on, Baby. Put on your coat first."

I quickly put on my new plaid coat Daddy bought me. My sisters were fuming.

CHAPTER TWO

In 1954, my family started breaking apart. I didn't understand why.

My parents were having problems, fighting about religion and morals. My mother was only 32 and already a grandmother. Sydney, who was four years older than I, had been date-raped and got pregnant. She loved the young man in spite of this.

I also discovered Flordnette was really my mother's sister, not mine. Their mother died when Flordnette was only 7. When she also got pregnant, amid my parents fighting, she moved in with her older brother. I had no idea where she went or why until we visited my uncle's house and there she was. I was so happy to see her. I ran to hug her.

"Hi, Flordnette, I miss you."

She bent down and said, "I miss you, too. Janie, I am your aunt, so call me Aunt Flordy from now on."

I could just muster out, "Oh?"

"Your mother, Johnnie, is really my oldest sister," she said. I was shocked when she called Mother by her first name, Johnnie. The next time I saw her, she was married and in her own apartment. Everyone in her new neighborhood called her Flo. I really liked her new nickname. She has been called Aunt Flo every since.

Sydney hid her pregnancy well. She was just 15 when her first baby was born. My parents were shocked when they found out. She was already nine months pregnant. She still graduated from Burbank

Junior High on schedule. Sydney's full figure, along with big shirts, helped conceal her full-term pregnancy.

My dad was so strict with us girls. We just couldn't figure out how Sydney sneaked away long enough to even have a boyfriend. Somehow, she managed to do it. After Sydney's baby was born, we were all so proud. He was a smart, cute little boy. I was only 12 and had fun playing with my nephew after school and in the summertime.

Sydney was a sophomore in high school when she got pregnant again. When her second son was born, we had two babies to entertain us. We had so much love in our house. We ignored the gossiping neighbors. Earlie and I loved our nephews and we took them everywhere. Mother and Daddy were the proudest grandparents. They still fought each other but they showed off those grandbabies to their family and friends. They were fine, happy babies.

Sydney managed to complete high school on time with straight A's while we all cared for her two small children. Despite Mother's objections and advice, Sydney married the "man of her dreams," the father of her children, soon afterward. She loved him and believed they would be happy together. She moved out but moved back in with us every three months or so. It was a constant war going on between those two. Two years later, a third baby was on the way. We helped Mother watch Sydney's kids while she worked.

It wasn't long before Earlie followed in Sydney's footsteps. She was only 16—two years older than I—when she married and was expecting her first child. She and her new husband were both very good-looking. They were the most striking couple. They were very happy, too. At first.

He was a mama's boy. He was the best-dressed drunkard around and didn't want to work. Earlie stayed with him for about six months but couldn't take the interference from her mother-in-law so she came back home, pregnant and looking for a place to stay.

The old neighborhood biddies said it would only be a matter of time before it happened to me. I heard through the grapevine the old women had made a bet—they swore I would get pregnant before I finished high school. I knew they were waiting for me to mess up.

I overheard the older women on the block talking about my family as I walked by one day.

"Those Lightfoot girls are so fast! Two of them are already married with babies."

"That little one over there," one said, pointing at me as she spoke. "She will be next if Mrs. Lightfoot ain't careful."

I was very popular at the time. It didn't look like I was going to make it.

Cute boys from all over the East Bay were coming over regularly to see me.

My mother and sisters guarded me like a sentry.

"Teen boys are like dogs in heat in the springtime," Mother said. "Jest watch how a pack of male dogs chase one female dog until they finally get hold of her." I did watch. That was one of the best lessons in life for me. I was still a virgin and planned to stay that way until I married.

I dated plenty but I wasn't that serious. And I showed those biddies a thing or two. I did finish high school with no babies.

* * *

One day, when I was 13, I got home from school and found Daddy sitting in his favorite armchair. He looked lost.

"Janie, do you know where Mother went?" "No, Daddy."

"When I got home from work, she was gone," he said. "She left me a note saying she needs to get away for awhile."

He got down on his knees in front of his armchair and began to pray.

"Father, I don't know what happened, Lord, I've done my best to be a good husband¼"

Earlie snatched me into her bedroom, quickly closing the door behind her. Her eyes were big as she patted her bed for me to sit down. I slowly sank down.

"Daddy doesn't know where Mother is," she whispered. "Aunt Carrie knows but she isn't telling. She said we can call her if we have an emergency."

I was flattered that Earlie confided in me for once, but I wasn't happy with the way they treated Daddy. He was my friend and he never would hurt anybody, not intentionally.

"Why did Mother leave?"

Earlie shrugged her shoulders.

"Is she coming back?"

"Yeah, she is only going to be gone for just two weeks."

I was fine because my Daddy was still there. I didn't find out where Mother had gone until I asked her when she returned one month later.

"I went to see cuz'n Gladys in Los Angeles," she said.

"In Los Angeles?"

"Yes and don't ask me nothing else, you hear?"

There was a hard lump in my throat when I tried to speak. I just nodded.

Shortly after she returned, things changed. There seemed to be something missing. We never laughed or had fun anymore. We sat politely at the dinner table every night in silence. Daddy didn't bother to tell his favorite stories. Mother didn't fuss at Daddy anymore. They never talked to one another. I watched them slowly grow apart.

Although they'd had problems for years, the rift between my parents widened beyond repair when my father discovered Sydney was pregnant again. That Sunday as we drove to church there was a lot of quiet tension in the car. Sydney sat very grim in the back seat, biting her fingernails. Earlie kept hugging her. I kept asking what was going on, but nobody would tell me anything. Earlie would only say, "Mother's mad at Daddy."

When I asked her why, she said, "You'll see."

When pastor offered the altar prayer, my Daddy took Sydney by the hand and led her forward to the front of the church. I looked at Earlie and asked, "What's happening."

"You know Sydney's pregnant again," she said. I didn't know.

"Why is she standing up there, though," I said.

"She has to ask God for forgiveness," Earlie said. "The first time was a mistake, Daddy said. The second time is not."

Sydney was flushed, crying and breathing heavy.

17

"I have sinned," she said, her voice soft and trembling, speaking through her sobbing. "I'm pregnant again. This time it's my fault. I thought he was going to marry me this time. I'm asking God and the church to forgive me."

The pastor asked everyone to bow their heads in prayer. The whispers started before the prayer began, their hushed whispers soon turned into soft mumbling. It grew so loud until the pastor had to admonish the congregation. Someone snickered. Pastor commended Sydney for being brave and humble enough to stand up in front of the church and admit her sins. He said, "Most Christian wouldn't do it. Pastor cleared his throat. He said, I planned to preach on a different topic today but when he stepped into the pulpit, God spoke to me. I am going to obedient to God. I am preaching from John 8:7. "He Who is without Sin."

When the prayer finished, the pastor hugged Sydney and she returned to her seat. My father went to his chair at the pulpit—he was one of the preachers—while my mother scowled at him from her seat in the choir.

As we left the service that morning Mother seemed so composed and proud with her shoulders erect, her head held high, with a beautiful smile plastered on her face. Sydney always stood straight and tall. This Sunday her head was slightly down and her shoulders slumped over. I held her hand and cried silently with her. I loved my big sister so much. I had never seen her cry like that before. I felt like a cold knife was stuck in my heart. Earlie hugged her on the other side as we made our way through the staring crowd. Some of the mothers grabbed their teen daughters, pulling them away from us as if we were poison. Mother gave Dad a scowl as she climbed into the passenger's side of the car. We climbed in, Earlie first, Sydney next, me last. I held on to Sydney's hand as though I was going to lose her. She gripped me tightly to her side.

"Don't cry, Sydney," I said. We all clung together as though it was our last day. It hurt me to see people treat her that way. She was always so sweet and kind to everybody. Before this happened we were the popular family in the church, always looked up to. But after that Sunday, everything changed. Sydney was no longer an usher, we found out, and Earlie didn't want to be one. I was the only one who still wanted to go to church but no one would take me. Mother stayed in bed on Sundays. Daddy would still go to church, but no one went with him.

CHAPTER THREE

I 'll never forget the day he left.
"Baby, I have to leave. If you girls want me to stay, Mother said I could. But only if I you girls want me to. I love your mother and I love all my children; but your mother says I am too strict. She says she's tired of all those hypocrites at the church." Then he said, "If you talk to her, she'll listen to you." I felt pity for my father. That is the first time he didn't smile. He had dark circles under his eyes.

He looked so tired and much older.

"Your Mother said that I have to go."

I bawled like a baby.

Daddy tried calming me but I just continued crying.

"Don't cry baby. Please, Daddy cannot stand to see you cry." He held me close.

We should be happy now, I thought. We finally had more money. Daddy had a new job, and we wore nice clothes. Because Daddy spoiled me, Mother nor my sisters liked me. If he left, I would be in trouble.

"Talk to your sisters for me, Baby." Daddy said. "Try to convince them to let me stay. If that doesn't work, then talk to Mother. I love your mother. I don' t want to leave my family."

My heart thumped so ; I felt weak in the knee.

I knew my sisters hated it when he woke us up in the wee hours of the night to pray. I knew they were ecstatic over Daddy leaving.

I was confused. Why didn't they tell me?

Just the past morning, I walked in the kitchen catching Earlie and Sydney sitting in a huddle whispering and giggling about something. They jumped as if they had stolen something when they saw me.

"What you guys laughing about?"

Earlie said, "You'll see, just wait. You will see."

Sydney snickered. "Nothin', why?" Quickly, I ran from the room.

Dad coached me before I went inside to see my family. I needed answers. What happened? Why is my daddy leaving?

"Talk to your sisters," he said. "Tell them to talk to Mother. Please, will you try, baby?" Daddy's dark eyes penetrated right through me. He searched my face desperately for an answer I could not give.

"If they say no, then I won't bother them; I'll just leave."

Bursting through Sydney's bedroom door, I stood there breathing loudly. Before I chickened out, I blurted, "Daddy is leaving us! Did you know?"

Sydney lay face down on her bed. She looked up at me, picking her teeth as usual. She stopped long enough to say, "Yeah, we knew it."

"Earlie knows about it, too?"

"Yes," she said, still sucking on that toothpick as if it was candy.

"Why?" I asked. "I want Daddy to stay." Earlie entered the room as I spoke.

I searched their blank faces. "We need to talk to Mother!" I said. It did not work. They did not move. "We have to talk to Mother."

Sydney said, "No. I think I'm going to like it here when Daddy's gone." I couldn't believe my ears.

"I thought you loved Daddy! What is wrong with you guys? Daddy is out there begging to stay but he says Mother wants him to leave.

"That's not true, is it?"

"Yes, because he wouldn't let me have any boyfriends." Sydney said. "That's how I got pregnant, I had to sneak dates. He said, 'Don't be kissing on any boys, that's how you get pregnant.' Well, I kissed him and nothin' happened so I went further because I did not believe Daddy anymore. If he had let me go out then we could have talked about boys."

"We never had the chance to go to dances or anything," Earlie added. "We never had any fun. Now we can finally go to the parties."

I yelled, "Uh-Uh! Mother won't let us go out either!"

"Oh, yes she will," Earlie said. "She said so." She placed her hands on her hips. Her defiant stare made me shudder.

Sydney stared off, as though looking into a mirror of her past.

She turned and looked at me as she snapped back to reality.

"You remember when he beat me with a leather strap?" Before I could answer, she said, "Just because he caught me kissing my boyfriend."

"Janie, it was you who begged Daddy to stop beating me. That's when my purse caught on fire! It fell into the open lit burner on the stove while he was beating me with that strap!"

I felt like I was on the witness stand before the prosecutor.

"Don't you remember?"

I nodded in affirmation.

"He stopped just long enough to put out that fire. Then he whipped me some more."

Her dark eyes burned with such hatred. I had never seen Sydney like this.

She was so hostile, not at all like the sweet big sister I knew.

"I love Daddy." Defiantly, I looked into her eyes. "Daddy doesn't have anywhere to go!"

"Sydney, you have to forgive him like the Bible says."

"No! I will never forgive Daddy! I did not deserve that. I did not do anything wrong. It was only an innocent kiss. It was my first kiss, too, and… and… Daddy made me feel dirty!"

She shook her head. "Uh! Uh! Let him go! I want to dance and have fun." Sydney started popping her fingers and dancing the Cha-Cha all around me.

Sydney was a good dancer; funny I had not noticed this before. I turned watching her as she twirled and did fancy moves.

"He made me stand up in front of all those church members and ask forgiveness for my sins. He found out I was pregnant! He acted as if it was only my fault. My boyfriend never got in trouble for it. It is always the girl's fault. All those dried-prune-faced women passed judgment on me. They wouldn't allow their daughters to even sit by me in church or talk to me anymore. I was so embarrassed! Mother begged him not to do that to me. She knew those old sorry hypocrites. Both the men and the women are." She folded her arms in front of her chest. Her pouting bottom lip quivered. "I'm never going back to that church again. Mother says we're not going back there anymore either! I'm glad Daddy's leaving."

Earlie then put her two cents in, "All we ever did was go to church seven days a week. All day on Sundays, BYTU on Monday nights; Tuesday night was business meeting; Wednesday night, Bible study. Thursday night is senior choir rehearsal and Friday night is deacon board meetings, Saturday afternoons, junior choir practice."

Sydney chimed in, "Ooh yes! We're finally going to have some freedom, have some fun. I can wear the brightest red lipstick I want now and…"

Earlie interrupted; "He whipped me with that leather belt, too! Just because I wouldn't give you any of my candy, Janie!" She looked accusingly at me. "I'll never forget that day."

Instantly changing her facial expression, she went into an impersonation of Daddy. She pursed her lips speaking in his deep baritone voice.

"'Earlie, you mean you're not going to give your baby sister any of that candy? You have too much. You can give her one piece, can't you?'"

"I just kept licking on my red lollipop. I didn't say a word. I just kept staring at Daddy like he was crazy."

Earlie stood up just then, changing her stance. She pushed her chest out with her shoulders back to mimic Daddy: "'Earlie, baby, Can I please have a piece of your candy?'"

Earlie continued on, "I kept right on licking on that pop. I knew he was trying to trick me so he could give it to you."

"Then he really got mad, I could tell because he looked so mean. His thick brows looked like they were knitted together." (Earlie went back into her father-like persona)

Sydney was laughing so hard she doubled over in pain.

"'I bought that candy and you ain't going to share with your own father? You got a whole bunch of it! Ump, Ump. Ump. Lord have mercy on this child! I work hard to give you everything.'"

"I looked upside Daddy's head and said, 'Daddy, you didn't buy this candy! I worked hard cleaning houses, baby sitting and walking dogs for this candy.

"Ooh! He was really mad now," she said." 'You getting smart with me, girl,' he said. 'You don't talk back to me. You give me respect.' His face was red! I knew he was mad at me then. He said to Mother, 'Johnnie, did you hear that girl sassing me? Lord, my own daughter! None of my other children ever treated me like that. You're being selfish and I am going to whip your butt.' He had started pulling that leather strap out of his pants." Earlie demonstrated how he pulled off his belt. "'Girl, you get over here. Now!'"

Earlie changed back to normal.

"I made up my mind right then and there he wasn't going to whip me never again." Earlie's full lips changed into a pouting position. "I hadn't done nothing wrong. So when he went to hit me with that belt, I grabbed it and reached for the big butcher knife mother left on the table. I told him, 'I'm tired of you whipping me. I didn't do anything. Why do I have to give Janie my candy?'" Earlie held her imaginary knife in her hand as she backed up against the bedroom wall. "I bought this candy myself. Humph! I don't care! You can whip me if you want to. I don't care. Now!'"

I looked out the bedroom window.

He was still waiting, pacing on the sidewalk.

Earlie then changed her stature and her expression again, but this time she did an impersonation of our mother.

"'Calvin, why don't you leave that gal alone? Janie has to learn that she can't have everything she sees. She is too spoiled. You've ruined that girl.'"

Earlie then bucked her eyes wide, imitating Daddy again.

"'Oh, Lord, have mercy! My daughter! She's going to hell! Lord, forgive her for she knows not what she does. Earlie, you had better get down on your knees and ask God to forgive you! In the book of Exodus, 20:12, It says: Honor Thy Father and Mother; that thy days may be longer. None of my children, but you, Sydney and, and my baby, Janie, she never even talk back to me like you did. They have never talked back to me! You the only one that threatened me with a knife! You could've killed me. Ump, Ump, Ump. Lord have mercy on her!'"

"Mother snatched the knife from me then." Earlie then mimics Mother.

"'Calvin, I told you to leave that gal alone! All this about some stupid candy? Earlie, you go somewhere and sit your butt down before I whip you myself. And put that candy away, now!'"

Earlie then changed back to herself.

"Besides, Janie, you are the only one that don't get whippings. Remember? You're the baby; that's why you want him back."

Her accusations ripped through my stomach walls. I tried to keep my composure.

Earlie and Sydney were staring at me as if I were the enemy.

My world had dropped out from under me. I didn't know how to tell them I enjoyed going to church functions. It was so much fun! What's wrong with them? I hadn't realized how serious this was. Out of desperation, I said, "I'm going to ask Mother."

"Go ahead," Earlie said. "She said it was up to us! And we don't want him here!"

I headed for the kitchen. I knew it would not be easy to convince Mother to let daddy stay.

Mother sat quietly at the kitchen table, drinking her morning coffee. She listened to me with a disconcerted look on her face. After I finished talking, she sat there silently. My eyes focused on the large clock hanging on the kitchen wall. Time was moving too fast. My heart beat in rhythm with the loud ticking hands of the black timepiece. It was only 10 a.m. I thought it was earlier than that. Usually Daddy woke me up on Saturday mornings to have a nice hot plate of Mother's homemade sausage patties, hot buttermilk biscuits, with mounds of melted butter and two over-easy eggs served on top of grits. That was my special time with him. He would read the bible with me after breakfast. We would listen to our favorite Bible stories on a religious radio stations. We would sing Gospel music together.

We couldn't afford a television at that time. He always woke up early in the wee hours of the night praying. I was the only one who didn't complain when he woke us up to join him at 3 a.m. I loved talking to Daddy anytime. I didn't believe Earlie when she cheerfully announced, "Daddy is leaving."

She always enjoyed teasing me so I usually ignored her.

Somehow, I knew it was true this time. I have got to convince Mother to take Daddy back. I could not live without Daddy.

Mother sat stirring her coffee. She seemed to be far away in thought. Mother took a deep breath then exhaled. Before I could speak, she said, "No Janie. I can't take it any longer." She shook her head slowly from side to side. "Daddy says, 'If you just wear lipstick, you are like Jezebel in the Bible. If you wear a dress just past your knees, then you are indecent.' He is too sanctified. He wants to raise you girls like his Grandma raised him. This is 1955 and you would think this was 1925. He will not change."

"Please, Mother," I cried. "Please let me talk to him. Maybe he will listen to me. He will do anything to stay here. Daddy is crying outside. He asked me to talk to you.

"Mother, I never asked for anything before but please let Daddy stay." Tears of helplessness spilled out from my eyes. I didn't bother to wipe them away. Daddy would usually grab me and hug me whenever I cried. It never seemed to bother Mother. She believed Daddy had spoiled me rotten.

"I'm so tired, Janie, tired of living out of a shoebox. Daddy bought a new car. Then he puts most of his paycheck in the church. Yet my girls have to wear worn-out shoes. Daddy had to put cardboard to cover the holes in the soles of your shoes. He had to tie wire through Earlie's shoes to keep the soles from flapping. We always have to wait until another payday. Me? I have only one good suit, that black satin one. I have worn that to church for the last 10 years. He bought that suit when we came to California. We have been married over 18 years. He still lives by the same old-fashioned rules. That's how his grandmother raised him and he refuses to change."

Mother shook her head then gazed up at the ceiling. "What he did at church that Sunday—Uh uh! That was not right. He said,

'The Bible said to confess your sins in front of God and the church.' I ain't never seen nobody else in our church do it. I don't know if I will ever be able to forgive him for what he did to poor Sydney.

"He talked her into standing up in front of those so-called Christians—in front of the whole congregation—and beg for forgiveness for her sin. There they sat, their noses turned up in the air, like they smelling something, judging her, acting like they were so-o-o perfect, like they never sinned."

I slumped down in a chair at the table facing Mother. I could tell this wasn't going to be as easy as I thought.

"The Rev. O.P. Smith preached that sermon on Sunday. Pastor, his wife, and only a handful of members came over and gave Sydney a hug after church. The members seem to have forgotten about pastor's sermon on forgiveness and unjust judgment. They really need to remember that Scripture. Most of the people in church have done any and ev'rythang, now they pretend they never done nothin' before."

I had no idea then just how hurt and angry Mother was until her Mississippi accent thickened.

"Why, I know for a fact some of those same snooty women who held their noses up in the air sent their daughters away for a few months. First, you'd see them same gals wrapped up kissing on some fast tail little boy. Next thang you know, that same gal done gained a lot of weight around the middle. If the boy denies it, then she is quietly sent to stay away to live with some sick aunt or grandmother faraway. On the other hand, there is a quiet wedding. The father threatened the boy that if he does not marry his daughter, he will kill him. Now that's called a Shotgun wedding. Then six months later, here a baby comes—early. They claim it's premature but anybody knows a fine nine-pound baby is full term."

Mother poured herself another cup of coffee from the coffeepot on the shiny white stove before sitting back down in her chair.

"These same old biddies done played around before they got married and some of them while they still married! Now they done ran out.

"They are too old and tired now. They done got amnesia. Now they acting like holy saints, like nothin' bad ever happened to them.

Well, like my mother, Tempie Youngblood Partee used to say, 'The reason you ain't, is cause you can't.' So don't tell me nothing about your daddy staying here."

I knew Daddy and I just had lost our battle.

I hated this. Why did I have to bring him bad news?

I dragged myself outside where he stood waiting for the final verdict. I felt like a judge reading a death sentence. He was still pacing back and forth on the sidewalk until he saw me coming. I will always remember that dismal day as long as I live. Storm clouds hovered overhead. He looked so handsome in his crisp laundered white shirt with a tan paisley print tie that covered his buttons. He looked so young for his 49 years.

How can my mother dislike such a compassionate man like my father? He is always so kind and sweet, so good-looking. His dark mystic eyes twinkled with anticipation as I walked over to him. He bent down to hug me. I swallowed hard. Tears ran down my cheeks. He wiped them away with his hanky. I took a deep breath before blurting out, "They said, 'No, Daddy.'"

Tears ran down his cheeks now. Shaking his head in disbelief, he wiped them away with his handkerchief.

"Oh, Lord, forgive them, for they know not what they do!" He wiped his tears away. "Lord have mercy."

My body shook as I fought back tears.

"Daddy, please don't cry."

He squeezed me tightly, so tight until I could hardly catch my breath. I grabbed hold of his nice brown tweed suit coat. He took my hands away.

"Daddy," I cried out. "Take me with you! Please!"

"I can't, Baby. I have to find me a place. As soon as I can, I will come get you. Okay?"

I could only nod my head.

"Daddy promise you. Okay?"

"Okay, Daddy. I'll wait for you."

"You do what your mother tells you, you hear?"

"Yes, Daddy."

"I love you and I love my wife and chil'ren. You tell them that for me.

That no matter what, I ain't mad at them. Okay? One day, they will understand why I made them go to church. Baby, promise me you will stay in the church, you hear me?"

"Yes, Daddy, I promise."

"I got to go now, Baby."

I stood there feeling so alone and helpless. He held his head high and proud as he walked away. I watched him until he drove away. I stood there staring at his bright shiny Black Buick Sedan until it was only a blur in the road.

At first, he came to see us every weekend. I found out Daddy moved to Vallejo. He had a new job at the Naval Weapons Station.

It was fall 1956. He took me to buy a pair of white suede shoes called 'Bucks'. They were the most popular pair of shoes then and everybody had a pair. Mother couldn't afford to buy me any so I asked Daddy to buy me a pair. That was the last time that I saw him.

He took me to a small exclusive shoe store on San Pablo Avenue in Berkeley. I picked out an expensive pair of white Suede Spalding Bucks with pink rubber soles. That was my first expensive pair of shoes. I didn't know I wouldn't see my father again until after high school graduation. I called his apartment one month later. A strange woman answered the phone.

"I'm sorry, but Reverend Lightfoot moved and he did not leave a forwarding address," she said.

I lay across my bed crying. I felt so empty inside. I wanted to go look for him. I knew my daddy wouldn't just leave here without telling me. Something must have happened! I couldn't even afford bus fare to go find him. I made a vow to find him after I finished high school.

CHAPTER FOUR

After Daddy moved away, we didn't hear from him for a long time. I felt like he had divorced me, too. My heart ached with loneliness.

Shortly after my parents separated, Mother became very sick. She had an allergic reaction to a tuberculosis test. Within a week, she complained of pain. Her right arm was swollen and very sore. She couldn't bend it or stretch it out, and was forced to keep it up right.

She was unable to work after that. The monthly child support Dad sent wasn't enough and Mother had no choice but to apply for welfare. She came home from the welfare office furious they asked her so many questions. My mother, a proud, independent woman, had to swallow her pride in order for us to eat.

For a long while, she tried to hold out and "make do" with what we had. The county welfare aid barely paid our rent and there wasn't enough to money to buy groceries, clothing, or transportation.

However, our kitchen cabinets were never empty even though there was no money. That's when I really begin to grow up.

After Daddy left, Mother made me help clean and cook. Before this, my father spoiled me rotten. I never had to do anything before. He always let me have my way because he would remind my sisters that I was the baby. Until I was 12, Sydney had to bathe me. Most of the time, she forced me into a hot tub of water. When I complained loudly, my father would investigate. My sister would quickly run cold water so by the time he arrived in the bathroom, it was only lukewarm. She's always say, "Feel it, Daddy! Janie is just acting like a baby!"

I would run and tattle on my sisters about every little thing. They got in trouble a lot. They threatened me, saying, "When Mother and Daddy goes to choir rehearsal this Thursday night, we are going to get you." They couldn't touch me for fear of a scolding or a whipping. Once he was gone, they treated me differently. They would remind me constantly: "Your daddy ain't here, he can't save you now."

"I'm glad he's gone," Sydney said one time. "We can listen to the blues; listen to Fats Domino, The Platters, James Brown, Chuck Berry, and Big

Mama Thornton, too."

"We can listen to the love songs on the radio station," Earlie chimed in. "'Oh What a Night' is my favorite song." Earlie moved her hips in a slow gyrating movement.

I cut in, "Daddy said that's the devil's music."

She just ignored me. "I can date boys and go to the movies now."

Me? I didn't understand. I didn't have a problem with going to church and singing church songs. The music and words of love always soothed me. I wanted Daddy to come back home.

My mother didn't believe in spoiling her girls. There was very little hugging and kissing from her. She was too busy making sure we had food on the table. For a long time I didn't think my own mother even liked me.

The day after my father left, I woke up, expecting to find him back in his room. It was empty. I went to the kitchen. I found Mother and my two sisters sitting and talking at the table. They sat staring at me. The room was still. Anxiously, I stood there wide-eyed wondering whether to run and hide from their cold stares. I knew what was coming next.

"Here she comes, looking jest like her Daddy," my mother said. I felt cursed and confused. Before Daddy left, she was proud I resembled my father so much. I was despised for looking like him after he was gone. What a reversal! Sydney and Earlie snickered at me as I stood there, wondering whether I would be safe in the same room with them. Should I go to the living room where I felt safe?

I wanted to scream, it wasn't my fault. Mother married Daddy and they made me. So why are you all mad at me? I didn't dare say anything. Butterflies fluttered inside my stomach. Next, nausea came, then chills took over. I trembled involuntarily.

Hot tears traveled down onto my high cheekbones spilling into my mouth. The salty tears were strangely soothing to my downed spirit. I tried hard to stop them but my big dark eyes surrendered to my emotions. I tried to hide my fear and the hurt caused by their rejection.

Earlie sensing it, teased me even more. "Janie, what are you crying for now?"

I was choked up and couldn't speak.

"She is always crying," Sydney added.

My chest swelled. Sharp pains stabbed my heart. Swallowing hard then gasping for air, I tried to speak. My lips moved but nothing came out. I managed to squeak out, "Nothing." My body trembled as I sobbed.

"What did you say?," Mother said. "Girl, you better stop that crying and speak up!"

So, I let go full force, bawling like a two-year-old.

"She's just like Lightfoot," Mother said. "He's so emotional, he cries about everything, too."

Their insults became my morning ritual. The more they talked about my daddy, the more I missed him. I would have given anything to have my daddy home. They wouldn't treat me like that if Daddy were home. After he left, I cried about everything. I became super-sensitive to the least little thing.

Sydney reminded me, "Daddy can't help you so stop being such a cry baby."

But sometimes Sydney would comfort me when we were alone. When no one was looking, Sydney would hug me, and wipe my tears away with her hands.

"Please don't cry Janie. Please. Don't say anything but I miss Daddy, too. Sh-h-h-h."

Sydney could be very kind. Sometimes, Earlie could be nice to me, too. She shared her candy when she got paid from babysitting. She always invited me to come with her when she cleaned our neighbors' houses or walked their dogs. Whenever she had a late-night babysitting job, she brought me along. We would play double solitaire and checkers together. We had a lot of fun.

We found out Earlie could really fight. One day this big bully pulled her scarf off at school. He was a tall stocky boy. It didn't matter to Earlie. She was so embarrassed! She closed her eyes and began swinging her fists hard and fast. When he tried to hit her back, with both feet flailing in the air, she kicked him. Then she knocked him out. That is how she earned the nickname "Little Light Feet."

Earlie attended Burbank Junior High School at the time. She showed up at Berkeley High School just in time to defend Sydney. Sydney always got in trouble when she spoke because her words were like a sharp sword cutting you down. She wasn't much of a fighter but a fast talker. Often, she would talk herself into a fight that she couldn't finish.

I was very tiny for my age so I learned to fight big girls and boys who bullied me. They started to bully me after Earlie went to junior high. I was in the sixth grade. They thought I couldn't fend for myself. They were wrong. I would fight long and hard and, luckily, Earlie would show up to even the score. You would find her at the high school defending Sydney. On the same day, she would ride her bike over to the elementary school to defend me if necessary.

Sisters are funny. Right before junior high school, Mother took me shopping. She tried her best to find mature clothing in the latest styles. I was 13 and still wearing a child's size 8. She couldn't find anything to fit me. I refused to wear those girlie pinafore skirts or dresses. I looked like an 8-year-old in them.

Earlie took one yard of black percale fabric and made me my first tight skirt. She pressed my hair until it was shiny and so straight. I felt pretty for the first time in my life. My sisters showed me their love in a funny sort of way. I was just confused about when and how.

After my father left, my sisters acted like runaway slaves. They had too much freedom. I wasn't accustomed to living like that. I kept waiting for God's wrath to come down and strike us dead.

My sisters wore lipstick now. This was an unspoken declaration of freedom from the Holy Roller lifestyle they'd lived by before. They cut their long hair into new short pixie styles.

With four women in the same house, ooh wee, our hormones were kicking! My sisters and I fought over clothes, the phone, everything. Daddy never approved of us fighting. And cursing, oh, no, we weren't doing that. I believed Daddy when he said, "God will strike you down." My sisters used four-letter words only when Mother wasn't home. Our morning rituals always ended up with Mother beating us with a wooden broom-handle to break us up. This day and age, we call it child abuse. Back in those days, they called it discipline.

My mother dated discreetly until I was 17.

I didn't know she had a steady boyfriend until I finished high school. She always demanded respect and believe me she got it, too, from everyone.

Mother had admirers proposing to her all the time. On many occasions, I heard her male friends say, "Johnnie, you sure can cook. I want to marry you. All you have to do is say the word." I wasn't sure if they were kidding her. She would just crack up. She thought it was funny. She treated them like old friends. Mother was a pretty woman with a cute figure. She lost a lot of weight after my daddy left.

He used to tell her "I like a woman wit' some meat on her bones". He would also say, "I like you like that Johnnie. You look good!"

Mother never seemed happy when she was married. She very seldom smiled then. While Daddy was at work, she would sleep all the time. She would only stay up long enough to cook meals.

After their break-up, her doctor put her on a low-fat diet. She followed it diligently. She ate baked and broiled foods with no salt. Within six months, she had gone from a size 18 dress to a size 10. She never did get fat again. She had a tiny waist and a round, firm backside, which we all inherited. Mother preferred male friends to women. She was raised up right along with her brothers; she felt more comfortable with men. She treated them as old friends and they visited my mother often but they left at a decent hour. She was a natural born hostess and could cook. There was always a lot of food on the stove at our house. She could take anything and make it taste good. All our friends came over regularly, too. They would talk to my mother and tell her things they couldn't tell their own parents. Everyone was always eating and drinking, laughing and talking about the good old days while they drank whatever they brought with them.

My mother didn't buy or drink alcohol. Cherokee blood didn't mix well with alcohol; it caused a personality change. She would change from a sweet lamb into a growling she-wolf.

If someone handed her a drink, we would all yell, "Oh, no! No liquor for her." We guarded her like soldiers. She avoided it, too, after the adverse effect it had on her.

Our friends would all sit down around the table and play Bid Whist with my sisters after dinner.

I would listen to them making bids. "I pass," one player said as he rapped his knuckles lightly on the table. Someone else would bid "four uptown or downtown." I didn't understand the game but it was fun watching anyhow. Just to feel the camaraderie was exciting. My mother didn't play cards either. She was the perfect hostess, making sure everyone was enjoying themselves. When it grew late and she felt tired, she wasted no time telling her guests to leave. She would say as she ushered them to the door, "Well, time has run out. All you Wools are leaving heah!" That is how she earned the nickname Mother Rawness. She never bit her tongue. The grandchildren said, "She will get loose like a goose. Mother is raw! Mother Rawness! She will tell like it is. She don't care, she is going to tell you about yourself. You won't have to worry what she's thinking because you will already know."

By the time I was 16, I could date, but when the poor fellows came to pick me up, they went through pure Hell. My mother didn't have to say anything. My sister Sydney was the chief interrogator. She treated them as if they were in prison camp or something. She fired questions so fast the poor boys could only stutter and stammer.

"How old are you? Where do you live? Are you in school? Well. Do you have a job then?" My poor date. He couldn't answer fast enough for her. Then Earlie would threaten them so until they were afraid to do anything to me. They respected my mother and my sisters a lot. Believe me, they were no joke. "And you had better have her home before 11 p.m." Sydney always yelled out the door before slamming it. I was so embarrassed! My date was sweating before we left my house.

I wasn't serious about any of those boys. I just enjoyed all the attention I received. I was merely having fun. I demanded respect and I got it. Before I would step out my door, I made it clear there would be no sex or discussions about it. The man I married would be the only one to even touch me.

CHAPTER FIVE

Family members looked to my mother for spiritual uplifting as well. She had a way about her that made you laugh and see the humorous side of any situation, while giving you the insight to solve your own problems through prayer and Scripture. Her favorite prayer was the 23rd Psalm. It is now one of my favorites. She would counsel the young men and women in our community because she was so wise.

She also had a dry sense of humor. She could bring a person out of deep depression. Before they realized it, they would bowl over laughing with her.

After she finished talking about wolves, or the "wol's," as she called them, telling you what a wol' was and how to handle them, her guests would crack up!

One time, one of my girlfriends was going through an ugly divorce. Her husband cleaned out their bank account and moved away, leaving her practically penniless.

Johnnie sat at the head of the kitchen table drinking a cup of coffee. She listened attentively while my friend told her about her last escapade with her husband. She cried and she cried. My mother waited until my friend calmed down.

"Let me tell you something about wol's," Mother said. "They will tell you they love you, win your trust and then they attack when you least expect it." My friend looked puzzled. Without hesitation, she asked, "What's a Wool?"

I'd always wanted to know what it meant, too. I always thought it meant wooly hair.

Johnnie looked exasperated. A long sigh escaped her thin lips.

"You mean to tell me you don't know what wol's is?" she said. "They travel in packs and have a lot of fur; they look something like a German shepherd. They sneak up from behind and before you know it, they got ya'll.

"You gotta watch out for wol's."

There was a long silence. You could hear a pin drop, then something clicked in my mind. I yelled out: "Oh! You mean like a wolf?"

"Yeah, W-O-L-V-E-S spells wol's, doesn't it? That's what I said, wol's. You know I'm tied-tongued, gal."

I must have had a dumbfounded look on my face because just then, my mother burst into laughter. It came up deep down from the pit of her stomach before escaping from under her rib cage. A loud, hearty laugh shook her whole body. She tried to catch her breath between laughing spells, tears just rolled down her cheeks.

My friend laughed just as hard, not because of what my mother said but because she just looked so funny crying and laughing at the same time. When the laughter wore off, Mother became serious.

"Don't you know that you can't put your trust in a man," she said. "You got to put your trust in God."

She bowed her head and said, "Let us pray. Our Father, who art in heaven, hallowed be thy name. Thy kingdom come, Thy will be done."

She then quoted the 23rd Psalm and instructed my friend to read additional verses from the Bible.

Mother loaded my friend's car with bags of food to take home. She reached into her bosom and pulled out her old tied-up handkerchief from her bra.

She gave my friend a wad of money. She'd been complaining about being broke and not having enough money to live on. I couldn't hide the look on my face. I was totally shocked she would give away all the money she had. She looked at me with that don't-you-say-nothing look.

"The Lord will provide," she said.

I learned a good lesson that day. A miraculous thing happened after my mother gave my friend her last bit of cash.

That very same day, two male friends who worked at the racetracks came over after work. They groomed horses for the jockeys at Golden Gate Fields and would only come over during the racing season. They brought bags and bags of groceries to her. They only wanted her to cook for them. They told her they wanted to give back something to her. She always made them feel at home. They offered to pay her for cooking their food. She refused to take anything. After they left, she discovered they had slipped a $100 bill into her apron pocket. They brought enough groceries to feed us for at least another month. They filled up our freezer with fresh meat, chicken, and fish. Fresh fruit and vegetables were in the bins. They left cases of carbonated drinks and gallons of punch for the grandchildren.

Mother even received a lump sum of money in the mail she wasn't anticipating. She looked at me in her cool, quiet manner and then said, "God will provide all our needs." She rolled the money up into her old hanky and placed it back in her bra. "Just trust in Him and he will direct your path."

My mother read her Bible every day. I know that was how she stayed strong. Her loving spirit kept us a close-knit family. We were always laughing, joking, and fooling around. There were always lots of love and good times at our house.

CHAPTER SIX

People who say they love to hear the pitter-patter of little feet never lived with my sisters and their children. Almost every waking hour, toddlers ran up and down the halls, into rooms and out squealing and screaming. And the pitter-patter? More like baby elephants stomping around. It felt more like an earthquake.

I have to admit I did help spoil my nieces and nephews, though.

Mother was a proud devoted grandmother who gave them all the love and affection there was to give. She never seemed tired of holding them on her lap or kissing them. She never seemed to have much time to sit and talk to me anymore; she didn't even have time for herself.

Sydney always came home after a big fight with her husband. She dragged her babies behind her, crying and complaining.

"He won't go to work. And, and, he hit me." Between her usual barrages of tears, she tried to explain what happened.

"He's always beating on me and cussing at my boys. I'm tired of it!" I asked, "Why do you keep going back to him after he mistreats you?" Sydney ignored me. She yelled out her usual obscenities.

"When she gets enough of it, she'll leave," Mother said. "Sydney, you don't let any man beat on you! You stay here until you can move."

The following day, Earlie sat at the kitchen table, telling Mother how tired she was of her husband. My mother was still very angry with my father, too. I stood there, perplexed and confused over this continuing soap opera. "The Young and the Restless" had nothing on the Lightfoots. Earlie and Sydney sat at the kitchen table with Mother for hours discussing their husbands. The phone rang constantly because their husbands were begging them to come home.

One time, Earlie had a screaming contest with her husband over the phone. She yelled at the top of her lungs at him, "Nigga, you had better get a job. That spells J-O-B, job, just in case you forgot how to spell. If you can't pay child support payments, at least buy milk and diapers for your baby.

"Your visitation rights are suspended," she said, slamming down the phone.

Their husbands always dropped by at the most inconvenient times. They came demanding to see their babies. It was always mass confusion at our house. Babies cried constantly and diapers hung all over the place, outside on the clothesline, inside the bathroom over the shower bar, just about everywhere. We had an old wringer washing machine at the time and we couldn't afford a dryer.

I would try to discreetly make my way down the hallway into my little escape chamber—the living room—to quiet serenity. I gently closed the door behind me to escape the furiosity of the moment.

My Daddy had bought us an old upright piano when I was about 6 and we all took piano lessons. To my family's surprise, I was a natural. I had found my niche. I sat at that old piano picking on the keyboard. I was in my own little world. I composed my own music and wrote songs of love.

My mother and my sisters were busy men bashing and I didn't want any part of it. This included talking about my father. In order to drown them out, I would hit the keyboard harder and sing even louder. I stayed out of their way and avoided the anger. If I walked into the kitchen for any reason while they were talking, their laughter ceased and the talking stopped. Their eyes focused on me. There was complete silence.

I felt like an outsider.

Quickly, I darted back my safe haven.

I prayed, "God help me. Why do they hate me so? I just want them to love me."

I did my homework in the living room, too. Afterwards I wrote lyrics to my music. I played the piano into the wee hours of the night until I fell asleep at the keyboard.

I worked hard on my musical career. I sang in local talent shows. They called me "Little Janie, the little girl with the booming voice." If the microphone was off, everyone could still hear my strong tenor voice. A local talent scout heard me singing at a talent rehearsal. He offered me a recording contract. I was so excited! I sang rhythm and blues on weekends at nightclubs and on Sundays, I sang spirituals in our church choir. For once in my life, Mother showed me how proud she really was! She supported me in my singing endeavors. Sydney and Earlie bragged to their friends about my singing engagements. Sydney fixed my makeup and Earlie made my clothes and did my hair. I felt so pretty and special again. We were almost a family.

At the tender age of 16, my musical career was taking off to new heights. Mother signed a contract for me on a small record label. That summer, my manager drove me and another local singing group to Los Angeles to a recording studio.

My goals were to finish high school, then, go on to college, and become a singing star.

After waking up one morning, I discovered it was only the two of us at home. It was rare for Mother and I to be home alone together.

"A-a-ah!" I said, with relief. It felt nice to have peace and quiet for a change. In fact, I was enjoying it very much. I swore I would never have children, well, at least until I was 25 or so.

I woke up to an abnormally quiet house. I thought I was dreaming at first. I looked around my bedroom to make sure I was in my own room. I could actually hear the tick-tock of the alarm clock on my night stand.

The phone rang, interrupting my thoughts. I heard my mother as she answered in a business-like tone, "Hello, Lightfoot residence." I could detect by the change in her voice that this was a close friend or family member. I quietly listened through the thin walls of my room.

"Oh, hello, how are you?" she said. "Oh, fine, thanks. Well, I ain't doing nothing. It's quiet here today. Listen to this, Sydney took her kids and spent the night with her friends. Earlie called home last night, said she was spending the night at her friends, too. I'm so glad they took the kids with them. Um hum! Otherwise, I would've been the built-in babysitter. You know, it feels good not hearing all that noise in the morning. I could get used to this, girl!"

She laughed, "Oh, yes, Janie's home with me though." The conversation faded out as Mother walked away into another room.

I hurried into the shower, then dressed as fast as I could. I headed to the kitchen to make breakfast. I was sure hungry. I could still hear her talking on that phone.

"One of those wol's took my favorite red blouse. I can't have nuthin," she complained while opening and slamming the drawers. "I was going to wear that today. Just wait 'til I see them." I could actually hear the hangers in her closets. They rattled and clinked as she slid them back and forth searching for her blouse. "Can't find nuthin' when I need it. Can't keep nuthin' neither. Those girls take all my stuff."

I poured a bowl of corn flakes into a bowl. It seemed strange to actually hear the sound of the crisp cereal as it fell into the glass bowl. I heard birds chirping outside the window. I peeked from the kitchen window. I saw a blue jay flitting around a rose in the yard.

I decided to ask Mother to take me shopping or to visit Aunt Carrie or just do something. I peeked into her bedroom. She wasn't there. Where did she go?

I spoke loud enough for her hear me, "Mother, I'll be glad when you get off that phone. Maybe, we'll do something together, for a change."

"Mother? Where are you?" I checked the living room. She wasn't there. Where did she go?

I pulled back the drapes. She is probably talking to a neighbor. That is when I saw Mother running to her car. She was rushing.

She quickly slid in behind the steering wheel. She started the car, anxiously looking out the window before pulling off. She knew I would want to go. She was leaving me! This must be one of her can-I-just-go-by-myself days.

I darted out the door, running down the front steps and out into the street. I inherited my father's agility and speed. My little, short bowlegs picked up.

I waved my right hand wildly as I chased the car. Surely she could see me from her rear mirror.

Desperately, I lunged forward, using my arms as a propeller. I was short of breath but sheer determination pushed me forward.

Mother drove midway down the block.

"Mother, wait for me," I yelled. My loud voice echoed on our quiet, tree-lined street.

Embarrassed, I looked around, but I kept running. I had to catch her. I got my chance. She slowed down for a stop sign ahead. I gained speed and caught up. I ran alongside the car. When I caught up with her she was near the corner. Flailing my arms wildly, I jumped right in front of her car!

"Mother, wait," I shouted.

Mother's reaction was swift. To avoid hitting me, she stepped on the brakes, swerving the car away from me.

I stood there, my mouth agape. The angry look on her face told me I was in trouble.

Mother took a deep breath.

"Janie," she yelled. "Get over here, now. You must be crazy. You ran in front of my car? I could've hit you. What do you want?"

Wisely, I made my way to the passenger's side. I leaned my head inside the open window. Peering in at my mother, I asked, "Where are you going?"

Mother gave me a petulant stare.

"Don't you have anything better to do than to chase me?"

"Can I go with you?"

"Why you wanna' follow me?" Mother said. She put the car into neutral, leaving the motor running. Making sure her right foot was on the brake pedal, Mother ranted on.

"You are usually on the phone talking to your friends, if you ain't singing and banging on that piano. Sometimes I need to get away by myself, you know, sometimes."

Mother leaned over to unlock the door.

"I can't find you wol's whenever I need you. Now you want to follow me. What's the matter? You done broke up with that boyfriend of yours or something? Get in the car, gal. I ain't got all day."

I waited until the frown left her face. I wasn't crazy. I wouldn't get into the car, not just yet.

I cautiously eyed her through the open window of the vehicle. She still seemed slightly irritated by the expression on her face. My mother was biting her lip now; her right eyebrow was slightly raised—a true indication of how agitated she really was. I could see Johnnie attempting, unsuccessfully, to suppress her anger. I just knew if she could reach me, she would slap me silly.

I turned the handle on the car door, and quickly answered, "No, Mother, I'm just bored, and anyway, you know I don't like to stay at home by myself. I could tell you didn't want me to go because you sneaked out."

I slowly slid in the car as I closely watched her.

"I don't have to sneak out," she said. "I am grown, girl." She released the corner of her lip and relaxed her brow.

"Oh, yeah, I almost forgot about the last time I left you home alone. There were policemen all over the place. They were searching around my house and yard as though a fugitive was on the prowl.

"They said someone called them, claimed someone was outside trying the back door and was walking around on the back porch. When I found out that it was you and they didn't find anything, I beat your butt."

Mother changed the subject, to my relief.

"That's what I like about you, though. You have good sense. Looks like you are going to finish high school without worrying about a baby. I don't need to worry about you. You did listen to me. Them other wol's, Sydney and Earlie, they did not listen. Oh, no! They were in love. They wouldn't listen to me."

I always felt uncomfortable whenever someone complimented me so I changed the subject.

"Anyway, Mother, will I be able to go to the senior ball?" There was short silence. Mother exhaled loudly.

"Gal, you know I ain't got no money. Your daddy never sends any money anymore. I haven't heard from him in years. I just can feed you. It's a good thing you can sew, otherwise you wouldn't've had any clothes to wear.

"You're so little for 16. You don't weigh but 80 pounds. I can't find nothing to fit you in the department stores. I can't afford the House of Nine dress shop. There ain't nothing in that store under $100. Maybe you can make your prom dress. You can sew. Your dress will be the prettiest one because it will be different from all the rest."

We rode in silence for a few more blocks. I didn't have anything else to say. I knew the last request had upset her. When she couldn't give her girls what we asked for, she would snap at us, not out of anger but frustration. I was afraid to ask where we were going.

"I figured I'd go spend some time with Mrs. Piggis," Mother blurted out. "She called me this morning and asked me to come over for prayer."

Mrs. Piggis was my mother's best friend. On the drive over, she told me how she met Mother P, as we called her.

"I met Mother Piggis while she was waiting at a bus in Berkeley, right there on San Pablo Avenue. Ooh, wee, those winds were blowing so hard until the trees branches were bending and that rain was just pouring down. She was holding her umbrella out in front like she was fighting the devil himself." Mother chuckled and shook her head still keeping her eyes on the road ahead. "I pulled my old Plymouth over to the curb and asked, 'Would you like a ride?'

"I reached over and opened the door and in she jumped right in the front seat. It was so fast I don't remember her answering me. I introduced myself and she smiled as she gave me her street number.

"'I live in North Oakland on 40th Street near the park.' I could feel Mother P. staring hard at me. I felt funny-like. I turned my head slightly to look at her from the side of my eyes. She said, 'God is blessing you. You ain't never going to go hungry or want for anything. You are getting married again.'

"'Johnnie, you were very hurt by something that your first husband did to your oldest girl. He loves you and his daughters. He felt he was doing the right thing by her. That is your past but I see you married again and it ain't going to be long. He is a good friend. There is someone who has always admired you and he is in love with you. He is a lot older than you.'"

"I stopped the car," Mother said. "I told her, 'You must be crazy!'"

"Mrs. Piggis then said, 'No, I'm not crazy. God told me to tell you that. He also told me that He sees you crying, you are worried about your children and your grandchildren. He is saying, "Fear not, for I am God."'"

"Tears came to my eyes and I tried to blink them back. They fell anyway. I told Mrs. Piggis, 'I haven't cried like this in a long, long time. I didn't even cry when my Mama died.' With the tears falling and the rain pouring down so hard, I couldn't see where we were going."

"Mrs. Piggis looked at me with compassion and said, 'I'm in no hurry. I know that this was no accident meeting you like this. God meant for me to talk to you. Do you believe that, Johnnie?'

"I jest said, 'Yes.' I pulled over slowly and parked to wait for the rain to stop. I told her, 'I cain't see nothin'.'

"Mother P said, 'Let us pray while we're waiting for the rain to stop. The Lord is going to bless you, Johnnie. Bless you with more than you could ever imagine.'"

Mother continued telling me her story.

"I couldn't find anything to say to her. I just sat there with my head bowed as Mother Piggis prayed for me. I was shocked that this woman was asking God for the very things I secretly desired in my life. Only God could know those things. From that day forward, we were the best of friends."

I knew there was something special about Mother P because Mother didn't take to many women. The only women my mother talked to were her sisters, Carrie and Flo, and sisters-in-law, Daisy and Vernice. And my mother very seldom visited anybody.

On the ride over, Mother also explained how God gave Mother P the gift of prophecy. I didn't believe in it nor did I understand it. I knew I didn't have the strong faith in God my Mother had.

"As a child, she would tell complete strangers her visions from God. People avoided her and her family because they feared her peculiar ways. She was very frightened and confused. Her parents pleaded with her not to tell a soul. She complied. God came to her in a dream. He told that she had a special gift that let her see into the future. Through prophesying she would be able to tell them about Jesus, the Son of God. He asked her to tell all about Him, through prophecy. He gave Mother P. scriptures to read.

"Immediately upon waking from this dream, she called her parents into her room and told them what had happened. They tried to convince her it was only a dream. Again, they begged her not to tell anyone about this. She kept hearing God's voice talking to her all the time. She tried to ignore it. It was now happening in the day as well as at night.

"She would quote Scriptures whenever these visions would appear. She begged God to go away but she knew He was there. She didn't tell her parents anymore about it.

"Later, she married a handsome young Texan. They had five children. She talked to God on a regular basis. She confided in her husband who just humored her about it. She would hear God talking. She begged God to leave her alone and let her live a normal life. God wouldn't go away, He wouldn't leave her alone. She tried to block him out. She couldn't sleep from fear. He would talk to her in her dreams.

"Then one night, He spoke to her again, insisting she teach the Gospel through prophecy to sinners and believers alike. When she woke up the next morning, she felt the spirit of God in the room but dismissed the thought. She had overslept. Her children had all gone to school, and she would have to hurry to make the bus in order to get to work on time. As she tried to get out of bed, she was paralyzed from her neck down.

"She could barely talk. She called for her husband but he had left for work earlier.

"She called for her children but they had left for school. Tears welled up inside. She cried out, 'Oh, God, where are you now, why have you done this to me?' There was no answer. She knew God wasn't far, He constantly talked to her before.

"In desperation, she called out to Jesus for help. Mother P. pleaded with the Lord to remove the pain in her head, to remove the numbness from her body. She apologized for ignoring his advice and told God how frightened she was. People had teased her when she was little. Her own family didn't believe her when she would tell them. God promised her if she obeyed Him, he would not only remove this affliction, but He would bless her abundantly.

"From that day forward, she told everyone about God and his wondrous works. Through Scripture and intercessory prayer, she would foretell their life stories, never forgetting to give God the praise and the honor. People came from near and far to meet Mother P.

"Shortly after she started prophesying, teaching the word, God blessed her as He promised. Her husband, Kevin, got promoted to foreman on his job. This was a first. Ordinarily, they didn't let the colored workers give out orders to the white man. Ironically, Kevin was the first black man at his plant given this position. She was able to quit her housekeeping job.

"Her family was able to move out of the shabby two-bedroom projects in West Oakland to an exclusive neighborhood most blacks couldn't afford in North Oakland. The white real estate agent didn't usually show these houses to coloreds, but God had touched his heart.

"They now had enough room in their three-bedroom home for their five children. They were now teenagers and needed their own space and privacy. She had a large living room, formal dining room, eat-in kitchen, two bathrooms, three bedrooms, and a large backyard with plenty of fruit trees. There was a special room allocated for prayer in her lovely home.

"Mother P. thanked God daily and continued to administer to others at her local church who started to call her Mother P. She never charged anyone for her services, but most left a donation anyway. She would even pray over it so the money would multiply for her many clients."

On this particular day, as we pulled into the driveway, we spotted Mr. Piggis sitting on the porch of their Victorian house. He was smoking his pipe as usual. The light gray smoke that flowed from his ebony wooden pipe had the essence of cherries. I loved that smell.

We spoke as we walked up the stairs to the house. He never said much.

Usually, he would just nod his head in a polite gesture. Today was different.

He said, "Go on in, the door's open." Amazing! He actually spoke!

My mother looked at me with her mischievous eyes to let me know she was just as surprised as I was about his verbal response. We both giggled softly as we entered their lavishly furnished home. Their children had grown up, married, and moved out. Mother Piggis and Mr. Piggis were proud grandparents. Mrs. Piggis was about doing God's work and Mr. Piggis was very much retired, enjoying his life finally.

My mother and Mother P hugged, then followed their usual routines of complaining about not calling or about who visited whom last. It would go on and on. It was all in fun.

I found my favorite spot on their French provincial loveseat across from the matching sofa. It was very soft and plush. It was made from the most beautiful brocade fabric I had ever seen.

While I sat there waiting for my mother to return from the prayer room, I daydreamed about my future. I hoped to be a famous singer one day. I was known for my heavy tenor voice, and I loved to sing in public.

After daydreaming, I became restless sitting. Mother Piggis always told me to make myself at home. If I wanted something to drink or had to go to the bathroom, she'd always say, "Gal, you know where the fridge. Jest go and make yourself at home."

On this visit, I went to the bathroom. On my way down the hallway, I peered into the room where she and Mother were in fervent prayer. They were bowed down before her makeshift altar. I had never been in the prayer room before. I had sneaked a peek several times while Mother and Mother Piggis babbled on in the living room. This room held a certain mystery to me. I knew there was lots of praying done in there. An open Bible lay on the table. I smelled incense burning.

It appeared dark but it really wasn't. The reason was because there were two lit candles on the table. I overheard them as they called out, "Jesus, Jesus, Jesus, thank you, Jesus." Mother P started speaking in a language I'd never heard. Later, I asked my Mother what language she spoke. She spoke in Tongue, Mother said. God understood her.

I never had a desire to go in that room. I merely wanted to come along for the ride and to taste Mother P's Hermit Cake. It was my favorite.

They came from that room smiling up a storm.

Mother P was laughing, then she turned, gazing directly at me. I felt uncomfortable but managed a polite smile.

"How old are you, Janie?" she asked.

"Sixteen, I'll be 17 in October of this year," I answered proudly.

"I see you have a lot of boyfriends but you're not serious about any of them." After she took a deep breath, she continued with her eyes closed.

"Janie, I see you are worried about your finances; you want to attend college. God told me to tell you will attend college. He told me to tell you not to worry. You will be able to buy the wardrobe you need and the books. He told me to tell you to trust in Him and he will direct your path." With her eyes still shut, she then said, "Oh, thank you, Jesus! Thank you, Lord!" She continued her revelations.

"God is showing me you are going to meet a nice young man. He is a dark-skinned, handsome man. You will fall in love with him and you will marry him, but not right away."

With her arm around my shoulder, Mother Piggis gently steered me toward her prayer room.

"Come with me. Oh, thank you, Lord, thank you, Jesus."

I obeyed her but looked back at my mother for reassurance. She smiled and gestured for me to go on. I was so very frightened. I followed her down the hallway, not knowing what to expect. A chill went all over my body. I shuddered. Yet, I felt I had to follow.

Immediately after entering the prayer room, Mother P. had me repeat a Scripture with her. I felt such comfort as we read along together.

The Lord is my light and my salvation
Whom shall I fear?
The Lord is the strength of my life;
Of whom shall I be afraid?

Tears of joy rolled down my cheeks as we quoted this Scripture. God was truly in that room. I could actually visualize what she was predicting to me.

"Yes, Janie, God is going to bless you with a baby. He is going to be different than other children. It is dark around your child, and he seems lonely. God is going to use you through your child."

"I'm not married yet, and I don't even have a boyfriend now," I said. "I'm still a virgin. I'm saving myself for the right man and besides I'm not ready yet. I plan to finish school first, then go to college."

Mother P ignored me, then preceded on with her prediction.

"You're going to meet a young man who is very intelligent. He is not very tall, in fact he is short. He has a strong desire to be somebody. You're going to get pregnant before you marry him, though, because I see you in a green maternity smock. There is a lot of people there, seems like some sort of party going on. I see you talking to one of your friends. You're telling her, 'We are getting married but we are waiting until he finishes college and gets a good job.'"

I protested loudly.

"No, I'm not getting pregnant. I promised God and my sisters I would finish high school and go to college. I'm waiting until I'm married. Sydney and Earlie will be upset with me. I am not going to disappoint them."

I prayed silently to God, "Please, Lord, don't let this happen to me. Please."

Mother P went on with her prediction.

"Don't worry, I don't see it happening soon. You are going to finish high school. You will be very young when this happens. God is leading me to tell you this: You will marry this young man. I ain't going to take it back. God is going to bless you through this union.

Oh, thank you, Jesus! He is showing me this young man. He has a large head. His hair is cut very short. He is a very clean-cut young man. Very smart. Yes, thank you, Lord. I see him in a blue uniform. I can't tell if it is an Air Force or Marines uniform. He loves you very much. I see you in a park-like setting. You have on this pink dress. I can see you now. You have your little son with you, too. You and your husband are holding his hands. It looks like you are walking in a beautiful green park. You two look so happy! When you marry him be sure and wear pink that day."

"I didn't want to hear no more. I didn't want to seem disrespectful but I didn't want to believe any of this. I wanted to scream out, "NO! This is not going to happen to me." I felt so hot and tears kept falling from my eyes. I just wanted to run from that room but I was glued there.

Finally, Mother P led me back into the living room where my mother waited. My mother had an anticipatory look on her face. I didn't want her to ask me anything. Mother P never said a word to Mother about our encounter in that room. They gave their usual good-byes and we were on our way.

We were quiet during our return ride.

"Don't worry, I am not going to ask you what Mother P said," Mother finally remarked. "Mother P won't reveal it to me neither. She says it is only God that knows all. She keeps all her readings confidential. It doesn't matter none to her that I am your mother, she ain't going to tell. You don't have to tell me. She has never been too far off in her predictions, I can tell you that for sure."

I never mentioned it again. Neither did my mother.

CHAPTER SEVEN

I went on a blind date with my best friend from Oakland in February 1960 that changed my life. Mayola had just gotten married a few days before. She called to invite me out to the drive-in movies in east Oakland. She told me about this "fine young man" who was a friend of her husband's. Against my better judgment, I agreed to meet him. My mother and my sisters agreed to let me go only if I picked up my cousin, Dorothy, to be a chaperone. I knew they meant well, but it was embarrassing for me. I always tried to obey my mother and my older sisters because I knew they were only trying to protect me. They insisted Mayola and her new husband pick up my cousin on the other side of town to accompany me.

This dude, my blind date, turned out to be in love with himself. On the way to the movies, he kept up a constant conversation about himself. He had an "I-I-I" complex. "I did this and I did that" and "I know that I am fine." This was the bulk of the conversation. The first chance I got, I whispered to my cousin that when we got to the movies, she and I would disappear into the snack bar.

"I heard there were some really cute guys there," I said. She readily agreed.

After the car was parked, the newlyweds started smooching in the front seat. Dorothy and I excused ourselves. The conceited guy just sat there, staring at us, with his mouth hanging open in total disbelief. The two of us were just giggling about the whole scenario.

Dorothy and I were a sight to see. She was 5'8" with a very nicely formed petite figure. Her golden copper skin with light hazel eyes was a contrast. She had on a cute light blue sailor dress with the matching shoes. I think that she only weighed about 100 pounds.

I, on the other hand, was 4'8" tall, also very petite. My hair was cut into a cute pixie style and I had dark eyes that appeared to look right through you. I was always told my constant smile gave me a very mischievous look. I weighed about 89 pounds. I had on a short and tight white skirt, with a split in the kick pleat near the hem. I was always given compliments whenever I wore that skirt with my matching cashmere sweater. I had on a pair of high-heeled pumps that gave me the appearance of being at least 5'1".

We walked up a steep slope in the dark, trying to find our way to the snack bar. This was our first time to this drive-in.

As we approached the entrance to the snack bar, a group of guys started flirting with us. They casually stood around, blocking the entrance, and someone whistled as we assertively made our way through the group.

One of them, a dark-skinned guy, gave me the once-over. My heart started thumping fast. He was sort of cute, I thought silently. All of the other fellows looked a little too rough for me, not my type at all. We were from Berkeley and the guys from Oakland were more aggressive. They called us "Those Seditty Berkeley Girls." Seditty was a slang word for sophisticated. My cousin and I both changed our stature so they would not think we were intimidated. I guess it worked, because they moved aside and let us through.

As we made our way toward the doorway entrance, the same dark-skinned guy said, dripping with sarcasm, "Excuse me." I knew he was merely trying to get my attention by the devilish smile on his face. I didn't feel anything, but I may have bumped into him accidentally. I turned and quickly apologized.

"Ooh, baby," he answered back. "It's okay. You can bump me anytime."

"I am not your baby," I snapped back, annoyed. "You certainly are not my father."

"Well, excuse me then, Little Mama," he answered back curtly.

His friends found this entertaining. I was furious because I thought they were making fun of us.

"And I am certainly not your mama, I did not give birth to you," I said abruptly.

"Hey, baby, why you want to put me down? I find you attractive and I am only trying to make conversation with you."

"Okay, you did, now excuse me." With that, I walked on into the snack bar where Dorothy was waiting for me.

We laughed with relief that we had made it through the maze. We discussed how we were going to get back through without another encounter with "The Boys."

We ordered our food and walked out the exit doors on the opposite side of the snack bar. We were so relieved we didn't have to see those guys again.

However, I did find the one who had teased me very attractive. We found our way back through the dark to the familiar car. To my relief, Mayola informed me my blind date had left to join other friends in another car. I made a remark to let her know I was glad that he had left with his "I-I-I" syndrome. I started mocking him and how he kept rubbing his finger-waved hair.

Mayola felt bad and insisted on finding me the perfect date for that night. Despite my objections, she left at intermission to go get this "sophisticated gentleman" who was one of her best friends. She told me he was a smart dresser and very handsome with dark skin. He was clean-cut, lived in Alameda and a senior at Encinal High School. He was from Oakland but had moved in his junior year.

It wasn't very long before she returned with him, literally dragging him by the arm. He didn't look very happy. I confided in Dorothy that I didn't want to meet anybody else. I'd had enough blind dates for one night. She invited him into the car but he stopped suddenly at the door—as though he had seen a ghost.

"You want me to get into the car with her?" he said. "She just cussed me out a few minutes ago, called me a whole bunch of names, talked about my mama and told me I was an ugly baby and she wouldn't be seen with me!"

He was the guy who teased me in front of the snack bar. He had that same mischievous sideways smile on his face.

Dorothy and I started laughing.

"He is lying," I interrupted, trying to explain what really happened but he kept fast-talking me. I couldn't get a word in.

He was kind of cute, I thought to myself. Mayola nudged him to get into their two-door sedan, because it was windy and cold out.

"Get in, David," she said. "Get in the car; it's too cold out here. We need to close the door. I'll introduce you after you get into the car. Hurry."

He jumped right into the back seat with Dorothy and I. His friend climbed in, too. Dorothy wasn't about to move for this guy. Mayola suggested I sit on

David's lap. At least I knew his name was David now. After we got situated in the back seat of the car, we were formally introduced to the two gentlemen. Even to this day, I couldn't believe I actually sat on this strange boy's lap. I didn't have to worry about Mother, my sisters would have killed me if they had seen me.

Well, it turned out to be just an innocent night of laughter. I sat on David Bess' lap. He kept us in stitches during the movie we were watching. To tell you the truth, I don't even remember the movie. He was a born comedian. He had the nerve to demand complete silence when the cartoons appeared on the screen. He was serious too. We had a lovely time. When he asked for my phone number, I gave a lame excuse. I thought he was kind of cute, nice but just not my type. It was just a wild, funny night.

❧━❍─◦◦❀◦◦─❍━❧

Graduation was just a few weeks away, with the prom coming. I had passed my finals. I made a point of walking over casually to tell the old fuddy-duddy neighbors that I was graduating.

I greeted them with respect, then proudly announced, "By the way, my graduation date is June 6, 1960."

After their dry congratulations ended, I dropped the bomb on them.

"In case you are interested, I am still a virgin." My little tartan-plaid skirt fit every curve. I topped it off with a candy-red waist-length top to show off my slim figure. I swished off across the street. I could hear them whispering, "Now that one is going to be somebody! You know, that girl can sing. She made a recording, too."

For my senior prom, I wore a gorgeous pink dress. It was strapless with tiers of chiffon ruffles that stopped just above my knees. For the first time in my life, I looked glamorous. Earlie made my prom dress. It was so beautiful. It fit my hips well. Mother bought my satin pumps that Sydney dyed the same color as my dress.

Earlie did miracles with my fine hair. She colored it a soft ash brown then pressed and curled it. It looked thick and pretty.

She was attending beauty school. She used all her new acquired skills to make me glamorous. My date, Greg, was due shortly.

Earlie was more excited than I was. I know she wanted me to have fun. She couldn't attend her senior prom because she was pregnant. My sister loved me; she was so proud of me.

My family was all excited. I was so very happy. My date was due any minute. My heart thumped loudly. I was trying to calm down when the doorbell rang. There stood my date. He had on blue jeans and a Ban-lon shirt. I couldn't believe it. I asked him why wasn't he ready.

"Where is your tuxedo?" I said.

After Greg stammered and stuttered, I went berserk. I ran back to the kitchen to get something. I grabbed flowerpots off the stair ledge and began throwing them at him. He ducked just in time. Quickly leaping over the rail, he ran to his Thunderbird parked in the driveway. He quickly jumped in and sped off. I stood there, not believing what happened. Nothing anyone said made me feel better. I couldn't stop crying.

Just then, Mayola called to see if I was still going to my prom.

Between my loud sobbing, I explained what had happened. Mayola immediately went to work. She tried to get in touch with David, the guy I met at the drive-in. She told me, "David has a tux. He rented it for his prom yesterday. He has been trying to reach you every since that night at the drive-in."

I was desperate now. I wanted to go so badly. I said. "Call David for me, please. Ask him if he would go."

I doubted he would call. After all, I wouldn't give him my number even when Mayola kept bugging me for it.

She tried to contact him but he was out. I ended up staying home with my mother and my sisters who tried to comfort me. Later, I found out why my prom date showed up without a tuxedo.

Earlie kept bugging me to give her Greg's number. Well, after all the excitement, I did not want to see him ever again. I never called his number but Earlie did.

When I was dating him he promised Earlie tires at a discount price. He said his father owned a service station where he worked.

"I'll get you a good deal, for cheap," he promised.

She called and a woman answered.

"I am trying to find Greg," Earlie said. "He told me he could get me a good deal on some tires."

An uneasy silence followed.

Earlie rambled on, "You see, Greg told me he worked at his father's service station and…"

The voice on the other end quickly interrupted her and said, "Greg's father is dead."

Earlie then replied, "Oh, then maybe it is Greg Jr. He was supposed to escort my sister to her prom but he forgot to go by the Tuxedo shop and…"

The woman interrupted Earlie again.

"Greg Jr. is 5 years old. But Greg Sr. is my husband. And he is 25."

"Oh, no" Earlie said in shock. "He told my sister he was only 19. That dirty dog is married?"

"Yes, he's married. In fact, I found out about his secret prom date. When he went to pick up his tuxedo, he found out I had cancelled the rental."

Earlie could hardly wait until I got home that day. She was sitting on the brick stairs waiting to tell me what happened to Greg.

I heard through the grapevine that Greg's wife was a short, obese woman. That answered all my questions. She beat him up pretty bad, I heard. That served him right for trying to take advantage of me, a naive teen.

CHAPTER EIGHT

With my diploma in hand, my girlfriends and I wanted to do something different to celebrate graduation. All the graduates went their separate ways. Since one of my friends got a car for her graduation gift, she suggested that we go somewhere. I suggested the drive-in movies. I told them about my encounter with this certain young man. His name was David Bess, I said. I was hoping that I might run into him again. When I mentioned all the good-looking guys hanging outside the snack bar, they were game.

Well, I didn't see David that night but one of his friends was there and recognized me from that time before. He told me David had been trying to contact me ever since. This was my chance to see him again. He asked me to give him my phone number. He said, "I promise, I'll make sure he gets it." So I did.

Lo and behold, the next day, I got a call from him. He asked me to go to a mambo session with him. I accepted. We set a date for the following weekend. He said we would double date with his brother, Johnny. And his fiancé.

This was my first time ever going to a dance where they played Latin-Cuban music. What an experience! I didn't know how to dance like this elite group. They were mostly college students. I was doing the Cha-Cha. I felt so clumsy. I felt like everyone was staring at me. David danced at a much slower tempo. moving smoothly with fewer steps. Me? Well, I seemed to be running with my little short legs. I was moving way too fast for the beat.

Then I accidentally stepped on his foot. That is when he took control. He said, "Just take my hands, slow down a pace and follow my lead." He gave me his sexy, sideways smile.

He explained he went to "sessions" all the time. I just had to learn this dance. It didn't take long before I got into the groove of it. I loved the way his arms felt around my waist. It felt very natural to be in his arms.

He slowly led me into different steps with him. He was a smooth dancer yet I could feel his untamed energy as he swirled and twirled me around. I liked the way he took control on the dance floor. He guided me gently with confidence to this new tempo. I had a ball that night! I was floating by the time I arrived at my doorstep.

He made one mistake. When he reached my door, he grabbed me and passionately kissed me.

"I sure would like to know you better," he said.

For some people, that is a pretty tame expression. But for me, that phrase just sent off alarms. I had a date with a boy from Richmond before and he had said the same thing to me. Only, he just wanted to get to know me better sexually. He started getting fresh with me after one kiss on my front porch. I kneed him in the groin and punched him in the eye. That was the end of our relationship.

David was doing fine before that. He kissed me gently at first, then he started French kissing, I was okay with that. too. I rather enjoyed it.

But when David said, "I want to get to know you better ¼" I had flashbacks of that Richmond dude. I slapped David's face so hard it scared me. He stood there stunned. I ran up the stairs to my door and yelled, "You have known me as well as you're going to."

He had this puzzled look on his face. I stood in the front entryway, pondering if I acted irrationally. He was so polite and a gentleman all night. I peeked though the small porthole window looking down at him. He stood in front of my house staring up at the closed door. He scratched his head, turned and then walked off.

The next day, Mayola called me.

"What happened?" she asked. "David said you two were having a good time. He said he only asked you if he could get to know you better and you slapped him! He said he didn't know why you were mad."

I told her about my experience with the other date. She cracked up.

Once Mayola explained that boys from Oakland, like David, were more direct in asking for sex, I knew I had made a mistake. I had to talk to him.

I told my cousin Dorothy about my date and how I slapped his face. She cracked up at first then said, "Just call him and explain."

I was hesitant at first.

"He must have thought I was really crazy!' She kept insisting that I call him.

Finally, we came up with an idea. We would pretend we were a popular radio station that sponsored a contest called the $64,000 Question. They called up listeners randomly and asked them to give the correct answer to a question. If they got it right, they won $64,000.

I sat at the piano just playing around while trying to think of a tune when I got a bright idea. Using the letters to David's name I composed an up tempo tune. Dorothy grabbed the opportunity and called David. When David answered the phone, she immediately put on her professional voice. That's when the charade began.

"Is this David Bess? Congratulations! Your number was randomly picked for our contest, the $64,000 Question. For $64,000, can you name this tune?"

I began to play the piano and sing a song using the letters of his first name. It went D-A-V-I-D, D-A-V-I-D-. I was singing so fast. I knew he couldn't distinguish the words from the song.

"Can you tell us what the words of the song?" Dorothy said.

He chuckled, then asked Dorothy, "Can I tell you who is singing?"

"I'm sorry but you have to tell us what the words are to win the contest."

"I don't know what she is singing, but can I tell who is singing instead?"

Dorothy couldn't hold it any longer. She broke out in laughter and handed me the phone. From that day forward, David and I were inseparable. Mambo sessions became one of our favorite pastimes.

I started Merritt Business College in fall 1960. David was attending school at Laney College. Our campuses were about 10 miles apart. He caught the bus to meet me after class; we would walk together to my house every day. We would joke and horseplay all the way.

He told me his family had promised him a car but hadn't given it to him yet. He was the youngest of three brothers. His oldest brother married young because he and his girlfriend were having a baby. To do the right thing, he quit school to take care of his new family. The middle brother finished school but didn't walk across the stage to receive his diploma. David was the only one to finish school and formally receive his diploma. His parents were very proud of him so they had promised him a car. But they hadn't been able to buy one. I didn't care; I loved him so much and was just happy to be with him. We had fun walking, holding hands and planning our future together.

David and I did everything together. Our families finally met, they hit it off really well together. Everything seemed to be going along smoothly for David and I.

Early that spring, David's parents kept their promise and bought him his first car, a yellow Oldsmobile with a black top. We were so excited because we could be alone together now. Before, we always double-dated.

One of my friends was curious about David and I. We had been dating for more than a year and hadn't had sex yet. She told me she felt this was an odd relationship. She advised me to find out if he was gay. I explained to her we had a special kind of relationship; sex wasn't an issue. We were waiting until after college. We planned to marry after he got his associate degree in architectural drafting.

She kept telling me: "Girl, you had better check him out. He may not make you happy sexually."

"I know he can satisfy me," I'd say.

"You mean to tell me that, you have been going with him for over a year and you haven't done anything? There is something definitely wrong with that.

"You better do 'it' soon to see if he is the one for you. You may be disappointed."

I said, "I might get pregnant."

She reassured me.

"No, you won't get pregnant the first time. I've done it several times and nothing happened."

"My mother and my sisters will be mad at me."

"They don't have to know. You won't get pregnant, girl."

She kept after me and I began thinking seriously about it. My sisters had already threatened David. "Do you know Janie is a virgin?" they asked. He said, "Yes, she told me."

"Now we warn you, if you even try anything, you will have to answer to both of us," Sydney said.

David looked down at my sisters who were both under 5 feet 2 inches tall.

He chuckled at them as though they had told a joke.

"I'm not afraid of you little women," he said. "I'll take both of you on at the same time."

He should have never said that.

It was late. They coaxed him into the living room, and then barricaded the door. Sydney turned out the lights. Both Sydney and Earlie took the Rainier Ale bottles they had been drinking from and beat him all over his head. I could hear him yelling, "Hey, man, why'd you turn the lights off?"

Earlie said, "You said you could take us both on."

"I can't see. Turn those lights on. OW! You're hitting me with those bottles. Ow. That is my head, you know!"

I heard Sydney giggling. Then there was a loud thud.

"Ow! That hurts! Take it easy!"

Earlie said, "You will not touch our sister, you understand?"

"I was just joking with you guys. God!"

I heard Sydney and Earlie laughing.

"Let me in," I yelled. "I'm telling Mother on you."

I tried to rescue him but they had locked the door. I couldn't get in to help him. When he came out of that room, he was a changed man. He showed respect for my sisters from that day forward.

CHAPTER NINE

One Saturday afternoon, my mother had to leave. Earlie was at the hospital having her second baby. Sydney wasn't home either.

My family already accepted David. They never worried about us being alone together anymore. We were planning to get married the next year.

Well, it didn't work out that way. I kept hearing my girlfriend's voice prodding me to "try it to see if you'll like it."

David dropped by that afternoon just to sit and talk with Earlie and Sydney. This was a usual routine for the three of them. David had no sisters and we had no brothers. So, they really enjoyed each other. Sometimes I would just sit and listen while they gave him advice.

But my sisters weren't home and my mother was running out the door when David arrived. After Mother hastily drove off, I put on some slow romantic music. I thought this is the right time. So I started dancing to the slow music, moving my slim hips in a suggestive manner. It wasn't long before I had convinced him what I wanted to do.

It wasn't like I pictured it would be. I felt dirty and ashamed. David was remorseful and kept apologizing. I felt worse. I'd broken my promise to God and my family.

We promised after that night never to do this again until after marriage.

We went on double dates after that last escapade. We kept our promise to never do that again. Our relationship was strained. He stopped visiting with my sisters. I think his conscience bothered him also. I tried to avoid my sisters as well. This was impossible for me because I was being drilled by them daily. They kept asking me if I had done anything. I denied it. They were suspicious. They stayed on my back: "David must have broken up with you or somethin'." "What happened to David?" "Why doesn't David come over as much now? He used to be here every night. What happened?" I would just make some excuse about his final exams taking up his time or something. I didn't have to make excuses for long. A short time later, David's car threw a rod.

He was driving to my house when it happened. His father had it towed back home. He spent most of his time on the weekends fixing his car. It took over two months for him to fix it. Finances and lack of experience was the main factor behind that. That gave us plenty of time to think and to be alone.

Meanwhile, I had focused back to my singing career. Our singing quartet consisted of four girls named The DeVells. We were practicing faithfully and diligently for three whole weeks. We had been invited to sing at an Easter concert. Immediately after the show, we were scheduled to sign a contract with a famous recording studio. We were just extremely happy. We had been waiting for this break.

We were featured alongside Martha and the Vandelas, Ray Charles and the Raylettes at the Oakland Auditorium. Oh! I couldn't forget Etta James! She was my idol! She was scheduled to give a cameo appearance during the show before intermission time. This was the moment I'd been waiting for. We were finally going to make it big! My dream was coming true.

Two days before the concert, I came down with a fever. My temperature was so high I couldn't even sing. I left for home early that night from practice to get some rest. I assured everyone I would be fine.

My mother went to work to break the fever. She rubbed me down with alcohol before applying Mentholated rub all over my body. She used her special formula. Mother then wrapped me up from head to toe with a warm blanket. I hated the smell of the mentholated rub.

Mother insisted I stay home the next night, too, because she said that my eyes still looked peaky. But she promised me I would be ready for the concert on Easter Sunday. Again I was rubbed down with the same stuff. I could hardly wait till morning so I could take a nice shower and get that eucalyptus smell off me.

Easter Sunday I leaped out of bed and grabbed my giant green bath towel, wrapping it around me as I hurried to take a shower. I was so excited. We were to perform at the Easter concert that very night. But first, we were to meet at the Oakland Auditorium that morning for dress rehearsal.

I almost collided head-on with Earlie as I rushed for the bathroom. She stood there, frozen. Her mouth was hanging wide open; her eyes appeared as though they were popping out of her head. She just kept staring at me. I became annoyed with her. Sometimes, Earlie plays too much, I thought.

However, I wasn't in the mood. Not today. I was just about to give her a piece of my mind, but she started calling for Mother.

"Mother, oh Mother. Come here. Please come see Janie."

By the time Mother arrived down the hallway from her bedroom, Earlie had snatched my towel from around me. The movement was swift like a matador moving his red cape off the angry bull without much effort.

"Look, Mother, Janie has red bumps all over her body. What is that? She can't go like that. Can you get rid of the bumps for her so she can sing on stage?"

I had always been a big crybaby. It was no different on this day. The uncontrollably hot tears were now streaming down my face. I was upset with Earlie. She always had to blab on me! Earlie always noticed everything! Mother simply gave her prognosis.

"Girl, stop that crying. It isn't going to help none to cry. Looks like you got the measles. You will be all right."

I then started begging her to call the doctor.

"Mother, please, I am probably allergic to that mentholated rub that you rubbed all over me last night to break the fever. Please call the doctor."

Mother looked at me as if I had stolen something.

"Girl, I know you must have lost your mind! I haven't got any money. I only have enough money to last us the rest of this month. You think that money grows on trees."

"But Mother, remember, I am getting paid tonight if I get a chance to perform. I just know it isn't the measles. Didn't I have the measles before? We will be signing a contract with our agent tonight. And we are getting a lot of money for this show. I'll pay you the money back, right after the show. Please, Mother, call the doctor."

"It is Easter Sunday," Mother said. "If the doctor comes out, he is going to take the pants off of us. Do you know how much that cost for a house call? It's Easter, girl."

I was really sobbing loudly now.

"Please, Mother, this is my big chance. I've got to be there. The girls are waiting on me. I can't let them down. Please!"

"All right, all right. You want me to pay a doctor. I already told you what it is. But, no, you need a doctor. You are going to pay me back my money, you hear?"

It took forever for that doctor to get there. My mother just sat quietly in a chair nearby my bed as he examined me. She had this knowing look on her face. He took my temperature first and then checked my heartbeat. After taking my blood pressure, he examined me thoroughly from head to toe. He then confirmed that I, indeed, did have the measles. My mother didn't say a word after the prognosis. She didn't have to. Her eyes gave me the "I told you so" look. I was just dumbfounded. I was instructed not to leave the house.

"You are on quarantine, young lady," the doctor said.

Just as he was packing to leave, Sydney entered my bedroom. She was bringing me a hot cup of tea. He looked at her impregnated figure and asked, "How many months along are you, young lady?"

I had forgotten all about Sydney because she was unusually quiet. I could tell she didn't like the attention being diverted toward her. She was expecting her fourth child and didn't wish to discuss it.

"I'm seven months along," she answered. "Why?"

"Oh, it doesn't matter, you are far enough along. Seeing that you are well into your pregnancy, the measles won't to be detrimental to you or your unborn child."

VISIONS

I wanted to ask him what he meant by that, but I didn't want mother to know I had missed my period. I just had to ask him a question in private. My chance came when my mother and Sydney left my room shortly.

"Doctor," I said, peeking around the doorway, "my period is late. Could the measles cause that?"

"Well, yes, when was your last period?"

"Six weeks ago, sir."

"So, how late are you?"

I watched d him writing in my records, praying my mother couldn't hear me.

"Just two weeks."

"Well, yes, that could cause a delay or you could possibly skip a month. Have you any reason to be concerned about your period?"

Mother walked in and was standing there listening.

"Uh, no, sir. I was supposed to start this week but I'm late. I have never been late before. That's why I asked you."

"Oh, don't worry about it then. If you haven't started your menstrual cycle by next month, contact you regular doctor." He was putting his tools away and his file. "Everything will be fine. Just make sure you don't let anyone pregnant, excluding your sister, be exposed to you. Stay indoors for seven days. You are on quarantine." He picked up his bag, handed Mother the bill, then he left

I kept thinking, I should have told him the truth; that I might be pregnant. Then I reminded myself: you had sex, but it was only one time. I can't be pregnant. Relax, Janie.

⁂

Meanwhile, my mother was seeing an older widowed friend named Henry Prather. He was a quiet and pleasant man. My mother seemed happy. I could see it in her eyes. It made me happy to see her with a nice man. She didn't date often because she always said she did not want just any man to raise her girls. She was very protective of us.

Mr. Prather was an old family friend who belonged to our church. He had lost his wife, Mary, a few years before to diabetes.

She was a sweet caring women. We all loved and respected her. When I was younger, while my father was still there and we lived paycheck to paycheck, Mary made sure Henry delivered a tree and presents to our house every Christmas.

During Mary's long illness, she lost her sight and couldn't walk. Mother went over there every day. She prayed with Mary, and gave her medicines too. She cleaned, washed, and cooked for her. Henry offered to pay my mother, but she wouldn't take anything from him. Mother felt she could never repay them for all their kind deeds. She enjoyed going over and talking to Mary. She was an older wise woman who gave my mother sound advice. Mother truly missed her when she died. Henry would come over and sit with my mother and talk for hours at a time.

When he asked her to marry him, I wasn't surprised. I was very happy for my mother. I had never seen her truly happy before. This was the first time she didn't have to want for anything. He showered her with expensive gifts.

She was finally enjoying her life. I saw a change in her. She would laugh and her eyes sparkled with excitement. Ironically, I was the only one who approved of my mother's friend.

Earlie and Sydney made fun and teased my mother.

"He's too old for you, Mother" or "Why would you want to marry Mr. Prather? He's old enough to be your father! You must be desperate, Mother."

I, on the other hand, reminded Mother Earlie and Sydney were adults and living their lives to the fullest. I told her it was time for her to live. I also told her not to worry about me, I was going to be all right.

Mr. Prather and mother got married that summer, a few weeks after the measles ended my singing career. She made me promise not to tell my sisters. It was during that time I actually bonded with my mother. She moved in with him, but so as not to arouse suspicion, she left some of her clothes and belongings at home.

My sisters were still living at home, unaware of Mother's marriage. They resented the fact she was staying with that "old man." They pretty much ran things at the house. My mother was very proud of me. She seemed relaxed knowing I was in college. She didn't have to worry about me anymore.

CHAPTER TEN

B ut she did have to worry. Three months after Easter, still no period. I knew for sure I was pregnant. I had to tell Mother and I had to tell David. What should I do? Should I tell Mother first? Naw. She'll tell Earlie and Sydney. I'll tell David first. Lord! I'm scared. What will he say? What if he rejects me or accuses me of lying? I heard of guys lying, saying, "It ain't mine!" I was so very frightened!

I remembered what happened to my oldest sister. Her boyfriend had lied about her and said she had sex with all his friends. Because she was only 14 and he was 19, my parents pressed charges. They took him to court on statutory rape charges. He denied the baby until he was born. In the courtroom, he told the judge my sister had lied about her age. He also told him he thought she was 18. He brought his buddies with him. They stood in front of the judge and said she had sex with all of them. The judge then told the guys they were going to jail for statuary rape along with her boyfriend. They changed their story quickly and told the truth. The father of her child went to jail for statutory rape for six months. When he got out of jail, he came to see his son. He looked just like him. That's when the rumors stopped.

My poor sister. She loved this man in spite of what he had done and continued to sneak out to see him. That's how she got pregnant again. My parents were heartbroken over it but there was nothing they could do. Once she made 18, they got married. I knew David would not do anything like that but I still worried about how he would treat me. My sisters' boyfriends all changed once they got pregnant and they were married. My sisters were mentally and physically abused by the men who swore they loved them. I didn't want this to happen to me. I asked God to forgive me. I prayed and asked Him to help me to say the right things at the right time.

David and I had a date the night I decided to tell him. The YMCA gave a hayride party to the San Francisco beach for a wiener roast. The Berkeley Teen Club that I belonged to sponsored it. I had warned David I had something important to tell him that night. I had told my best friend, the same one who told me I wouldn't get pregnant the first time. She was the only one who knew.

We rode in the back of the hay wagon. On the ride to the beach, the tension between David and I was thick. After we had put our blankets down on the beach, we took a little walk alongside the ocean water. I needed to be alone with him to talk.

I had butterflies in my stomach and then the chills started. My teeth chattered loudly. Goose bumps appeared on my arms and I couldn't stop shivering. I had on a red halter-top and white shorts. I felt so stupid because Mother had warned me before I left it would be cold. I wish I had listened to her.

"Janie, gal, you had better take a jacket or something. I ain't particular about you going on this wiener roast anyway! I ain't never heard of no such thing! A wiener roast, huh?"

Mother turned her head to look at me sideways. "Anyway jest whose wiener are you going to roast?" Embarrassed, I shrieked out: "Mother-r-r!"

My girlfriends broke out laughing. They thought it was funny. I didn't. I rushed them out the house so fast until I had forgotten my sweater.

David quickly took off his jacket and gently placed it around my shoulders without uttering a single word. After a very short while, I just blurted it out.

"I'm pregnant, David. You don't have to marry me. I can manage it. I'll be 19 this year so I am considered an adult." The words rushed from my mouth. This wasn't the way I planned it at all. I had rehearsed it over and over again in my mind. Now I felt like a fool.

He reached over and hugged me close to him. He kissed me passionately.

"What are you worried about? I love you," he said, looking me straight in my eyes. "We will just get married sooner than we planned to, that's all."

I took a deep breath of relief. I knew then that everything was going to be all right. We both decided we would have a family gathering to discuss our future plans about the new addition. We would announce our engagement and the news about the baby. We decided not to marry for another year, though. David had almost completed his classes and only had a few credits left.

David tried to reassure me. He said, "I have to finish school but I will work part-time."

I said, "I'll attend school for as long as I can,"

"We both went home that night with a new perspective on life.

We met with David's family the following month. They lived in the Alameda Naval Housing projects. We only told our families that we wanted to announce our engagement. Both families decided to make it a festive occasion. After we announced our engagement, we threw in the news about the baby. David and I were surprised at how well they took it.

Before me and David made our announcement, Mother said, "First, I have an announcement to make—me and Henry Prather got married this summer." I saw the exchange of looks between my sisters when Henry let them know they'd been married since June. Sydney and Earlie were shocked that I, knew about their marriage.

Thank God. It made it easier for David and me to tell them about our baby.

Mother cooked Creole gumbo for the party. They loved it. The Bess family prepared enchiladas. My family had never tasted enchiladas before. We had a feast. This was the first time we had come together as a family.

Both families found they had a lot in common. They exchanged good conversations and family recipes before we left. This was the beginning of a tradition that lasted through the years.

"Why you taking up for Mr. Prather?" Sydney asked.

"Because he is good for Mother! You just jealous 'cause you don't have a nice husband. Sydney, maybe you and Earlie should marry an older mature man, too"

Sydney said, "You just wait 'til David finishes with you," Sydney sneered. "He hasn't married you yet."

"Yeah, at least James married me right away," Earlie added.

David and I were not together as much. Our relationship seemed to have slid downhill. I couldn't concentrate on my classes anymore. I had an incomplete in all of my classes. I dropped out of college. I resigned from the singing group. I had started to show. My plans were changed. I really focused in on my problems: I was pregnant, with no money. I was really worried about my future. Mother's friend, Mother P, had been right about me being an unwed mother-to-be. He was not in the Air force or the Marines, that's for sure. Her prediction, I thought, was just a coincidence.

Meanwhile, my sisters were having a hard time financially because Mother had moved in with her husband, Mr. Prather. One night, I came home from school later than usual. They started in on me.

"Where have you been? Probably up to no good. You probably have been doing you-know-what with that old, ugly, black boy David."

They really knew how to hurt my feelings.

"Do you have any money to pay for your food while you're staying here?" Earlie asked.

I was shocked.

"Of course I don't have any money," I said. "I don't have to pay you anything. Mother buys all the food here."

"Things have changed from the time that you left for school," Sydney said.

"Since you don't have any money, you will have to move," Earlie added.

I was just devastated. I didn't have anywhere to go.

"This is my mother's house. She pays the rent here, not you! I don't have to leave!"

Sydney then retaliated, "I must inform you that from now on, Earlie and I are roommates. We pay the rent here now!"

"How can you pay the rent? You can't afford this house," I said.

"Oh, yes, we can. We made Mother give us back our money that we receive from welfare for our babies. We told her that we could handle our own money. We know how to budget."

I realized I wasn't wanted there so I called Mother, sobbing. Mr. Prather told Mother without hesitation that I could come. I could live in his house and finish my education.

Henry Prather then took the phone from Johnnie to reassure me.

"You have been always respectable to your mother and to me, as well. Pack you things. We're on our way. We will be right there."

I packed so fast I couldn't believe it myself. They came and picked me up immediately. My sisters just stood in the doorway with their mouths agape. Both of them had this stupid look on their faces when Mother and Henry Prather pulled up in their brand new Mercury Marquis. I was so happy to see them and surprised that Henry had bought Mother a new car.

Things certainly changed after that. I had my own room. I was so happy there. I started calling Mr. Prather Daddy.

Before their marriage announcement, I wasn't sure what to call him I felt awkward calling him Mr. Prather but I couldn't call him Henry. I never called Johnnie by her name. We all (including the neighborhood children) addressed her as Mother. I was taught to respect my elders. So I just couldn't call him Henry. Shortly afterward, we moved into their new home, me included. I asked him could I call him Daddy. He seemed so flattered. That's what I called him ever since.

David would come over and both Mother and Daddy treated him with a lot of respect. He asked for my hand in marriage and permission to marry me.

My sisters started to visit more frequently at the new house. Sydney noticed my expensive, new wardrobe hanging in my closet.

"Where did you get those pretty outfits from, Janie?" she said. "I saw these same clothes and those same heels at Macy's in downtown Oakland." Sydney shuffled the clothes back and forth, examining every piece hanging on the rack.

Without thinking about it, I answered, "Daddy bought them for me." Sydney had this scowl on her face now.

"Daddy? I know that you ain't talking' about our daddy. Not Daddy Lightfoot! He hasn't bought us anything since you went to visit him the summer you graduated. We don't even know where he is now."

"I'm not talking about him. I'm talking about my new Daddy, Mr. Prather," I said.

Sydney started laughing, "Shoot! Humph! I'm going to start calling him Daddy too!" She practiced saying, "Daddy. Oh Daddy…" as she made her way to the living room looking for him. Henry chuckled light-heartedly about it.

"Yes, you can call me Daddy, too," he said proudly.

From that day forward, my sisters called Henry Prather "Daddy," too.

CHAPTER ELEVEN

I will never forget the baby shower my mother gave me. I was due in February but I didn't last that long.

My middle sister Earlie greeted each and every lady as they entered.

"We are going to play a game," she said. "Here, first, take the clothespin. Whatever you do, don't cross your legs. Whoever catches you, takes your clothespin. The one with the most pins will get a surprise later. So don't cross your legs."

Mother Piggis arrived early. While I rushed around helping set up, she followed me around the dining room as I placed Mother's fine china and silver out on a lace tablecloth.

She stood next to me as I arranged the table buffet style.

"Yep, God showed me," she said. "You are going to marry a man in a blue uniform. You were only 16. I remember that look in your eyes. You were so scared you were shaking. You told me I'm not getting married and I ain't having no babies. That's the first time you came into the Prayer Room."

She looked around to see if anyone was listening, then said, "Is he dark-skinned with a long head?"

"Yes. Did God tell you that, too?

"Yep."

"You were shore right 'bout that. Matter of fact, his nickname is Head. His brothers always teased David about his big head."

"Well. God showed me the boy is going to marry you. And I ain't going to take it back."

"But he hasn't said nothing about going into the service, at least not yet," I said.

"Well, God showed you married with a little boy and you guys were walking in a big park. It was green and pretty there! He had on a blue uniform. God is going to use her. I don't know how but I just could feel it."

"Well, I don't think he's ready but I'll wait until he gets a job before we marry," I said, making my way back into the crowd of ladies standing around talking.

Most of the guests sat in a semi-circle around my special armchair with pink, blue, and yellow colored balloons tied to it. Earlie's dark eyes gleamed with excitement as she beckoned for me to stand up.

"I made Janie her first tight skirt for junior high and look," she said proudly. Without any warning, she lifted up the green pleated maternity top. "I made her first maternity outfit, too."

I found myself staring down at my pointed stomach peeking through a hole in the tiny skirt held only by a drawstring tied neatly into a bow.

As I pulled my top down, one of the ladies said, "Janie, how much do you weigh?"

"Hundred and ten pounds," I answered with my head still down, wanting to avoid all of the staring eyes focused on me.

"She doesn't even look pregnant," someone said.

Then the questions began:

"When are you due?"

"February 1962."

"What do you want?"

"A girl."

"What does the father want?"

"A boy."

I'm sure I answered more questions, but I don't remember what I said. I excused myself and went into the kitchen to escape.

Mother scurried back and forth between the kitchen and the dining room. She scooped thick, brown liquid from a large aluminum pot into a gravy bowl. Sydney lugged in a huge oblong-shaped pan heaping over with golden brown stuffing, placing it upon a silver trivet adjacent to the carved turkey. Meanwhile, in the kitchen, Mother painstakingly arranged the pineapple-glazed ham slices onto her best serving pieces.

"Johnnie, I don't know how you managed to cook all this food by yourself."

Mother smiled politely as she slid past Mother Piggis with a long oblong pan of enchiladas. "Excuse me."

Mother Piggis stepped back, turning sideways to allow Johnnie to whiz by.

"I didn't cook everything," Mother said. "You know David, Janie's boyfriend? Well, his father, Mr. Bess, cooked over three dozen enchiladas. David brought them over early this morning. He tried to stay but you know Earlie and Sydney made him leave."

Because Earlie's best friend, Sederria, brought all of the latest music, she was the proclaimed disc jockey for the day. She had purchased all of the latest '45 records and continuously fed them to the revolving spindle of the phonograph. Once the music started, some of the ladies broke off into different little cliques. Practically everyone was talking and some were dancing to the latest songs. Everyone relaxed and soon after, there would be a shuffling of feet. People forgot about the clothespin game and then someone would pounce on an unsuspecting victim to claim their clothespin. Most of the ladies were on the alert, watching, waiting to claim another clothespin for their collection.

"Ride Your Pony. Get on your pony and ride" blasted from the speakers. I started galloping like I was riding on a horse. Everyone broke out in laughter. I became lost in the music.

Soon it came time to open my presents, but it also opened up a subject I didn't want to think about. While I opened gifts, Earlie and the other ladies related birthing horror stories. They regaled me with their experiences like old fishermen with their tall tales of struggle and size, each trying to outdo the other.

"Janie, you had better listen to me," Earlie said. "It won't be long before you will be at Highland."

"I don't want to hear that," I said. "You're scaring me!"

"Girl, I thought I was going to die this last time. I ain't having no more babies."

My heart skipped and fluttered. "I don't want to hear anymore!" Quickly, I changed the subject.

"Look! Isn't this pretty?" I said, holding up a blue sleeper set. My short, fat hands trembled as I envisioned her in the labor room.

"But Earlie, I was told that the second time is easier," said Sederria, Earlie's best friend. "That was your second pregnancy, wasn't it?"

"Yep. But that's a lie. My second pregnancy was the worst. First, my pains were light as I lay quietly in the hallway waiting for a room at Highland Hospital."

She took a deep breath and kept right on talking. "Anyway, I had on this little see mo' gown…"

I said, "What's a see mo' gown, Earlie?" Earlie's opened her mouth in shock.

"Janie? You mean you don't know what a see mo' gown is? Well, let me tell you. You see mo', MO' of everything.

"Gurl-l, I saw this one woman in her see mo' gown. You could see everything, I mean everything. She was cussing, screaming, hollering and kicking the cover off as they wheeled her into the delivery room. It was disgusting. That gown was off her butt, she didn't care. I rolled my eyes at her. I wuz so embarrassed!"

"Earlie, that's enough," I yelled. "I don't want to hear any more. I'm opening the gifts now!"

Earlie had her audience captivated.

"Wait, Janie. Look. Let me show you guys. I'm going to give you a real demonstration."

Earlie got down on the floor enacting the whole scene moaning and groaning as if in labor.

"I tried to keep quiet. I wasn't going to act like that lady. I was trying to keep the blanket on me and keep my see mo' gown over my butt. Then those pains started coming fast and hard. I heard the nurse say something about dilating. My back was splitting in half. It was going to split wide open!

"Girl, I was kicking and a holl'ing as they wheeled me into labor. My little legs were jest agoin'. Now I understood why that lady was acting like that. I had forgotten all about that see mo' gown. It was moving as fast as my little legs could go."

She described an ol' baldheaded white doctor who wouldn't admit Mother into the delivery room.

"'Young lady, you had better calm down,'" Earlie recounted. "'Yelling and kicking is unnecessary, in fact, it interferes with your delivery. I know that you are hurting but you will have to stop it.'" She said she cussed him out for snapping at her.

One of the late arrivals sashayed over to me while I sat eating.

"I never met your boyfriend. Is he here?"

"No, he's at his parent's house."

"Oh. So… when are you getting married?"

I knew that was coming.

"Oh, we're waiting until David gets a job. We don't want to get married just because we're having a baby. He wants to make sure that he can support a family."

I finally opened my present from Earlie. She surprised me. She made me a green maternity dress just like Mother Piggis had seen in the vision she told me about two years before. She saw the dress, too, and looked at me. When things had quieted down a bit, she came over to speak to me. She wanted to talk with me later and invited me over to see her. We set a date for the next morning.

"It is important that I talk to you tomorrow. Come to my house please so I can pray with you."

She had told me of my future when I was young. I wasn't sure if I wanted to hear what she had to say now, but I promised I would get Mother to drive me over their first thing in the morning.

I never made it.

CHAPTER TWELVE

That night, after the shower, David stopped by to see me. He told me he was heading south to Los Angeles to try to make it as a singer. I started crying. I couldn't understand why he was leaving when I only had five weeks to go. I begged him to say. He said he'd be back in time for the baby.

But the next morning, Dec 5, 1961, I woke up with cramps. I told my mother, sure it wasn't anything to worry about. She started timing me. When the cramps started coming five minutes apart, we knew.

"I'm scared, Mother," I said.

"You weren't scared enough," she said. "You kept dancing and prancing to that song "Ride Yo' Pony. Well, looks like you gonna' ride that pony on in here. That baby is comin' today. When I say, let's go now, that's what I mean."

I held onto the front door knob trying to stall her.

"I've got to pee," I yelled.

"No, you can't go in the bathroom. Your baby might fall into the toilet."

"It is not time yet. Earlie said I would feel my back splitting open."

"I tol' you 'bout lis'nin' to that girl. Earlie ain't got a bit of sense. She was jes' funnin' around with you."

"Uh-uh. She was serious."

"Your labor is almost five minutes apart and I am not delivering no babies at home. So let's go, Janie. Gal! I mean it. Now!"

Opening the car door for me, she gently led me in the back seat.

"You just had to lay up with that boy, so you shouldn't be afraid to have his baby. You got to face the consequences."

Slowly I slid down, going into a fetal position on the back seat as the cramps hit me in lower part of my abdomen. I groaned and prayed for David to call home. I had called his mother to let her know I was on the way to the hospital. I assured her it was only false labor even though my mother insisted it wasn't. When he called, his mother would tell him about me.

We drove in silence to the hospital. She ran inside and a nurse came running out with a wheel chair.

"My mother says I'm just about ready," I told the nurse. "I'm scared."

She smiled.

"My sister says my back will feel like it's split open. Will it?"

The nurse giggled.

"Birth pains are indescribable. It is different for everyone.'"

Oh Lord, I was really worried.

She zoomed me into the hospital labor room to prep me.

Afterward, standing over my bed, Mother looked so tired. It seemed as though she had aged a few years since this morning. She had just returned with my records.

"They just told me I can't go with you," she said. "It has to be the husband only. I told them you were not married yet. So they said, it had to be the baby's father in delivery with you."

"Did you tell them he went to Los Angeles?" "Yes, Janie." She looked pissed.

"I'm going home," she said. "I'm not going to sit out in that waiting room all day. Have them call me when you have the baby."

I didn't want to worry her but my trembling body gave me away.

"You'll be fine."

"What if I have a caesarean?"

"They would have told you before now, Janie. Don't be acting crazy now. It's time for you to have that baby. Do what they tell you. You'll be fine. I've prayed for you. God will take care of you."

I watched her trudge slowly from the room. I turned my head away as the tears burst forward. Through the tears I saw all the sharp shiny implements on an aluminum tray shining brightly from the giant overhead lights.

They changed me into one of those see mo' gowns.

I closed my eyes. Visions of Earlie, with her legs up in the air kicking hard and fast, popped in my head. My knuckles were rigid as I gripped the crisp white sheets tighter with both hands.

When they transferred me on to a gurney and began to wheel me into the delivery room, I became hysterical.

"I want my mother, ple-e-ase," I begged them. "Please call my mother back. I need her here with me."

They just shushed me.

"You're going to be okay. You're going to be fine."

They put my legs in some silver stirrups and adjusted the leather straps around my ankles.

I tried to appear calm, but loud whimpering noises escaped my lips.

"I don't want to cause trouble," I said. My voice trembled when I spoke to the doctor. "I'm not having hard pains. It's not time yet, is it?"

"Oh, it's time all right, young lady," he said.

My voice echoed loudly off the walls.

"But I'm scared!"

"We can see the baby's head," one of them said.

That's when I lost it.

"Can you please put me to sleep," I begged. "I don't want to feel my back splitting open."

"You will experience some pains but I want you to concentrate on taking deep breaths in and out slowly, this will help you to have a smoother delivery," the doctor said. "Come on, breathe in and out, in and out." He warned me about the shot before he numbed my lower spine with a cold long needle. "When I tell you to push, then push. But not until I tell you."

"Okay," I managed to say between the pains.

One nurse with a lock of curly hair peeking from under her surgical cap stood over me, rubbing my hands, trying to comfort me. I dug my nails into her hand as hard pains hit me.

"It's okay," she said. "You squeeze as hard as you can. I'll be here with you."

Another nurse appeared with a large rubber contraption. They tried to place it over my face, Apprehensive with fear, I pushed it away.

"What is that?" I asked. My heart raced. I felt faint.

"It's only an oxygen mask. It will help you breather easier."

"I am fine," I insisted. "I don't need it." They wouldn't listen to me. She placed the oxygen mask over my face. Sweat poured from my body.

"Now inhale slowly, then exhale slowly. This oxygen mask will help alleviate your pains. You can breathe through it. Relax."

I started out inhaling and exhaling in a slow rhythmic beat. Just then sharp pains struck me in my lower back, my thighs began to throb in pain. My lower abdomen felt strange. It was moving as excruciating pains hit me repeatedly. I really began inhaling not bothering to exhale the oxygen.

I started hallucinating. Screaming in my head was Earlie's voice, talking about her back being torn apart. I closed my eyes. I could see her bald-headed doctor. He was standing over me now, yelling at me. "Earlie, young lady, stop that noise. It doesn't hurt that bad."

I moaned, "I'm not Earlie. I'm her baby sister. We look just alike." My moaning soon turned into loud wailing.

"Please don't let me feel those awful back pain," I cried. "Please, doctor. Oh Lord, help."

Then a nurse said, "It's okay, we know who you are. You're Janie. Just take your time, and don't breathe so fast."

"Okay," I said.

"Janie, I am going to take the oxygen mask away now. Just relax." She tried to remove the mask from my mouth. I had a death-grip on it. She pulled hard. I wouldn't let go.

"If I let go, I'm gonna feel the pain," I said. "My sister said my legs would practically tear from their sockets."

"No, it's almost over. We can see your baby. Just be ready to push. Just keep breathing in and out."

I kept breathing and clutching that mask, desperately hoping and praying the terrible pain would go away.

"Not too fast now, slow it down."

"No, no," I yelled as the nurse tried to snatch my oxygen mask away. I still held on. I wouldn't let go.

A small black circle formed in front of my eyes. It kept growing until a dark tunnel surrounded me. I cried out, "Help me, Lord."

I was swirling around and around inside that deep tunnel. Then it swallowed me up into a pit of darkness.

I passed out.

❦

I woke up screaming. I looked around. I thought I must be dreaming. Two older ladies came scrambling over looking down at me lying in a strange bed.

"Where am I? Who are you?"

They both looked at each other in total bewilderment before giving me an answer. The white middle-aged woman was first to speak.

"We're patients here, too. You're in the recovery room." She had a few strands of gray on the sides of her temples, a few wrinkles on her forehead, and a few around the corner of her mouth. Her hair was a pale blond. She lit a cigarette, took a few puffs and then said, "Why are you in this recovery room? You must have lost your baby, too."

"I-I don't know," I stammered.

The Negro woman was very young, probably in her twenties. She had beautiful cocoa brown skin. Her hair was long and silky black. She had big expressive eyes and a nice smile.

Agitated, she rolled her eyes up in her head.

"My God, why'd you ask her somethin' like that? Don't be so insensitive."

The white woman's voice changed to a softer tone. She apologized.

"I'm sorry. Have you talked to your doctor yet?"

"I don't know where my baby is," I said. "I must have passed out during labor."

"What?" The older lady said. She looked stunned.

"I don't even remember anything." I peeked under the covers to look at my stomach. It was flat. I lifted up my see mo gown. "What happened to my legs? They're all bruised."

"Where is my nurse?" I said. I tried to get out of bed but my legs were wobbly. My upper thighs ached as if I had run for miles.

"You don't know what happened?"

"No, I was having a baby but I must've passed out or something."

The white woman reached and pushed the red button over my bed.

"There is a young lady here and she don't know what happened to her baby."

"Yes," a voice on the intercom said. "A nurse will be there to talk to her soon."

It seemed like forever before someone came.

A nurse walked in. She had on a crisp white uniform with a small, white cap. I recognized her when a small red curly lock fell over her eye. She swooped it back with her right hand.

"Hi, Janie," she said. "You finally woke up, huh?"

Without waiting for an answer, she said, "You had a beautiful boy this morning. He's in the preemie ward. He only weighed 4 pounds 2 ounces and was only 17 inches long. He has a lot of black curly hair." She walked over to an empty chair and wheeled it to my bed.

"The nurses are spoiling him already." Her blue eyes beamed. "Get into this wheel chair and I will take you see your newborn baby.

"You had us worried for a while," she continued. "First you held onto that oxygen mask and passed out. We finally got that away from you. But then somehow, you managed to take your feet out of the stirrups. We don't know how you managed to do that. Your feet were strapped in. So we forced your legs apart for the delivery. You slept through the whole ordeal. Unbelievable.

"Oh, by the way, the pediatrician will be in to see you later."

I only heard bits and pieces of her conversation.

I glanced up and said, "Thank you, Lord. Oh, thank you, Father." I knew God was right there with me.

"Yes, Janie, you really gave us a scare. You see this was the most unusual delivery. I've never seen anyone take her feet out of stirrups but you did. I don't know if you fainted or what. We had a time getting that oxygen mask out of your hands. I had to practically pry it from your fingers. You just wouldn't let go, miss."

I tuned her out. My baby is alive! I just wanted to see my baby, to hold him and let him know I was here. I felt cheated because I missed the most important part. The delivery of my baby. I felt so useless. Why didn't the nurse give me smelling salts or something?

"We're almost there."

"I noticed black and blue marks on the inside of my thighs. What happened?"

"Well, just when your baby's head was coming out the birth canal, you closed your legs. So the nurses forced them open again while the doctor used forceps to pull your baby out."

"What? You mean I didn't help at all?"

"No, ma'am, you were out. We couldn't wake you no matter how we tried. We think you may have been traumatized."

Traumatized. I thought of Earlie and all her stories. I didn't bother to explain.

Finally we made it down the elevator to the nursery. There were lots of babies. I peered inside this huge window that looked like a picture screen. I wanted to see if I could spot mine. While putting on a pale green surgical gown and mask, I found myself peering in to try to see my baby. Proud fathers were inside, holding their babies. I longed for David. Did he get my message yet? There was no phone where he stayed. I prayed David would sense my urgency and call my house. Sometimes I felt we had mental telepathy. We did think the same way at the same time. Mother hadn't called me either. It seemed like everybody had forgotten about me.

Oh, please, Lord, don't let me cry. Oh, God, my stomach felt queasy as I fought back tears. I wanted to see my mother. I wanted David to be here. My sisters hadn't came to see me, either.

This was not at all like I planned. I could taste the warm salty tears as they rolled down my cheeks and into my mouth. I wiped them away, hoping the nurse didn't see me crying. I hated this part of me. I felt it was a sign of weakness. Just then, the nurse interrupted my thoughts.

"Well, here we are. Look. Isn't he cute?"

There's my son, I thought. Poor little baby. I wasn't there for you. Some mother I am. Only by the Grace of God you are here, Little Man.

I promise you, son. I will make amends to you. I will never let you down again, so help me God.

CHAPTER THIRTEEN

I looked at my little son lying in a small glass bed with a special light over it. He was pushing up on his legs while lying on his stomach. He looked just like his father. I knew then to name him David Bess Jr.

His coloring was deep reddish-brown. He had a long head, just like his Dad. The nurse was right. He had plenty of hair, black as coal, with the most beautiful curls covering his head. He had the tiniest lips I'd ever seen. His beautiful eyelashes were long and plush, like black fans resting on his small round cheeks. He didn't open his eyes. I was dying to see his eyes. I couldn't believe this little creature actually came from me. It was truly amazing. A product of our love, yet, an indication of our sin. It was then I realized how much I loved my baby. He depended on me for his every need. I asked God to help me be a good mother. Please, Lord, I want to make sure he is happy and successful. I felt so ashamed of how I acted during David Jr.'s birth.

"When will he be able to come home?" I asked the young pediatrician the next day. He was examining my baby as I entered the nursery. The stethoscope he used was very tiny. It actually looked like a toy.

"We will have to wait on this little guy to gain a few more pounds. He has to weigh over 5 pounds. I can estimate at about six to eight weeks from now."

"Why does he have to wait so long?".

"Your baby was six weeks premature so he needs about the same time in the incubator to finish developing as if he was still inside your womb."

"Oh, I never heard of that before. This is the first premature baby in our family. My sisters all had big babies. They weighed from six to nine pounds. So this is new to me."

I went home three days later without my baby.

I was up bright and early running to see my baby at the hospital every day.

David rushed home from Los Angeles right away. He was so proud.

"Man, he looks just like me," he said.

David's mother showed me David's birth certificate. She wanted me to compare all the similarities between father and son. David Sr.'s birth certificate and our son's birth certificate bore similar statistics. Both were born at Highland Hospital. At birth, both weighed 4 pounds 2 ounces. Both were born premature. How ironic.

⁂

The big day had arrived. My baby was coming home! My mother drove David and me to the hospital to pick up Little David. We were so excited! I couldn't wait to get him home. Sydney and Earlie were there when we arrived. That's when the examination began. All three of them, my mother and my two sisters, started checking him from head to toe.

"Janie, be sure that you rub his head every day to give it a nice shape," Mother said as she checked the shape of my baby's head. "That helps to mold it."

Earlie was looking at his fingertips, examining his knuckles.

"His knuckles are darker than his fingers. And look around his ears. They are darker around the edge of his ears."

I was becoming agitated.

"Yep, he is going to be black like David," Sydney responded. I was getting furious.

"Well, I don't care," I said. "I didn't want no light-skinned baby."

I was just about to take the baby from Earlie when she said, "Janie! Look at his eyes. They have a gray ring around the outer rim of his pupils." Sydney and Mother came over again to look at David Jr.

"That's different," Sydney said.

"Mrs. Bess, David's mother, says that her father-in-law had gray eyes.

Maybe that's what it is. David Jr. is going to have gray eyes," I explained.

Earlie wouldn't accept that.

"Janie, you had better call that doctor now, let him know about those gray rings around the pupil of David's eyes."

I reluctantly called to make the appointment. It was really done to just pacify Earlie so she would shut up. Amazingly, I was able to get in the following day for an appointment.

I had no idea what I was in for. At first it started out as a routine examination with the pediatrician. He examined my baby. I had nicknamed him Junior, but everyone called him Li'l David. It stuck.

Three hours later, I was still in that room. They asked me to help hold Li'l David still. I stood, crying quietly, wiping the tears away. My poor baby was crying out in pain. They kept stretching his eyes wide. The whites of his eyes were red and irritated. I couldn't take any more.

Poor Li'l David was so strong it took seven nurses and two doctors to hold down a six-pound-seven-ounce infant. A slew of young interns had come to observe. At first, I didn't suspect anything was really wrong but after the first round of young interns left the examination room, about 10 more doctors entered. The pediatrician then asked me would I mind sitting out in the corridor so they could have enough room to complete their examination. My baby was hoarse from crying and his cry was always faint; now there was no sound just tears coming from his eyes.

I was a young naive 19-year-old. I did as the doctor asked. I didn't want to be difficult. As I sat out there in the hallway, another group of interns waited to go into that small room. The first group stood in the hallway discussing my son's case. They acted as though I was invisible, as if I didn't even exist.

Nobody bothered to tell me anything. I was growing impatient. I rose slowly out of my chair. I walked up to the pediatrician who was talking to an older mature doctor with graying temples. None of these white men bothered to even acknowledge me. A new group of interns appeared and examined his eyes. They stood out in the halls using their medical jargon. It sounded like a foreign language to me. I had become furious and frustrated. Nobody bothered to tell me nothing! Finally I yelled out, "What is wrong with my baby? Will someone please tell me something? I am not invisible. Look at me. Look at me. Somebody had better tell me something, damn it!"

The older mature doctor came running because I had now pushed all those ugly young indifferent interns out of the way.

"You're not going to experiment on my baby, you hear!"

Without another thought, I quickly wrapped my baby up in his new fluffy blue blanket. I then put on his matching hat and ran past all of them, those young white prejudiced bastards. As I ran to get into the nearest elevator, the older doctor jumped in front of the door of the elevator to block me from entering.

"Mrs. Bess, I need to talk to you. It is important. I apologize for every one of the staff. That includes me. We were totally engrossed by what we discovered. I am the head ophthalmologist and that was my staff of interns. Are you aware of the medical problem that your son has? I need you to come to my office. I need to ask you a few questions."

He gently took me by the arm and opened the door to his office. I slowly sank down into a chair as he pulled it out for me. I wanted to get out of there.

"Mrs. Bess, we discovered that your son David has an unusual eye disease. He has congenital cataracts on his eyes. Do you know what cataracts are?"

I couldn't stop my tears. I couldn't talk just then. When I tried, nothing would come out except loud whimpering noises. I sounded like a wounded animal. My body shook involuntarily with each sob. I must have looked like one of those sad-face masks that hung on theater walls. The tissues the doctor gave me earlier were in a crumpled mess in my hands. The older doctor gave me fresh tissues from a neat dispenser box on his desk nearby. Without a word spoken, he held out his small white plastic receptacle. I quickly dropped the old wadded-up tissues into the flip-lidded wastebasket.

Finally, I was able to speak.

"How did my baby get cataracts? I thought cataracts were only something that happened to old folks' eyes." Without waiting for an answer, I continued on, "Isn't that a white film that grows around the pupil of the eye? Doesn't it eventually cover the whole eye, causing blindness?

"I remember one of the ladies at our church, she was our piano player; well, that's how she lost her sight. They said she waited too long and the cataracts had completely covered her pupils. You said my son had cataracts? You called them con-ge-nit-al cataracts? Did I pronounce it correctly? What does con-ge-nit-al mean?"

"Mrs. Bess, we need to perform surgery as soon as next week. I know this is a hard decision for you to make but we have no other choice. It is of the utmost urgency that these cataracts are removed soon. Otherwise, your son will most definitely lose his vision permanently."

"I'm afraid for my baby. He is only two months old. Are you sure this operation will save his sight? Are you absolutely sure? Will he be able to see normal? Will he need glasses?"

"No, ma'am, we cannot guarantee what his range of vision will be but I assure you he will be able to see clearer than now. We cannot run the normal vision tests because David cannot tell us what he sees. We feel that his vision at this time is merely a blur."

The doctor then handed me all these sheets of paper to read.

"This medical form states our prognosis of your son's medical condition," he said. "In order for the ophthalmologists to perform the eye surgery, I need you to sign here stating we have permission to do so. The first open date is Jan. 20,1962. I advise you to take it. Otherwise you will have to wait for at least six months. Right now we are fortunate to have an eye specialist on staff from Germany. He is one of the best in the world. His name is Dr. Svenzkoff.

"I have to admit this will be the first time that this type of surgery will be done on an infant. This is a highly unusual case."

I don't know how I made it home. I heard that doctors' voice repeating in my head.

"I'm so very sorry, Mrs. Bess, we don't know the cause for this. We have to operate."

All those doctors kept questioning me; they were drilling me.

"Are you sure you didn't take any medications? Were you sick when you carried your baby? Did you have a cold or the flu during your pregnancy? Did you consume alcoholic beverages? Do you smoke cigarettes? Did you ever smoke while you were pregnant?"

"No. No."

"Does or did any members of your family on either side have any sight problems?"

"No."

"Blindness?"

"No."

"Did you or any members of your families have cataracts at birth? How about David Sr.?"

"No." I felt like I was being interrogated. All those doctors in the same room. It must have been at least 15 at one time. There seemed to be no consideration for my feelings. They were glaring, coldly staring at my baby and me. I felt like we were in a circus.

I held my poor little baby so tight to my bosom he started squirming to try to free himself. I have only been able to hold him for two days.

As soon as I reached the front door of our house, I could hear the phone ringing. Oh, no, I bet that's Mother calling me. I had forgotten during the excitement, she was picking me up.

I ran to answer the phone. I picked it up just before the last ring. "Hello?"

"Janie! What are you doing home?

I recognized Earlie's voice.

"Hi, Earlie."

"Mother is still at the clinic waiting on you."

"Oh, no," I said.

"She got worried. She wanted to know if you called me. Mother sat there in her car for least two hours. She looked all over that eye clinic for you before calling home. There was no answer. She just called me from the eye clinic to see if I had talked to you. I'll call her back and let her know you're okay."

I found it hard to talk. I was shook up. I tried to speak but no sound came out.

Tears fell rapidly; quicker than I could wipe them way. I tried to explain in between sharp jabbing pains stabbing at my heart. My throat muscles closed and I could hardly breathe. My stomach muscles fluttered like crazy. I felt my esophagus muscles tighten up and I felt sick. After taking deep breaths, I was able to use my voice again. I managed to force the words out.

"They, I mean the doctors, said that they have to operate on Li'l David as soon as possible. I had to take him to the lab for blood work and for his urine specimen. Mother probably came looking for me then. It took forever, at least two hours in that stupid lab. I had told Mother it wouldn't take long, it probably wasn't anything. I wanted to believe Li'l David probably inherited his grandfather's gray eyes. Now I find out there is a major problem. They're going to cut on my baby's eyes." Loud sobs now racked my body.

There was a quiet stillness on the other end of the phone.

"I'm on my way over," Earlie said, determined. "Just hold on Janie. You hear me, Janie?"

"Yes, but Earlie, I'm so scared. Oh, God, help me."

"I'll be there in just a few minutes."

I put the phone back on the cradle.

Slowly, I sank to the floor still clutching my baby close to me.

Earlie have drove like a bat out of hell. It seemed like I'd just finished talking to her when I heard the clunking sound of her old Chevrolet. She slammed the car door and quickly ran in.

"I have got to put this car in the shop when I get enough money," she said.

I was unaware that I was still a crumbled mess on the kitchen floor.

"Girl, get up off that floor. Quit acting like a baby. And, and stop all that crying."

"Poor Li'l baby. He is sleeping through all this."

She took him from my arms, cradling him close to her. She kissed him on his fat cheeks.

"He doesn't even know what's happening." Her smile left. The concern in her voice was there.

"Janie, are you sure they going to operate on him? He is too little. I've never heard of anything like this before. He is only two months old. You had better wait and get a second opinion. I think they are rushing this; they're taking you a little too fast."

"I-I don't have time for a second opinion, Earlie. They said that is was imperative to perform the surgery by next week. They have him scheduled for next Monday on Jan. 20 at 7 in the morning.

"Oh, I almost forgot! David said he was going to the post office today to see have a job opening, if they don't he's going across the street to check with the Air Force Recruiter. He says he might join the service now. I've got to get in touch with him today so I can tell him that Li'l David is having eye surgery. He's been busy trying to find work. I have got to take my baby to Children's Hospital in the morning. They think he has an enlarged heart. They're going to give him an EKG. Everything has to be done quickly. I only have three days left."

"Okay. I guess you're right." Earlie was thinking fast. I could see it.

"Janie, why don't you come live with me for a little while? I could help you with the baby. And you can help me with my children. I'm almost done with my classes at Laney Beauty College. Just two more months and I'll have my cosmetologist license. I'm going to pass my tests when I go to the state board. I'm sure of that. Do you want to do that? We can split the rent."

"I don't know. Let me concentrate on this first. I've got to talk to Big David. I'll let you know after the surgery. That's a promise.

Okay? Meanwhile, I'll stay with Mother until then." I was talking out loud mainly to myself now.

"I guess we'll have to wait to get married after Big David gets back. We have too much to worry about right now."

Just then Mother walked in. She queried me anxiously. I answered her the best I could before the tears started. It was basically the same questions over and over again.

I called Lessie, David's mother, to tell her about the baby's eyes.

"I wonder where he got that from," she said. "Nobody in our family has anything like that."

I wanted to say something but I didn't know what. There was a sick hollow feeling in my stomach now. I felt like she was trying to put the blame on my family.

"I don't know" was all I could manage to get out before I started crying.

"It's okay, baby. I'll tell David to call you as soon as he gets here. Don't worry, I'll let you tell him. You two will need to talk and to be alone. Bye, now." With that she hung up the phone.

I felt so alone just then. Everyone had left except Mother. I could hear her on the phone talking to one of her sisters. She called someone else. She was explaining about Li'l David's eyes and about the upcoming surgery.

I heard her when she called Mother P. She then asked to speak to me. She asked me to come over before his surgery. As an afterthought, she mentioned there would be a prayer and healing service that very same night in Oakland. She invited me to come with Mother and be sure and bring my baby for healing, she said.

I didn't want to go.

"It ain't going to do any good, Mother. God must be angry with me for not keeping my promise to Him. I should have never had sex before marriage. I shouldn't have listened to my friend. Now look at what happened. God won't listen to me now. I sinned and it's too late."

Mother was growing impatient with me.

"Girl, you stop that mess. You aren't the first to ever have sex before marriage and have a baby. Believe me, you won't be the last either. Why do you feel like you're so special that God is punishing you exclusively?"

"You see, Daddy had always told me God had anointed me to sing the Gospel for Him. I started singing Rhythm and Blues and everything else. Now look what has happened. My baby has something the doctors never heard of and-and-" I broke down, I was sobbing so loud until my head was hurting.

"Girl, I couldn't tell you anything. Now look. Is that boy going to marry you or not? What are you two planning to do? You know that you don't have to marry him. You ain't the first young lady that had a baby out of wedlock. At least you finished school and have a year of college under your belt now."

"Don't worry, I am talking to David tonight, Mother. We are going to get married after he gets a job."

"How y'all going to pay for the baby's eye surgery? You know that cost money. Daddy and I don't have any extra money. We are already buying the baby's milk. That little can of Mull-soy costs $4. It only lasts for one day. Call David's parents and ask them to help us buy that milk. We can't afford it. Daddy Henry is retired now and we are on a fixed income too, you know. Call them right now."

Reluctantly, I dialed the number. Before the phone could ring, I heard David's voice, "Janie, did your phone ring?"

"No."

"I just picked up the phone and I heard you talking in the background to your mother. The lines must have crossed. How is Li'l David? What is wrong with his eyes?" I was crying again. I just couldn't answer him.

"Mom told me the doctors are going to have to operate on within a few days. Is that right?"

I couldn't tell that story again. It was too much. I waited for him to blame my family, too.

There was a short pause on the line, then he said.

"I'm coming right over."

CHAPTER FOURTEEN

We talked at length once he arrived. He held me close to him as we discussed our son's dilemma. That was the main topic of our conversation and, of course, our plans to marry later.

Mother kept walking around us as we sat on the living room sofa. She placed fresh red roses into a vase nearby. She made sure the drapes were closed neatly within the folds of the pleats. She arranged her "Look" and "Ebony" magazines neatly in a fan-like assembly on the coffee table in front of us.

After awhile, she just stood there. My mother always belched loud whenever she was nervous or contemplating something.

She was doing it now. Her belching grew louder with time. After she belched a few more times, she looked directly in David's eyes as he sat on the sofa. She had the Oakland Tribune newspaper open to the want ads section.

"I see they're hiring at the Post Office. Also, they need policemen. They need them badly, too."

David answered back respectfully.

"I already went there. I passed the test with a 90 percent score, but they aren't hiring now. They always have that ad in the paper. It's immaterial. Actually, I have other possibilities.

"I am going to see about some other jobs. I don't want to be a cop, Mrs. Prather."

I held my breath. I knew what the next question would be. Mother belched again. It sounded like a deep growl coming up from the pit of her stomach, then you could hear a higher pitch growl before the air escaped.

"Excuse me," she said absently but she was more interested in her questions. "When are you getting married? You have a baby now. He is sick and he will need the best medical care possible. I had Janie call your father just a few minutes ago for some more milk. That milk costs $4 a can. We can't afford it. Daddy is drawing his social security now. That's our only means of support."

David didn't say much but I could tell it bothered him, too. I knew he felt awkward whenever he came over. He felt as though Mother didn't believe him. He was determined we wait until he could support us.

"Yes, Mrs. Prather, I know. As soon as I get a job, I will come and get my family and take them with me. I am going to marry Janie. We just agreed to wait until we had something. I am not getting married just because we had a baby."

He then stood up to leave.

"Don't worry Mrs. Prather, I will make sure that David Jr. gets his milk every day. I have to go now. I've got to get up early for an interview."

He took a deep breath before turning to speak to me.

"I've got to go now, Janie. I'll call you tomorrow. I know you will be busy with Li'l David's appointments. If I finish in time, I'll go with you to Children's Hospital tomorrow. Is that okay?"

"Oh, yes, that would be fine."

I walked him outside where we could be alone on the front porch. Before sitting down on the red concrete steps facing the street, we just stood there momentarily holding hands and just smiling at each other. It was such a quiet, still night. We could hear the crickets chirping. They seemed to be singing a love song to us. We found ourselves quietly gazing up into a deep, blue sky. An exquisite crescent-shaped moon emanated a smile of approval down on us. The constellation of stars embellished the sky with poetic twinkling.

"I need you to go with me," I said quietly. "I am sick and tired of the way doctors treat me. They think I'm just a typical fast girl who had a baby, and don't know who or where the father is. I feel that must be the reason for acting as though they can't see me, like I'm invisible, or something."

He tenderly pulled me toward him and hugged me tightly. My head fit perfectly inside the crook of his arm. I took a deep breath as I nestled up close to him.

"Whenever you're with me, I feel the difference in the way they address me. They treat me with respect."

"Okay, then, that's a promise," he said. "I'll try my best to get there as fast as I can, so I can give you support." He then kissed me tenderly at the front door before leaving. I watched him as he got into his yellow Oldsmobile. He blew me a kiss as he drove off.

I dreaded going back inside. I knew Mother wasn't through with me yet.

"Janie, you are going with me tomorrow night. Elder Bruner is here from Georgia. He is having a healing service at the Oakland Auditorium downtown. When you get back from Children's Hospital, I want you to get dressed for church. We are taking that baby there."

I knew there was no use arguing with Mother.

"Okay, Mother, I'll be ready."

⌖

David did go with me to Children's Hospital as he promised. The doctors there were so understanding and showed so much compassion. We discovered in the electrocardiogram that David Jr. had a heart murmur. Surprisingly, David and I discovered we both had heart murmurs as well. What a coincidence.

After leaving the hospital, we spent the rest of the day at David's parents' house. His Aunt Thelma came over while we were there. She started reminiscing about the good old days. I discovered Mr. Bess used to be a singer. He had traveled with the chit'ling circuit singing with Count Basie and others. David's parents, Lessie and John, sang together. These were old love songs by Bessie Smith, Billie Holiday, so many I can't even remember. Aunt Thelma accompanied them on the piano. She could really make a piano talk.

Suddenly, Aunt Thelma changed to a faster tempo. She started playing boogie woogiemusic and then sang John Lee hooker's old blues tunes.

"You young people don't know nothing about this," she said. Her fingers flew across the keyboard. She sang another song and John and Lessie joined in. They started dancing a dance I'd never seen before. I was amazed. I never knew old folks could have so much fun. We had a good time that afternoon. Li'l David slept through the whole thing.

"Your baby sure sleeps good," Aunt Thelma said. "He didn't even stir through all this."

"I know," I said. "He doesn't react to noises, too. I am going to have his hearing checked. I read when they don't react to loud noises, they may have a hearing loss."

"There you go, looking for something," David said. "Stop worrying. There is nothing wrong with Li'l David's ears. Our baby has enough problems."

I tried to explain my suspicions to him, but he wouldn't listen.

David took me home so I could attend the prayer and healing service with Mother. She insisted I attend. On the way home, I tried to persuade David to come with us. He declined. I knew it was awkward for him to face my mother again. He didn't have the heart to tell me. I was trying hard to be supportive but it was becoming more difficult as time went by. I felt he was taking this whole thing too lightly.

"I hope you can understand, Janie," he said. "My brothers, Johnny and Freddie, and some of my old friends are going out. Are you okay with that?"

"Yeah, it's okay. What else can I say?" I said. I turned away folding my arms in front of me. "We never go out much since you returned from Los Angeles.

"I just wish that you would come with me to the prayer meeting first," I added. "Then you could go out afterward."

He growled under his breath. I could see he was annoyed with me. I felt like I was only holding on to him by a string. Before I got pregnant, he would go with me everywhere.

"I will just have to go with my mother by myself," I said.

I clammed up on the ride home. I got out. I refused to kiss him when he walked me to the door.

I knew I made him angry then. I wanted to hurt him like he was hurting me.

He handed me our son and sped off before I could close the door.

We were among the first to arrive at the prayer meeting. Mother and I sat in the front pew despite my begging her to sit closer to the back.

"I'm not hearing that," she said. "I'm going to get as close to God as I can."

I turned around in the sanctuary and watched as throngs of people came in on crutches, wheelchairs, on cots. They were brought up front near us. I felt uncomfortable sitting there. I felt such pity for those sick and crippled people. Soon everyone became engrossed in the bishop's sermon on faith healing. He was dressed like one of Jesus' disciples. His beautiful ebony skin was so smooth and his pearly white teeth just sparkled when he smiled. He reminded me of the great African Kings majestically dressed in his long white flowing robe.

After he completed his text on Romans 10:17, "Faith Cometh by Hearing and Hearing is by the word of God," he closed the sermon out.

Next, he asked for those who wished to be saved to come forward. In a few minutes, a throng of people came up to the altar. Next he asked those who wished to be healed to come forward. I had Li'l David wrapped up in a blanket and clutched him close to me. I prayed, Please, don't let him see me. I didn't want all those people staring at my baby or at me. I didn't want any pity. Please, Lord, don't let him ask me to come up there.

That preacher had to have X-ray vision because out of all the throngs of people, he spotted me in the pews. He spoke in a loud authoritative tone, "The Lord has spoken to me, there is a young lady in here with a baby that needs healing. God is telling me the doctors want to perform surgery. I understand he needs it as soon as possible." He started preaching again.

"I don't know about you but I know God can do all things but fail. Ha! All you need is to have faith the size of a mustard seed and, ha, God will move mountains out of your path. Don't be afraid, young lady. Please step up here."

I looked around over my shoulders to see whom he was speaking to. Surely he wasn't talking to me!

"Yes, you, young lady, and please bring the baby with you."

My mother prodded me in my side with her elbow. I froze up.

"Go on up there, Janie. He's talking about you."

"No, Mother, I'm scared. You gotta' come with me."

"Okay, come on, girl," she said under her breath as we slid out of our seats. She made her way through the crowd with me following close on her heels. I kept my head down. I hope nobody recognizes me.

Next thing I knew there was a whole bunch of ladies dressed in white surrounding us in front of the congregation. I shuddered. I was so embarrassed. Some spoke in tongue, others spoke in English.

The preacher put a light gold oil on all of the participants who desired healing. He explained, "This olive oil had been blessed by God." He applied to my mother's forehead, then mine and on Li'l David's forehead, too.

He uttered verses from the New Testament of the Holy Bible as he touched our heads firmly with the palm of his right hand. He then went through the throng of people standing in front of the church.

"Heal in the name of Jesus! Oh Lord! Heal right now! I order you to come out of this woman! Satan, come out in the name of Jesus!" He then came back over and touched little David. He took him in his arms and held him up high.

"In the name of Jesus! Give this infant child his sight back now, Lord, if it is Your will." He touched my head with his left hand and held up his right hand as if he was reaching up to God in the heavens.

"Give this young mother faith in you, Lord. Oh Jehovah Raffia." He held his right hand up even higher toward the sky. His left hand rested firmly on Li'l David's forehead. "Let the Spirit of God in. Now!

In the holy name of Jesus! I see the doctors plan to perform surgery, then let them be skillful with their surgical tools, Lord."

The reverend said a silent prayer over us then made his way through the masses of people. Thousands of people had come to see this great man of God. I felt such comfort from the words he had spoken. They seem to come straight from the Lord himself. God was surely in that place. After what seemed like forever, we were allowed to return to our seats. I kept looking at my son, who did not focus or look at me.

I waved my hand in front of Li'l David's eyes. He still couldn't see! I prayed hard. I was ashamed to be here, Lord. I was too ashamed to praise you out loud. I was afraid someone I knew would recognize me and make fun of me… Lord, punish me, not my child.

Tears of anguish flooded my eyes. My soul was filled with remorse for denying Him.

"I know I have not been a good Christian but my baby didn't do anything. I believe You can give him back his sight, if it is Your will. You must surely be angry with me. That is confirmed by the fact Li'l David still needs surgery. I saw lots of other people healed right then at the service, but not my baby."

I truly believed God was surely disappointed in me and I just knew I was being punished.

That night, at home, I got back down on my knees. I had a personal talk with God.

"Well, Lord, I'm asking you to forgive me. I know what my mother told me but I know I did wrong. I'm asking you to forget about me and concentrate on my son, Li'l David, because tomorrow morning he's to have eye surgery. Please Lord, it's not because I don't have the faith in you, I do believe in you. I know just like you gave the minister healing powers in his hands that you also gave the doctors skilled hands, minds and the tools to use them as well. Let them be ever so accurate with Li'l David's surgery. Let them be skillful and, and compassionate with my baby tomorrow. Just don't let David suffer because of me. Please forgive me if I am doing the wrong thing by having this surgery, but I have got to give him every chance to see.

A chance to see the flowers, birds, trees, my face, his father's face and the rest of the family's.

"I hope you understand me, God. It's not that I don't trust you but I want to believe that you are the One who sent those doctors to me as well as the minister to heal. Thank you, Lord, in advance for my son's successful surgery. Amen."

I went to bed feeling such peace and serenity. I just know God heard my prayer that night.

CHAPTER FIFTEEN

When I woke the next morning, I felt a weight off my shoulders. But then I rolled over, looked at the alarm clock and realized the alarm had not gone off. Oh, God, I'm going to be late. I had to get David Jr. to Highland Hospital within an hour. I scurried about as fast as I could. Mother was up making breakfast for us already.

"Mother, I'm going to be late. Why didn't you wake me?"

"Gal, you have plenty of time. Daddy is ready to drive you there as soon as you eat, so stop your yapping."

I arrived just in the nick of time. The doctors were ready to prep him for surgery. The young intern explained they were anesthetizing around the optic area only.

I really wish he had kept that bit of information to himself. That only caused me to worry more. What if the anesthesia wore off while they were still working on him?

I shook the thought away. David always admonished me for my negativity. Whenever I worried too much, he'd say, "Think positive, Janie."

I sat out in the waiting room petrified. My baby was not quite three months old and he was being cut on. I had never had surgery in my life. I would have done anything to save him from this if it was possible. I kept praying I was doing the right thing for my baby.

What if he dies? I don't know what I'd do...

Every time a doctor came out of that room, my heart would just sink. It must have been at least seven hours before the head ophthalmologist came out of the operating room to talk to me.

"Mrs. Bess, we were able to remove a lot of the tissue from the right eye. I have to advise you, though, he must lie very still so as not to disturb his eyes. So we will keep him anesthetized for several hours in recovery. You will be able to see him in a little while.

"This was a very delicate operation, I have to say. We will have to keep David Jr. here for at least two weeks in the pediatrics ward. You have the finest doctors on the staff. The pediatrician will be down to talk to you in a few minutes."

"Can my baby see now? Will he be able to see?"

The doctor took a deep breath. He cleared his throat before he answered. In the most compassionate tone he said, "It is too soon to tell what the outcome will be." I hated that. I hoped his answer would be filled with optimism. Instead, I was hearing the uncertainty in his voice now.

"You mean you cut on my baby's eyes only to tell me that you don't know what the outcome will be?" I was furious as these evil thoughts entered my mind. He probably humored me just to use my baby for an experiment. I continued ranting.

"I had read how the white officers in the military required these black soldiers to be injected with a serum of syphilis. They were used to experiment on to see what would occur in the human body. The results were many of them died after suffering from blindness and dysfunctions of other organs. Now you expect me to trust white men? You didn't tell me all this before! Why did I trust you to cut on my baby? I must be a fool! Lord, help." I turned away.

"Mrs. Bess, I assure you, we will do all that we possibly can to make sure he will see. We just can't promise you what the exact range of vision your son will have. Only time will tell."

I walked to Earlie's house. She only lived two blocks from the hospital. I needed time to think. By the time I arrived, I had made some very important decisions.

First, I was going on welfare until David could support me. Li'l David's milk was expensive and it wasn't fair for me to expect our parents to take over our responsibility. I knew I wouldn't be able to work right away. I couldn't leave my baby now. He was going to need a lot of attention and medical care. Medical bills from his birth arrived. I had given them to David.

Second, I needed to set a date to get married even if it wasn't until a year later. And I made up my mind to stay with Earlie. I didn't want to deal with Mother then. I was too stressed. I couldn't bear to hear Mother ask the same questions over again.

"Have you guys decided when you getting married? What you gonna do 'bout the milk."

Earlie had given me a spare key to her apartment. I knocked first, then I opened the door.

Earlie peeked out from the kitchen. She was standing over the kitchen sink washing dishes.

"Come in. Why did you knock? Haven't you figured out yet why you have a key?"

"Thank God you're home, Earlie," I said. "I'm not ready to go home, not just yet. Mother's been on my case about David again."

Earlie had taken the day off from school.

"I just couldn't sleep last night. I was worried about you and the baby." She had cooked a beautiful meal. I peeked inside her favorite black cast iron skillet. There was hot steaming smothered steak. Two more aluminum pots had mashed potatoes and collard greens. In a glass bowl in the center of the round table was hot-water cornbread wrapped up in a brightly colored kitchen towel. I sat down and ate lunch with her and her children.

That's when I told her I would take her up on her offer stay with her in exchange for babysitting.

"I am going to turn in my welfare papers. I will be able to pay you some money by next month. I will be able to pay you half rent if I am accepted on welfare. I'm ashamed that I need charity. I had sworn in the past that I would never go on welfare¼"

Earlie interrupted me.

"Have you heard from David? Has he said anything about when you gettin' married."

"No, I haven't heard from Big David. He told me he was going for an interview today and if it didn't work out, he was thinking about the Air Force. But I don't know what he's doing anymore. I am going to go by and see him when I leave here."

"A bus leaves here within an hour." She had a sly smile on her face as she spoke. The suggestive look she was giving me gave me more than a clue. I knew she was hinting I should go see him.

"Earlie, I ain't going to chase him down. He knows where to find me when he wants to see me."

"Yeah, but you ought to come down off your high horse and go talk to him, make some plans. He keeps telling you you're getting married but time is flying by."

Quickly, I changed the subject.

"I am more concerned about my baby right now. Li'l David is still in the hospital. He has these aluminum shields with little tiny holes in them. They are taped over his eyes. It looks awful, like something from outer space. His little face is practically covered with those ugly bandages. His fat little cheeks and his little cute lips are about all that I can see. I went to visit him, I picked him up and held him as close to me as possible. I wish that I could take him home. They had him tied to the bed like he was a dangerous animal. He was crying and tugging at the strips of white cotton that were attached to the crib. He looked like a caged animal. He was trying to free himself.

"Well, this nurse, she's colored, she gave me a hard time. She's about Mother's age. She came into David's room when I was there. It might be my imagination, but it seems she enjoys interrupting my time with Li'l David. The minute I untied those ugly strings from his wrist and feet, she was back, out of nowhere! Just as I picked him up, she entered the room. I spoke to her and she didn't even say nothing! Turned her nose up and said, 'Time to change his bandages.' She didn't ask permission to take him. Instead, she just reached over and rudely snatched him from my arms. Of course, he started crying for me. He was scared and didn't understand.

"That cow! She just ripped the tape and bandages from his little face as though he didn't have any feelings! She had no regard for him. Even I could feel the pain myself. You know me, Earlie! I started crying. Once I cry, it's over. The tears were falling fast. It was too much for me to watch. His fragile little body jumped involuntarily after each pull of the tape. His little cheeks were irritated and red from the adhesive. When she saw me breathing loud and my hands on my hips, she said, 'I have to change his bandages every four hours.' That's what she said.

"It was apparent by the way I looked at her I wasn't very happy her handling Li'l David that way. I watched her with quiet hostility. He was screaming! I couldn't stand it anymore. I acted like Mother when she gets mad, I got loose like a goose. I said to that woman, 'Excuse me, but that is my son whose skin you are pulling on.' She looked up at me surprised at my change of attitude. I could tell from the look on her face she really thought I had flipped out. I said, you tied him up like an animal and you now you're treating him worse than a dog.

"She replied back huffily, 'Well, ma'am, we had to tie him down to prevent him from tampering with his bandages. He was trying to rip off the bandages. I had no other choice. We are only thinking about his welfare.'

"'I know that you're doing your job, but can you at least show some compassion. Have some consideration for his pain. Most of you professionals on this ward seem to have such insensitivity toward my child.'

"I had my hands on my hips and was breathing loud. I was so mad. She looked scared. I could tell she was nervous.

"I said, 'Damn it. Give me my baby.' I took Little David out of her arms.

"'I could have taken those bandages off and changed them myself. And he wouldn't be crying in pain like that.' She started picking her tools up off the tray and putting them away. I wasn't through with her yet. I said, "And you always give me dirty looks whenever you come into this room as if I've done something wrong to you. I don't care what you think, but I know this. You are going to treat me with respect.' She stood there with a shocked look on her face. I could see her thinking, how could she have the nerve to talk to me like that!

"'I feel so bad for my son. It's as though you resent working with him, as if you blame me for what happened to him. You never did ask me what happened to him. I never volunteered to tell you either because you don't care but after today you will! I am going to administration to see about somebody showing compassion around here. I don't want him here. I didn't have a choice. So if you have problem with my son, then get out.'"

I seemed to be talking to myself now. Earlie was preparing dinner but she seemed to thinking about something else. I could tell she was just being polite. She only uttered an occasional "uh huh" every now and then.

"Well, Earlie, that nurse, she looked at me like I was crazy and flew out of that room. I didn't see her no more. And the next time, you know, she better show respect.

Earlie said, "Then what did you do?"

"I didn't do nothing. She left out of there in a hurry. I just sat and held Li'l David close to me. I rocked him until he fell asleep."

"Are you feeling better today?" she said.

I just looked at her momentarily. Then I said, "Yeah, thanks. I feel a little bit better.

"Well, I've got to go let Mother know I'm moving in with you," I said as I headed for the door.

"Bye, girl, you ain't even listening to me." I slammed the door to piss her off and ran down the walkway. She ran to the door as I went down the stairway.

"Hey, did I hear you say you are moving in with me?" "Yep," I said as I walked on out into the sunlight.

Mother faked indifference and Daddy predicted we wouldn't last three months in the same house together. He reminded me of when I stayed with both Sydney and Earlie before and how they had mistreated me. Needless to say, it was a useless conversation. I had made up my mind.

"Don't say I didn't tell you," Daddy Henry said.

I moved in with Earlie the very next day. David came over and while I unpacked my things, we talked well into the night.

Earlie asked, "David, have you thought about going into the Army?" Before he could answer, she said, "My cousins went in. One went into the Army and the other joined the Air Force. They took their families with them. They traveled to different states. They have medical, housing, and all their benefits paid for." Her piercing eyes bore a hole through David's.

"You should think about it," she said.

"I already have. Didn't Janie tell you?"

"No, Janie didn't tell me nothing." She gave me an accusing look.

"I have an appointment with the recruiter's office early tomorrow morning." He was toting his black attaché. Inside the attaché were official military papers showing proof he was active for two years in the Army National Guard. He beamed with pride when he explained what he trained for. His modesty overshadowed his pride as he talked.

"Yeah, shoot, I was a little thing. I couldn't have weighed more than 100 pounds. Let's see, I was only 5 feet 1 inch tall when I joined.

"When Eisenhower was President in the White House, he recruited teenage boys into the National Guard. It was during the Korean Conflict."

David stood tall and proud as he talked. I sat in a chair nearby, excited, just hoping and praying he would go in the service.

"Eisenhower sent recruiters to junior high as well as high schools," David said. "He needed to make sure he had enough troops to guard the home front."

"How were you going to guard the home front at 13?" Earlie said. "We did weekend duty. They called us 'Weekend Warriors.'"

"So you served time in the National Guard, but I am trying to figure out why you need those records?"

"I found out from the recruiter my two years prior service in the National Guard would entitle me to higher pay."

115

The next morning, I visited Li'l David at the hospital then decided to take a bus out to see David. I figured he should be back by the time I got there. They lived in Alameda in the old estuary housing known as Gibbs Naval Housing. I had tried to call David earlier but discovered that his phone was disconnected. As I rode through the dark estuary tunnel on the bus, I prayed he'd be happy to see me. I figured he would be at home. He wasn't due to leave until the next day. The huge identical two story apartment buildings seemed to tower over me. I searched for the big numbers that were painted in big bold black letters on each corner of the buildings. I found my way through the winding walkway. When I reached 301 Gibbs, I looked in the parking lot searching for David's car. It wasn't there. Neither was his parent's car. Lord, have mercy.

My heart beat fast as I walked through the old housing area. They lived on the second floor in the three-story bungalow. I timidly tapped on the door. There was no answer. I started knocking frantically after there was no answer. Where is everybody? A feeling of desperation came over me.

I ran up the stairs to the third floor and knocked on one of the neighbor's doors. I recognized the young lady. She had attended Merritt College with me last year.

"Hi, Janie. You looking for David?"

"Yes, do you know where he is? His parents are usually at home."

"Oh, you didn't know?" She held her hands up with her palms facing out. "David left with his older brothers this morning. Freddy and Johnny returned a few hours ago. When I asked them where David was, they said he was leaving for the Air Force today. Then they left following Mr. and Mrs. Bess' car about an hour ago. They said they wanted to see David off. I heard them tell my parents he was flying out this evening to an Air Force Base in Texas."

"You sure that they said David's flying out today?"

My eyes searched the parking lot for his car.

"Yep, that's what I heard them say."

"He would have told me if he was leaving today."

"I heard them say he left with the recruiters. I think they said somethin' about going to the Oakland Airport.

"He said he would call me before he left."

I started crying as I sank down on the curb in front of their apartment. He was gone! I didn't get a chance to kiss him goodbye! My stomach felt like it was tied up in knots. Why didn't he call me? I sat down on the steps bawling like a baby. The girl squatted down and hugged me. I knew she was trying to console me.

"Come on inside. Wanna' use the telephone or something?"

"Yes, thank you. I need to call David's Auntie Thelma. She's probably home. Maybe she can tell me if he's leaving or not."

But no one answered at his aunt's house.

"May I use the phone again? I want to call home, if that's okay." I wanted to check and see whether David had tried to call my house. I clutched that phone to my ear listening intently to the ringing. No answer there either. My heart was thumping now.

"Maybe, he called and left a message with my parents," I said nervously.

No answer.

"Apparently there's no one home, either."

Where was everybody? David should have at least called me. I felt so alone, like the only person left on this earth.

I started walking, not even aware of what my next move would be. I just knew I couldn't tell my mother David had left without even seeing the baby or me. Maybe he's not coming back to marry me. Mother was right. I was so stupid to believe him.

I was standing at the bus stop crying when out of the blue David's parents drove up.

"Janie, where have you been?" Mrs. Bess said. "I talked to your mother about two hours ago. She left with your father, Mr. Prather. They are looking for you. Mrs. Prather told me you had probably caught the bus out to Alameda. I told her you were probably on her way to her house. She insisted I would find you here. Thank God! David was having a fit! He went to take in the papers and they kept him there. He wasn't allowed to leave after the swearing-in ceremony. He was told they were shipping him out this evening. He's at the airport. He's due to leave within the hour. Jump in! We have got to hurry."

I jumped into the back seat of the car. I was so excited and so very happy. David does still loves me. He had sent his family looking for me. His family accepted me after all.

Mr. Bess drove off as soon as the back door of the sedan was shut. His wife and three sons all called him Mr. Bess. When I was introduced to him, I was afraid of him because he always had a mean expression on his face. David and his brothers addressed him as Mr. Bess whenever they spoke of him. At the first chance, I asked David and his brothers, "Why do you call him Mr. Bess? Is he really your father?" All three of the brothers broke out in laughter. "No. He is our real father all right. That's our old man." I didn't understand their lighthearted attitude. They gave each other knowing looks. I later discovered his genuine kindness behind his mean exterior.

We rode along in silence. I could see his face in the rear view mirror. He had this smile on his face. He very seldom said anything but he spoke just then.

"I had told David this morning that you are going to make it. You two have a good sense of values. You and David are going to make it in this relationship. You are an intelligent young couple and you have stable goals for your family. Out of my three sons, you have the best one of my sons. You have the pick of the crop, Janie. Take my word for it."

Lessie, who was sitting next to him in the front seat of that big old Pontiac, gave her objections.

"We tend to differ, Mr. Bess, when it comes to the boys. I feel that all of my boys are going to be something. So don't start nothing, you hear me."

Nothing else was said after that. We pulled up into the parking garage and walked swiftly into the airport where David was waiting anxiously.

I ran to hug him and to tell him about Li'l David's progress since his last visit. David listened attentively as he stroked my hair. He hugged me close to him as we sat in the airport terminal. We were like lovebirds wrapped up in our own little world. I had mixed feelings about this. I hated to see him leave yet I was happy to see him go. I truly felt this was a signal from God that everything was going to work out now.

"When I get back, we're going to get married and I'll take you away to see the world," he said.

He explained to me all the benefits the military had to offer. He would be able to finish college while in the Air Force.

David was rattling on. He was so excited he was talking more than ever.

"Li'l David will have the best medical care. And it won't cost us a red penny. We'll be able to afford the expensive milk he needs."

He hadn't finished his last sentence when he heard his name over the intercom.

"The recruiter is rounding us all up to leave now. You know, I have to admit this is my first flight and I am a little jittery. You take care of our baby. I'll be back for you."

He hugged his parents, Aunt Thelma and my parents, who had just showed up right when his name was called.

"Mrs. Prather, don't worry, I'm going to marry your daughter," Davis said when he hugged my mother. "I love her and I plan to take her and my son with me when I get back from Lackland."

Mother, surprisingly, didn't say a word. She just nodded her head to show approval. David then shook my stepfather's hand before giving him a big bear hug and a firm pat on the back.

"I'll be back. Take care of my future wife." He turned and walked briskly through the entranceway to the plane.

Tears streamed down my face. I held them until I knew he had boarded the plane. Once the plane was in the air, I broke down and just cried.

CHAPTER SIXTEEN

It was six months before David made it back from basic training. Then he pulled his right knee jumping a creek while out with the boys. He had to have major surgery and rehabilitation before he could report back to duty. Big David was home for at least six months. It gave him time to become familiar with his son.

Meanwhile, Li'l David was in the hospital the same time his father was in the hospital recuperating from knee surgery. Li'l David had two more eye surgeries while Big David was home on medical leave. That's when I realized how much his son really meant to him.

At first, Li'l David didn't know his father because he was always gone somewhere. First, Big David left for Los Angeles to try for a singing career. After joining the Air Force, his military training kept him away. Li'l David was afraid of him. Big David was hurt and couldn't understand why Li'l David kept trying to get away from him.

"Honey, he doesn't know you," I tried to explain. "You're always gone. That's why he is afraid of you. Try to understand."

David wouldn't accept that. He would grab Li'l David, who would try to escape his father's grip by squirming. Failing to free himself, he would roll over on his back while crying and look at me for sympathy. I felt sorry for both of them. Was I relieved when Li'l David began to recognize Big David and to accept him. Finally, he went to him with out stretched arms signaling to be picked up.

Li'l David was 13 months old and weighing less than 15 pounds when David and I took him to be fitted into a pair of custom trifocals The glasses were as thick as coke bottles. The frames were attached to adjustable black elastic straps secured by metal snaps so the glasses would stay on his tiny little face.

Poor baby. He hated those heavy things on his face. At first, he pulled the glasses off, throwing them across the room. He didn't understand. Whenever Li'l David was hot or frustrated, he would snatch the glasses off. That only lasted for a few minutes. Ignoring my loud objections, Big David would spank his little hands then shake his finger at his little face saying "NO! NO!"

as he forcibly set the tri-focals back on the bridge of his nose. Li'l David showed no reaction, not even a blink of his eyes.

"David, he doesn't understand," I said. "Don't scold him like that."

"He knows what he's doing. This boy is smarter than you think he is." Big David just glared at me.

"Leave me alone. I know what I'm doing," Big David shot back defensively. "David Jr. is very smart! Smarter than you think."

I jumped in front of little David to shield him from David Sr.

"You're not going to touch my baby," I yelled. "You're too rough with him."

David Jr. was sitting on the floor crying. Big David had bent down in front of Li'l David, pointing his finger at him with a threatening stare.

"He doesn't even know what you're saying. I know you think he is stubborn but, poor baby, he can't hear you and he can't see that good, either!"

I knew David had heard Earlie and Sydney chastising me earlier.

"Janie is just spoiling that boy," Earlie said. Sydney would nod her head in agreement.

After recuperating from knee surgery, David flew to Mc Chord Air Force Base in Tacoma, Wash., for his very first duty assignment.

The night before he left, we sat in the living room at my Mother's house, on her orange brocade sofa in front of the fireplace. I leaned over and gave him a big hug.

"I am so excited. We can make plans for our wedding now."

David looked at me with an air of uncertainty. He didn't say a word. In my excitement, I failed to see the signs. He was unusually quiet as I rambled on about our marriage.

"Are you coming home for our wedding or will you send for me?" I said.

David's mood shifted to a stranger responding with acrimony.

"Why are we rushing into marriage? How many times do I have to tell you that we can't get married until I..."

I pulled away from him, fighting back tears. With my head bowed, I nervously toyed with my hands that rested in my lap.

David slid over on the couch, placing his arms affectionately around my neck.

"Once I arrive at McChord, I will schedule a meeting with the base chaplain for marriage counseling," he said.

"Marriage counseling?" Placing my hands on my hips, I stood up glaring at him.

"Why do we have to wait?" I asked. "I thought that right after basic training we were getting married." I shook my head in disbelief. "This is the first time I had heard this one."

"Janie, the Air Force requires us to have marriage counseling."

"I am tired of waiting. First, we had to wait for you to get a job. Next, we had to wait for David's surgeries. Then we had to wait six more months, until after you recuperated from knee surgery. Eighteen months later and we still have not tied the knot. I have swallowed my pride and tried to conceal the hurt and disappointment from everybody but I am tired of this game."

David stood up as he tried to reason with me.

"Janie, I told you I was going to marry you and I am. I am not going to marry you without a job or a future. I don't plan stay around here the rest of my life. I need to get settled in Washington, then I will send for you."

David wiped my eyes as he tried to reassure me.

"Baby, I love you. I want to be able to show you the world. I want to take you with me all over the world. I want to be with you to raise my son."

I hugged him close.

He tipped my chin up and gazed deeply into my eyes searching for an answer.

"Do you believe me?"

I nodded a yes.

"Are you going to wait on me?"

My stomach did flip-flops as I stood staring up into his eyes.

"Yes, of course I'll wait."

"I have to report to duty in just a few days, so as soon as I talk to the chaplain, I promise I will be back for you and Li'l David. Okay?"

I simply nodded the affirmative.

"I love you, Janie."

"I love you, too," I said as I gave him a quick peck on the cheek.

He grabbed me tightly into his arms and we passionately kissed. Laughing with relief, David led me outside and before we realized it, we were walking hand in hand down the lighted streets of Berkeley like two happy love birds under the beautiful fluorescent moon shining down from the dark midnight blue sky.

David left for his new assignment a couple days later. We both promised to write every day. But once he left, I spent my time waiting for a letter from David. I could hardly wait for the postman. He had been our mailman for many years. He knew all of my family's names by heart. The minute I saw the red, white and blue mail truck pull up to the curb in front of my house I rushed outside.

"Hi, Felix. Any mail for me?" I said while trying to read the names on the envelopes he held in his hands but the writing was too small.

"Expecting something important?"

"Yes, my fiancé is in the Air Force and I'm expecting a letter from him."

"No, I'm sorry Janie. I don't have nothing here for you today." He sorted through the letters in his hands. "Here's something for your parents, Mr. And Mrs. Prather, though. That's it." He handed me a couple of business letters and magazines. My heart sank. Every day I wrote David telling him how much I missed him and how I couldn't wait to be married; So far, I'd got nothing in return.

Mother took the mail from me but not before she noticed my tears.

"What's the matter with you, gal?" she said between belching.

"Oh, nuthin'."

"Gal, you cain't fool me. I'm Johhne Ree! Remember?"

I rolled my eyes.

"What's the matter? Expecting a letter from that boy. Humph!" Didn't get it, didya?" Without waiting for an answer she said, "Done tol' you dat wol' weren't ready to get married."

"The mail is probably slow, Mother."

She muttered an "um-hum." It dripped with sarcasm.

"He's in Washington state, not Timbuktu," she said.

Without another word, I rushed to my room, closing the door behind me. Laying across my bed, my mind drifted away. I should never have moved back home with Mother. I had almost forgotten why I left in the first place. Earlie had already worked my nerves. She would stop by to see me every day after work. She pressured me daily.

"You've got to tell David he'd better marry you, now or never," she said. "I'm not going to rush him," I said. "Will you leave me alone?"

Sydney, who was in the kitchen talking with Mother, overheard us and added her two cents to the conversation.

"I know this girl, Marlene, who had this baby for this guy and he went into the Navy. He promised her he would marry her, then send for her and the baby. Well, after basic training, he went overseas, got stationed in Paris, France. Well, he met this French girl over there and married her. Had the nerve to bring her back home for her to see. There Marlene stood looking pitiful holding their son as this fool told her, 'I'm sorry. But I couldn't help myself. I fell in love with her. But don't worry, I'll take care of my son.'

"I felt sorry for her. I had told her to go with him in the beginning but, oh, no, she said, 'I'm going to wait on Warzell to come back for me.'"

Sydney looked deeply into my eyes searching for the tears but I was not going to break down.

"So what's that got to do with me," I spat back at her.

Sydney sat down on the bed next to me.

"Well, she almost lost her mind. She was very hurt and embarrassed because it was like a slap in the face." She hugged me close to her and held my tiny face in between the palms of her hands.

"He brought that French mademoiselle back here to the states flaunting her like she was a trophy or something."

I distanced myself from Sydney by sitting up on the bed.

"David is not like that," I said. "We dated for one year before I had our baby and he was faithful to me. I trust him. I will wait until he's ready."

Sydney stood up and headed toward my bedroom door. I heard her mumbling under her breath.

"It doesn't appear to me he'll ever be ready."

"What?" I yelled out the door. "He is going to send for me as soon as he gets settled at the new base." Quickly, I climbed off the bed and followed her into the kitchen. "He is in training now and is busy but I know he is coming back for me."

"He keeps making excuses," Sydney said. "First, it was he's looking for a decent job." Sydney placed her hands on her hips. "Next, he was singing in L.A., trying to make a record with his singing group. Then, after he went into the service, he said he's going to marry you. The last time when he came home, then he says you'll have to wait to see a marriage counselor. How long are you going to wait, Janie?" Sydney's long hair was swinging back and forward while she popped her neck talking. "Don't be a fool like me."

"Sydney, if he doesn't marry me, it's not the end," I said. "I'll get a job. I can take care of my own child. I've got my diploma and almost two years of college under my belt so I am not worried. I will not be like you."

Sydney looked at Mother for support, while she spoke to me. "Like Mother told me, 'Wake up, girl, and smell the Coffee.'" I popped my neck back at her.

"And like Mother told me, 'If you have a little bird and he wishes to be free, let him go. If it is truly yours, it will come back to you'."

Clicking her lips, Sydney walked out of the kitchen into the dining room to sit next to Mother and Earlie.

I followed them. They had to hear me out.

"I know David loves me. It's not what you guys think!"

"Janie, I don't want to see you hurt," Sydney said. "There are plenty of guys out there. You are pretty and you don't have to wait on him. If he doesn't want to marry you, it's okay. You are so cute and tiny. A lot of guys would grab you up, baby and all. You demand that he better hurry up. You guys have a son and he needs to be with his father."

"I don't want him to feel obligated. We didn't want a shotgun wedding so that's why we waited. It has to come from his heart."

Earlie's arms were folded in front of her chest and she rolled her eyes as she sighed loudly.

"Humph! What heart? Men don't think with their heart. They only think with their you-know-what."

I snapped back.

"He's waiting until he settles down at his new duty station then he going to send for me." I truly trusted and believed that. I didn't feel the need to rush him. Earlie was tapping her right foot unconsciously as she mumbled a chilly "Um-hum" before walking off.

The days seemed to drag on and on.

It was on a Thursday morning, I woke up with a strange feeling. It went all the way down into my stomach, call it intuition or whatever, but I just knew there was a letter from David coming that day. Holding out my hands in front of me, I said to the mailman, "I know you have a letter for me. Just give me my mail."

"Yes," he chuckled, "matter of fact, you do have a letter from McChord Air Force Base in Washington here, I see."

I snatched that letter out of his hand so fast and took off running toward the house. My heart leaped with joy as I sailed inside with my letter in my hand. I yelled to my mother. "I got a letter! It's from David!"

Mother eavesdropped as I started reading out loud. I turned, giving my mother a smug look.

"My dear Janie,

"I really miss you and Little David very much. How is he doing? How was his last eye surgery? I have done all the necessary paperwork to start an allotment for him. You should be getting a check for his support soon. I am sorry that I did not write you sooner but I have been struggling within myself for an answer concerning our future. I have been very busy learning about my new career field. There is so much to learn. What I have to tell you is not good. I want you to sit down before reading any further."

I tried to walk away from Mother. She followed me.

"What's wrong Gal? You cain't fool me. You gots ta' wake up early in the morning to fool me."

My stomach flip-flopped as I rushed blindly to my room. I stared momentarily at Li'l David sleeping peacefully in his crib. I envied him just then. I needed time alone. Mother was standing in the doorway with her unusually loud belching.

"Mother, I can't think when you are standing over me, belching. Will you please go?" Hesitantly she left. After her loud belching sounds faded, I knew it was safe so I turned back to reading my letter:

"I went to talk to the squadron chaplain for marriage counseling. He recommended we wait another year because by then, I will make another stripe. Then we can afford to get married. Right now, I don't make enough money to support a family. So I am asking you to wait until next year at least. I hope you understand.

"Love always,
"David"

I dropped the letter like it was hot lava spewing from a volcano. Strange, that I had been praying for a letter. But I didn't expect this.

I couldn't believe this was happening. I felt deserted, abandoned. Why me, Lord? I was so gullible. I believed him. Now it sounds like David has had a change of heart. My family had come at me from both sides. To think I defended him! Now I would have to face them with bad news and listen to them say, "See? I tol' you so."

I felt David had tricked me out of two years of my life and Li'l David, too. I broke into a cold sweat followed by chills. My head felt like it was going to split open and my stomach felt queasy. I ran into the bathroom. I had to vomit. Afterward, I sat on the toilet stool just staring at the walls and the large gold beveled mirror on the bathroom wall above the vanity. I wet a small hand towel with cold water and blotted my forehead first and then blotted all over my face. I must have sat there for over an hour.

As I sat there reflecting back over the past year, I saw the handwriting on the wall. Without any warning, the emotional shock, suddenly transposed into to a deep, furious anger. I stormed into the kitchen looking at Mother and Daddy Prather holding that letter like it was contaminated.

"Read this. I am so mad! I can't believe he's asking me to wait another year. I'll be 21 in October. If I wait any longer, Li'l David will be 3 or maybe even 4 or 5 by the time we say I do. To think that I have wasted all this time. Humph!"

Mother and Daddy Prather both stopped eating and stared at me. I had never talked bad about David before.

"He gave me an engagement ring before he left. I feel like a fool. Well, I am a fool believing everything he told me. I told everybody we're going to wait until he gets a job to support us. Now he has a job. He is in the Air Force making money. Now he tells me, it isn't enough money so I have to wait again, he says."

Mother stood up from the table belching loudly.

"He wants you to wait again?"

Daddy Prather, who never says anything, spoke up.

"You done waited long enough. Do you want me to talk to him?"

"No," I said. "I am going to write him back. If he can't marry me by October of this year, then forget it."

"When that wol' came home from basic training, I felt it. I could tell something was up. He kept saying he had to get permission from the Base commander and…"

I cut in, "Yes, I know, and I believed him but…"

Mother was tired of all the excuses. She clicked her tongue against her teeth loudly, displaying disgust. I could see her chest rise and fall as she inhaled and exhaled through her nostrils. She reminded me of an angry bull breathing loudly, clawing the earth with its hooves just before it lowers its horns to attack.

"There you go, making excuses for that boy."

To relieve the tension, I exhaled myself. I decided I had better keep quiet.

"He sho' didn't ask permission to make a baby, did he?"

She gave me a contemptuous stare.

"Here, girl, stop looking stupid at me. Come on over here. Sit down and eat your breakfast. There's bacon, eggs, grits and hot buttered biscuits. Daddy and I jest sittin' here talkin' and enjoyin' breakfast."

I could feel Mother and Daddy's eyes on me as I made my plate. Slowly I slid into my chair at the table. The aroma from the crispy bacon floated up to my nostrils enticing me to take a bite.

Daddy teased. "I'm surprised you're hungry, girl." "Me, too," I said.

Mother chuckled, "That girl, now she can eat! It takes more than a bad relationship to ruin her appetite."

Smiling, I took a bite of buttered toast then picked at the fluffy yellow scrambled eggs with my fork before tasting them.

Mother poured Daddy another cup of coffee then stood behind him resting her chin into his soft curly gray hair.

"You telling her or what?" Mother said, twisting her head around to look into Daddy's eyes.

Daddy blurted out, "Me and Johnnie talkin' 'bout going up to Weed."

"When? What for?" I searched their faces.

No answer, just smiles appeared.

"Where is Weed?"

"Right up close to Mount Shasta."

Daddy looked smug and Mother was smiling like a new bride on her honeymoon.

"Who lives in Weed? I've never heard of that place before." Daddy just kept talking like I hadn't said anything.

"Then we might just drive on up to Washington State to McChord Air Force Base."

I almost spit a mouthful of grits out when he said they were going to McChord.

Looking from one to the other, I said, "What you going there for?" While buttering her biscuit, Mother said, "Wanna go, Janie?"

"Yeah! You going to see David, aint you?" I said, stirring cream into my coffee as I watched them.

"When we going, Daddy?" Mother asked while looking at me.

"We leaving day after tomorrow. And Janie, you cain't go." Daddy looked smug as he sat in front of his now empty plate. His arms were folded in front of his broad chest. His bottom lip stuck out like a pouting child's.

Before I could protest, Mother said, "That's Saturday morning. We only have one day to get ready?"

"Yep, if you're going with me." Daddy was trying hard to conceal a smile.

"That's not fair." I searched Daddy's face. "Why can't I go?" He showed no emotion at all.

"He's my fiancé."

"Cause we ain't taking no babies," Daddy Henry said with his mouth poked out, still pouting. "You can go if you can find someone to watch the baby."

"You're talking about going to see my fiancé and I can't go? On top of the fact he has written me a Dear Jane letter. Oh, I've got to figure out a way to go!"

"Mother, what do you think?" Daddy asked.

I answered, "I'll call Earlie and Sydney. Maybe they'll watch David Jr. for me."

Mother picked her teeth with a toothpick, stopping only long enough to say, "Earlie's always busy at the beauty shop on Saturdays. You gone and lost your mind?"

My mind was racing. "Well, I'll see if Sydney can watch them." Daddy said, "Sydney got her hands full already with her four."

Mother said, "Let me call Flo." She picked up the phone and began dialing while talking. "She may watch him. I don't think she'll mind. You always babysitting her kids so I'm sho' she'll do the same for you."

After talking to Flo, Mother handed me the phone. She gave me a warm smile indicating a positive response.

"Janie, I'll watch Li'l David. All I ask is you don't wake me up early. I know Johnnie and Henry will be up before the chickens, so bring David Jr. over Friday night. Okay?"

"Okay. Thanks, Flo. I love you!"

"Love you, too."

"Well, I had better start packing."

"Wait! Wait! Now how long you goin' to be gone?"

I turned to Daddy Henry. "Daddy? How long are we going to be in Washington?"

Daddy scratched his head.

"Give me the phone. Let me talk to Flo," he said.

"Oh, we'll be gone for about a week," he said. "I'm stopping over in Weed, Calif., on the way back."

Daddy turned to me.

"Flo said for you to be sure to bring all of his milk, baby food and changes of clothes to last two weeks."

I listened as Henry continued his phone conversation with Flo.

"Flo, I ain't rushing back now." He looked at me while he talked to Flo. "We gonna get away for a change to enjoy ourselves. Me and Johnnie."

Filled with excitement, I ran to pack Little David diapers, pajamas, and clothes, making sure to pack more than enough to last him.

After packing my bags, I dragged my luggage into the living room so I wouldn't forget anything. Daddy's eyes were twinkling as he teased us.

"Girl, you only gonna be gone for one week. You and Johnnie look like you planning to move away for good."

I sat down at the breakfast nook table to write a long letter to David.

Mother stood over me belching just as I began to write.

"Janie, Daddy said he wants to surprise David. So don't you tell him we're coming."

"I was just writing to tell him I had changed my mind about marrying him.

"Mother, I said, was just thinking, maybe God has something else planned for us."

Mother smiled. "Now you sound like the old Janie I know." She bent down to hug me, laughing with relief.

When I wrote David back, I gave him the option of marrying me right away or else.

"You can just take care of your son. I'll be okay. I have had several guys propose to me but I told them I was waiting on you," I wrote.

It took everything I had to keep from telling him we were on our way to Washington State.

CHAPTER SEVENTEEN

It was a refreshing ride. I sat in the back seat with the window down, letting the air blow in my face and through my hair. We drove for hours only stopping for gas and food. As we sped down the highway, Daddy spotted a giant archway in a golden yellow color hovering high into the sky. He managed to merge over to the nearest freeway exit to a new hamburger place with a large neon sign attached to it. Bright red letters flashed the name at us.

"McDonald's HAMBURGERS! 29 cents FRENCH FRIES 19 cents! MILKSHAKES 19 cents."

That was the first time I ate at McDonald's. It was a large hamburger place, nothing like the little smoky hamburger joints in the Bay Area. It had a drive-through window just like A&W Root beer stands except nobody came out to serve us. Instead, we drove right up to the window and they handed us our food right then and there. That was the biggest hamburger I ever had. It was big as a saucer and had the best mustard on it. It was the best I had ever tasted. I didn't realize how hungry I was. I wolfed that burger down in only a few bites. I crunched on the fries and slowly sipped on my large strawberry milkshake in the bright colored container. Satisfied, I dozed off to sleep. I woke up when I felt the car slowing down. The car wheels made a crunching sound as we turned onto a graveled road. I overheard Daddy talking to Mother.

"We're just a rock's throw away from my friend's house."

Mother turned around in the front seat looking back at me slumped over in the backseat as I groaned. I stretched, then sat up in my seat rubbing my eyes open. We pulled up in front of a tiny rundown country house with no porch, just a concrete walkway leading up to the front door hanging on loose hinges.

Curiously peeking out the window of the car, I asked, "Where are we, Daddy? Are we in Tacoma yet?"

"No. Matter of fact, we are just outside the Oregon border."

I couldn't hide my disappointment. "Oh. But I thought that we were going to Washington state."

"We are," Mother said. "But first Daddy wants his friend to meet us."

Daddy stepped slowly on the brake, coming to a complete stop almost at the front door.

"I called my old Army buddy Jesse and tol' him we were comin' this way so he said, 'I know y'all gonna stop by fer awhile.' We grew up together in Mississippi. Right after the war we both moved to Oakland but he kept right on driving, came up here in these mountains. Right here in Weed, Calif., and been here ever since."

"Who lives here?" I peered through the window like a curious little child. "My friend, his name is Jesse and his two daughters. One's your age." Daddy's friend rushed out to meet us.

We ended up staying there for a couple of days while they caught up on old times. I learned from their conversations around the fireplace in his tiny front room about their past. I also noticed that both Daddy's and Jesse's accent had transgressed into a slower Mississippi drawl.

Daddy Henry's best friend had lost his wife a few years back. Daddy explained, "And he "raised his two chil'ren by himself." He lived only a rock's throw from the Oregon state line. There right in front of us stood a beautiful giant snow-capped mountain. I became mesmerized. "Ooh! That is a beautiful mountain! It is huge." I said, with my head reared back looking up.

"That's Mt. Shasta," Jesse explained

Closing my eyes I said, "The country breeze is nice and refreshing."

He explained, "In Weed, you don't need a air conditioner."

That was the farthest I'd ever traveled. I was excited but when we finally crossed the California state line, I was ecstatic.

We arrived at McChord Air Force Base 10 hours later.

The military police at the front gate peered into our car. asked, "What's the purpose of your visit?"

"Daddy Henry said, "We're coming to visit Airman David Bess, Sir,"

The soldier saluted us through the gate after the Daddy showed him his driver's license and car insurance papers. After giving us directions to David's barracks, I was excited, but uneasy. Wild thoughts invaded my happiness: What if David has found someone else? He may not want me here.

Daddy got out of the car and walked into the Civil Engineer Squadron office. David came bopping out of the office with a tall, slender man who walked with him to our car. The surprised look on David's face gave him away. His sideways smile slowly appeared on his face as he spotted me sitting in the back seat near the open window.

"Hey, Janie! Your dad didn't tell me you were here," he said.

"This is my first sergeant. I want you to meet Mrs. Prather. Oh, yes, and my fiancée, Janie."

Teasing him, Daddy said "You met me already,"

We all burst into laughter. The first sergeant let David off for the whole weekend. Daddy was amazed at the prices for food at the cafeteria. David took us shopping at the Base Exchange and in the commissary with a special pass. We stayed there for only four days. One whole day, we spent driving for miles trying to reach Mount Helen, another snow-capped mountain. We soon tired of the long trip. We stopped and ate at a quaint little restaurant before returning to the base. David got us a room in guest housing. It was very nice and cozy with expensive furnishings.

We spent the next day picnicking at Point Defiance Park in Tacoma. We walked through the zoo looking at the animals—tigers, elephants, everything. The chimpanzees entertained us the most. There was one who had the cutest personality. He really put on a good show to earn the goober peanuts the small children held out for them Through an opening in the cyclone fence, they threw them in every time he did his acrobatic stunts from the trees. Everyone was laughing. He was so cute!.

While in Tacoma, we ate out every day. The first day we were there, David took us to the Base Chow Hall with him as his guests. There was so much food until I felt full from just looking at all the different dishes. They heaped man-sized potions onto our plates as we pushed our trays along.

Time flew excessively fast for me. After the third day, Daddy said, "There's a Chinese proverb, it goes like this: House guests are like fish. After three days, they stink. So, I don't want us to start stinking up the place. It's time to go now."

We cracked up!

David tried to talk him into staying longer but it didn't work.

"Now, Janie can stay, but I am taking my wife home now." He stood up, towering over us. Pulling up his belted slacks further over his waist, he said. "I've got work to do at the house."

"I thought you retired, Mr. Prather," David said.

"I retired from Judson Steel but I still work on my own. Besides, I need money for this woman," he said, pointing at Mother. "She's too expensive. I've got to work to just clothe and feed her."

We all laughed again.

David and I held each other close that night. He stayed with me all night in my room. We talked long into the morning. I didn't want him get too close for fear I might give in to my lustful feeling.

I dreaded the fact I had to go. I waited to see if he would talk about our future. I didn't even mention marriage, not one time while I was there.

Wouldn't you know it? That mean, nasty letter I wrote him arrived the day I was leaving. He surprised me by pulling it from his pocket that morning.

"Oh, I got your letter today," he said. He tried to sound casual but I knew he wasn't happy with what he read.

"What? I mailed that letter just before we left." My heart skipped a beat. "You're just getting it? I tried to sound as casual as possible too. I thought you had it already."

He said, "No, but we need to talk." Frowns over his eyebrows was a sure give-away.

In the letter, I told him I felt he was using marriage counseling as an excuse to keep putting me off.

"You don't have to marry me," I wrote. "I just want you to take care of your child."

I explained I would be able to work once Li'l David's eye surgeries were over, and he was old enough for day care. I told David he needed to start an allotment for his son as soon as possible. I needed his financial support. I stressed in the letter not to worry about marrying me because of Li'l David. I had suitors coming at me and I made sure I told him so.

I mailed the letter the day before we left for Washington State.

At that moment, I wished I had never sent it.

David said, "I read this letter over and over. I hope you didn't mean what you said."

I dropped my head in shame.

He pulled my chin up, staring into my eyes.

"Why did you tell me there were other guys trying to date you? That hurt me so. I love you, Janie. I still want to marry you."

"You have to understand. I was so angry and hurt; I wanted to hurt you, too. Besides, I don't feel we really need a marriage counselor."

"That's what the Air Force requires, before we get married."

"Yeah, but we're not like most the couples here. We have already faced financial difficulties, medical problems and other obstacles which has blocked us these last two years, but our love has not died. We've been together too long. I know you love me and I love you, too."

"I do?" he teased.

"Yes, you do," I said. "If you stayed with me after my sisters inflicted pain and suffering on you, you can make it with me."

"You are right. Your sisters put me through hell. It was a full-fledged war the first day I met you. First, you slapped my face on our first date, then you just about raped me later after your sisters nearly killed me in the front room hitting me with those ale bottles. Just because I hinted about us having sex."

"No, I didn't." I giggled happily. I could see my smiling happy face reflecting off his sunglasses.

"Your brothers are no joke either," I said. "Especially Freddy. He'd come to Merritt College every day at noontime while I was walking across the street toward Jo Ethel's café..."

"You mean Smoky Joe's Café," he guffawed.

"Yeah, everyone called it Smokey Joe's because Jo Ethel's was always filled with smoke. Well, anyway, he scared me to death. I would feel myself being lifted into the air and then thrown over someone's shoulders. When I finally recognized Freddy, it was too late. I had punched and kicked him so hard. He was running with me on his back. He thought it was funny,. until I yelled, 'Put me down.' Then some of my admirers came running over to rescue me. They took me down from his shoulders I was screaming and kicking all the way.

While reliving about our past, we laughed so hard.

I quickly changed the subject, "We already discussed how we want to raise our kids."

"Yeah, I believe in spanking if they get out of line."

"Me, too," I said.

"I read child psychology books after I found out you got pregnant."

Surprised, I said, "You did?"

"We have a son to raise together. I want to make sure I understand that little guy." He gave me a lingering kiss. "Besides, I want lots of children."

"I know we both love God," I added to the list.

"I am Catholic, you are Baptist. How's that going to work?" I reminded him," You promised you would go to my church with me."

He said, holding his hands out in front as if to ward me off. "Sometimes-not all the time." He explained, "You see, when I was a little boy, just about 10 years old, this fat lady got 'happy' in church. She started shouting and dancing. She flailed her arms around in the air and she made these weird sounds. I was holding onto my mother's hand for dear life.

Then all of a sudden, WHOP! She swung her large arms and hit me right up side my head. Man! I took out running! My mother had to chase me outside before she caught me. I was headed home."

"Really," I said. I laughed so hard until tears sprang from my eyes. I just couldn't stop laughing. I could picture him, a little boy with his eyes bugging out his head frightened to death when the lady screamed. I could see him breaking for the front door to escape the madness.

"She was happy!"

"Happy?" he said. A puzzled look appeared on his face

"She was filled with the Holy Ghost."

He shrugged his shoulders.

"I never went back," he said. "Instead, I chose to go to church with my cousin, Doris. It was nice and peaceful in the Catholic church. I just had to repeat after the priest, 'Holy Mary, Mother of God, pray for us sinners now.'"

Teasing him, I said, "Oh, well, I was going to teach you the 'old time religion.'"

David looked worried.

"I'm going to have to work with you on that. I said, You see, I love the church that praises God out loud. In the Bible, it says make a joyful noise unto the Lord…"

"Okay, let's get off the subject of religion." He was serious again. "That's too controversial for me."

"We both respect our parents," I said.

"Yes, Mr. Bess would knock your head off if you talked back to him."

"Well, we have covered everything," I said. "What else is there for us to know?"

"Nothing, I guess," he said. "So you still gonna wait for me?"

"Yes," I said, then kidding him. I said, "But only a few months. Your time is expiring quickly."

He laughed.

"Sounds like a the expiration date on a can of corn or something."

"Then I am going to have to start looking for an available young man."

His soft and tender lips caressed mine. I pulled away.

"Uh uh. Not until we're married this time," I warned him, smiling.

We held each other close. I hated to leave him, but I knew he would be back for me now.

CHAPTER EIGHTEEN

David wrote me promising to come home to marry me on my birthday. I wrote back telling him I wouldn't want my wedding on my birthday.

"I admit, it would be a nice birthday present, but I would rather celebrate our wedding day separately," I said.

I only had two weeks to find a dress for my wedding. I refused to wear white because tradition required only virgins wear white.

Mother Piggis said, "I see you wearing pink. That color looks good on you. So you wear pink."

We had no luck looking for wedding dresses. Traveling all over San Francisco, Berkeley and Oakland with Mother searching for that certain dress with only a little money and no time proved challenging. Being short and tiny created even more problems. Finally, we found the perfect dress but it was much too large for me. It was on sale in Macy's Bargain basement. After trying it on, Mother looked at me while I sat on the wooden bench in the dressing room with my head down, achy feet just throbbing, frustrated beyond description, while Mother stood shaking her head at me.

"I got an idea!" I said grabbing the dress up and putting it on. I grabbed a handful of the material on both sides.

"I can take this dress up and hem it and then it'll be okay." I turned to show her. "What do you think Mother?"

Mother shook her head.

"Gal, for that much money, you can make your own dress. You talkin' bout taking all that material and cutting it down. You can

141

make your own dress and it will fit you better than that. You made your prom dress and it looked better than those in the store."

I put the dress back on the rack.

Mother was right as usual.

After bathing and feeding Li'l David that night, I fell into bed exhausted. I dreamed it was my wedding day. The dress I wore was a floral design embossed with pastel pink and aqua blue roses surrounded with rich green leaves. The fabric was soft with a matching bolero. I had never seen such a unique dress as that one.

The next day, I ran to the fabric store around the corner.

When the salesclerk flipped the CLOSED sign over to OPEN over the door at the fabric shop, I was the first to enter.

"Good Morning,"

"Yes, it is a good morning," I said as I eagerly walked through the door, up and down the aisles of neatly stacked bolts of fabrics.

The tiny woman wearing a red candy-striped apron followed me as I made my way. Walking up to me as I stood in front of a display, she looked over her spectacles, and said, "What can I help you with?"

"Well, I'm getting married next week and I'm trying to find the right fabric and a pattern, too."

She led me to the bridal section where all of the white sateen brocades and silk-laced materials were displayed.

"Oh, no, I'm not wearing white. We already have a child and it is going to be a very simple ceremony with just family members present."

Remembering what Mother Piggis told me, I said, "I want to wear pink."

The once helpful sales lady's disposition immediately changed. She actually smirked at me.

"Well, there's a lot of pink fabric all over. If you'll excuse me."

I could tell by the look on her face what she was thinking—*Here's another Negro teenager with an illegitimate child. When will they learn?* She quickly headed off in the opposite direction to assist another patron who had just entered the store.

Relieved to be alone, I searched for the fabric I envisioned in my dream. I strolled casually down the aisles until I found myself in the back of the store at a bargain table searching through a large bin with assorted materials. As I pulled them up to examine and feel the different fabrics, I spotted a speck of pink peeking from beneath another fabric in the bin. I reached down and pulled it up

I liked what I saw. This was the actual fabric I saw in my dreams! There were the same identical pink and aqua roses with the green leaves surrounding it. I couldn't believe it! I even found another remnant in the same bin, a beige satin fiber that was perfect for lining the dress and bolero jacket. I looked through all of the Simplicity, Vogue, Butterick and McCall Pattern books. As I flipped the pages, I saw a basic sheath dress with a bolero jacket. It was not what I really wanted but it was close enough. I could design it myself. I found a soft pink organza fabric in the bridal section, a perfect match for the pink roses in the material. I dropped it into a shopping cart and wheeled it up to the front of the store where the clerk was cutting fabric for the patron who entered the store after me. I waited patiently until she finished her transaction.

"I'm ready," I said. "I found just what I wanted." She looked surprised.

"Where did you find that? It is an unusual design. I have never seen that fabric before!"

"God showed it to me in my dreams last night."

Her mouth flew open and she appeared speechless.

"Please come back when you finish it. I would love to see it!"

"I will just do that."

"Promise?" she asked.

"I promise."

After paying for my purchases, I left with my bag tucked tightly in my hand, skipping like a little child all the way home.

I proudly showed Mother and Daddy my materials and pattern. They gave their approval. Mother was holding Li'l David on her hip.

"You had better get started. Don't worry, Daddy and I will take care of the baby so you can finish your dress. You only have three more days to make it."

My sisters came over and gave me some good suggestions.

The form-fitting bodice had spaghetti thin straps accentuating my tiny waist. The gathered skirt fit snugly at the waist and flowed softly into gathers but had a center pleat that gave a balloon effect at the knee length hem showing off my nicely shaped legs. The short bolero jacket buttoned down the back with soft pink pearl buttons. I made my veil out of the matching pink organza fabric. I had a few problems but I found a pair of pink satin pumps. I even found a matching evening bag at Leeds Shoe Store. I was now set for my wedding day.

David came home on my birthday. He brought many birthday presents for me but the best present of all was the beautiful engagement ring. Before he presented it to me, though, I almost swallowed my tongue; he scared the life out of me.

"Take off your engagement ring," he said.

"Why?" I asked. My voice quivered. I was still wearing the one he had given me when I was pregnant. I never removed it, except one time when he had lied to me. He had trouble finding it after I had thrown it in his face. He couldn't find it for a week. It fell down into the back seat of his Buick and he had to take the back seat out to retrieve it. He made me promise never to take it off again unless we decided not to marry.

"Because my brother Johnny gave it to me and I was to pay him for it later. He had broken up with his fiancée so he asked me did I want to buy it. I didn't have any money or a job so I took him upon it. Now, I am giving it back to him."

"Why?"

"Just take it off, Janie."

I reluctantly handed him to the ring. He then whipped out a blue velvet box from his coat pocket and opened it.

"This one was made for you. It is exclusively yours."

Inside the box was a beautiful engagement ring with a matching wedding band. He kissed me tenderly then placed the engagement ring on my finger. It fit perfect. He kissed me again. Tears fell from my eyes. I didn't bother to wipe them away. I took the ring off my finger to admire it. I noticed the inscription "Eternally Yours" etched inside. There were three smaller diamonds on both sides of a quarter karat stone in the center of the ring.

He then gave me the wedding band still in the velvet box to examine. I knew he had spent his whole paycheck and his savings on this one. It was gorgeous. The diamonds seemed to blink back at me.

"They are beautiful."

David wasn't exactly the romantic type; he very seldom showed outward affection. I knew this was his way of showing me how much he really loved me. I was just ecstatic.

He stuck his chest out promenading around the room.

"Now, I need to talk to Mr. Prather and your mother. I can't wait to see the look on her face when I ask permission to marry you."

We laughed together.

I tried to warn him. "Don't play with my mother. She's no joke!"

"I'm not afraid of her," he said, laughing. "I just want to mess with her. She kept asking me, 'When are you getting married?' So, now she'll know. Ha! Ha!"

We walked hand in hand into the kitchen where Daddy and Mother were having an afternoon snack.

"Mr. Prather," David said, saluting him as if he was a military officer. Henry just busted out laughing. He stood up and saluted back. "Yes, sir!" he answered back,

Mother then stood up next to Mr. Prather with a look of expectation written all over her face.

"Mr. Prather. Can I ask you and Mrs. Prather for your daughter's hand in marriage?"

"'Bout time!" Mother said.

Daddy chuckled, "Yes, of course, you don't have to ask me, ask her mother."

Mother smiled, "Like I said, 'bout time!"

I was so happy. Mother hugged David. He looked surprised. Daddy shook his hand then embraced him.

We got married on a Friday night, Oct. 23. We went to the Rev. O.P. Smith's house to be married. He was the pastor from the same church who consoled Sydney when she stood bravely in front of the congregation to ask forgiveness. I missed them so much. When Daddy said, "Call Rev. Smith, he'll want to do the honors. He is always asking about you, Janie," I ran and dialed their number. I still remembered it. I sang lead in the junior choir there from the time I was 6. His wife was like my godmother. Every year, she sponsored my trips to summer camp with her. I spent a lot of time with them at their house as a little girl. When I asked the Rev. Smith to officiate our marriage ceremony, he said, "Why, I would be proud and honored to accommodate you. It will be good to see you again, Janie."

Shyly I said, "Thank you, pastor."

That Friday all of our families stood there in the Smiths' living room anxiously waiting for us to say, "I do." It was a small family wedding. After he said the traditional words, he pronounced us man and wife.

David looked so happy and proud as he stood there cajoling with his brothers. Pastor Smith didn't like it and made it clear, "This is a very serious time in your life."

David continued to make faces.

That's when Pastor said, "Janie, you see this marriage license I hold here in my hands. This is your ticket to keep David in line."

David asked, "How she going to do that?"

"I was raised on a farm back in the Deep South," he said. "We raised all sorts of animals in Alabama. Well, we had these mules and horses. Mules were the most stubborn at times. Well, the way we tamed them was we put blinders on them so they could only see in front. That way we kept them focused on the road in front. That's called a bridle. That is what your marriage license represents. It is your bridle."

David mumbled something to his brother Johnny, who was the best man.

The Rev. Smith noticed. He was a wise man.

"Not only that, we use a whip when we train a young stallion. When we get on him for the first time, we have to break him in. The minute we straddle his back that stallion begins to buck. H e will try to kick hard enough to kick you off.

"Then, we have to use a whip to stop him from kicking and bucking. Sometimes he refuses to move. When they get out of line and start kicking, trying to throw you off, we whip them.

"This marriage license is your bridle and your whip, Janie. When your young buck gets out of line, you whip him with this marriage license. Pastor waved it in the air. "He'll calm down, I guarantee."

David said, "Oh, yeah? This horse has a mean kick, sir."

Mother said, "If you kick my daughter, then you'll have to answer to me."

David retorted back, "Hey, mother-in-law, I have the papers on her now."

"My name is Mrs. Prather, not mother-in-law. And she ain't no horse. If you're going to mistreat her, then you send her home."

Mother was serious, too. Daddy had to hold her back. I think if she could have gotten hold of David she would have whipped his butt.

Mrs. Bess said, "David, stop it. This is serious,"

"I'm just playing with Mrs. Prather, Mom," he said.

We all laughed after everybody hugged.

"What should I call you, Mrs. Prather?" David said.

"You can call me Mother like everybody else."

"Oh, no, I can't call you Mother. I know you really don't like me."

"Then, like I said," Mother looking at David like she could choke him, "call me Mrs. Prather."

"No, I think I'm gonna call you Mother-in-law."

"Then that'll be fine," Mother said, as Daddy led her away.

That is what he called her from that day forward. He knew that would irritate her.

CHAPTER NINETEEN

A few days later we left for Washington in our new car. David's father had given us his pride and joy, his 1956 Pontiac, as a wedding present.

"We just bought a new car. We don't need two, so you can have the older one. We got it serviced and it runs like new."

That was truly a blessing from God. We needed it because we had no transportation at all. David and Henry packed that Pontiac so tight with all of our wedding gifts. My parents gave us a new black and white television set. That was a luxury item back then. That was before color televisions existed. It was packed in the trunk, cushioned between several large soft pillows. When the trunk was packed to maximum capacity, Daddy Henry ordered David to sit on it to hold it down. We just could squeeze into the car ourselves. We had only enough room for Li'l David to sit in the back seat on top of our bed pillows. That was before the seat belts were invented. He was so tiny he only took up about a foot of space. He stretched his little head to the maximum, to enjoy the scenery as we drove.

Lil David sensed something exciting was happening. I felt cheated because we had no way to explain to him what was happening. David drove for more than 10 hours as I sat close to him in the front seat. Daddy and Mother were in the lead in their blue 1960 Mercury. They went with us right up to the boundary lines of California and Oregon.

Daddy blew the horn and Mother waved as they turned their car around to head back home. I looked back, still waving, until their

Mercury Monterey was nothing but a blur. The car descended into the hills, and then disappeared out of sight. I cried silently as I looked out the back window. I couldn't see the car anymore. My mother was gone. The tears were starting. I wiped them rapidly away with my right hand, at the same time using my peripheral vision to see whether David noticed. We traveled up and around narrow and steep mountains. There were large rocks on one side of the long stretch of highway. On the opposite side of the highway were beautiful giant trees with large dark green leaves hanging from massive branches. The trunks of the trees were too large to describe.

I missed my Mother already. I made a mental note to call her as soon as I could get to a pay phone. I kept wiping the tears away. My eyes were now red and puffy from crying. I kept my face turned toward the passenger side of the window of the car so David wouldn't be able to see my tears. However, David did notice. I expected him to tease me; instead, he smiled at me.

Suddenly, without warning, he grabbed me around my neck and pulled me close to him with his free right hand. He skillfully maneuvered the car around a sharp curve, and then stepped gently on the brakes to slow the vehicle down. A huge 18-wheeler cargo truck blew its horn impatiently as he passed us just before another curve appeared. David pulled off the highway to the side of the road, carefully checking in his rearview mirror for traffic. He hugged me close and turned my face toward his. He stared at me intensely with his deep-set brown eyes. He seemed to look right through me. He seemed to have X-ray vision. He could read my mind.

"Do you want to go back home?"

"No," I answered as I lowered my head in shame.

"Then why are you crying, Janie?"

"Be-cause I-I-I mi-miss my mother." My lips shook and I tried to hold back my emotions.

He lifted his hips up slightly and pulled out a handkerchief from his right back hip pocket. David gently wiped the tears away and kissed me tenderly.

"Don't worry, Janie, I plan to make you very happy. I am going to take good care of you and my son. I don't want you to worry. You hear me? I love you, Janie."

He held me close and wiped my tears away. Then he pulled back onto the long stretch of highway. I turned around to check on our son, who had been playing with his miniature cars earlier, had now fallen asleep.

David was getting tired. He changed the radio station merely out of boredom. There was nothing but static on the radio then. We were out of range. He turned it off because the noise was irritating to the ears.

I knew this was a long drive for him. I didn't know how to drive yet so he had to drive the whole 1,700 miles to Tacoma. I was the co-pilot. I read out loud the directions on the map. David patiently followed the instructions. The night before, Daddy and David had outlined the route in red ink. He looked tired I just kept talking to keep him alert.

"I only left my mother one time and that was to visit my real father, Calvin Lightfoot."

"You never told me much about your real father before." David glanced over at me as he waited for an explanation.

"Oh, that's right. You never did meet my father before. Everyone says I look just like him." I beamed with pride. "He is a minister in Los Angeles now. When Dad and Mother broke up, that's where he moved to. I visited him in June 1960, right after graduation. Then he moved to another address. The last letter that I sent him last year came back with return to sender on it. We lost contact after that. When Mother married Henry, well, we moved to another house. Like I said, I went to visit him after my high school graduation. I haven't seen him since.

"I hate myself when I cry like this. I feel like a little girl my first day of school. It was the first day in kindergarten. Mother took me to my classroom and left me there with this old, mean, white teacher. While mother was still there, she was extra nice to me. 'Hello, Janie, it's so nice to have you in my class.' "After Mother left, the smile left her face instantly. Her facial expression instantly changed. She turned into a mean, ugly witch."

To fight sleep, I continued talking. I needed to stay awake. I needed to make sure I kept David awake and alert on our long journey. I chattered on and on about my childhood days.

"That teacher, she spoke to me in a harsh tone. 'Go sit down in your seat, in the back row, young lady.' I still remember that day. It seemed like just yesterday. There were only two Negro children in her classroom. This one boy, Joshua and me. She would smile at the all the white children with their blond hair, blue eyes. Even the red headed freckled—face little girl, who later hit me for no reason. I was chided for crying by Mrs. Brighton, in front of everybody. All the little white children then snickered and laughed at me. Joshua, the little Negro boy, stood on the sidelines looking frightened, fearing that he might be their next victim. They then started chanting, 'Crybaby, crybaby! Suck your mama's tittles.' They formed a circle around me. I put my hands over my ears and closed my eyes so as to drown out their angry words but I could still hear them. I was crying so hard my body trembled with each and every sob. The teacher then shook me hard and made me go stand in the corner. I was so scared. I didn't tell Mrs. Brighton I had to go to the bathroom because I thought she might scold me again. The children might make fun of me again. I tried to hold it. I shifted my weight from one leg to another until I was actually dancing a jig. 'Keep still, Janie. You are to stand erect in the corner with your face to the wall.'

"I tried to tell her, 'But I have to go to the bathroom.'

"She said, 'I told you to turn around, young lady' so I obeyed her. My daddy always told me to obey your elders. So I stopped trying to explain. I tried to hold it, but my stomach was aching with pain. Next thing I knew, pee was running down my legs into my socks and down into my shoes. She then had the janitor come and mop it up. My mother had to come and pick me up from school. I could hear the urine squishing inside my shoes, sloshing as I walked out to get into the car. My socks were soaking wet, too.

I told my mother what had happened but she thought I was exaggerating. I only went to that school for a little while. My mother went to talk to the teacher and the principal. I heard her talking to my aunt on the phone the next day. Johnnie said, 'Yes, Carrie, I told that principal when my daughter says that she has to go to the bathroom, you had better let her go. Girl, I got loose like a goose in there. That principal made Mrs. Brighton apologize to me and Janie can go anytime she wants. I know they are prejudiced. But they are not going to treat my baby any old way and get away with it.'

"I was moved to another classroom shortly afterward. My new teacher was nice. I wish my mother had X-ray vision, so she could have caught that teacher while she was shaking me and yelling at me. She would have slapped that teacher's face. Believe me, I know my mother."

David looked at me seriously, then asked me, "Don't you want to go to sleep? If you want to sleep, it's okay by me. I will be fine. Don't worry. Trust me. Go to sleep! You are driving me crazy. I never knew that you talked that much!"

"No, silly, I'm not sleepy. I just get sentimental from time to time. I want to make sure you don't fall asleep at the wheel."

We rode on for several hours before I started to doze off. I felt like my neck was no longer attached to my shoulders. I would wake up every time my head would roll to the extreme right or left. My head would roll backward then forward. It felt as though it was going to fall off my shoulders. I tried my best to fight sleep but after a short while, the white striped line in the middle of the long winding highway hypnotized me. It seemed like we would never arrive. It was now dark. I looked at my watch. It was almost 5 p.m. I dropped my head forward for the final time before falling into a deep sleep. Before I knew it, we were pulling up into a sloped driveway.

"Wake up, Janie. We're home. Wake up, baby. Look right directly in front of you."

I looked out of the front windshield again. There was a white-shingled cottage with five red wooden steps leading up to the front porch. I got out of the car and quickly walked up the steps. David was right behind me.

"Is Li'l David still asleep?" I said.

"Yes, let him sleep. I'll bring him in as soon as I can. But first let me carry you over the threshold." With that said, he picked me up, all 98 pounds and carried me into our fully furnished flat.

"How do you like your new home?" David asked anxiously. He still had me in his arms. He peered into my eyes. I was surprised to see him like this. He always had this cocky way about him. He always had such an air of self-assurance. David hands were actually shaking as he put me down. He was fumbling with his keys nervously. He looked like a little boy looking for approval. He looked so cute just then. I loved him even more.

"I like it!" I said. I smiled and nodded my head in approval. "The apartment is very nice."

"It is very nice," I said again to reassure him.

He smiled at me, just then, with his sideways smile.

"Oh, I had better get Li'l David out of the car." He bolted out the door. He returned in a few minutes with Li'l David fast asleep in his arms. A blanket was dangling haphazardly from around our little son.

We only brought in our bedding that night. We were very excited, but also very tired. We both agreed we could unpack all of the other stuff in the morning. We quickly made our bed and then laid Little David down in his crib. I gave him a goodnight kiss after I pulled his favorite blanket over him. He had his own bedroom now. This was his first night sleeping alone.

Li'l David didn't like being separated from me. Before I could climb into bed with David, he started whining. His cries gradually shifted from annoying whining to a loud, insisting caterwaul. The inflection of sound modulated until it was totally unbearable.

"He is afraid. He is used to sleeping with me. He always slept on top of my chest in my bed when you were gone."

David insisted that Li'l David sleep in his own bed.

"He'll stop if you don't go in there. Just ignore him. Janie, come back here!"

I ignored David's orders and ran to pick him up.

"My poor baby," I hugged him tight to my breast. "Hush, baby, your Daddy just doesn't understand." I looked up. David stood in the doorway, leaning on the doorjamb. He was shaking his head in disgust.

"Janie, I took child psychology. I read and studied books about babies before we got married. You have to be firm with him. You are just spoiling that boy."

"I keep telling you, he can't hear so he doesn't understand. We have to be patient with him."

"Your sisters were right. They said you wouldn't let him cry for a minute before you're picking him up."

I just tuned David out. I sat down in a rocking chair nearby. Li'l David clung to me. He had a firm grip on my nightgown. I held him in my lap while I rocked him and rubbed his perfect shaped head. He finally fell asleep. After putting him back into his crib, I slowly tipped-toed out.

I crawled back into bed with David who was waiting impatiently for me. This was our first night together in our own bed. I snuggled up to him. He pulled me closer than close. Before long, we were smooching and kissing. We were having so much fun making up. His warm lips on mine were not enough to convince me we were man and wife. I was aroused just thinking about making warm passionate love, just as we were getting into it, we heard a loud knock at the door. I was frightened out of my mind.

"David, is this a good neighborhood?" I asked.

"Yes, Janie, I checked before renting this place. I am paying high enough rent here. It is the best I could find. Why?" He kissed me on my neck and my lips. Between our hot breathing, I asked, "Did you hear that loud knocking at the door?" He kept on kissing me until I was like putty in his hands. I returned his hot kisses.

"Yes, it's probably the neighbors hammering or something." I was trying to concentrate on consummating our marriage but the loud sounds interrupted us again. My heart thumped hard and fast.

"David, go see who's there! Li'l David is in the room by himself, go see about Li'l David, please." I pushed him away.

Sighing loudly, he got up to check the door. There stood Li'l David preparing to knock as David opened the door. He grabbed him up like he was a sack of potatoes. He spanked him on his legs and Li'l David squealed. I couldn't stand for David to spank my baby.

I protested about the way he handled him. It only made matters worse for Li'l David.

"You have spoiled this boy and he's going to learn to mind me," David yelled. Fearful from the angry look on his Dad's face, Li'l David really cried out.

David started spanking his son and with every lick I winced. My heart ached for my child. I am sure it was not hard but I knew Li'l David didn't understand.

I wanted to yell stop but from past experiences, I knew it would only make things worse. My yelling would just infuriate him more. He would spank him even longer to prove his point. After a few more taps on his legs, David laid Li'l David back in his bed and shook his large index finger in his tiny face. David stomped his feet so hard on the hardwood floors until the bed vibrated. Li'l David's the eyes were filled with terror as he watched his father leave. David ushered my unwilling body out the room, closing the door behind him. He led me back to bed and locked our bedroom door. I was just furious with him.

I lay there in our bed fuming in the dark, crying my eyes out. David ignored me completely. He didn't talk to me and I certainly had nothing to say to him. I felt he was too rough on my child.

While I lay there, thinking, maybe I had done the wrong thing by letting David spank him.

All of a sudden, we heard this loud crashing noise at our bedroom door. Bam! Bam! Bam! I trembled with fear. David jumped out of bed immediately.

"What the..." he said. He unlocked the door and looked out. There stood Li'l David in the doorway. Over his head, he held his little yellow Mexican ladder-back chair with the woven hemp seat. David took him firmly back to his room, laying him firmly back into his bed.

I was laughing so hard until I wasn't even angry with Big David anymore. He had to laugh himself once he returned to our bedroom. He fell onto the bed chuckling, holding his stomach trying hard to hold back the laughter.

"See, I told you that boy had plenty of sense."

We all went to sleep soon afterward. We were truly a family now.

CHAPTER TWENTY

T he whole state of Washington was green and pretty, just like Mother Piggis saw in her vision. She told me she saw the three of us walking together in a park, laughing and having a good time.

"I see that you will be very happy there. While you are walking in that park, say the twenty-third Psalms as you walk with your little family. There will be blessings given to you."

Tacoma was so lush and green with lots of hills and mountains. We moved from the little cottage because it was too much for our budget. We now lived on a hill in the Salishan housing projects. Tall beautiful trees surrounded us. It was a defunct Army housing that had been sold to the city of Tacoma. The Housing Authority ran it. Rent was paid according to your income. David and I would walk with Li'l David. The plants and flowers were just beautiful. The birds would always be chirping. I had never been conscious of birds before. We held hands as we walked through our neighborhood. Li'l David would run ahead playing with his German Shepherd dog named Brownie. A dog that had adopted us. He jumped into our car one night while we were at the country grocery store. When we opened the door of our car to put in our groceries, in he jumped! All the coaxing, pushing, pulling, tugging and calling would not persuade him to leave. We went all over the parking lot asking every available person if they had lost a dog. We went back into the store to have it announced over the intercom. There was no response. So we kept him after making sure the word was passed around in our small community we had a lost German Shepard. Nobody ever claimed the dog so I figured that God sent Li'l David a companion to play with.

It didn't take long for Li'l David to figure out when his dad was at home, he had to be on his best behavior. When his dad was at work, however, he would give me a run for my money. I soon discovered he possessed an awesome sense of time. He would lie in his bed, patiently waiting for his father to leave for work. As soon as David had driven the car out of our driveway, he would start! I'd hear his little bare feet as they hit the hardwood floor. First, he'd run to the bathroom to rid his jaws of last night's dinner. He looked like a little brown squirrel scurrying about. Due to the fact he was storing unwanted food back in his mouth, his cheeks jutted out just like a chipmunk's.

He would first peek into our bedroom to make sure the coast was clear. He would adjust his glasses on his nose in able to see clearly. He would squint eyes as though he was staring at the bright sunlight. I would feign sleep. After he made certain only Mommy was in the bed, the fun would begin. I could hear him as he ran to the bathroom. I knew I had to watch him. He moved very fast! I sneaked out of my bed and followed him into the bathroom to see what he was doing. To my surprise, he was leaning his head over the toilet bowl. He looked like a little squirrel with nuts stored in his cheeks. With his index finger, he was raking the unwanted food out from his mouth. I had cooked steak, mashed potatoes with gravy and spinach and now it was all being shoveled out. The night before, Li'l David had locked his mouth like a vise and refused to open up to eat his meat and vegetables. David squeezed his jaws open and forced him to open his mouth wide. David then shoved a large spoonful of food into his tiny little mouth. Despite my loud objections, David used his leather strap to convince Li'l David to finally chew it up. After a few good licks on his butt, David inspected his mouth to insure he had swallowed it. There was no evidence of food in his mouth. Then and only then was he permitted to have his favorite drink: grape Kool-Aid. Afterward I would serve him ice cream for dessert. How he managed to keep his dinner separate from the ice cream is beyond my wildest imagination.

Who would've ever thought a deaf toddler had the capabilities to conjure up such an ingenious way to conceal food? The most amazing part of it all was, he was cunning enough to figure out how to get rid of the evidence. I wouldn't have believed it if I hadn't seen it with my own eyes. I could hardly wait for David to come home so I could tell him forcing the food on him didn't work as I had warned him. He only figured a way to outsmart him.

I was constantly taking Li'l David back and forth to Madigan General Hospital for his pediatrics appointments. During these frequent visits, I asked the pediatrician on duty about giving him a hearing test and evaluation. The pediatrician said he would have to be referred to a speech and hearing center located in Seattle.

"Could you please refer my son to the hearing clinic," I asked. "Li'l David doesn't speak or use any words. He makes a sound like a bird."

"It is not unusual for toddler boys to be what we call late talkers."

"I know my child and he do not make sounds like other children. You see, I have helped raise my nephew. I was an aunt when I was only 11 years old. I babysat all of my nephews all the time. In fact, they lived with us from the time they were newborns up until they were about 7 or 8. I was like their second mother. My sister went to work and I babysat, changed their diapers, read to them, and played with them. My oldest sister was a single parent with four boys and one girl. My middle sister had one boy and one girl. So believe me, I know about babies! I have five nephews and two nieces. None of them acts like my son. My little cousins, I babysat them, too, from the time they were only three months old. There are seven children in all. They were all talking before they two. I mean in complete sentences. They all said Mama, Dada or something! They imitated whatever they heard. So I disagree with you."

The young intern's face changed from chalky white to crimson red. He stared at me so hard I felt as if his deep blue eyes bore a hole through me. His lips pursed up tight, giving me that phony smile.

"Like I explained to you, Mrs. Bess, all children are different." It was so obvious he was not happy. I knew he was trying to keep his composure.

"Well, could you please explain why David does not respond to toys that make noises, only action toys, the ones that move?"

"I can't explain that, Mrs. Bess."

"He doesn't even react or respond to loud noises. His cry is so soft you can hardly hear him." The doctor subliminally doodled on a blank notepad. "I noticed this when he was only three months old." While trying to hold back my tears of frustration, I told him why my suspicions were aroused. "Just the other day, he was playing near me on the kitchen floor. In my kitchen, I have linoleum over sub-concrete floors. Well, while drying my dishes, I accidentally dropped a cast iron skillet on the floor of my apartment. As the heavy skillet hit the hard concrete surface just missing his him by a margin, the floor actually vibrated! The sound was earsplitting. My son just casually looked at it. The loud crash had even startled me, and I ran to him thinking he would be frightened out of his wits. I wanted to give him reassurance, but he showed no reaction at all. Don't try to tell me this is normal! I have been doing research on deaf children. Sir, I sent for pamphlets and information from Washington, D.C. on how to detect deafness in a baby. Li'l David fit all of the symptoms that were described. Please listen to me! My baby needs help!"

I was practically screaming out of frustration.

"I'm sorry but I can't help you. There is no actual proof he can't hear therefore, I don't feel that it is necessary for David Jr. to be referred to a speech and hearing clinic or a doctor in ENT clinic."

"Excuse me, but what is the ENT clinic?"

"Ear, nose and throat clinic, ma'am," he said impatiently. "ENT is where you would be referred if he has had a lot of ear infections with fever, etc. or his eyes are giving him trouble or something. It is also for sore throats. I'm very sorry, but we do not have the auditory equipment or the facilities here to check for a hearing loss for anyone under the age of 5."

"Well, now, how do I manage to get an appointment with a doctor in the ENT clinic then?"

The young white doctor didn't show the least bit of interest in what I was saying. He didn't even look at me. He just kept writing something in David's medical records.

Huffily I exited his office. I practically knocked him over as I ran out.

I was persistent. I tried everything to get him an appointment in ENT. I kept making appointments for David hoping someone would detect his hearing loss. I feigned an ear infection. I hoped and prayed at least one doctor would have a genuine interest in David's ongoing health problems. No such luck. I suggested and begged for them to give recommendations for my baby to have hearing tests. They gave no examination; just the same old explanation that boys sometimes are slow talkers. The same thing every time: Medications were prescribed for him that would rid him of the infections he supposedly had. There was nothing ever mentioned about the suspected hearing loss. Each and every time I took Li'l David there, they would give me some weak excuse. I never could get help. I grew discouraged. I just kept praying and asking God to help us.

One day soon after we arrived in Washington I woke up with David shaking me.

"Get up, Janie, we have got to get out of this car!"

"What happened?"

"It's smoking. It might blow up!"

My head was pounding. "What happened? Where am I?"

"We crashed," he said. "I've got to get you out of here." I screamed in pain as he tried to move me.

"Wait, David, I can't breathe." I wondered if he could understand me. I saw wires hanging over my head. I knew somehow I was under the dashboard of the car. I panted, trying to catch my breath but I felt like someone had punched the wind out of me. My head felt as big as a boulder and began to sing. I heard sirens, then drifted into a fog.

I started to hear strange voices.

"Let's get them out of here."

"Quick, the car is smoking."

I saw blue uniforms and heard David trying to describe what happened.

"As I went downhill, these guys in another car started blowing at us, then as we sped up the hill to escape them, they forced my car into a parked car lane. I tried to get over. Oh, my God, it was too late."

David held his chest, gasping for air.

"Are you okay," a paramedic said.

"Yes, but I'm having chest pains." He forced his words out. "I tried to move over, to get out of that lane, but they blocked me in. After I hit two parked cars, they blew and kept going."

The words kept getting louder then fainter as I tried to maintain consciousness. They loaded me on a stretcher and placed me in an ambulance. I heard someone calling my name. I looked over and there was David with an oxygen mask.

"Where's Chuck and Pat?" I tried to ask. They were the couple we'd been driving with. We were attending their wedding but they didn't have a car so we were driving them to their reception.

"Lie still, Janie," David said, holding my hand. "Another ambulance picked Pat and Chuck up off the front lawn of somebody's house. They were thrown out of the car."

My eyes stretched wide. I covered my mouth with my free hand. The other hand had an IV inserted into it.

"Is, is Pat, I mean, are they okay?". The sounds I made were unintelligible but David seemed to always know what I was thinking.

"I don't know yet, Janie," he said. "Just lie still. Try not to talk."

David wiped his forehead. The frown lines on his face told me this was serious. I tried to talk again. He held my hand and shushed me.

"I can't breathe," I forced out. Someone placed an oxygen mask over my face. I didn't remember anything after that. When I came to, I was in a hospital room near an open window.

"Hi, Janie," someone said. I tried to turn to see who it was but cried out in pain.

"It's me, Pat," the voice said. She was in the adjacent bed in the hospital.

Tears of joy filled my eyes.

"Thank God you're alive," I mumbled. I couldn't speak more clearly. "Where is David? Where's Chuck?

"They're both here, too. They're at the admittance desk."
"Where are we? What happened?"

"We're in a veterans hospital," she said. "That's all I know. You were out. Chuck and I were found laying on the lawn still holding hands." Pat had trouble talking, too. Her voice sounded muffled just like mine. It was unbelievably strange how we understood what the other was trying to say. She tried to speak again but grimaced in pain.

I forced a smile, then waved my hand in the air to tell her to forget it. Neither of us could really talk. I could see she was in a bad way, too. Her right cheekbone was huge with black and blue marks, and she had a black eye. I didn't have any idea what my problem was yet but from the look on her face, I was worse. I just thanked God we were still alive.

As I closed my eyes my mind took me back to Easter vacation. Mother, Daddy and Earlie drove up to visit us and brought Earlie's kids, Trena and Jimmy, who were a little older than Li'l David. I was so happy they came because they understood him. He now had his cousins to play with. Mother spoiled me, cooking all the meals while she was visiting. She took us shopping for nice, new clothes and Li'l David and the other grandchildren got new toys, too.

The time went too fast. I cried when they left. To cheer me up Earlie said, "We'll be back in the summer. Trena and Jimmy can come and spend the summer with you guys. In June or July, I'm going back to Chicago with Mother and Daddy so I need you to watch the kids for me, anyway."

After they drove off, the only thing that made me feel better was when David reminded me that our friends Chuck and Pat were getting married. We were going to their wedding the next weekend.

Pat and Chuck had a small ceremony. It was nice but I had a strange feeling. I just wanted to rush home afterward. I had this urgent feeling. I told myself, *"Maybe it's Li'l David. I've never left him with anyone but family before."* I asked David to take me home. He insisted we go to the reception, which was in Seattle. I didn't feel comfortable going that far.

I wasn't usually this anxious to go home but a voice said, *"No. Go home."*

"Li'l David is probably worried, wondering where we are," I said, trying to make up an excuse. I knew David wouldn't believe me if I told him about the voice. He didn't believe me when I told him about Mother Piggis.

David ignored me as he led me to the car. I figured once we got in our car, I could persuade him to take me home. But the bride and groom got in the car with us. They didn't own a vehicle so David offered them a ride. It was dark when we left the wedding and I was tired. Finally, I tried to tell David that I felt funny.

"There you go with the voice of doom," he said.

I tried again.

"Li'l David will be looking for me."

"David will be fine. Stop worrying," David said, frowning at me.

Now, laying in the hospital, I started to worry again about Li'l David.

"How will he know where I am?" I thought as I started to cry. I needed to see my son, to assure him I was still here. I thought about it. I was really the only one reacting about Li'l David. I knew he was fine. Funny thing, he never cried when I left him. From the time he was born until he was 2 ½, I think God preconditioned him to be absent from my life. It started with his first six weeks of life in an incubator, then back and forth in his long hospital stays for eye surgeries. He stopped crying for me and accepted it as routine.

David came in and told me our car was totaled. He cried as he looked at my swollen face and black eyes. I had always took pride in my nice, white, strong teeth. I was told by so many that my smile melted the hardest hearts. Now I couldn't even open my mouth to speak.

The doctors and dentists who visited me refused to give me anything for the pain, saying I'd suffered a severe head injury and they couldn't prescribe any heavy medication. They also told me the accident fractured my left ribs and broke my jaw in three places.

"Do you know where you are?" one said.

"Yes, I'm in a hospital," I mumbled.

They stuck a thermometer into my mouth and I tasted blood. I spit out white particles. I knew they were fragments from my teeth.

I wiggled my tongue around in my mouth. I knew by the feel of my tongue my front teeth were smashed together.

"Doctor, can I get my teeth repaired," I asked.

"We need to worry about repairing your jawbone first, Mrs. Bess."

"Can you fix it?"

"We have to wait until you're better."

"Can I go home until you can fix it?"

"No, ma'am, you had a concussion and were out for several hours so you have to stay here. We have to perform surgery when you're feeling better."

The doctors then went to talk with Pat, who also had a concussion. She'd broken her right cheekbone when she hit the ground. As they murmured together, David spoke to me.

"It's all my fault," he said. "I should have taken you home like you asked me to."

"No, David, you couldn't know this would happen, you can't blame yourself." I tried to reach over to hold him but sharp pains in my rib cage took my breath away.

"I talked to Mother-in-law and she is on her way," he said. "Before I could explain what happened, she asked, 'Did you hit my daughter?' 'No, Mrs. Prather,' I said. I told her what happened and that you were admitted to a hospital. I told her you were hurt bad but the doctors were taking good care of you."

"When is she coming to see me?"

"She didn't say, Janie, she was so upset. I just know she thinks I did something bad to you."

I shook my head. "No, David, she doesn't think that."

"Oh, yes, I remember. She threatened me at our wedding. I told her, 'Don't worry, Mrs. Prather, I didn't hit your daughter.'"

"Where is Li'l David?" I asked.

"He's still with Verdell," he said, referring to the friend who agreed to watch David while we attended the wedding.

"Why didn't you bring Li'l David to see me?"

"This hospital won't allow children in here under 12."

"David, you better get Li'l David. He's probably too much for Verdell."

"Oh, she insisted he stay with her. Besides, I have to bum rides here because we don't have a car anymore."

I started to cry again, thinking how long it might be until I saw my son again.

Pat and I were the only women in the old veterans hospital in Seattle where they ambulance took us. The doctors and nurses put a shield around us to keep the veterans away from us. I never quite got it. Some of them were old enough to be my father or grandfather.

After the third day, Pat and I got into our wheelchairs and took a private tour of the hospital while waiting on the nurse to bring our dreaded liquid diet. We were very bored. We had no television or radio in our room. When we discovered there was a TV room in the hospital lounge on our floor, we went there often to watch it. The nurses came looking for us to give us our liquid Jell-O and soup and scolded us for leaving our room.

"You can't leave your room because there are nothing but old men in here. You are in your hospital robes, but you are young, pretty women and you still excite these old men and there might be trouble."

I told them if they put a television in our room we wouldn't leave. "We're bored laying there," Pat added. "There is nothing for us to do." "Can I go home, please," I said.

"That's impossible," a nurse said. "You are a long ways from being healed, young lady."

I felt neglected and homesick. I envied Pat because her parents and friends came to see her every day. This was her hometown. My family and friends were all in California. I felt imprisoned. They wouldn't let David bring our son to visit. He tried to smuggle Li'l David in but he made cooing sounds as they passed the nurses station and they caught him. I tried to sneak out to see him but they kept their eyes on me after the TV incident.

Four nights later, my mother, Earlie and my cousin L.C. walked into my hospital room. Tears of relief and joy flooded my eyes.

"Oh, Janie, what happened?" Earlie said. I could tell by the look on her face I wasn't a pleasant sight. But I was thrilled to see them.

The months dragged by. I ended up spending more than three months in the hospital. They finally wired my jaws shut after two failed attempts. I fainted at the first try because they told me they couldn't put me to sleep or give me medication because of the concussion. I prayed for strength but the minute I was wheeled into surgery fear overtook me. As I stood up to sit in a dental chair, I got rubbery legs and they fell from under me. Everything went dark. I woke up back in my hospital bed.

"What happened?" Pat asked from her wheelchair.

"I don't know," I stammered. "I was standing there getting ready to sit in a dental chair when all of a sudden my legs felt weak, I felt hot and sweaty, then the lights went out."

Pat looked frightened because she was due to go next. The nurse wheeled her out to the elevator. Next thing I knew, she was back in her bed.

"Did you get your surgery?" I asked.

"No, I fainted, too."

Our jaws hurt but we managed to laugh in spite of it.

The next try, I threw up in the elevator on the way down to the dental clinic. Finally, they were able to give me aspirin and because of my heart murmur penicillin. When they performed the surgery, I was fully awake without sedation. I heard my jawbone popping and cracking as they forced it into place. I yelled out in agonizing pain but they ignored my cries as they continued to work my facial bones into place. It was a grueling, painful procedure. With a strong, forceful push, they finally snapped my jaw. I screamed.

I'd prayed the night before for strength and He gave it to me. I made it through. I will never forget the pain, though. My jaw wasn't even after the surgery; one side was lopsided. I knew I would have to grow my hair long to hide this but that would take a few years. I was able to cover the scars on my forehead with bangs but I couldn't hid the big, vacant space between my remaining teeth. I lost five of my front teeth.

Finally, I was dismissed. I went home. My jaw was still wired shut and I was on a liquid diet. My ribs were still tender but I could breathe easier. I had to report back to the hospital in six weeks.

I was too ashamed to leave home. I became an introvert. The neighbors already stared at my son. I didn't want any more pitiful looks. I played with Li'l David and later, when Verdell got a job, I baby-sat her son.

My family did come back to visit during the summer. I was surprised and happy to see them. We still had no phone so they couldn't call. It was like Christmas for me. They brought Earlie's children, Trena and Jimmy, and like I promised, I watched them for her when she went to Chicago with Mother and Daddy.

Trena and Jimmy were so much fun. I went out after they arrived. We went to the park and the zoo. I was so relieved my family came. I'm sure that is what saved me from mental depression.

David's friend let him use his car to take me back to Seattle for my return appointment. My body stiffened every time we passed an 18-wheeler or bus. I reached up to the roof of the car while stepping on imaginary brakes. David tried to understand but I know it was annoying him.

"Janie, what's wrong, why are you grabbing at the ceiling? Please stop it. You're making me nervous."

"I can't help it. Whenever you step on the brakes or pass those big trucks, I freeze. I'm sorry." David was used to my muffled voice. He responded to me with his crooked smile.

"I know it's hard but try to relax."

He laughed a bit then. "I can't believe I get to speak without you interrupting. I could get used to this."

I closed my eyes and tried to relax but I couldn't so I sang a gospel song in my head. The song seemed to help me loosen up.

I finally exhaled after we reached the dental clinic. The doctor talked with us after he removed the wires.

"We couldn't snap your jaw back all the way so when you can, maybe later, you can have corrective jaw surgery. They can cut away some of your jawbone but I don't recommend it yet. Just wait a few years, maybe modern science will find a less painful way."

I wasn't about to go through that pain again.

"Oh, no, that's OK. I'll learn to live with it." It felt strange talking without the constraints. I laughed, realizing I was free. I covered my mouth self-consciously because of the missing front teeth.

When we arrived home David told me he'd scheduled an appointment for me with a dentist downtown.

"I borrowed from Air Force Aid," he said. "I can make monthly payments.

I miss your beautiful smile. I want you to have it back."

The next week I went and received a partial plate. I could smile again. I was so happy to have my smile.

"I think I'm going to regret this except for your beautiful smile," David teased me. I punched him in the arm and gave him a grin.

I had to learn to talk again. I had to adjust to eating with a smaller bit. I had trouble eating apples and other large, round fruit because my bite was smaller than before. But I was back home with my family. God had shown me just how precious life was. I was just thankful to be alive.

***

Five months later, in March 1964, I woke up, looked out of the steamy bedroom window and saw snowflakes falling! I had never seen real snow. After David had gone to work, I took a long warm shower, then dressed warmly. I gave Li'l David a shower, too, and dressed him in layers of clothing. I put him in his snowsuit, mittens and snow boots and put a warm cap with earmuffs on his head. Holding tight to his little fat fingers, I led him out onto our slippery walkway. It was icy and we slipped a few times. Determined to have fun with my son in the fresh snow, I started trudging out until the deep snow was up to my mid-calf. Before I could think twice, Li'l David had somehow managed to climb onto my leg and had wrapped his legs around my legs. I couldn't walk! I lost my balance and we fell head-on into three feet of snow. He frantically shook the white flaky substance from his mittens. He looked so frightened when he saw the white substance clinging to his mittens. Lord, I wish I could explain to him what it was. All of the other housewives were out making snowmen with their children. They stopped and stared at me and my son. By the time I was able to pry David from around my legs, he hightailed it back into the house. He stood on the living room sofa and just peered out of the living room window at me. I beckoned for him to come out. He wouldn't come. I started building a snowman hoping he would join in. No such luck.

One of the women was having fun with her small children. They were throwing snowballs at each other. The children were laughing loud and were rolling in the snow. I felt so alone. I wish I could laugh and talk to my son. My poor little boy. Lord, how can I explain anything to him? He must be so confused. He thinks the white stuff will hurt him. I could see the fear in his eyes as he jutted back to the house. Defeated, I went back inside

None of the neighbors really talked to me. I lived in a predominately white area with the exception of maybe two families. I tried to act like it didn't matter, but it did. They all turned up their noses and stared at my son like he had horns or something. I sensed they thought I had a retarded child. They didn't know he could put his shoes on correctly. The right shoe went on the right foot, the left shoe on the left foot. He was able to distinguish this all at the age of 2. They didn't know he ate his foods with a fork and was completely toilet-trained before he was 2. I saw their big boys still in diapers and still holding a bottle. David drank from a cup. Even with his sight problem, David walked at the age of 1. David just couldn't talk because he couldn't hear me.

"Why, Lord? Nobody believes me. They suggest that maybe our baby is a slow developer. David and I both know this isn't true. Our child is very intelligent. First thing in the morning, when Li'l David wakes up and gets out of his bed, he makes his bed. Then he puts on his own clothing and goes into the refrigerator and gets his own fresh fruit. If there are cookies in the cookie jar, he will get a stool or a chair to reach it. After eating his fruit, he will take off running to the home of a neighbor who gives him treats and candy. He looks back to see if I am following him. His little short legs can go. I can't keep up with him. Brownie follows him wherever he goes. The dog waits outside patiently for him. That's how I am able to find him later. Thank you, Lord, for giving us Brownie.

The day after the snow fell, Li'l David woke up with a cold. He was sneezing and sniffing. I gave him children's aspirin to help combat the cold. His head was stuffed as well. I kept him indoors. He was frightened of the white flakes anyway. It was still snowing so at least I didn't have to worry about him running outside, at least not until after the snow melted.

Big David came home early. He was on snow removal at the base. They had let him come home due to the increment weather. We couldn't sleep that night. Little David had a fever and coughed all night. He cried continuously and whined and whined. We were up all night administering medicine to him. The following morning, David stayed home from work to drive us to the clinic.

The doctors at the clinic insisted Li'l David only had a cold and a possible ear infection. I tried to explain he wouldn't eat.

"He has diarrhea and has just been lying down in the bed," I said. "That's not like him at all."

"Just continue to give him lots of liquids, a can of flat 7-Up drink and one children's aspirin every four hours," the doctor said. He ignored me with cold indifference. He continued to write on a page in Li'l David's medical records, never looking up at me at all.

The next day, David had to go in the "field" with his unit.

"We are required to practice these military exercises. We will be prepared in case of a war," he said.

I hated to see him go. I wouldn't be able to contact him for at least three to four days. I was scared to stay home alone. Especially now. Li'l David was not looking or feeling any better that morning. David offered to take me to the clinic at 7:30 a.m.

"Oh, no," I said. "It's too cold and slippery out there. I would have to take the first bus back, which would only take me as far as town."

David was so worried.

"What are you going to do if he is still not feeling better? I don't want you trying to carry him in all that snow."

"He is really scared of the white stuff," I said. "I don't even understand why."

"If you find out later that you will need me, call my NCOIC and tell them you need me to take you to the hospital. Now don't forget. Call me, you hear!"

"If you dropped me at the clinic, I would have to catch at least five buses to get back home," I insisted. "He will probably feel better in the late afternoon."

David stared at me annoyed.

"Okay, David, I'll be sure to call." He kissed me on his way out.

I looked out the window and waved as he drove away. The snow was coming down fast. The snow was so thick and high out. It could probably reach my knees, I thought.

Later that morning, I gave Li'l David some aspirin and checked his temperature. It was over 102 degrees. He was hot to the touch. I had to get him to the hospital! I struggled with his limp body. I had to literally force him into his quilted snowsuit. I then dressed into my warmest clothing. I slipped on my snow boots. Then put on my black woolen overcoat and wool stocking cap. I should have listened to David this morning. He offered to take me, but I had to open my big mouth and tell him he would probably get better. Now I have to try to get through to him on the phone so he can come and take us to the hospital.

I finally made it to the bottom of our icy driveway. It was as slippery as glass. It seemed like I had walked a mile. Li'l David lay motionlessly in my arms. He was so heavy. There is nothing worse than carrying dead weight. I only weighed 98 lbs myself. I was struggling trying to keep him close to my bosom while maneuvering his blanket to keep it tucked around him. Li'l David showed no reaction at all. He simply stared into space.

Not a soul was outside. It felt like we were the only people left on this earth. The snow was coming down hard and fast. I could hardly see in front of my eyes. That was my first time ever being out in the snow like that. Just as I made my way to the bottom of the icy walkway, I lost my footing. The ground was slipping from under me. I tried to catch my balance, but with each step I made on the icy walkway, my feet slid upwards. I put out my left hand to cushion my fall in case I fell. With my right hand, I clutched my baby in a football hold. I tried to walk swiftly. (I was irrationally thinking that maybe if I took quicker and shorter paces; it would enable me to erect myself upright again.) What happened in those few seconds seemed like an eternity. My free left arm flailed wildly in the air. In my right arm, I still clutched my baby close to me. My feet began to slide backward as I stepped forward rapidly. I couldn't get a solid grip with the ground.

It seemed like this took all of 20 minutes. My legs were growing tired as I did my survival dance on the icy sidewalk. I had to think fast! I couldn't fall forward, but it was inevitable that it was going to happen! Quickly, I gave in to the ice, making sure I leaned my body against the centrifugal force and fell backward. I landed with the back of my head hitting the hard concrete below with a loud thud. I shook my head to clear it, to fight off unconsciousness. My head was throbbing. I felt as though a big rock had hit me in the back of my head.

Miraculously, my baby was still cuddled up in my right arm. His body never touched the ground. I knew God was surely protecting him!

I rolled over on my left side. I looked around. I was totally embarrassed. I was hoping and praying no one had seen me fall. Well, I was out of luck! Across the street was Sarah, the nice white-haired lady out picking up her morning newspaper. She always waved at me whenever I came out for a walk or something. When we moved into our apartment, the same lady brought hot spaghetti and French bread over to us. Her husband Frank was retired military.

"Hello!" she yelled from across the street. Now both, the nice elderly woman and her husband were both peering at me. They were the only elderly couple living in the Salishan Housing Project. They mainly stayed to themselves. Mostly everybody else living there were low-ranking military families. There were only a few low-income civilian families.

"Do you need help?" Frank yelled, leaning over the first floor porch railing of their two-story apartment building.

"Uh, no, I'm alright now." I giggled nervously, trying my best to ignore the pain moving down my lower spine. I tried to compose myself.

"You be careful walking in the snow," Sarah said. "It is really slippery out there."

"Thanks" I said, giving a reassuring smile with a nod.

I walked slowly and ever so carefully to my next-door neighbor's house. Cassie was a young, black military wife I met just a couple of months ago. I felt comfortable because she was the only black wife who had befriended me. She told me if I ever needed anything to come on over. I never did though. I basically stayed to myself. There were always a lot of the military wives hanging over her house for the coffee Klatches. They were snobby and talked about their husband's rank as though it was a status symbol. I never understood that. Air Force and Army wives were all in the same income bracket. The men never brought it up. The wives also bragged about their baby's first accomplishments as though we were in competition. The subject was always the same: whose baby got their first teeth, which one took their first step, and their first words. I didn't like all the questions they asked about my son's muteness.

Today was different. I had to swallow my pride. I needed to use her phone to call David's first sergeant. I needed to talk to him. I needed David to help me. I had to get to the hospital as soon as possible. It was quiet. There was no sound at all from inside. I took a deep breath to gather up courage. I knocked hard on the door. There was no answer. I knocked a few more times. Perhaps she's asleep. I didn't want to wake her. I hated imposing on others.

Sarah across the street was watching me. She leaned over her porch railing and yelled over to me, "Hey, Cassie's not home. Her husband took her to the doctor for her appointment." Cassie was expecting their first baby. She was only in her first trimester.

I stood there not knowing what else to do. Tears were now coming down. I wiped them away with my mitten-covered hands. The wool fibers was irritating to my eyes. My eyes burned.

"Can we help you?" Sarah asked as she walked over.

"Yes, I need to use a phone. I have to call my husband's squadron. He needs to take me to the hospital. He is out in the field doing a training exercise. I need to get in touch with his first sergeant. My son is very sick. I've done everything the doctors told me, but my baby's temperature is high. He is dehydrated, too. He hasn't eaten or drank anything for two whole days. I have been back and forward to that clinic for the last two days. That's not like him. His nickname isn't Hungry for nothing!" She laughed with me on that one.

"They keep telling me to just give him liquid aspirin. I need to get there as soon as possible."

"Is that all you wanted," Frank said. "You're welcome to use our phone anytime. Go right ahead. Help yourself."

I felt a warm rush over my body as I fought back tears. "Thank you," I managed to say. Sarah handed me a steaming hot cup of English tea. It felt good going down.

"I was practically frozen!" I said, laughing in spite of myself. "And this tea is thawing me out." We all laughed at that.

The phone rang and rang. Finally, his first sergeant answered.

"May I speak to Airman David Bess?"

"He is in the field, ma'am. I'm sorry. I can't reach him."

"Sir, my baby is very sick. I need my husband to take me to the hospital. Please. 0He said you could get him if it's an emergency. Can you please send someone to get him for me?"

"Ma'am, he is in the field. With all this snow comin' down, it may take hours to reach him. Can't you drive your baby to the hospital? You will have to make other arrangements, ma'am."

"But, sir. I'm at a neighbor's house. And they don't have a car. I don't know what to do! My husband told me he would be able to take me. Now you're telling me you can't get in touch with him. You've gotten in touch with him before. My baby is sick. I've got to get to the hospital."

Tears streamed down my face.

Sarge spoke in a commanding tone.

"Ma'am, ma'am, you've got to calm down. Go ahead and catch the bus to Madigan Hospital. It leaves on the hour."

"But I'm scared, sir. I slipped in the snow already. My baby isn't able to walk and he is too heavy."

"You are a big girl, now. You will have to manage." I pleaded with him but it did no good.

"I've got to clear the phone in case of emergencies. I'm very sorry, ma'am."

I heard the click on the other end of the line. Still clutching the phone to my ear, I bawled right in the living room. The dial tone hummed in my ear. I hung up. I said wearily, "I better hurry and catch the bus."

"One should be here within the next five minutes," Sarah said. "Frank will walk you out and carry the baby for you. He'll wait with you until it comes. Too bad Old Bessie stopped on us last month. Otherwise we'd take you to the hospital."

I thanked her and wrapped my baby tightly before going out the door. The storm door slammed hard behind me. The snow was so thick until I could see nothing but white out. Frank ran out behind me.

"Wait! I'm going to help you. Here give me the boy," he said, taking Li'l David from my arms.

"Thanks," I said. Just then the bus rambled over the steep hill right in front of their apartment just as Sarah predicted. Frank handed David to me. I climbed onboard waving at them as the bus pulled away.

CHAPTER TWENTY-ONE

I arrived at the clinic two hours later. The receptionist sent me way on the other side of the hospital to pick up his records. After picking them up, I treaded back to the opposite side of the hospital grounds. I must have walked at least four miles one-way. Despite the cold temperature, sweat dripped from my body. By the time I arrived back to the clinic, with Li'l David, I had made up my mind those doctors would not send me home again. I was not leaving until they admitted him. I meant that.

I sat in the waiting room for about two hours. I became impatient waiting on the doctors scurrying past me as if I wasn't there. The receptionist ignored me too. She assisted another white lady before she waited on me. I overheard the lady complementing the receptionist for helping her so soon.

They weighed my son and took his temperature and blood pressure after I returned with his records. Even after the nurse said his temperature was 102 she still took her time. I told her, he couldn't keep his food down and he refused to drink any liquids.

Finally, they called his name. After they gave him a quick two-minute exam, they reassured me he would be just fine. The pediatrician on staff looked bored as he talked to me.

"His fever is at a little over 100 degrees. That is not really high for a toddler. We are overcrowded with children with colds and fever. Just keep giving him aspirin and fruit juices. Lots of liquids."

I saw red. I was furious. Before I knew it, I had cussed that young intern out.

"You are a sorry excuse for a doctor if you can't see that my baby is sick. You prejudiced white bastard! My baby is almost dead. He hasn't eaten in at least three days. He won't take even water. He spits out his medicine. He lies in his bed not moving. His temperature was 102 degrees, his color is an ashen gray, and you are trying to tell me that my baby only needs aspirin?"

Without waiting for an answer, I said. "Well, I am not taking him home. No, sir, if he dies, it will be here. You and your staff will be held responsible for negligence."

One of the other interns standing near spoke harshly to me. "Mrs. Bess, you must calm down!"

One of the nurses talked to me. too. "You cannot yell at a superior officer." "I don't give a damn what he is!" I said.

"Ma'am, that doctor is a colonel. You are disrespectful to an officer. If you keep this up, you'll have to leave." This nurse sat down beside me and talked softly. She rationalized with me.

I ignored her, screaming out every word.

"I don't care what he is. I don't wear any stripes. I ain't in the military. They can't do nothing to me. Anyway, if they take me away, then they will have to care for my baby!"

"Ma'am, we will have to call your husband if you don't calm down." Bingo! She said the magic words. I really started acting the fool.

"You can't reach my husband. That's what his NCOIC said when I called him." My neck moved back and forth with every word. "His sergeant is prejudiced, too." They glared at me. I stared back.

"He told me I was a big girl now, that my husband can't be contacted and that he was in the field."

Within a matter of a half hour or less, they had driven my husband David from the field directly to the clinic. They brought him right to me.

"Janie, what is the matter with you!?" He grabbed me firmly by my shoulders and looked dead into my eyes. He was furious with me. "Do you know that you were cussing out the colonel?" I shook my head back and forth, not able to speak. I was sobbing loudly.

"You don't disrespect an officer!"

I went into a rage.

"I don't care! I am not afraid of the military. He can't do nothing to me." I put my hands on my hips and stuck out my chin in defiance as I spoke out. "Do you know I am sick and tired of them giving me the run-around? They were trying to send Li'l David home again! I was not going anywhere until they really examined him. He is very sick. His temperature was over 102! He could die! I refuse to leave until they admit him. I am not taking him back home to die."

My next words were dripping with sarcasm. "Oh, I see the first sergeant located you after all."

"What do you mean by that?" David asked. I told him what the first sergeant had told me when I had called to ask for him.

David then told me the story about an altercation he had with his sergeant that morning.

"Sarge is all right but he is prejudiced," he said. "He is a redneck from Alabama."

"What happened, David?"

"Well, today Sarge made a terrible mistake. He said, 'Come here Boy.' I didn't understand why Sarge called me boy. I said, 'Boy? I looked around over my shoulder, pretending to search for the boy. I cracked up. Again, I said, 'Boy? I don't see any boy.'

"'You standin' there, ain't cha?'

"I laughed in his face, 'Do you see a boy, Sarge?'

"Sarge was angry now. He said, 'That's what I said, boy. You are a boy, ain't cha? Ain't cha?' Sarge gave me a dare-you-to-say-anything look.

"I looked dead into Sarge's eyes. I said, 'Hey, Sarge, no disrespect to you, sir, but why do I have to be a boy, sir?'

"He was pissed off now. I could tell by the snarl on his face what he was thinking, that I was just a young, cocky little nigger. He asked me, 'Where ya' from, boy?' I started looking around again as though I was still looking for that boy.

"Sarge looked puzzled. He asked, 'Airman Bess, what are you looking 'round for?'

"I looked at Sarge. I know I got his goat. I laughed again. 'I'm looking for that boy that you calling, sir.'

"'That was a witty reply, Airman Bess,' Sarge said. He turned a deep shade of crimson now. 'Ain't you a Boy?'

"I answered back again, 'Like I said before, sir, I am not a boy.' "He yelled at me, 'Well, are you an old man, then?'

"'Oh, I see,' I said, still laughing at him. I looked upside Sarge's head. 'So that's the way it's supposed to be.'" David demonstrated to me how he shifted his feet, touched his chin as if he was thinking. He nodded his head as he stood there staring defiantly at Sarge. "'Now I get it! I either have to be a boy or an old man.'"

"Sarge was fuming now but he tried to be cool "'Hey, Sarge, why couldn't I just be a man.'

"I had really pissed Sarge off now. Sarge was boiling, steaming mad! His face was redder than ever. He was breathing hard. First, I had challenged his authority. Now, I made jest out of his conversation. I knew I was in trouble now.

"Sarge cleared his throat. 'Airman Bess, I will talk to you later. Do you understand?'

"I answered, 'Yes, sir.'

"Sarge yelled like a drill sergeant, 'About face, Airman Bess. You are dismissed.'

"'Thank you, sir.' I stood erect in a military stance before I pivoted. I walked away with my shoulders pulled back proudly. Sarge walked away, too. I went back out into the field. I didn't know he had given you a hard time."

"Now, I understand why the Sarge was giving me such a hard time," I said.

We sat quietly waiting for the colonel and the interns to call us into the room. I held little David in my arms. The doctors soon called David to bring our son into the exam room.

They wouldn't let me in. The colonel insisted I sit outside in the waiting room. I could hear my baby crying out. It was a cry of pain. It was a loud cry filled with terror. I tried to go in the examination room but they stopped me. I was going to try to force my way into that room. My baby needed me. He didn't understand what was happening to him. I had almost pushed my way through when I saw David's look of disapproval, as he peered around the door at me.

"Go sit down, Janie! I have him. He is okay." When he gave me that look and spoke in a stern voice, I knew he meant business. So I went back to my seat in the waiting room. All of the other patients in the clinic had gone home. It was after 5 p.m. and the clinic always closed on time.

I knew something was terribly wrong with my baby.

I saw the nurses rushing back and forth from the examining room where my son lay motionless.

It seemed like forever before David returned to tell me anything. I watched the clock on the wall as the second hand slowly crept before moving on to the next minute. It was so quiet in that waiting room I could actually hear every tick of the second hand as it moved.

When my husband did return, he had tears in his eyes as he spoke. He sat down, leaned his head back on the back of the chair. He took a deep breath before he said anything. He didn't look at me. His eyes were closed as he spoke.

"Janie, you were right. Li'l David is very sick. The techs tried to draw blood for lab work. His veins had collapsed. They couldn't even draw blood from his fingers, foot or arms—they tried everywhere. No luck. Finally, they had me help hold him down while they drew blood from his neck. That was very difficult for me to do.

"Now I know how you must feel when you had to hold him still for them to look into his eyes before surgery! Damn! That really shook me up.

"Li'l David is a strong little something! It took six nurses and two doctors and me to control him," he said with fatherly pride. "I have a weak stomach, you know. It hurt me to see them do this. I couldn't watch.

"They now say they are probably going to have to keep him here to run tests. God, his skin looked so gray and ashen. He could have died."

"Now you see why I was acting the way I did," I said.

"That still does not justify your actions. You could have had me put out of the service, I could have lost my stripes, or been banned from the hospital. Anyway, the doctor would like to see you so they can get an idea about

David's health problems."

"Okay," I said. I took a deep breath. I had cried out so much I didn't have any more tears left. I slowly rose to enter the examination room where the doctor was waiting to talk to me.

"Have a seat, Mrs. Bess," the colonel said. "We are running tests on David Jr. now. There isn't anything conclusive at this time that I can tell you. We do suspect he has a viral infection, but without running tests on him, we cannot tell you much. He will be admitted to the pediatrics ward. Did your husband tell you?"

"Yes, he did," I answered solemnly. My head was down. I was so ashamed of the way I had acted. *Please, Lord, forgive me*, I prayed silently.

After all of the red tape, David and I left for home. His first sergeant relieved him of field duty for the rest of the week.

David was quiet on the ride home. I was so ashamed of myself. I was relieved he didn't say anything to me.

David finally asked, "Are you alright now?'

"Yes, but I miss my baby though. I will have to wait until tomorrow to find out what's wrong with our son. You should have seen the way the doctors treated me before you arrived, David. I couldn't take anymore."

The night went by way too slow for me. I worried about how they were treating my baby. I tossed and turned all night. I wanted to know how he was. I couldn't call the hospital. I didn't have a phone. It was too late to go over to anyone's house to use the phone. So I waited the night out. First thing in the morning, I insisted David take me to the hospital.

Li'l David looked so much better. His coloring had returned and he was sitting up in his crib playing with a bright plastic toy. He recognized me and reached out for me. They had him tied to the bed with these white strips of cloths. I went running to the nurse. She explained Li'l David had gotten out of the crib and was running down the halls and had gone out of the hospital doors.

"I think that he was trying to go home," she said.

It wasn't long before the colonel arrived to give us his prognosis— Li'l David had an intestinal infection.

"We will have to keep him here for at least five more days," he said.

"I knew that something was wrong with my baby. He is always so active.

He wasn't able to move at all yesterday. He looks better this morning" I said.

The colonel then asked with a concerned look on his face, "Has your son ever been tested for his hearing? He seems to have excellent motor skills. He is quite aware of his surroundings and is quite an intelligent little boy. Tell me, Mrs. Bess, have you ever had hearing tests done? I am going to look into having a hearing evaluation done on him as soon as possible."

"Oh, thank you doctor. I have been praying for this for a long time," I said.

"Good. By the time he is dismissed, I will have my medical assistant obtain all the necessary information and a scheduled date for a hearing test. It will have to be done at the Seattle Speech and Hearing Center in Seattle. It's about 30 miles from here."

"Thank you, Lord," I said with no shame.

CHAPTER TWENTY-TWO

It took two months but we were finally on our way to the Seattle Speech and Hearing Center. Li'l David had to attend there for five days straight at $25 per day for testing fees. That was a lot of money in 1964. David's Air Force salary was only about $250 for the whole month. Our rent was about $60 a month, groceries were $50. Our utilities, such as butane oil for cooking, cost about $60 per month. Car repairs, hospitalization and transportation to and from work, as well as other expenses, took care of the monthly paycheck. So I wrote a letter to the Salishan Housing Authority, requesting an extension in my rent until the next pay period. I explained that we had a large hospital bill to pay due to my son's unexpected illness. I also explained it was imperative he gets hearing tests done. I didn't think that it would work. Thank God! The housing authority approved my request. I ran to the mailbox to send off the $125 money order.

I had no idea how we were going to pay our rent the next month. Right before I mailed it, there in front of the bright U.S. Postal mailbox, I stopped in my tracks and I prayed, "Lord, I trust in You. I have faith that I am doing the right thing. Please, Lord, give me X-ray vision. Let me see through this dilemma. Please give me evidence I'm doing the right thing. Send me a sign, Lord. Please, in the name of Jesus. Amen." I sighed deeply, then dropped it into the mailbox. With renewed energy, I ran all the way home. My baby was going to have a hearing test done. Finally!

When I got home a delivery man was there to tell us we'd received a telegram. David and I drove to town to pick up the telegram. It turned out to be a $200 money order from my mother. It read: "I hope you can use this. Love, Mother."

God had answered my prayer and sent me a signal. I knew everything was going to work out. God had touched my mother and she sent money and it was right on time. I could pay the rent on time, too. I even had enough for traveling expenses. I could hardly wait to go to the speech center.

The day had arrived. I didn't know how we were going to get there. I couldn't afford to spend money for a hotel as suggested by the Speech Center. I asked my friend Cassie if she would drive me there. I offered to pay her for gas. Guess what? She said she and her husband were going to Seattle that week on business. She had to see a specialist. She explained she wasn't going to have her baby at Madigan Hospital. She had to travel back and forth every day for three days for special tests. She and her husband had different blood types so there was a possibility of complications. It happened to be on the same days as Li'l David's appointments. God had answered our prayer. Another couple, Jerry and Anita, had just moved to town. It was late at night when they arrived, and they had nowhere to sleep. They stayed with us for a couple of days until their house was ready. They said they would take me the two remaining days as a favor.

The ride over was quiet. Neither Cassie nor her husband said a word. My mind raced. I heard my heart as it beat so fast until I could even feel the loud thumping. Li'l David sat quietly in the back seat. He was sensitive to my moods. He anticipated something, but had no idea what it would be. I wished I could communicate with him. I dressed him in his best outfit. After the long ride in the car, he jumped out. He was so excited. He peered at me through his big glasses, anticipating my next move. He pushed them back onto his nose before taking my hand. He trusted me so much. I was his only source of communication. He depended on me to demonstrate everything to him.

We entered into the tall stucco building. It was an impressive two story that towered over the parking lot. The receptionist greeted us as we opened the door. We sat down and waited patiently in the nicely upholstered gray chairs. It seemed like forever before they

VISIONS

called Li'l David's name. We went into a room for an assessment orientation. The nice young lady asked me questions about David's health. I filled out tons of paperwork with questions about his medical history, habits, sleep patterns, his favorite activities, etc. She wanted to know who referred me and asked a whole lot of questions I felt were impertinent.

Finally, they told me they were going to run tests. The lady took him by the hand to take him with her. He looked back for me and as I reached for his other hand to go with him.

"I'm sorry, Mrs. Bess, but David has to go in the testing room alone. You will sit and you will be able to see him but he won't be able to see you. It's a two-way glass window. David will see a mirror on his side of the glass and you will be able to see how he is doing with the tests on the other side."

Through the glass, I saw them enter and sit down at a table. The tester handed David a wooden toy replica of the traditional red and blue mailbox. All around the sides and on the top were different shaped holes. In a little box were wooden blocks. They had shapes that coordinated with the ones on the mailbox. Triangles, squares, rectangles, and round blocks had to be put into the shapes. They placed these auditory earmuffs upon on his tiny head. David was given one of the shaped blocks to hold close to his head. Whenever he would hear a beeping sound, he was told to drop the correct blocks into the opening. An assistant demonstrated this. His first hearing test went awry. It was terribly frustrating for Li'l David. He didn't understand what they wanted him to do. We had our own way of communicating with him at home, but they would not let me into the room to demonstrate. They kept talking to him as though he could hear them. They wouldn't let me come into the testing room. The door was locked!

I knocked on the reverse mirror to try to get the audiologist's attention. She was giving the tests to David. She looked up annoyed, but ignored my taps of desperation. I was starting to cry. I told the assistant on the same side of the mirror my son was very intelligent but he couldn't hear the audiologist and didn't understand what she was asking him to do. The one evaluating David merely said, "You have no proof that he can't hear. That's what we are testing him for."

By the end of the long morning, with David failing test after test, I felt like this trip was useless. After we returned from lunch, they informed me they wouldn't be able to continue the tests. They felt David might have a severe learning disorder and there was no way to test his hearing, due to his inability to comprehend. They recommended I take Little David to the Seattle Neurological Clinic nearby for testing.

I insisted that my son had superior intelligence. He did far more than the average 3-year-old. I told how he always put his shoes on the right foot. I even bragged about how he dressed himself completely after running his own bath water. I told how he matched his shirt and pants, even his socks. I could tell that they didn't believe me. It really looked bad for Little David.

I asked them to tell me where and how I could purchase that wooden play mailbox and the different blocks that fit inside the holes. I could show him how it worked.

"Give me a week or two, he'll understand how the shapes fit into the corresponding holes." I promised if they let him come back for another test, he would understand how to use the mailbox.

"I'm sorry. We cannot give you that information. It is only made and sold to special education classes and for teaching coordination skills."

I prayed, *"Please Lord, help me find those blocks or something similar to those for my son."*

The very next day, the postman came by to deliver our mail. I had to sign for a certified package. It was a free catalog and a complimentary charge card from Sears Roebuck. I couldn't wait to see the wish book! I immediately opened up the catalog and started skimming through the many pages as I walked back inside my apartment. There were all kinds of goodies I would like to buy. This is going to be my wish book, I thought. I can't afford anything in there. We just can pay the rent and buy heating oil for the winter and for cooking on the old oil stove.

Li'l David was looking at the pictures with me as he sat on my lap. I would point at the pictures and he would imitate me. I was sure he understood. He would hit the page really hard with his little fingers. He would point at pictures of little boys and then point to himself.

Oops! The catalog fell from my lap and crashed to the floor. I bent down to pick it up. I noticed that the book had fallen open to a page full of educational toys. There, on that open page, was the Playskool mailbox, sold EXCLUSIVELY by Sears catalogue services. The same one that the hearing center used to test him on. The cost was $49.99.

I couldn't wait until David came home. I was too excited. I ordered the Playskool mailbox on our new Sears charge card. I will have to tell David later, I thought.

My rationalization was that my son needed this toy as soon as possible.

David agreed with me when I showed the catalog to him later that evening.

Sears Catalog became my best friend. Li'l David's quick comprehension of the shape matching game was such a great accomplishment. Within only one day after receiving the mailbox, he was able to conceptualize the idea of matching the correct shapes into the right hole.

For example, at first, David would try to force a rectangular shaped block into a round shaped hole or a round shape into a triangular one. He was becoming frustrated. He wasn't the only one. As tears were starting up in my eyes, I fought them back. I heard an inner voice saying, "Stop being a crybaby. Your son needs you to be strong."

Just then, I got an idea!

A simple tap on the floor was my only means of teaching him when to drop it in. I demonstrated by inserting the blocks into the correct shape. Whenever I tapped my foot on the floor, I would drop it in. I then gave the blocks and mailbox to him and let him try it. He understood and imitated me. Whenever he did it correctly, I would scream with glee and would swing him up in the air. He saw the happy smile on my face and he laughed out loud. He was having a lot of fun while learning now.

It was a game we played every day. I enjoyed teaching him. It wasn't long before he became bored with the mailbox game. Later I ordered large wooden puzzles for preschool children from the catalog. He figured that one out after I had him feel the different shapes of the wooden puzzle pieces. I would then have him feel the ridges in the back of the puzzles frames. Every day, I would teach him a new game. He was learning so fast! I couldn't keep up with him.

We received a notice in the mail, for Li'l David to return to the Speech and Hearing Center in Seattle for a second time. He would be evaluated the same way as last time. Only this time, it would be a one-day evaluation. This time around, Li'l David made me proud. He was doing really well on his evaluation. He was eagerly following the examiner's visual signs and instructions. He now understood the concepts of putting the correct shapes into the mailbox. There was, however, one thing that was wrong with this picture. I sat there quietly and observed Li'l David on the other side of a window. He went about his business putting the correct shapes into the correct holes. He would nod his head to show approval. That was exactly what we did when he was instructed at home. I had taught him how to insert the proper shapes into the mailbox holes. He was sailing right along. Due to a reverse mirror, he couldn't see me, but I could see him. I realized my clever little son had mentally memorized and timed the intermittent beeps coming from the headset placed on his small head. He had somehow figured out the exact timing. Even when the sound was so weak I couldn't hear it, he would still insert the blocks. The sounds of beeps had grown weaker and weaker;

still Li'l David was dropping the wooden shapes into the box. Even when the sounds were inaudible, he still managed to pause rhythmically before dropping the shapes into the correct hole. I was thinking to myself, maybe he felt slight vibrations from the ultrasonic beeps through his headset. Then again, the odds of David actually hearing those mute sounds were nil.

Instantly, it hit me square in the face! He couldn't possibly hear those last beeps. They were not audible at all!

David was simply timing the frequency of the beeps and dropping the blocks into the Playskool mailbox. I had to get through to the other side of the mirror to talk to the examiner. I tried to convince the evaluator to let me go over to the other side of that door to talk to her. I needed to inform the examiner on the other side what I felt was happening, that David had memorized the timing of the beeps.

"She needs to change the frequency of those beeps," I said. "My son can't hear that. You and I can't hear it."

The evaluator was sitting nearby writing and recording the timbre of sounds he was supposedly responding to.

I was having a hard time convincing her he couldn't possibly hear it.

"Believe me, ma'am, he has it timed down to a science. He now knows the frequency of those beeps and are dropping them it in at the correct time! I know my son."

She pretended to ignore me. She kept writing on a form as if I had not said a word. I was growing impatient.

"I am not going to let anyone walk over me," I said. "I paid for these tests. You have $125 of my money that I couldn't afford to even spend! You are going to listen to me."

I ran past that lady, straight through that closed door that lead me to my son's examination room. I walked swiftly over to that evaluator. I looked her straight in her eyes as I spoke to her.

"Do me a little favor," I whispered as if my son could hear me. "Change the frequency of those beeps. I know my son couldn't possibly hear those faint little beeps that you just made." I continued staring dead into her eyes now.

I could see she was going to put up a good argument.

The other evaluator burst through the door.

"Madam, you will have to leave this room," she said, out of breath. "We can't test him with you interfering." She tried to convince me by threatening to discontinue the tests.

Her shallow threats just went right over my head.

"Be truthful, if this were your son being tested, and if you had to pay someone to bring you 70 miles round trip for a series of tests, wouldn't you want a fair evaluation? If you had to spend over $150, and that's what it costs me to come here, if you had sacrificed and gave up your rent money in able for your son to get the best education possible, wouldn't you want every speck of doubt erased from your mind that your child can or cannot hear? I already know you owe me some money back. I only used up one day the last time that I came. I spent $125. Nobody gave me any change back, so I am not only going to insist my baby have an accurate assessment but that I also get a proper refund for services not yet rendered. I have only spent $50 for these two days. I must insist that you give me what I paid for and my change, or I will see what can be done legally. I'll will sue you. Don't play me cheap."

Then and only then did she agree to do as I had requested.

At first, she insisted there was a possibility he could have heard the acutely faint beeps.

I spoke quickly before she could attempt to patronize me.

"Why not play a trick on Li'l David? You'll see, I know my son. You have nothing to lose. Just try alternating the timing of the beeps then you will see he did not hear the last sounds."

The evaluator barely opened her mouth to speak again. I could see she was annoyed with my rude interruptions. I ignored her looks of irritability and kept right on talking. Quickly I said, "He has a perfect sense of timing. He has it all figured out."

Nervously, I pointed at the mailbox.

"Change the timing and see if he still drops the shapes into it."

She reluctantly did as I requested. She changed their rhythmic sounds patterns. We all watched tensely. After a slight pause, Li'l David put an object into the mailbox slot. I then requested they just keep the machine quiet and just observe him to see if he still put the blocks in. There wasn't even one sound made. He paused, then still dropped it in. That was how I was able to convince the audiologist and her accomplice that my son was truly deaf.

That very day, his hearing loss was confirmed. Victory at last! He was pronounced profoundly deaf.

We would now be able to apply to have Li'l David attend a deaf preschool I'd read about in the local newspaper. It was about a new concept that speech and sign language should be taught as early as possible in the beginning stages of development. This was contrary to age-old customs. The theory before 1963 was deaf children were unable to be taught speech and sign language until the child had reached the age of 5. This article told of how it had just been introduced on the West Coast. This practice was already being used in European countries and on the East Coast. They found that children more easily grasp and retaining information when taught at an earlier age, the earlier the better. Small children have fewer inhibitions. Parents show pride for the smallest efforts made by an infant or toddler; therefore, this age group has fewer fears of being teased or ridiculed. An older child has been reprimanded, scolded and yelled at by parents whenever they made a mistake. We expect more from an older child. They are frequently teased by their classmates or friends also. Unfortunately, some teachers ridicule students if they give the wrong answers. This inhibits their learning abilities.

The article described this program and showed pictures of children and teachers in a deaf preschool class at Birney Elementary School located right smack in the heart of Tacoma.

If I could only get Li'l David placed in this classroom environment, he would be able to learn, to laugh and play with other deaf children, children like him. These children wouldn't beat him up at the playground or throw sand in his eyes because he didn't speak to them.

I went to work immediately. I wrote to that school. I inquired about their program. I asked what the requirements were for my child to be admitted to this program. It took forever to get an answer.

In retrospect, a couple of weeks seemed like eternity. I waited anxiously. I ran out to meet the mailman every day, to see if he had a letter from that school. It got so bad that when he saw me coming, he would slowly shake his head, indicating I had no mail from the school.

The day finally arrived! The mailman was just as excited as I was. He had probably grown tired of seeing my long face.

I could feel it in the air. I was so happy this particular day. I had an anticipatory feeling when I awakened that morning. It was a perfectly beautiful day outdoors. I knew my letter had come when I could see the postman's big smile a block away. It felt like Santa Claus had come to bring presents. Only this time, Santa now donned a blue postal uniform instead of traditional red and white.

He yelled to me from down the block.

"Hey, Mrs. Bess! I have that letter you've been waiting for! It's the one from that school for your son!"

I anxiously tore open the large manila envelope. A lot of literature with colorful photographs fell out of the envelope. They had sent a campus brochure and an admission application. They stated in the letter this new class was a pilot program. This was only the second semester and they were accepting applications for preschool age children.

They had me bring him there for testing. Would you believe, the tools used for his evaluation were the same wooden mailbox and wooden puzzles we had purchased for him earlier?

Li'l David sailed through the tests with flying colors this time. I was so excited for him. He looked so happy when he saw me smiling after the tests were over. I grabbed him up and hugged him. The staff informed me they were anxious to get started with him. The superintendent looked over his test results and seemed so surprised at all of the findings.

"Has David Jr. ever been to a preschool or had any kind of formal training?"

"No, why do you ask, sir?"

"Well, it is truly amazing at 3 ½, his motor skills are similar to those of a hearing child, not those of a profoundly deaf child with impaired vision." He kept leafing through the reports as he spoke. He looked up at me with this serious studious look

"I read David's medical report before this testing date. I find it unusual for a small infant to have had cataracts at birth."

"Yes, I know. I don't know why. And none of the doctors could explain to me the reason for David's birth defect."

The superintendent closed up the David's thick medical file. He shook his head in disgust at the five-inch thick file. He then looked directly into my eyes. He looked so serious. It didn't look good for David Jr.

"This is an unusually thick file for such a little fellow." He shifted his position in his burgundy office chair, then said, "Do you have any questions, Mrs. Bess?"

"Yes, when will I know if he will be able to attend the deaf school?"

Leaning forward over his desk, he took a deep breath as if he was trying to think up a way to tell me disappointing news. He tapped his pencil lightly on his desk. I could feel the tension; the air was so thick in that room. I started feeling hot. The heat seemed to rise from the bottom of my feet and ascend straight to the top of my head. I unconsciously responded to this by fanning my face, quickly alternating between both my hands. I started with my right hand, and then my left. I pursed my lips and blew out air. As if subconsciously wishing this action would cool my body off.

"Well, Mrs. Bess, your son David will not be able to start this semester; however, he will be admitted in early August of this year." The supervisor then leaned over his desk as he handed me a slew of papers to fill out. "I recommend that you return these papers as soon as possible. They are needed in order for your son's admission to Birney School for this coming semester."

Right then and there, I sat cheerfully filling out the papers.

Finding a school for Li'l David came as if had been special ordered by God himself.

CHAPTER TWENTY-THREE

I discovered I was expecting a baby. The doctor said I was about 16 weeks along. David and I hadn't even noticed I missed my period because so much had happened within such a short time.

We had lost one baby. I had a tubular pregnancy earlier that year. We were stressed over the loss. We had wanted another child so badly. David had taken me to the hospital doubled up in pain. I thought it was a chronic bladder infection. Instead, I was rushed into surgery. Just before I was wheeled into the operating room, the doctors warned me I might have had a ectopic pregnancy. If so, I wouldn't be able to have any more children. It depended upon what happened. He said he wouldn't be able to tell until after I was anesthetized. He was going to have to open me up and see what was going on inside. After the surgery was performed, they told me they had to remove one of my fallopian tubes. Thank God, I still had my ovary left. Only one of my tubes ruptured so my chances of having children were good. If both tubes had been removed, I wouldn't have been able to conceive. I cried and I cried.

"Lord, please let me at least have one more child. A little girl will be fine if that is possible." I prayed hard before going under the surgeon's knife.

After the surgery, one doctor told me I had the finest doctor on staff. He was the only one who correctly diagnosed my problem. At first, the other doctors had decided I had a kidney or bladder infection. I kept insisting it couldn't be. I had never felt any pains like that before. They were on their way to sending me to the lab for tests.

David started complaining to them.

"I want a full examination by an ob-gyn right away," he said. After he had carried me on his back from our apartment, he knew it was serious. He had found me coiled up into a tight little ball on the bathroom floor. He attempted to pick me up. A piercing scream escaped my lips. It was a death-curdling yell of agony and pain. I couldn't bear for him to even touch me. David finally convinced me to wrap my arms around his neck as he knelt down low enough for me to reach him. I don't remember how he managed to carry me out of the apartment and put me into our car. I rode curled up in the back seat of our car. An Air Force buddy drove us there. The quiet, tense ride to Madigan Hospital seemed to take forever. His friend drove very fast. I could feel every little bump and crevice in the road. I felt the tires rolling over every little pebble or rock. I cried out in pain whenever the tires rolled over uneven pavement or even a small crack in the road. I can't explain the pain but I have never had anything like it since.

After one week in the hospital, the doctors released me. Finally, I was able to go home. My doctor warned me not to try for any children for at least another year. I didn't listen. Being a young and vibrant couple, we couldn't wait. I was pregnant by my six-week return appointment. We were so happy. The doctor was furious with us. I didn't care. I was a little worried but I had more than a little faith in God. I knew God had given us another chance to have a baby.

During my first three months of pregnancy, the doctors in the Ob-Gyn clinic ran several lab tests on me. I was so sick of having blood drawn. Those needles hurt and stung so when they were injected into the bend of my elbow. I later saw my blood specimens in labeled glass tubes and the urine specimens taken back into the laboratory for analyzing. It really made me nervous. I kept asking the nurses why were they shooting me with all those needles and taking all of my blood.

A young nurse dressed in her stiffly starched uniform smiled at me.

"I understand how you feel," she said. "But we are only making sure that you and your baby will be fine. The doctor just discovered through those specimens that you and your husband have the RH factor. He will be in to talk to you soon."

I prayed silently, *"Oh, Lord, please let my baby be okay. I can't, I just can't stand any more problems. Not right now."*

Once the doctor was seated, he immediately started flipping pages. He kept skimming over information until he came upon something of interest. He read my medical records. He asked a million questions before explaining the reasons for it.

My voice quivered involuntarily when I asked, "Doctor, what is the RH factor?"

"It means your body might reject the blood of your unborn child during delivery. The reason for this is because your blood type is A negative and your husband's is O positive."

"Why wasn't I told this before? I had one son who is three years old and nobody ever mentioned it before. I recently lost my second child in my fourth month of pregnancy." I explained it was a tubular pregnancy. I told him emergency surgery was performed and how they removed my left tube. "I still have my ovaries and my right fallopian tube."

"So you should still be able to have children."

My doctor said they would have to give me an injection in my last month to ensure my baby and I would not have complications during my delivery.

A new world started for Li'l David that August when school started.

Li'l David is the happiest 3-year-old in the world now. On his first day of school we stood waiting patiently at the bus stop conveniently located directly in front of our housing complex. He looked like a little man in his brand new outfit, chocolate brown twill jeans accentuated a gold cotton turtleneck shirt. He had on his brown tartan plaid raincoat with a matching hat and scarf. He looked so cute even with his bifocal glasses on. I had to take a picture of him with our new flash camera. He gave me the most beautiful smile that I had ever seen.

"Thank you, God," I exclaimed. He's finally going to learn how to read, learn sign language.

The bus pulled up and he jumped on, without even looking back. That boy has no fear!

I waved at David as he peered through the big window at me. He waved back with a big smile on his face.

I stood just staring and waving at that bus until it was out of sight. I didn't bother to wipe the tears away because this was the first time, in a long time, I was crying tears of joy.

I went back into the unusually quiet apartment to finish cleaning. I also had to pack my bags because my delivery date was growing nearer!

I'd been in and out of the hospital several times already with false labor.

They had to give me injections to stall my labor pains.

The doctor said it was too early for the delivery.

"Your baby needs to grow more," he said. I was just seven months along.

In a few days, I thought, I will be eight months along.

I didn't understand the big deal about waiting. I was so big I waddled like a duck.

My baby was almost born in our old 1963 Renault. Soon after we'd moved to Tacoma, we'd lost the car we got for a wedding present in a bad accident. David bought the Renault for cheap. We were going to need transportation to the hospital.

It's a wonder I made it there safely.

When the time came, I insisted he call our dear friends Mike and Paula who lived next door.

"No," he said. "I'm not calling Mike and Paula. We would have to wake them up. It's 5 a.m. I'm not calling them to drive us again. They took us the last two times and you didn't even have the baby. What if this is another false alarm? I am too embarrassed. The last time, poor Mike, he almost turned us over; he was flying, going through green lights, yellow lights, and red lights, too. He was speeding past speed."

In the end, we did call them to watch Li'l David. But David barely gave me enough time to do that.

"The Renault is warmed up. Here, let me sit your suitcase outside by the back door. I am going to have to push the car up the hill first and when you see me coming back down the hill, be ready to jump in. Don't forget, grab your little bag and jump in."

No wonder I had the baby two weeks early. After bouncing up and down on the freeway in that raggedy little blue car traveling at a speed of 70 miles per hour, I had no other choice.

The minute the nurse spotted me from the hospital window attempting to maneuver my short legs out of the little car, she came running with a wheelchair. I'm sure I must have looked a sight. The pains were shooting through my back and lower abdomen. I had to stop and rest my now impregnated body before continuing my now desperate attempt to get out of the small car and into the wheelchair. It seemed like I would never make it between those sharp-shooting pains in my lower back. I was sweating profusely now.

As the nurse rushed me down the long corridor to the delivery room, she yelled back at David, "Go get your wife's records and take them to admittance with her military I.D. card. By the time you get back, she will probably be prepped and ready to have the baby."

David rushed back with my medical records, but was still too late.

"You have a healthy, beautiful baby girl," the nurse said.

I was in the recovery room with only a white curtain separating me from the nurses' station. I could hear everything they were saying but couldn't see them. I wish I could have seen David's facial expression as she continued on with the vital statistics.

"She weighed six pounds, eight ounces, and has a head full of beautiful black curls."

David shook his head in disbelief. "No! No! You're lying! I don't believe you! She couldn't have. I took me less than five minutes! Did she really have the baby?"

The nurse chuckled at his loud outburst.

"Yes, she did. Matter of fact your wife is right behind the first curtain to your right. I know she must be anxious to see you. Your newborn is getting cleaned up now and as soon as they take her to the nursery, you can go see her."

David couldn't wait. He went to see the baby first, then came to see me. David looked so sweet just then. He came into my room smiling with is chest stuck out. He was The Proud Father.

"She is so beautiful!"

I was very tired after the delivery. I just felt numb. I merely nodded my head in agreement and held onto his hand. I fell asleep with him sitting alongside my bed. I remembered saying, "Thank you, Lord."

<hr />

After three days in the maternity ward, I went home with our baby girl. David was truly the proud father. Upon my arrival at home, he put me to bed in a nice clean bedroom. The entire apartment, I noticed, was immaculately clean and neat. My heart was thumping. Lord, this is too good to be true, I thought.

"Baby, I bought you a new washer and dryer." I was thrilled because previously, I only had an old used wringer washer machine. The chipped paint on that old round monstrosity was an ugly olive green. After washing and squeezing the clothes, you had to hang them outside to dry. But in Washington, the sun very rarely shined. It mostly rained every day in Tacoma. You could hang your clothes out on the clothesline early in the morning and by the late afternoon, if you were lucky, they might be just damp. Otherwise, the light rains would come down and soak them good. We would have to dry them indoors by hanging them over a heater, or in the bathroom, on anything so they could dry by the next morning.

I was truly happy for a new washer and dryer.

We were so happy with our little family.

My mother and stepfather drove up to see the baby. Mother and Daddy made over her like she was the first baby born. We named her Terri Minjon Bess.

"She looks like she's going to have more of your coloring, Janie," Mother said. "She's going to look more like you."

"She is a pretty baby," Daddy said.

We decided to call our little girl Terri after Mother showed us how difficult it was to pronounce her middle name.

"You pronounce it like this, Mother. Men-Yon, Mother, now repeat it, Men-yon."

"O.K. Ming-yown."

"No, Mother, Men-Yon."

David listened as long as he could until he couldn't stand it anymore.

"Mrs. Prather, just call her Terri. Okay?" he said.

Mother and Daddy stayed for only a few days. They drove back to California. I sure did want to go with them to show off our beautiful baby girl.

CHAPTER TWENTY-FOUR

For once in our lives, everything was going well. Too well. I should have known something would happen. It always had.

David got orders for Vietnam. First he had to get us back to California.

then he had to report to Cannon Air Force Base, N.M., for survival training.

Li'l David was almost 4 by then. Terri was about 2 ½ months. David only had two weeks to get us home. Those two weeks flew by fast. We were forced to practically give everything away. My new washer and dryer, our infamous Renault car. Our bedroom, dining room and living room sets. We sold everything for only $150. David was only an airman second class, so Uncle Sam didn't pay to ship our household goods. We couldn't afford to ship anything. We called his parents, The Besses, to see if the kids and I could stay with them while David was in Vietnam.

I was surprised Mr. Bess agreed. We told his parents we had a Maltese terrier named Pepper for a pet. Brownie had died in a car accident and we'd just got Pepper before the baby was born. They still said it would be fine. David explained our dog would come later. We had to leave her with friends because he still needed shots in order to fly on the plane with us.

David was home with us on leave for 30 days. He stayed through Thanksgiving and he left right after Christmas.

David Jr. started Hawthorne School in Oakland. It was only about 10 minutes from where we lived.

Everything seemed to be going along just fine. David was 4, going to school and seemed very happy. Terri was crawling and teething now. She was such a happy healthy baby.

Mr. and Mrs. Bess both seemed to enjoy us staying there with them. We were all very happy. I helped her decorate the apartment and Mr. Bess and I exchanged recipes. After about the middle of March, I started feeling restless. Five months had gone by so fast. I felt it was time to get my own place. My kids needed room to play. Li'l David was hyperactive and Terri was getting into everything. That two-bedroom apartment was becoming too small. My dog Pepper finally arrived. It had been over three months, she was running all over the place. I finally called my parents and they let Pepper stay with them.

I wrote David and told him I needed to find a place before the in-law relationship became sour from such a long stay. We were still getting along, but I could feel the tension whenever I didn't discipline the children. Sometimes when I did, they didn't endorse it.

The same day I wrote and mailed my letter to Vietnam, I received one from him. It read:

> *Dear Janie,*
> *I was just thinking that maybe you should start looking for an apartment soon.*
> *I will be coming home within a few months time. I realize from the photos you have been sending me that our children are growing bigger. They need their space and so do you. Write me soon and let me know how you feel about this.*
> *Love and I miss you, Baby.*
> *David*

I talked to my Aunt Flo and explained my dilemma to her. She took me directly to the Oakland Housing Authority office. The rent was subsidized; it was determined by your income. She helped me find an apartment near her. It was in the West Oakland Housing development off of West Grand Avenue. They had just been recently built. They had modern appliances, nice draperies and blinds at every window, with upgraded linoleum throughout the living room, kitchen, and the bathroom. There was security and everything.

We were able to move in within a week's time.

I went out and bought a white vinyl sofa. I needed something that was childproof. I fixed my new place up. My color scheme was in white with black and red accents.

I kept my little place so clean and neat.

Time flew by. Li'l David was still attending Hawthorne School when one day, the principal called me. He said he needed to talk to me right away. I went expecting something positive, but instead, it was bad news. His teacher told me Li'l David didn't seem to be able to sit still long enough to learn

letters or to learn the alphabet. He said they weren't staffed or trained to work with a legally deaf-blind child.

I retorted back, "David is not blind. He wears glasses and is able to see well with them." I told them how well he did at Birney School in Tacoma. He could recognize his own name by sight. He had learned how to trace his name in raised letters on the classroom door with his index fingers before entering back into the classroom.

"There, at Birney School, David was learning his alphabet, colors and learning how to count, too," I said proudly.

The staff wasn't the least bit impressed. "Had their noses up in the air like they were smelling something." That's what my mother said as we walked back to the parking lot. She had driven me there for the meeting, so she came in to see what it was all about.

Li'l David continued going there. But I didn't see the same kind of curriculum that the school in Washington State offered.

"He doesn't sit still," they complained. "He is hyperactive and he will not sit still long enough for us to teach him. I am so sorry, Mrs. Bess, but we feel that David will not be able to grasp the conceptual value of sign language. He is disrupting my classroom."

I wrote David to inform him of Li'l David's latest episode with the educational system. We were both at wits end. We were told they didn't have a program for David in the Oakland School district.

I was devastated. They promised he could finish out that school year before he would have to transfer to the California School for the Blind in Berkeley. They didn't expect that to happen until the following year. To attend the school, students had to be 6 years old, toilet-trained and able to feed and dress themselves. I was told transportation would be provided. A yellow school bus would pick him up and transport him there for classes. I couldn't wait for him to start there. There was a long waiting list so I didn't get my hopes up too fast.

CHAPTER TWENTY-FIVE

David finally came home from Vietnam, just before Christmas 1966. We were all so happy that he was able to survive 'Nam.

We gave him a surprise party at Aunt Flo's house. He was truly surprised. We were so happy. The first couple of weekends, while David was on days leave, he went out celebrating with his brothers to San Francisco to the new topless clubs and to the Hippie joints on the corner of Haight and Asbury streets.

He was to report to duty at Hamilton Air Force Base near San Rafael in a small town called Novato.

I tried to outsmart God and Mother Nature. Three months before David's expected return from Vietnam, I went to the obstetrics clinic at Oak Knoll Naval Hospital. I explained my husband was due home soon. I wanted to make sure I didn't get pregnant. My daughter was only 13 months old and I already had a small toddler at home, I explained. I asked for advice on birth control. The gynecologist suggested I start taking birth control pills at least three months in advance of my husband's arrival. He then warned me I would have to come back for a Pap smear within three months before he would write me another refill for those pills.

I made an appointment with the receptionist on my way out. My appointment date was for around Jan. 15, about the same time I would need to get my birth control prescription refilled.

"If I don't see you back here for your pap smear in January, young lady, I will not be able to renew your prescription," the doctor said. "You are overdue for it. I'll let you slide for now. But don't forget."

"I promise, doctor. Don't worry, I'll be here Jan. 15," I said as I quickly made my way out of the clinic door.

Well, I forgot all about my appointment. I was so enthralled about David's safe return it was the last thing on my mind.

I was down to my last month's prescription. I had about 14 pills left in a cute little round purple plastic dial pack. I was on the phone talking to my mother when Terri came to me. She was spitting out a white powdery substance from her mouth. She had this look of distaste on her face.

As she held out her hand to give me my purple pill box, she said, "Nasty candy! Mama, I don't like it. Here!" She shoved the empty pack into my hand as she continued spitting out my birth control pills from her mouth. They were all crushed. It was apparent she had swallowed some of them. There was not a one in the dial pack. I just dropped the pack down. I was still talking to my mother when this happened.

"Mother, I've got to go. Terri has swallowed all of my birth control pills. God, I don't know what to do. I don't know whether to spank her before or after I call the ambulance. I needed those pills, too. I can't get anymore until I have my pap smear done. I missed my appointment because David came home on the night before. I had completely forgotten about it."

Mother tried to reassure me everything would be all right but I couldn't listen to that mumbo jumbo. I quickly hung up the phone and called the gynecologist.

"Sir, my 15-month-old daughter just ate my birth control pills. Should I bring her in?"

"Yes, she needs to be checked. Please bring her into the pediatrics clinic right away."

Mother rushed us to the hospital. Terri was playing with her doll and chattering leisurely in the back seat. After the examination, Terri received a clean bill of health.

"There's nothing to worry about," the pediatrician said. "She should not have any side effects. She must have swallowed only a small amount. It will come out in her stool."

My next visit was to see the gynecologist. He looked through my records, and then he said, "Oh, yes, I remember you. It shows here you missed your appointment for a pap smear. We will have to reschedule this for the following month. We are booked up solid now."

"Can I please have just a 30-day supply until I can get in? My husband just got back from Vietnam and I don't want to get pregnant right away. We want to wait a while, at least another year."

I pleaded with that doctor, but to no avail. He merely said, "Use another form of contraceptive until that time or just abstain from having sex during ovulation.

Now, how was I supposed to hold off from sex with my young, virile, sexy, good-looking husband? We hadn't been able to have sex for 13 months. That doctor must be crazy, I thought.

I knew David wasn't going to wait for a whole month. Neither could I!

Despite using a new contraceptive foam and other contraceptives, I got pregnant. In denial, I returned for my Pap smear appointment and to get my prescription for my pills. After the examination was over, I sat in the doctor's office waiting while he skimmed over my medical file. The gynecologist kept turning the pages in my records.

"Well, Mrs. Bess, I see you returned for your Pap smear. The nurse says you wanted a new prescription for your birth control pills. Is that right?"

He peered up over his glasses to look at me. Without waiting for me to answer, he continued on, "After examining you, I got the results back. Your pap smear was good. No problems there. But…"

I interrupted him. He was taking too long. I wanted to yell for him to the point but instead, I asked, in a near whisper, "Then doctor, what is it?" My lip quivered.

I leaned forward. I waited nervously; impatient for him to finish speaking.

He looked me dead in my eyes.

"You won't be needing those birth control pills after all. Your lab tests show that you are pregnant."

"But, but, sir, I used foam like you told me to and, and my husband used condoms. I just don't understand how I got pregnant. We were so careful."

He cleared his throat and looked at me as if to say, Not careful enough, ma'am. I could almost read his mind.

"Well, as we all know, none of these contraceptives are 100 percent sure, not even the oral contraceptive known as the pill," he said, pushing his glasses back upon the bridge of his nose. "I want to see you back next month. I'll expect to see you in the obstetrics clinic. Here's a refillable prescription for prenatal vitamins and iron supplements. Go to the receptionist and she'll schedule your next visit, within the next 30 days. Thank you, Mrs. Bess."

With that, he closed my file and placed it on a neat pile along with the other patients' records lying upon his desk.

I sat there totally numb. He opened the door for me and stood there, politely, waiting for me to leave. I slowly rose up out my chair and walked out.

"Thank you, doctor," I said as the hot tears just seemed to explode from my eyes. I ran sobbing out of the hospital doors, down the stairs and outside. I had to tell David. I didn't know what he would say.

I pictured him saying, "We can't afford another baby. Not now, Janie.".

I went to my mother's house from the hospital. She suggested I go with her to see Mother Piggis for prayer.

She led me back into the prayer room. After a Scripture was read from the Bible, she said, "Janie, God is going to bless you with a beautiful baby boy. Ooh! Thank you, Jesus! I can see him. He is going to be a blessing to you. Your son, David, and your daughter, Terri, are going to love their little brother."

All of a sudden, she changed her tone. She was looking at me intensely as if she was looking through me. Her voice seemed to go up an octave, as she asked me, "Janie, has Little David been complaining about pain in his eyes?"

"No. Why? He can't tell me about pain. He doesn't know how to explain that to me. We don't even have a home sign for pain."

"Just keep a eye on him. I see him holding his hands up in front of his face like he is trying to see them.

"God is going to use this child," Mother Piggis said. "I ain't going to take it back." She closed her eyes and said, "Thank you, Jesus."

I was having cold chills now. I didn't say a word. She continued talking with her eyes closed.

"Yes, I see Little David. Ooh, wee! He is a smart little boy. I see him helping you with his little sister and the new baby, too. Oh, yes, thank you, Jesus. God has shown me something else. He is a grown man now. God is showing me something. Wait! It looks like he's standing up in front of a class. He's a grown man and he appears to-to—be teaching little children. Oh, thank you, lord! I see him on TV, too. He is going to be famous. God is going to use that boy. But right now, he looks lonely sometimes. I see your daughter Terri holding his hand. She talks to him and plays with him. What I see now is Terri showing him or she's leading him around. Sometimes, though, I see him in a room all by himself, he has nobody to play with; there is no one to talk to him. God help him. There is something wrong. Janie as soon as you can, take him to see an eye doctor. God is showing me that his eyes are bothering him. He is in pain. If David isn't in pain now, I see that it won't be long. So remember, take him back to the doctor's office as soon as possible. You hear me? I ain't going to take it back. God has shown me this, so you obey God, don't obey me."

Mother had joined us in the prayer room. I hadn't even noticed her until she proudly said, "I know that Little David is smart. You are so right about that. He can't talk but he can do almost everything that a hearing child can. Sometimes, he does more."

Mother started searching in her purse for something. She pulled out a pack of her favorite spearmint gum.

"Would you like some gum?" she said, looking at me and Mother P. We both declined.

"He goes outside with Janie and they hang the clothes out together on the clothesline. He knows his clothes from everyone else's, too. When they are dry and ironed, he goes and stands on a chair and hangs them up in the closet. Honey, David is neater than the most kids. These other wol's, well, they won't do nothing until I tell them to. When they finally do it, they half do it."

She busted out laughing really loud. Mother Piggis joined in, laughing right along with her. They sounded like two cackling hens.

"Yeah, Johnnie, I'm raising my grandchildren, too, you know, since my daughter Vera died," Mother Piggis said. "These grandchildren of ours, they ain't nothing like our children, are they? Johnnie, I have to tell them over and over again, then I have to stand over them to make sure they do it right. And still end up doing it myself."

"Girl, I know," Mother nodded in agreement. "I am getting too old for this myself. But like I was saying, Janie and David spend a lot of time with their children. She teaches that boy how to fold clothes and to run his own bath water. He can dress himself and everything matches, too. He puts his shoes on the right foot, too. That's 'cause Janie, she has a lot of patience. Big David keeps those kids in line. He don't spoil them now. Uh! Uh! Although I don't always agree with the way he disciplines them. I think sometimes he too strict. And don't think for one minute that I don't tell him about it either."

Mother was chewing that gum hard and laughing in between every other sentence.

"They're shore good kids, though. David Jr. and Terri are so mannerable and neat, too."

I just loved to see Mother laugh. Her tiny teeth were so perfect and white. She had a beautiful smile. Mother Piggis was still chuckling as she walked us to the door.

Mother drove home, not saying another word.

After the prayer session, I felt such comfort. Mother Piggis said a special prayer for Li'l David. I did not feel like talking. I was gathering my thoughts, re-thinking the day's events. I truly marveled at how God had sent me an important message. I couldn't get over it. It was amazing how He told Mother P what to tell me.

VISIONS

I made a mental note to really watch Li'l David and to make sure he got an appointment to see his ophthalmologist soon. But in the end, we didn't get there.

David was fretting and agitated when I finally got home. I told him what the doctor said, that I was pregnant. To say the least, he wasn't happy. He yelled and screamed at me. He accused me of doing it on purpose because he'd wanted me to go to work. I hadn't, of course. I wanted to remind it that it takes two people to make a baby and I didn't see him staying away from me and our bed. But I didn't. In the end, he warmed up to the idea. He had to. I was pregnant and you didn't do abortions in the 1960s. Even if it had been legal, I could have never killed my baby, anyway.

CHAPTER TWENTY-SIX

T he months rolled by fast. David made another stripe. He was an airman first class and now he made staff sergeant. More money would come in handy with the new baby. I was due in September.

We could now live in base housing. We moved to a three-bedroom cottage located about one mile from Hamilton Air Force Base in Novato, only a couple miles from San Rafael.

Our families came out to our place to celebrate Memorial Day.

This was the first time since we had been married that were able to entertain our family. We barbecued right in our carport. There was lots of food, lots of good music and games to play.

My sisters got into a heated argument over something. That was stopped before it got out of control and everything went just fine.

Everyone agreed this was the perfect place to have a 4th of July picnic.

Plus, the military was putting on an air show at the base for the holiday.

When the 4th rolled around, everything was going just fine for us. But lately, my sisters had been having a lot of arguments. My mother was worried. She told me she had to break up a fight at her house between the two of them a few days earlier.

Mother said she felt Sydney was upset over the ways things had turned out for her in contrast to Earlie.

Daddy Prather had helped Earlie open her first beauty shop. He loaned her a large sum of money to have it built and furnished from the ground up. It was a modern salon with new furnishings. We were all proud of her.

Sydney, however, felt life was unfair. This really put a damper on things. I felt anxious whenever they were together in the same room. I loved both my sisters very much. It tore at my heart to see them fighting like that. I knew it troubled my mother more than anyone. When we would fight as children, she would discipline all of us, not taking sides with anybody.

We all knew Sydney was ashamed. She stood by her man even when he treated her wrong. She always said the same thing. "He was raised without his mother that's why he is like that. He just needs someone to love him and to trust him."

Earlie had always warned her to not let him run over her. Sydney's husband left her for another woman.

Sydney wanted to prove the world wrong. In the end, she felt alone like everyone was laughing at her. She tried to escape By blaming everyone for what really happened. She grew depressed. She was a single parent and the sole provider for a family of four. She was having difficulty on her job with some of her co-workers because Sydney was a dedicated worker. She moved up fast on the ladder shortly after being hired because she was very adept at her job as an IBM keypunch operator, Today, we call it a computer. Within a record time of three months, she was promoted on her job to a supervisor. The co-workers gave her a hard time after her promotion.

At the same time things were going very well for Earlie. Her clientele accelerated once she had opened her new salon. She named it Angel's Haven. Sydney felt like everyone was turning against her. She was on the defensive about her estranged husband. She seemed overprotective of her children.

Sydney showed up first at the 4th of July barbecue. She and her children looked good. I was so happy to see her. She was very pretty. Her full figure was well proportioned. She always dressed sophisticated. Sydney hair was long and pretty. Earlie had dyed her dark brown hair an Auburn color. It really complemented her dark olive complexion. I hugged her. I told her how proud I was of her promotion. She said she wanted to surprise me. She told me that since she had gotten a promotion she purchased new furnishings for her apartment.

"Oh, yes, I bought a new car," she said, gesturing with her hands toward the shiny blue Ford Pinto.

My mind wandered back over the last year. I thought about my big sister and how she always spent quality time with me while David was overseas. She always came to see about my children and me. She would pick us up and take me shopping or to my endless doctors' appointments. We would drive to a local park and talk while the children played. We lounged on a blanket on the green grass. She and I would just lie there, laughing and reminiscing about our past. We would talk about our dreams and ambitions too.

While I stood there on the lawn talking with Sydney that day, at least five cars drove up in front of our house filled to capacity with our friends and relatives. I felt overwhelmed with all of these people.

David's parents drove up in their shiny new Burgundy Pontiac with the white vinyl top. After we greeted them, John Bess immediately headed to the kitchen and went right to work marinating his spareribs and steaks. The retired chef then prepared his special Italian marinara sauce to add to his famous spaghetti casserole. He worked tediously to make sure there were alternating layers of the Italian marinara sauce, cheese, ground beef and hot Italian sausage with its many herbs and spices. Large strips of sharp cheddar cheese were laid on top into a lattice design.

My mother and stepfather drove up a short time later. Their new Mercury Monterey was filled to capacity with most of the grandchildren.

Mother was always the head chef in my family. She came with all of her spices and condiments to make her infamous Southern style barbecue sauce. She, too, found her a spot in the kitchen to prepare the sauce with its many spices.

I was nervous about her working alongside Mr. Bess in the kitchen. I prayed she and Mr. Bess would get along together. They were both critically outspoken and if anyone else cooked anything, they would find something wrong with it.

"Not enough seasoning," he'd say.

"It's too salty," she'd say.

I wanted to run and hide from embarrassment whenever they did this.

Earlie had a reputation about being late. I always thought my parents should have named her "Late" rather than "Earlie." It was no different this time, either. It was the middle of the afternoon when she finally drove up. She really caught me off guard. I spotted the new two-door sports car with tinted glass windows. It was a brand new 1967 white Mercury Cougar with a custom-made leopard top, solid beige leather interior and matching leopard seats. She drove the car up our sloped driveway right into our carport.

When the passenger door opened, out stepped this tall, handsome man. He had on a white lace shirt and white jeans with white boots. He was very light skinned with beautiful, wavy hair that was cut into a medium-length shag. This 6-foot-5-inch gentleman walked around to the driver's side of the car, then opened the door.

Out stepped Earlie looking like a model from Ebony magazine. I didn't recognize her at first because her hair was cut into a high fashion asymmetrical style. There were copper brown streaks of color alternating throughout her beautiful shiny black hair. It was a perfect coordinated look. She wore a leopard fur mini skirt with a matching bolero jacket and white lace-up boots.

I knew my mouth was wide open when Sydney punched me and then said, "Close your mouth, girl, flies could get in."

We both laughed hard before I ran over to hug Earlie.

Everyone was talking and having a good time. Earlie was busy making potato salad while I stirred Mother's barbecue sauce.

"Janie, I am going to Los Angeles to a hair show and convention next week," Earlie said. "I am going to look for our daddy."

"Oh, really, our real daddy, Calvin Lightfoot?" "Yes, do you still have his old address?"

"I have the old one but my last letter came back 'Return to Sender.'" I ran to my room to get it from my address book. "I hope you find him. I miss my daddy."

Sydney agreed. I was excited just thinking about my long lost father.

Sydney was having fun laughing and talking with other family members. She seemed relaxed for the first time in a long while. Her three boys were running and playing outside at first. Then they ran inside playing tag. They were knocking things over as they ran. It all started with Earlie telling Sydney to watch her kids, who were running around unsupervised.

Sydney retaliated back by talking about Earlie's children and about her new boyfriend, who was sitting right next to her.

Earlie then struck back with derogatory remarks to Sydney. Earlie talked about Sydney's no-good husband and how he never kept a job, and on and on until Mother said, "Okay! That's enough. Ain't neither of your husbands any good, if you ask me." Mother started her loud belching then continued on talking. "So neither of you can talk about the other. Like the saying goes, how can the pot talk about the kettle? Y'all done ran out now. I don't want to hear no more."

During the course of the barbecue, Earlie and Sydney stopped talking but started rolling their eyes at one another. My heart was thumping fast and my stomach was jumping with butterflies. I could feel the tension mounting.

Sydney's mouth was twisted now into an ugly distorted shape as she spoke to Earlie.

"Earlie, it must be nice to have someone buy you a beauty shop," she said sarcastically. She walked over toward Earlie and continued to needle her. "I'm going to ask Daddy to buy me a shop, too." Sydney was now circling around her.

Earlie turned around in her seat to keep an eye on Sydney as she slowly circled her chair.

"I am paying Daddy back," she said. "Every month, I make a payment to Daddy. I plan to pay him off within a year, so don't worry about my business."

Earlie rolled her eyes back at Sydney and said, "You know, Sydney, why don't you try to sit down and relax. You ought to be glad that that no good, dog-faced man you called your husband left. He did you and the kids a favor. All he ever did was lay on his backside, drink, take food from the kids and then jump on you every chance he got. He never worked a day in his life and when he finally did work, that's when he ups and leaves you. Now that he's gone, you should be able to save some money. You have a good job with the government. You get better pay than I do. I didn't have no man staying with me. If I had, he would sure have to be working so he could help me. Now that your husband is working, he doesn't need you. He should be giving you money for his four children. And you need to be asking him to help you. Focus on that!"

Sydney didn't like that.

"I'm going to focus on you now," she said and hauled off and hit Earlie with her fist right smack upside her head. It was on then. Fists were flying. Hair was pulled. Next thing I knew, they were both rolling all over my living room floor, still socking each other. Sydney's eyes were closed and she stopped hitting, but she continued to hold on tight to Earlie's hair as if her life depended upon it. She screamed obscenities at Earlie.

"You let go of me, Earlie," she yelled. Earlie ignored her and kept punching with her right hand as she kept Sydney's long pretty hair wrapped and twisted into the palm of her left hand. With each lick, Earlie was talking to Sydney in a rhythmic style. With every punch to Sydney's head, she'd say something to her.

"You-Bam!-don't-Bam!-hit me!-Bam! I-Bam-didn't-Bam!—Do nothing Bam-Bam!—To you!—Bam!—I am-Bam!—Going-to-Bam!—Bam!— Teach-you Bam!—A lesson. Bam!

I was screaming Earlie.

"Let go of her. That's enough. You guys stop it now." I was so angry with both of them. I was very embarrassed, too. Our house guests and neighbors seeing my sisters fighting like that.

"Mother, come help. Earlie and Sydney are fighting all over my house. Now they are out on the front lawn." Most of the men had left earlier. They had taken all the children to a nearby park to play baseball.

They arrived back just in time to see Mother hitting both Sydney and Earlie with my kitchen broom handle. She was swinging that broom handle fast and hard.

"You wol's are going to respect me. I told y'all about that arguing and fighting. I ain't going to have it. Unh!" She was saying "Unh" as though it gave her power to swing that broom.

"Mother, stop hitting me. That broom handle hurts," Sydney yelled. "You wol's gonna stop fightin' then?"

Earlie answered back. "Well, tell Sydney she had better not hit me again, I know that. Humph."

Earlie tried to smooth out her hair with her hands. It was standing all over her head.

Sydney pulled her hair up into a bun. She had bobby pins in her mouth between her teeth. As she tucked her hair in, she would pull a bobby pin from her mouth and secure her hair until it was in a neat bun. She was breathing loud. Her white jeans were now black.

"I'm going home now," Sydney said. "I am tired of everybody talking about me and my kids."

She started rounding them up despite my pleas for her to stay.

"It is late and your kids didn't eat anything yet."

"Let her go," Earlie interrupted. "She has been starting fights with me and I'm sick and tired of it. I ain't leaving so she needs go."

Sydney was starting to reach for her again when all of a sudden, a loud male voice boomed from the kitchen. It was John Bess, David's father.

"Who put ketchup in my spaghetti?" He shook his head in disbelief as he threw down the potholder on the counter. "They've just ruined my recipe." He threw the big ladle back into the big large pot with a loud clanging sound.

Every one had forgotten about Earlie and Sydney now. All eyes were on him.

My mother put the broom back into the kitchen pantry, then turned around with a defiant look. Her chin was jutted up in the air as she looked up at Mr. Bess. She was only 5'2". She looked like an ant next to Mr. Bess' six-foot frame.

"I did it," she said, putting her hands on her hips. "That spaghetti had dried out in the oven. I couldn't find any extra sauce so I poured a little catsup and water in it to moisten it up a little bit."

"What! You mean you're the one who messed up my spaghetti. Well, I'll be."

Just then, there was a loud scream from the living room and we heard a siren from a nearby ambulance pulling up into our yard.

Out came two medics running up to our door with a gurney. One of our cousin's friends had gone into labor right under our noses.

The medics strapped her onto a gurney and carried her out to the ambulance. I heard them say, "We've got to hurry! She has dilated and her water has broken. I think we are going to have a baby very soon!"

They closed the passenger doors after getting her settled and off they went with the sirens blasting loudly. All of the neighbors and all of our guests were now out on the front lawn.

One of my family members came running up to me as I headed back inside. I dreaded going back into the kitchen because Mr. Bess, Mother, and David were still arguing about the spaghetti dish with the unwanted ketchup.

I heard someone yell, "Janie! Come quick! There is something wrong with Li'l David!" I didn't really hear them at first. I was listening to Mother and Mr. Bess and trying to sooth their tempers. But then I turned around and went back out the front. The screen door slammed shut with a disturbing bang. It was a foreboding sound. I stood there frozen in my tracks as I watched my son frantically spinning around and around in a circle on the sidewalk in front of our house.

"He is screaming and he seems to be disoriented," someone said. I don't know how long I stood there. I was in total shock.

David came running out from the side of the house and swooped up Li'l David. Li'l David was waving his tiny little brown hands in front of his eyes.

"Oh, my God, David, Li'l David can't see." I saw his blank stare and I realized he was reaching out for me. I grabbed him from David's arms without thinking and just crumpled to the lawn rocking him close to me.

"Don't worry, Baby. Everything is going to be alright," I said

David ran inside to call an ambulance to pick us up but my stepfather said, "Just drive your car to the base. Don't they have any physicians on duty at this base now? They have to have at least one doctor on duty."

David called Hamilton Air Base clinic and they instructed him to take Li'l David to Presidio Hospital in San Francisco. All of our house guests started leaving. Everybody hugged us and gave futile attempts to reassure us. David looked very worried and very tired. I felt numb, my stomach had started it's typical flip-flopping. It always occurred whenever I was upset. I felt nauseous and was having chills. I didn't want to give my poor husband anything else to stress over. He was trying to be strong for me and our son. He was breathing heavily. David didn't seem to be aware or even conscious of the distressful frustrated sighs coming from his throat. I was praying all the way there to San Francisco.

Due to the heavy holiday traffic on Highway 101, we crept across the Golden Gate Bridge. Under other circumstances, it would have taken us 20 minutes or less. This night, when we were in such a hurry, it took four hours. We finally drove into Presidio Hospital at 9:30 p.m. and parked in the empty parking lot.

The medic on duty appeared annoyed when we came in and disturbed his quiet serene nap. He stood up from his chair yawning and rubbing sleep from his eyes as we rang the bell on his desk.

David and I were visibly shaken as I talked to the physician. He showed absolutely no compassion about my son's sudden loss of vision.

The doctor's measly examination consisted of a small pencil-thin flashlight shined in his eyes. It gave off a reflection of a white spot that shone into poor Li'l David's eyes. There was no reaction from Li'l David at all. He just kept waving his right hand in front of his face. His eyes weren't focusing. He just stared into space.

"Why aren't you using more sophisticated equipment?" I asked. "At Oak Knoll Naval Hospital, the doctors use a big black machine. It has a lot of different instruments attached. They used it to look behind the cornea into the iris and into the pupil. Shining a small red light into my son's eyes couldn't tell you that much, could it?"

His arrogant attitude and treatment of my son's blindness just seemed to frustrate me even more. I became angry and insisted he call the head ophthalmologist at Oak Knoll Hospital Emergency room.

"You only peeked into his eyes with a little flashlight," he said. "They never did that before. When he went to Oak Knoll just for his follow-up appointment, they used expensive ophthalmic equipment. I've never seen anything like this before. My son is in a lot of pain. His eyes look swollen and I can tell that he can't see. Can't you call over to Oak Knoll? The eye doctors there are familiar with Li'l David's case. They have his medical records there.

"My husband brought us here because he thought that surely Presidio would have the best staff. This hospital was recommended by Hamilton Air Force Base. So that's the only reason we're here."

The doctor was adamant about his diagnosis. He ignored me completely and addressed his remarks to David only.

"Sgt. Bess, as I told your wife, I didn't detect any bleeding of the cornea of either eye so I don't feel like there is any threat to your son's iris or pupil. It is probably just a temporary blindness maybe caused by a fall. I understand he was riding in circles on his bike, well, maybe he fell and you didn't notice it.

"Your wife informed me that next month, David Jr. has an appointment with the ophthalmologist at Oak Knoll. So I recommend that you wait until his follow-up appointment to have him checked. It is a holiday and they are probably short staffed."

David looked at me with his I-told-you-so look. I was livid. I stood with my hands on my hips and spoke to the doctor, looking him dead in his eyes.

"Doctor, obviously you didn't hear what happened. My son was playing outside with the other children when all of a sudden, he started screaming. I could tell he was in pain. He was riding around in circles on his bike and he was waving his hand frantically in front of his eyes as though he was trying to see his hand. His eyes did not focus." I picked my son up from the examination table and start wrapping him into my coat. "I don't want to wait until his next appointment. That won't be for another 30 days." I glared contemptuously at that old doctor.

"Come on, David, we are going to Oak Knoll Hospital right now."

My poor husband was torn between doing what the doctor advised or appeasing me, who persisted on taking Little David to Oak Knoll.

The doctor looked down on me with disdain. After taking a deep breath, he said, "I can see that there is no bleeding behind the cornea, as I stated. It really won't matter if you take him now. I am sure that they will tell you the same. You might as well wait until his next appointment in August now."

How could these doctors be so cold and callous?

David was driving as I rode beside him in the front seat. I had not learned how to drive yet. I held Li'l David close to me, trying to comfort him. I must have fallen asleep because when I looked up, we were headed down the freeway. I assumed we were on the way to Oak Knoll in Oakland, until I saw that David was merging into the San Rafael-Sausalito turnoff. It was too late.

We were on the route back to Novato.

"David, where are we going?" My voice trembled. It was 11 p.m. and there was hardly any traffic. I looked at David. He had a determined look on his face. As we turned into our driveway, I asked him, "Why didn't we go to Oak Knoll? I told you his records were there so I thought that you were taking us there."

We started arguing. I wanted to go to Oak Knoll but David wanted to wait until next month as that eye doctor had recommended. We were all exhausted after the long exciting day so I at least agreed to go to bed then. But I wasn't through talking about it. As soon as I was inside, I stormed around the living room yelling at the top of my lungs. I took off my coat and threw my across the room.

"I am going to call Oak Knoll tomorrow. I want to speak to Li'l David's doctor. He is an ophthalmologist, not a medic like that quack at the Presidio. First thing in the morning, I'm calling."

At first, David just stood there and listened to me rave on and on. He stared at me as if he couldn't believe his eyes. I had never acted like this with him before.

"You should have listened to me, David."

"Janie," he yelled back. "I'm getting sick of your big mouth. Shut up and listen to me. That eye doctor knows what he's doing. He told us to wait until next month. Li'l David has his next appointment scheduled so that's what we are going to do, wait."

I was fit to be tied. I yelled back obscenities.

"That's what's wrong, you trust these doctors." That night I made a vow this would never happen again. I was going to learn how to drive. If I knew how to drive, I would have turned that car around and went straight to Oak Knoll.

Before we went to bed I found a note that said my parents had taking Terri home with them. We all went to sleep as soon as our heads hit the pillow. I kept Li'l David close to me. He held tightly to my nightgown and wouldn't let me out of his sight.

I woke up in the middle of the night seeing that horrible scene with Li'l David spinning around and around in a circle. He was screaming for help.

Oh, Lord, let this be a nightmare. Maybe I'm dreaming this. It's not really happening. Not to my son! Yes! Yes! That's it! It must be a nightmare.

I was screaming, screaming very loud. My loud shrills woke David from his sleep. He tried to calm me down. He shook me gently back to reality. He hugged me and talked to me in a soothing calm voice.

"It's all right, shh, shh, come on, baby, don't cry."

I sat upright in the bed we shared. I felt my eyes. I wasn't even aware I was crying.

"David, I dreamed Li'l David was spinning around and around as though it was beyond his control! He was going around so fast, so fast, until he landed on his head and it blinded him. When he got up from the ground stumbling, he couldn't see.

"I was running around trying my best to grab hold of him but he was going too fast. It was as if an evil centrifugal force had control of him. I heard this fiendish laugh. A red devil with a forked tail was standing over my baby. That's when I screamed. All of a sudden, that thing swirled around him. And then some red dust appeared in and surrounded Li'l David. I couldn't get through the dust and then that thing picked him up and flung him and, and down he went with a hard thud to the ground as he landed on his head. That's when I screamed. Oh, God. Was it for real or was I dreaming?"

"You were having a nightmare. Now try to go on back to sleep." "Was I dreaming? David can see, right?"

"Janie, I don't know what to say. I wish it was only a nightmare. David is blind but there is no devil here. Just try to sleep."

David held me close, patting like I was a baby.

"Oh, David, I'm scared for my baby. What going to happen now?'"

David took a deep breath. He seemed to have no solution for this problem.

"Janie, try to go back to sleep. Please."

I tossed and turned until the sun came through my bedroom window.

CHAPTER TWENTY-SEVEN

Early the next morning, I called Li'l David's doctor at Oak Knoll. The receptionist told me he was on vacation.

"The earliest appointment I have would have to be the first week in August." I accepted the appointment gladly.

I wrote the date on my calendar. I couldn't afford to miss it. I went through the motions of existing until that day. My mind stayed in a constant fog. I called his counselor Evelyn to tell her what happened to Li'l David. Ever since he'd started the California School for the Blind, Li'l David had stayed in the dorm there during the weekend and come home on the weekends. His teachers knew him very well and knew all of the things he could do, things many sighted children couldn't master at his age. The shock and disappointment in her voice brought tears again as I relived that day. I could still see my son on his bright red bike with training wheels turning around and round in circles terrorized by the sudden darkness that engulfed him. Now he was sightless and helpless. His sight was the only way he communicated with us. Now it was gone in a flash.

She tried to cheer me up.

"Until his doctor's appointment, keep him busy. Let him wash dishes and help you hang out clothes. We all know how he likes to hang up his clothing. The night staff at the dorm almost croaked when they found him standing on the top rung of a ladder-back chair in his closet. He has an unusual sense of balance for a deaf child. So, let him do something like that. Just keep him busy. Poor little fellow. It must be hard for him to not know what happened and everything has gone black."

"It's even worse because I can't even explain what happened, or worse yet, how you feel," I said.

"Thank God, he is already enrolled in the Deaf-Blind program there or else he would've had to wait another year."

After David left for work that next morning, I gently placed Li'l David's hands into the warm water. He smiled. I encouraged him silently to feel the sudsy water in the sink. I then took his hand and let him feel my hands as I went through the motion of washing glasses, then silverware, and then the dishes. He was so tiny he had to stand on our kitchen chair to reach the sink. I tied my plastic bib apron on his neck. He wasn't smiling. He was so serious. The water was practically up past his elbows. Water was everywhere! But he was seriously cleaning those dishes. I practically waded in water because he splashed it all over the kitchen floor. It took practically all day for him to finish the dishes. I had to mop and wipe up water from the floor and off the counters. It was worth it because when he finished, he simply laid his head on my lap while I watched the daily soap operas. I couldn't clean or do anything around the house. I had to sit there. If I tried to leave him for any reason, he was terrified and clung to me. He would grip my clothing so tight until I couldn't pry his fingers off. He didn't understand what was happening to him and neither did I. I let him hold me and even go into the bathroom with me for the first two weeks after he went blind. I felt him trembling from fear and I knew he was frightened out of his mind. I spent hours each day sitting on the living room couch, crying my heart out for my baby. I asked God, "Why? Why?" Li'l David would just lie there and stare into the deep dark world he was forced into. It was the third week when got a call from Evelyn.

"What are you doing?"

I was crying so hard until I could hardly answer her. I forced the words out the best I could.

"I'm just sitting here watching TV."

"Where is Little David?"

"He's sitting right here resting his head on my lap."

"Why?"

"Why? He can't do anything else, can he?"

"How about you getting up off the couch and leading Little David to the wall and let him trail his hands along the wall so that he will start to learn his way around the house?"

"He won't let me up from this couch!"

"Oh, just try it. He'll have to get up if you do. So stop feeling sorry for David, get up, and do it. Now!"

She sounded like a military officer.

"I don't think that it's going to help him. He won't understand. Why am I doing this?"

I simply heard a loud sigh of disgust and impatience on the other end of the phone line.

"Okay!" I said.

I jumped to my feet and tucked the phone under my chin so I could listen to her instructions. When I set David down on his feet, he began shaking. I hugged him first, grabbed hold of his left hand, then took his right hand and placed it on the wall and coaxed him to feel the wall as we walked along the hallway. I showed him how to trail the wall.

"Janie, Janie, are you there?" Evelyn yelled into the phone. "Yes, I have the phone under my chin so I can hear you talk." "Well? What is he doing?"

"David is so smart. He's trailing the wall with his hand! He just felt a open space in the wall. Now, he knows there is a door there. He is feeling everything! The bathroom sink, the toilet, and the bathtub. He is shaking his head in acknowledgment. He knows that I'm showing him the bathroom."

"Good!" Her excitement was contagious. I was ecstatic. "I don't want you just sitting there with him. It's no good for you or the rest of the family. Soon, David has to get ready to help you with his little baby brother or sister." Evelyn laughed loud, and then became serious again.

"By the way, when are you due?" she asked.

"Around the end of September. I've got a little two months to go."

"Good! I know the last two months seem to drag. Are you getting big?"

"Getting big? I'm huge now. The doctor said I can't gain any more weight.'

"Well, you have your hands full. All I can tell you is to keep David's hands busy. Give him things to touch and give him something to do."

"Okay, thanks."

"Continue to let him wash dishes and let him help you with the baby after it arrives."

"I do, but when he washes the dishes, he always spills water and I have to mop it up. Big David made me stop holding him all the time but he can't see anybody and it was already hard for him when he couldn't hear but this is too much. I'm taking him to his ophthalmologist appointment at Oak Knoll in August. It seems so far away. The time is creeping along."

I took a deep breath as I fought back tears.

"I'm so worried. I feel like each day he may have less of a chance of regaining his sight."

"Why didn't you just take him there in the first place?"

"Well, I don't know how to drive yet and this old mean doctor at Presidio examined him and persuaded Big David to wait until August to take him to Oak Knoll. I kept insisting we go to Oak Knoll that night but he wouldn't listen to me! That doctor said that due to the holiday, that no doctors would be on staff there; and that there was no evidence of bleeding or the cornea or the retina, there was no rush, so we had nothing to worry about.

"I tried to persuade David to take us on that night anyway but he trusted that doctor. Of course, he would. I didn't because of my past experiences with doctors who were indifferent.

"I don't know how to drive! But I swear that I'm going to learn how, very soon."

"Well, this is as good a time as ever to do it. Get someone to teach you as soon as possible." Evelyn let out a long sigh, indicating she was getting restless.

"Well, I've got to go to my class at U.C. Berkeley," she said with pride, "Did you know I'm working on my thesis to earn my degree in special education. Got to go. I will check back in on you in a few days."

I sighed with relief after she hung up. God had sent me an angel of encouragement.

From that day forward, Li'l David and I did everything together, washing and drying dishes, laundry, making beds, cleaning the bathroom, vacuuming, dusting, and polishing everything.

It was an ongoing battle with David. I insisted on taking Li'l David to the bathroom with me. Most the time, David won the war. David pulled Li'l David off me, prying his little fingers from around my dress tail. He would scream in terror.

"Let him go, David," I protested loudly. "Poor baby, he has to go with me."

It was so pitiful watching Li'l David lying on the floor whimpering like a wounded animal while waiting for me to come out the closed door. Whenever David wasn't looking, I would sneak him in. Whenever he caught me, we had our usual shouting match.

"He has to learn he can't go everywhere with you," David would yell.

"You don't understand. Li'l David can't see me and he's frightened. He wants to make sure I'm near, that he won't be alone. I am his mother. I know my son. Please."

David finally gave in.

"Okay, I am going to stay out of it," he said, shaking his finger at me. "But you're starting something you're going to regret later. I'm warning you, you'll be sorry."

I felt such relief the day we traveled to Oak Knoll Hospital. The days before the appointment seemed like years. I waited to tell the doctor my theory. David gave me a hunch to quiet me down. It was to no avail.

"I was thinking maybe he had cataracts again because he waves his hands in front of his eyes as he did before his eye surgery."

The ophthalmologist didn't say a word. He was busy examining Li'l David's eyes. I noticed he used the big black ophthalmology machine with lighted gadgets attached to it.

I rambled on as he worked.

David rolled his eyes back into his head. It was his signal for me to be quiet. I chose to ignore him.

"That doctor at Presidio, I didn't trust him," I continued. "He didn't use this equipment to examine my son's eyes."

"What did he use?" the doctor asked as he applied some ointment in David's eyes. "We will have to let this sit in his eyes for a few minute so they can dilate. Then we can see what the problem is."

He sat down on a stool nearby as I stood holding Li'l David's hand so he would know I was there.

"Doctor, what do you think caused his blindness?" David asked. "It is temporary? Will he be able to see again?"

"We will only be able to determine what happened after a complete examination."

"That doctor at Presidio said that he couldn't find anything wrong. He said he didn't find any bleeding in the cornea. He told us to wait for my son's scheduled appointment with you."

Another doctor was now putting on his white vinyl gloves. Our doctor introduced us to him. As he prepared to give David an examination, I prayed silently.

Lord, I know that you can heal him. If it's Your will, Lord, let the doctors find the cause for David's blindness and give him back his sight. Please Lord!

My heart beat fast. David grabbed my hand as we sat tensely awaiting the verdict. David gave my hand a firm gentle squeeze, then, he winked then gave me a reassuring smile.

The doctor began to speak then hesitated, disbelief showed on his face.

"It's hard to believe a doctor would tell you to wait 30 days to see an eye specialist. Are you sure that he told you to wait? It is obvious something is wrong. How long has it been since this occurred?"

Fighting back tears, I forced the words out, as my throat seemed to close in on me. I tried to be strong to explain. David finished the story because I lost it. I wept like a baby.

"Sir, would it have made a difference if I had brought him here sooner?" "It's hard to say. I don't want you blaming yourself. I just cannot understand why the doctor insisted on you waiting. You could have brought him to the emergency room."

"I wanted to come here but my husband listened to the doctor," I said. I looked at David. I whispered in his ear, "I told you so."

David let out a big sigh. He was obvious he felt bad about the situation. I wished I could take back what I said. He had beaten himself up enough already.

The ophthalmologist went down the hall discussing Li'l David's case with another doctor. It seemed like eternity before he returned. Two more doctors accompanied him. They followed him into the room where we stood over Li'l David. He looked so tiny and helpless sitting in that big chair. He held on to me with a death-defying grip. My son was frightened to death. The doctors took turns examining his eyes.

They shot questions from every direction. More doctors arrived crowding into that little room. Flashbacks of my first encounters with eye doctors popped into my head. These new young men were there to learn just like the first ones. They began firing questions at us, too. I was accustomed to this but I could see David was annoyed.

One of the young interns asked, "How did this happen? Did he fall or something?"

"Just tell us slowly what happened," another doctor asked me the same questions as he sat down on a stool in front of Li'l David. There was still another doctor, who couldn't have been more than 25, ready to write with his pen and paper.

A third intern then said, "It states here in his medical chart he had congenital cataracts. It also says he is profoundly deaf. Has any members of either of your families had any history of blindness or deafness?"

"No, nobody, sir," David answered.

I just shook my head.

"Because of the rubella syndrome epidemic last year, we found out from the newspaper our son's deafness and sight problems were effected by my wife contracting German measles during her pregnancy, sir."

The doctor nodded, showing acknowledgment as he continued writing on David's medical records. "Rubella syndrome is what they called the birth defect."

"Why didn't you bring him in earlier, right after the incident," another doctor asked. David explained again.

"Would it have made a difference if we had brought him in sooner?" I was looking at my husband.

"Time is always of the essence whenever there is any sort of illness. The eyes are made of such sensitive and delicate materials it is best to be expedient in receiving the proper medical care."

"Oh, so are you saying we shouldn't have waited the 30 days for his scheduled appointment?"

The head ophthalmologist didn't answer but diverted his attention to my son who was fighting the assistants as they tried to hold him down. Li'l David was putting up a good fight. He was squealing in pain while raising himself up off the examination table.

There were at least three nurses and two medics holding him down. "Well, let's see what the problem is before we continue our conversation."

He turned on the big bright light so it would shine directly into Little David's eyes.

I cried every tear my son cried while on that table. David took charge. He spoke sternly to me. "You have got to get yourself together, Janie. You are not helping this situation by crying."

He touched Li'l David's hand firmly. He recognized his father's touch and relaxed for the doctor.

Several more doctors came in to examine Little David. We were growing weary. I knew something was definitely wrong. It didn't look good. I was having flashbacks of when he had the first cataract surgery. These doctors were very considerate and compassionate yet professional. I felt more at ease this time.

Finally, they took us into an office and gave us the news.

"Sgt. and Mrs. Bess, after thoroughly examining your son, we are sad to say, that this is unfortunate but David had congenital cataracts at birth. We had never heard of an infant having cataracts. The problem we are dealing with now that is your son has an eye disease called glaucoma. You see, your son is in excruciating pain. This is due to…"

"Glaucoma? "David asked with a puzzled look on his face. He was frowning, trying to understand. He looked back at the doctor then said, "Doctor, what Is glaucoma? What caused him to have Glaucoma?"

"We don't know the cause for the glaucoma. I feel because he had congenital cataracts, this may have come from that. It is a highly unusual case. We are going to have to perform surgery. You see the pressure behind the eyes have built up behind the walls of the pupils. We need to go in and remove the pressure which in turn should relieve some of the pain."

"Will he be able to see again?"

"I can't say. But from looking at the x-rays, it looks as there is a small chance, but we won't know until we perform the surgery. He has to be in intense pain!"

I tried to speak but I was all choked up. Tears flowed down my cheeks. I simply wiped them away with my hand.

"Doctor, you said you have to operate to relieve the pressure behind the eyes. Once the pressure is relieved, will he be able to see?"

The doctor was sitting down with his hand on his chin. I recognized that look. It happened to be the same look the doctors gave me when they had to tell me my son had to have cataract surgery. He spoke in a soft professional manner. It seemed like he was trying to think of a way to soften the blow. He stood up from his chair as he answered me. His held his head down slightly and he looked into my eyes.

"I'm sorry, Mrs. Bess, we cannot promise you that he will be able to see. It appears from the X-rays the optic nerve has snapped due to all the pressure that had built up. The retina appears to be destroyed from all of the pressure.

"Your son, David, will need to stay here tonight. We will give him something to relieve the pain. Then early tomorrow morning, we will perform surgery."

"I'm still going to pray for a miracle. God can do anything but fail," I added.

"I'm sorry, Sgt and Mrs. Bess, I wish we had other alternatives but we don't. We are merely going in to remove the pressure from behind the eyes. We hope this will relieve the pressure. Mrs. Bess, we don't want you worrying. We want to make sure that you have a happy healthy baby. So try to sleep, okay?"

"Thank you sir. My baby is due in about four more weeks and we haven't even had time to buy the anything for our new baby."

"Is this your second child?"

"No, sir, we have a little girl who will be 2 this month."

"Well, you just go home and try to rest. Come back in the morning if you want to be here. Surgery should only take about three hours."

"Thank you, sir," David said as he escorted us toward the elevator door to the admittance office. I was sobbing without any shame. "My poor little boy. Lord, why is this happening to us again?"

David was trying to comfort me.

"Janie, get hold of yourself. This won't help David. You've got to be strong, baby."

When we finished filling out the papers, we went to Li'l David's room. He'd fallen asleep from all of the medication they had given him. He was exhausted from the long trip from San Rafael to Oakland. When all those doctors came in to see this rare case of glaucoma, he was fighting with all of strength to keep them from his eyes.

We sat by his bed in the pediatrics ward until he was fast asleep then we sneaked out.

"David, I just won't be able to leave him if he wakes up and starts crying."

We returned early the next morning just in time for David's surgery. Due to the traffic on the San Rafael bridge we were running late. We arrived just as they were wheeling him into surgery.

I couldn't help it. David tried to comfort me but I couldn't stop crying.

Looking at my little boy who was only 5 ½ going back and forth through surgery doors since birth was too much for me. He looked so tiny on that hospital cot as he went past us. He was under anesthesia so he didn't know what was happening.

It was a long, long wait. I counted. Seven hours had passed since they'd taken Li'l David into surgery. Afterwards, the doctors came over to talk to us.

"Sgt and Mrs. Bess, you are close to your due date. We're aware you're in your eighth month of pregnancy."

David proudly answered for me. "Yep! Knowing Janie, she is so active. She might have our baby anytime."

"We would like to recommend that David remain here for at least six weeks. You need the rest and also some time to adjust to your new baby, so if you'd like, we'll keep him here under our care. It is difficult for you, I am sure, to see your son like this but I assure you it will be in your son's best interest and yours."

I looked up at David who was standing behind me now. I didn't want Li'l David to stay there too long. I didn't say anything. I looked up at David, searching his face for an answer.

"Can we give you an answer later tomorrow, sir?" "Sure, I understand."

"We'd like to talk about it first. I assure you we'll get back to you. After we talk it over tonight."

"The reason we asked you this is, Sgt Bess, because the procedure we used to remove the pressure is a very delicate procedure. We need to keep David under observation. We need time to examine him on an hourly basis. We are aware of his heart murmur and wish to ensure that before he goes home, he is free from any more complications. For about six weeks, Little David will be in such intense pain. We want to staff to be available to administer his medications and keep him under constant observation. So let us know. He will have a private room with his own nurse. He'll be in good hands, I promise.

"By the way, he is a strong little guy. He is quite intelligent, too. The nurses here just adore him."

"Yes, he certainly is quite a character," David said with pride.

"Doctor," I said, interrupting their light-hearted conversation. "How was his surgery? Will he be able to see again?"

I could tell by the look in the doctor's eyes it was not good news.

My stomach felt queasy just then. I ran from the room straight to the bathroom. I felt sick and couldn't hold anything on my stomach. I hadn't eaten anything so I had the dry heaves instead. I didn't want anyone to see me cry again."

"Oh, Lord, why? Why? Why" I screamed out in the ladies room. David came running in after me.

"David. This is the ladies bathroom. You can't come in here."

"I want you to calm down and come out of here," David said, grabbing my hand to lead me out. "Get hold of yourself, Janie."

He then held me by my shoulders and looked firmly in my eyes and shook me gently as if to shake away my fears and doubts.

"You've got to stop this crying, Janie! You don't realize I am just as upset as you are. Try to calm down. You don't need to be upset. We have a baby coming soon and you need to concentrate on that. I will handle this. I only ask one thing. I need you to be strong and stay with me through this. Understand?" He hugged me close to him just then. "Come on, baby, OK?" He stared at me with his halfway smile.

"Y-y-yes," I managed to get out. My whole chest trembled. My loud breathing came from my mouth. I tried to stop crying. "David, I'm scared! Lord knows Li'l David doesn't deserve this. Whatever I've done, Lord please, I keep asking You to punish me! Not our son!"

David stormed out of the bathroom. I knew he was disappointed in me. He couldn't understand how I felt. I yelled out the bathroom door as he walked away, "You didn't know what I went through before. You weren't there."

I didn't care if I hurt his feelings. I wanted to strike out at someone. I was tired of pretending to be strong. I just wanted to crawl into a hole and just die.

I tried composing myself before returning to the doctor's office. David sat in a chair facing the doctor as if waiting on a verdict. I heard David as he swallowed hard. Leaning forward in his chair, he spoke softly, "Doctor, sir, is it possible for me to donate one of my eyes to my son and if my wife gave one of her eyes, too, would Little David see again?"

"Sgt. Bess," the doctor said, shaking his head. "I don't know if you understand what caused the loss of your son's vision." He took a deep breath then sighed. I could see him struggling, trying to think how to explain it to us in laymen's terms.

"Sgt. Bess, in this case, it is not a temporary loss of vision. You see, it was caused by the pressure building up behind the eyes, which caused the optic nerve to snap. This destroyed the retina, which takes a picture. Let's say, it's like a camera without a lens. You can put film in it but without a lens, it cannot take pictures."

David and I answered simultaneously, "Oh, I see." We always seemed to think alike. We looked at each other and laughed. Our laughter actually helped me to relax. Just a little.

CHAPTER TWENTY-EIGHT

D ays turned into weeks. They were still performing surgery to relieve the pressure behind Li'l David's eyes. He ended up staying in the hospital more than 60 days.

Meanwhile, on Sept. 13, 1967, I went into labor.

I had an easy natural birth. It wasn't very painful probably because I had the baby only 10 minutes after arriving at the hospital. David had to wait in the delivery waiting room. Then, the rule was that husbands weren't allowed in the delivery room. I hated that. I wanted my husband to be with me more than ever because Li'l was in the hospital at the same time. Wouldn't you know it, the laws changed shortly after Tony's birth? Soon after, fathers were allowed in the delivery room.

Tony was born at Hamilton Air Force Base in Novato at 9:13 a.m. He weighed 5 pounds, 13 ounces, and was 18 inches long.

We were the proudest parents on this earth. He was a beautiful boy. His big dreamy eyes were just so cute. His long curly lashes rested on his round fat cheeks. He looked like me. I was elated.

The doctors dismissed Li'l David one month after Tony's birth. The doctors said we needed the time to adjust to our new baby. David and I were eternally grateful to the doctors at Oak Knoll Naval Hospital.

Li'l David came home on the weekend. The following Monday, David started back to school at the California School for the Blind.

As we drove into the school's entranceway, I heard Little David chuckle. I turned around from the front seat to the backseat to look at him., I saw this big smile on his face. He could actually tell when we entered the school grounds at California School for the Blind. Whenever we hit the familiar speed bump on the long curving road leading to his dormitory, he burst out in laughter and nodded his head up and down as if to say, Yes, I'm at home now. A beautiful smile appeared on his face as we came to a complete stop in front of his dorm building. He could tell we had stopped there. He laughed gleefully, grabbed his backpack and darted out the rear car door before we could stop him. He sped up the curved walkway, laughing as he ran. When he reached the big metal double doors, he put both hands on the metal bar handle and pushed it open. He was so strong. In he ran, laughing out of pure joy.

"Janie, you had better catch him," David said. "He might hurt himself."

"David, can't you tell?" I said, trying to calm him. "He knows where he is."

"Janie, go get him. He can't see where he is going."

"But David, didn't you see him run out of the car and onto the school grounds, onto the curved walkway? He went straight through the double doors."

I was so excited because my son had not laughed or played since that terrible 4th of July. There had not been any signs of happiness at all.

"I don't care," David yelled. "You had better catch him. He might hurt himself or somebody else running wild like that."

I answered back as I chased after Li'l David, "He seemed to know where he was, honey. Besides, I can't catch him."

⚬⚬◦⦂🙢🙠⦂◦⚬⚬

Months rolled by fast. Li'l David was back to his usual routine at the school now. He adjusted surprisingly fast. Even after his loss of sight, he was back to his old antics. Before he could see but couldn't hear but now his world was dark and yet he still managed to stand on a chair and hang his clothes up in his dorm closet. I stood there and watched in amazement as he trailed his hands around the room to find his dresser. He unpacked his suitcase, carefully laying each piece of clothing neatly folded into his drawers.

He had learned to use his fingers for everything. He would touch our faces to distinguish the different characteristics and facial features of each person. He could decipher if you were short or tall. He was also able to sense where he was; whether he was at school, home or at relatives' houses.

We were not aware of how many capabilities he had until his teacher told us about her latest adventure with Li'l David.

We arrived at the dorm to pick Little David up for his weekend visit.

The first person we saw was Evelyn Greenleaf, my angel of encouragement, who was now principal of the school. She decided to become a teacher for the deaf because of her son was deaf and she wanted to learn how to use sign language to be able to communicate with him.

She sat talking to the other teachers and counselors at a long conference table in the dorm's playroom when we arrived. It appeared they were having a meeting or something.

Evelyn got up from the table and came over to greet us. As she hobbled over on her crutches to meet us, I looked down at her right leg. A large white cast covered the right foot and continued up her leg stopping within inches from her knee.

"Well, well, Evelyn, whatever happened to you," David asked.

Evelyn laughed and directed her looks at all the other teachers who were sitting there. They laughed, too, as if we had told a joke.

One of the dorm counselors looked at Evelyn very seriously and said, "Do you want to tell them or should I?"

Evelyn guffawed, then said, "Well, you won't believe this but it's your son's fault."

"What did he do?" we both asked. Our voices rang out in unison. David and I just stared at each other before busting out in laughter.

"Well, are you ready to hear this?" Evelyn asked. She always kept her glasses on a silver chain that hung around her neck whenever they were not in use. She took them off now and let them drop casually onto the front of her copper cashmere sweater.

I looked at David and he looked down at me. We both just nodded.

"Well, it started with Li'l David. He was running through the corridors as though he could see. He was feeling the walls as he headed straight for the double doors with the metal handlebars. I had to move fast because David was moving very fast. As we sat talking at this very same table, David flew past us headed for the double doors. I thought he was going to hit his head on the metal bars. He was running full speed ahead. Now, the left door was already held open with a large doorstopper but the right door was closed. David was running straight to the right door." Evelyn pointed with her long thin fingers to the door. The one side was closed. "I yelled out, 'Somebody stop him. He's going to crash into the metal door.'"

Another teacher, Martha, then cut in, "Oh, get to the point, Evelyn."

"No, you tell them," she said, shaking her head slowly back and forth as if in shock. "I can't stop laughing."

"Evelyn jumped up to stop David because he was headed straight for the closed door. She bolted from her chair, ran toward the door but lost her balance on the slippery waxed floors and went down with a loud thud."

The teacher was laughing uncontrollably now until tears were actually coming from her eyes. Seeing that her co-worker was having difficulty finishing the story, Evelyn took over again.

"Then what happened," David asked.

"Well, Evelyn lost her footing and, and went up in the air, landed on her backside and went sailing on her tailbone across the room."

Martha broke into hysterical laughter again.

"Guess what," Martha said. David and I both were anxiously waiting for the rest of the story. It was obvious by our wide-eyed expressions. My mouth was wide open in total disbelief; as they dragged on with the story.

Again, David and I answered in unison.

"What?"

"We stood there, frozen in our tracks. At the last minute, the little devil went through the open door on the left. As if he could see it."

"Poor Evelyn! We all helped her up and she hobbled to a nearby chair."

"That's the last time that I try to save him," Evelyn chimed in. "I could've sworn he actually detected that the right door was closed." She was still shaking her head in disbelief. "I can't figure out for the life of me how he knew that the door was open."

"God is looking out for him," I said.

"Li'l David is like a blind bat," David said. "He must have extra sensory perception. A bat can detect an open window or door yet he cannot see anything, either. That's where the saying blind as a bat came from."

We were all laughing now.

"Do you think that maybe he can see a little bit?" asked Martha.

"You know, no, but I believe God gave him extra senses since he lost his sight," I said, then laughed again. "I have to tell you guys the story about what happened to David this summer at my Aunt Flo's house."

All eyes were on me as I continued.

"I got a job this summer right before school started and my aunt volunteered to baby-sit There was two incidences that stood out in my mind letting me know God was leading David and protecting him. The first incident happened when Flo was in her living room lying down on the sofa. She was talking on the phone to somebody. Meanwhile, all seven of her children and the three of mine were sitting in a semi-circle on the carpet watching television.

"Flo's youngest son, Deanie, was only 3. He was annoyed with Li'l David who was constantly touching and feeling him.

"He said, 'Mama, Li'l David keeps touching me.' He looked to his mother for help. 'Mama, tell Li'l David to stop.'"

"Flo answered back, 'He's not hurting you, Deanie. Stop acting silly. It doesn't hurt. He's only touching you.'

"'Uh, hum, Mama, I'm going to hit him if he touch me again.' Flo reassured him. 'That's how he can tell who you are by feeling you.'

242

"Deanie had grown impatient with David. He hit Li'l David really hard and looked to see if his mother saw it. She did.

"'OK, Deanie, don't say nothing if he hauls off and knocks the mess out of you.'

"Deanie had a plan. After smacking David a second time, he repositioned himself on the other side of the circle mingling in with the crowd. He hid by moving in order to camouflage himself.

"Deanie boasted loudly, 'See, Mama, David can't see or hear so he won't be able to find me now.'

"He then began chanting as he relaxed next to his big brother. 'David can't see me, ya, ya, ya, ya. David can't hear me, ya, ya, ya, ya.' His big dark eyes were just gleaming with mischief. He was giggling hysterically. He thought he'd gotten away clean.

"But it wasn't over yet. David was busy caressing and touching each and every one of the faces sitting in the half circle. He nodded his head to show it wasn't the right person as he touched each child.

"Flo gave Deanie a fair warning. 'Okay, boy, don't say nothing if he hits you back, I done told you.'

"Finally, David reached Deanie. First, he felt all over Deanne's long head then next he trailed his fingers all over Deanne's thin face. He used both hands to feel Dean's distinguishably high cheekbones.

"With the biggest smile on his face, David chuckled. He nodded his head then reared his right hand back and smacked Deanne's face with a loud wallop. He slapped Deanie so hard Deanie's head practically went from one side to the other.

"Deanie was stunned at first. When he realized what had happened, he yelled, 'Mama, David can see. He can hear' It was completely quiet for about one half a second. Flo was trying hard but couldn't suppress the laughter any longer. She laughed so hard she had to hold her stomach in pure agony.

"Big tears rolled down her cheeks and as she wiped them away with her hands she said, 'See, I told you to leave that boy alone.' She chuckled again trying hard to regain her composure.

"She kneeled down and held Deanie by the shoulders as she looked into his eyes. She was still trying to keep her cool as she spoke to him. 'I bet you'll believe me now when I tell you that David can see you, huh?'

"'Yes, Mama.'

"Now all of the children were laughing hysterically. Deanie stopped crying and was looking forlornly at all the children and his mother, who was totally out of control now. There was complete chaos in that household at that moment.

"'It's not funny, Mama. Make them stop laughing at me.'

"'I can't stop laughing myself,' she said. Deanie went to bed voluntarily, not because his Mama made him, but from total embarrassment.

"Later that summer, Li'l David and my other two were still at Flo's place in East Oakland. They stayed with her the whole summer. Well, she lives in a housing project there. There are about 50 apartment buildings and they are all identical." I leaned forward in my chair to emphasize, "I get lost there sometimes myself."

"You remember I said my aunt has seven children, right? On this particular day, they all went to the park to play. They took Li'l David and my other two children, Terri and Tony, along with them. They were given instructions the larger children were to look after the smaller ones. They were warned they had better watch my three children, especially Li'l David. 'And you had better not lose any of them' was Flo's final warning.

"It was still light out when they returned home around 7 p.m. But in their haste to get home before dark, they had forgotten to count heads. Everybody assumed everybody was accounted for. As they entered into the living room, Flo took a head count. She immediately noticed Li'l David was missing.

"'Where is Little David?' she asked.

"Everybody started passing the buck. Flo grew impatient with them as they all made sorry excuses.

"'I want all of you to go and find Li'l David and you had better not come home without him. Now I mean that.'

"They all took out running. The four oldest children were sent back out to search for Li'l David. She kept all the other children at home. It was getting late and it was dark outside. No sign of them yet. She became worried and contemplated whether to call the police. Now there were five children missing. She couldn't leave the other children for they were now asleep on the couch.

"Just as she reached for the phone to call the police station, there was a loud knock on the door. Flo ran to answer it. Upon opening the door, she discovered Li'l David standing there. She looked outside on the porch thinking that someone surely must have brought David home. The other children were nowhere in sight.

"Just then her phone rang. One of her neighbors called to let her know that her oldest children were there. They told her that they were afraid to come home. They told the neighbor if they didn't find David they couldn't come home. They had searched all over the area for David and couldn't find him anywhere. After two hours of futile searching they had become frustrated and gave up. They were afraid to face their mother so they had gone to a neighbor's house, sadly anticipating a good whipping.

"My theory was that Li'l David must have smelled his way home because Flo was an excellent cook and you could smell her food from several blocks away. Flo also believed that's how David found his way home because all of the apartment units were identical.

"So that's my story. I believe David must have X-ray vision."

Evelyn then said, "I wish God had given me X-ray vision to see that David was going to go through that open door then I wouldn't have tried to catch him. It's David's fault. When he gets old enough I'm going to tell him how he caused me all this pain and suffering."

We all laughed and nodded our heads in agreement.

"My mother says God has a protective arm around that child," I said.

"I believe it, too," Evelyn responded. "We just can't figure out how he knew which way to go. And how did he know that one of the doors were open?"

"Beats me," said the other teacher, hunching up her shoulders.

"I hate to break this up, but we have to get going before the traffic starts on the San Rafael bridge," David said. Amid much laughter, we left.

CHAPTER TWENTY-NINE

G od gave me the extra help that I needed so badly—my toddler daughter. She was an angel from heaven.

Terri always amazed me. At the age of 2, she showed such maturity. She was such a big help to me. She would escort Li'l David around the house until he was accustomed to his surroundings. Terri would lead him outside so he could play with the neighbor kids. She would talk to him as if he could hear her. When it was time to eat, she would lead him to the table and would motion him toward a chair.

"Sit down, David," Terri would say as she patted the seat. He seemed to understand her.

She was very patient with her brother. For this I was truly thankful.

Li'l David was even more amazing to me. God was surely showing him things. If I didn't know any better I would have believed he could actually see. God revealed to me how he works through watching my son as he went about his new life adjusting to the darkness and yet being able to decipher things only God could have given him. He recognized familiar places. By touching your hands and feeling your face, he could distinguish your identity. To identify his cousins, he would make home signs to help us distinguish something about them that was a part of their character. It was so cute. My niece Trena visited us every summer. She always spent quality time with David. She would sit for hours just playing with his wooden puzzles and games using shapes. Trena was one of his favorite cousins. To ask for

Trena, he placed both fists on each side of his head while opening and closing his little hands to illustrate her hairstyle. Trena always wore her hair parted straight down the middle with Afro puffs on both sides of her head. He repeated this motion several times until she showed up. Once she sat beside him, he would smile, nodding his head.

After Tony was born, I could sense Li'l David knew the little bundle. Even when I was pregnant, somehow he knew the large bulge at my stomach was his little brother. I had no way to communicate to him but I could detect by his actions, he was aware the bulge disappeared. He felt my flat stomach after he came home from the hospital. He rocked his arms back and forth to communicate his wish to hold his little brother.

During the week, he stayed at the dorms at the residential school. On the weekends, David always came home from school. He was so excited to see Terri and Tony. He proved to be a big help to me. He was an expert at tracing the walls with his fingers and was constantly running from memory through he house with his little sister holding his hand. If we were out in unfamiliar territory, she would guide him through the crowds.

He knew the sign for baby. By folding his arms in front of his body as if it was a cradle and rocking his arms back and forward, he would demonstrate as if he were rocking a baby. That's how he asked permission to hold little Tony. He felt my hands often to decipher whether I was changing diapers, bathing or feeding Tony. He would dash off to the dresser drawer bringing a fresh diaper to me. We used cloth diapers in those days. He always took the soiled diaper from me to a diaper pail for laundering. He would always remember to wash his hands afterward. I could only stare in wonder.

Li'l David had gotten my daily routine down to a science. After the diaper change, I would arrange Tony in my arms to nurse him. David always took the cue. He'd run to the kitchen and open the refrigerator to get the baby's bottled milk. He knew where everything was. His next step was to place the cold milk into the bottle warmer on the kitchen counter. David and Terri always waited patiently until it was ready. Terri was his eyes. He always brought it to me once it was warm. Terri imitated me, testing it on her inner wrist before giving it to Little David. His little hands had become his eyes and his ears. His fingers were sensitized to heat and cold as well as textures. He used his hands to determine identity shape, size and height.

When I finished feeding Tony, David knew the next step would be bath time for baby brother. He would run and get the blue plastic bathtub from the bathroom and place it in the kitchen sink. He'd pull a kitchen chair up to the sink to reach the faucet and actually run warm water in the bathtub. He had observed me using my elbow to test the water so he imitated that, too. It was truly amazing to watch. He couldn't see a thing yet he moved around as if he had vision.

One weekend, my cousin LC. drove up on his shiny black Harley-Davidson into our carport. It was a beautiful warm day in October. David was outside raking leaves off the front lawn. He revved his motor loudly. David dropped the rake and went over to greet him.

"Hey, man, this is a quiet neighborhood," David said, joking with LC. LC stepped off his bike, hugging David. They laughed together. David gave him "Five" before LC removed his helmet and followed David through the side door. I was bathing the baby in the kitchen with Li'l David and Terri as my helpers.

LC was a short man, yet he walked as though he was six feet tall. He always stood up straight and proud. His dark slanted eyes always shined with mischief. His strong deep voice carried. His contagious laughter was surprisingly high and shrill. LC's dry sense of humor always made me laugh incessantly even when his conversation was insidiously ridiculous.

To identify LC, Li'l David touched his hands and then his face to feel his features. David felt LC's long wavy hair. Once he recognized LC, he nodded then smiled. He continued to feel his face. His smooth skin reflected his delicate features and distinguishably high cheekbones. Li'l David chuckled lightly as he felt LC's black leather jacket, the big ring on his left ring finger and his leather pants.

"Tell him that's enough," LC said. "He know who it is by now, don't he?" He snickered.

We both laughed as David pulled Li'l David away.

"Well, he has to touch you to see who you are," I said.

"Well, don't you think that he figured it out by now?" LC quipped back.

"Oh, shut up, LC," I joked and swatted him on his right arm.

"Damn, you are just like your son. Now I see where he got it from, touching everybody."

We both broke out in laughter.

David grumbled as he led his son away. He gave me a disgusting look. I had known David long enough to read his mind. His eyes said, "Stop Li'l David from touching so much. It's annoying." David and I had never set any limits on how long or where Li'l David could touch. I just shrugged my shoulders at him.

After all the formalities, LC sat down to have a drink with David. They watched TV for a long while. During commercials, LC had a surprised look on his face as he watched Li'l David.

"I heard little David had eye surgery."

"He did," I said.

LC interrupted me.

"Li'l David can see now, right?"

"No, LC, Li'l David can't see," David said.

"Didn't he have surgery? David, I thought you said the doctors had saved his sight when he went to that Navy hospital?"

"No, I didn't say that. I said they tried to save his sight."

"Them doctors lied to you."

David and I both sighed loudly.

"About what, LC?" I said.

LC ignored me completely.

"I know he probably can't hear very good, but I'm sure that boy can see."

Simultaneously, we rolled our eyes at LC.

"I've been watching Li'l David for quite a while now and since I've been sittin' he hasn't ran into nothin'. He ran through here like a bolt of lightening without touching any furniture or anything." He pointed at Li'l David who had pulled a kitchen chair up to the sink. He stood on the chair at the kitchen sink and was elbow-deep in suds.

"What he doing now? He didn't bump into nothin' and now he standing up there washin' dishes?"

We both insisted, "He can't see, LC."

"Ain't no way he can do all the things, washing dishes, getting the baby's diapers for Janie. Uh uh. Y'all tell that to somebody else."

"No, really," David said. "You remember on the 4th of July when we had to rush him to the hospital?"

"Man! All I remember about the 4th was I had to take Melba and her friends. Don't you remember? She nearly had her baby at yo' house. Matter of fact, it was right here, at this house. I was gone, man. I had to lead her family to the San Rafael Bridge 'cause they followed me over here and didn't know how to get back to Richmond. First, we followed that ambulance straight up to the hospital. She had that baby before we headed out, too."

LC had a faraway look on his face as he described the events. He laughed again. We laughed, too. LC exchanged glances with us.

"I found out about Little David later, just bits and pieces, though. I can't remember who told me, I think Aunt Johnnie did."

"Oh, yeah," I said. "Mother told me she had talked to you."

I knew it was coming. David always made sarcastic remarks whenever Mother's name was mentioned.

"Oh, yeah, tel-a gram, tel-a-Mother, tel-a-Everybody."

LC cracked up again. I swung at David, but he moved too fast. David talked, still shielding his face just in case I swung again.

"Like I was saying, LC, Li'l David's optic nerves snapped from the pressure, destroying his sight. They said it was glaucoma." It was hard for David to talk about, but he was doing fine. "So there is no way he will ever see again."

"Aw, that boy can see," LC persisted. His front tooth was gold. It twinkled with his mischievous smile. When he laughed, his slanted eyes would close.

"He has to be able to see something, the way he ran through this house. He didn't bump a thang."

I took a deep breath.

"Believe me, LC, David can't see. The doctor had to remove the retina from both eyes."

Tears welled up. I fought them back.

"What's the retina?"

Big David hugged me close to his side.

"That's the lens of the eyes," I explained through tears. "Without the lens, he can't see. The doctors said. 'it's like a camera without a lens.'"

Shaking his head, LC said, "I don't care what y'all say. Li'l David can see." He laughed, watching Li'l David move about unassisted.

L.C. giggled, "Hee! Hee Hee! That nigger can see."

I gave up it was nearly impossible to convince LC otherwise. To this day, LC still says, "Li'l David can see somethin', I know."

I believe God sent LC of all people to show us how well Li'l David was doing. David and I needed talk about it. Before that day, I felt nothing but pity for my son.

CHAPTER THIRTY

I t was a nice summer day when I wandered into the personnel office at the Base Exchange and put in an application while David shopped for garden tools. I had heard they were hiring for the fall. David suggested I wait until Tony was at least 2 before going to work. I only planned to buy Tony a play pen because he was starting to crawl and get into everything but once I did that, I walked across the street to inquire about openings. They hired me immediately and asked me to start right away. The part-time job I got that summer turned into full time in the fall.

I enjoyed working as a cashier at the Hamilton Air Base Exchange. I really liked my new job. It was set up just like a major department store except we were able to buy things at a tremendous discount. I liked serving the customers and folding the merchandise on the floor.

And I loved having my own money. I now had purchasing power.

That first summer I worked, Aunt Flo kept my children because Li'l David couldn't attend regular day care. The base nursery didn't have the staff or facilities to work with a deaf-blind child, so she volunteered to help.

In the fall, Li'l David returned to the residential program at the California School for the Blind so I didn't have to worry during the week. We only had one car. While on break, David always rushed home to take me to work, and then he scurried back to his job. We lived about 2.5 miles from the base.

After six weeks, David was showing signs of stress. He would yell, "You aren't ready? Janie, I can't be late."

I tried to explain and he never seemed to understand. It always ended with us doing the Blame Game.

Terri and Tony were regulars at the base nursery after Li'l David left for school in the fall. But almost every time without fail, Tony would soil his diaper or spit up just as David pulled into our driveway. Or we would discover Terri had secretly played hairdresser and taken her hair braids down. Her hair was so soft and fluffy like cotton. I would have to comb her hair again. Most times, he would return to work tardy with an excuse.

Soon, David grew tired of this gruesome task. He decided to give me driving lessons again. David promised me he wouldn't yell at me while I was behind the wheel.

David learned his lesson a couple years back. He made that mistake before when we lived in Tacoma. We had just bought that old gray Renault. He took me out on Portland Avenue to teach me how to drive a stick shift. It wasn't as easy as it appeared. I started in a vacant area just down from our house. David told me to push the clutch in first, and then shift to first gear. I was to push the clutch in and step on the brake then come to a stop. I took my foot off the brake and my foot off the clutch and stepped on the gas. It took off.

Then I tried to change gears.

"Don't you do that," he yelled. "You're stripping the gears. I told you to put your foot on the clutch before trying to change gears."

Finally, out of exasperation, he cussed at me because I stripped his gear.

Instead of watching the road, I looked down at the gear stick.

"Keep your eyes on the road," David yelled. I panicked. "Watch out, Janie. Look where you're going. Oh no!"

I looked up but it was too late.

"Step on the brake, step on the brake," David screamed. "The brake. The brake. Now!"

I meant to step on the brake but I stepped on the gas pedal instead. I made a new highway through that median. Over the concrete divider I went, traveling fast, astride the median tearing down all the colorful shrubbery and flowers as I plowed my way through.

At the first chance, David reached over and grabbed the steering wheel. He maneuvered it back onto the side of the road. My foot fumbled upon the brake pedal. I stepped down so hard on the brakes our heads went reeling toward the dashboard. We came to a screeching stop. God was surely in that car or else we would have been killed.

David took over from there, driving home in silence. My feelings were hurt and I swore I would never drive that Renault again. He was angry and very shook up.

"Do you realize how close we came to death?"

"But you scared me when you said, 'Step on the brake. I was looking down to find it.'"

"You don't look down Janie. You have to keep your eyes on the road."

I ran to our bedroom to escape David's loud ranting and raving. I didn't speak to him for the rest of the evening. I'm sure he was grateful.

That was the last time he took me out driving, that is, until I was employed.

Every Sunday David drove me out to the old flight line at Hamilton for driving lessons. On the weekends, it was empty there were no distractions at all.

I did well because he didn't yell at me this time, not once, at least not until I was back home with the car parked and safety brake on. Once the keys were in his hands and we were safely inside our home, he would start.

"You forgot to put on your blinkers or did you see the stop sign? Pay attention!"

I would laugh after apologizing to him.

Within a few weeks, I had my driver's permit. I would drive David to work then come home to get ready for my job. It gave me ample time to dress the kids and prepare for daycare. He was on time again, stress-free.

We were financially stable for the first time since we married. We had extra money and we bought things to decorate our place. The children wore nice clothes and had plenty of new toys. David called them "his poor, deprived children." I bought myself a new wardrobe so I could look decent for work. I passed my driving test with flying colors the first time around. I was relaxed and confident about driving. I was soon appointed the family chauffeur even on outings across the San Rafael Bridge to visit our folks.

One weekend, while David and I were visiting Earlie, she proudly announced, "I found Daddy."

With cynicism, I asked, "Daddy? You mean, our real father, Calvin Lightfoot?"

"Yes, Janie, our real father, Calvin Lightfoot."

I couldn't keep still. I screamed for joy, leaped into the air, hugged her then spun her around. After I calmed down, she told me what happened.

"On Saturday, I drove to Los Angeles for the West Coast Hair Show. While I was there, I looked him up in the telephone book. I drove over to his place. Daddy still looked the same. He was so happy too see me."

"What did he say?"

"He said he wrote us at the old address on Grant Street but the letter was returned. So he didn't know how to reach us. He asked about you and Sydney. I told him everything. He said his car was in an accident and he had to pay a lot of money for his deductible. He asked me if I could loan it to him. I did. He said when he gets it fixed, he was going to drive down to see us."

"Did you give him my address?"

"I didn't know your address. I just know where you live.

"You know he asked about his Ba-a-aby. I told him his Ba-a-by was married and had three children. I told him what happened to Li'l David. He cried. You know how emotional Daddy is."

I got his address from Earlie. When I got home and I had a quiet moment while the children slept, I sat and wrote my daddy a letter. I was so excited when he wrote me back. We exchanged letters for about two months.

In the last letter Daddy wrote, he told us he had married a young woman he met in Fresno. Two months after they met, they got married. They were expecting a baby. The baby was due in the late summer. It was hard to believe daddy with a new baby. I knew he was up in age, I just couldn't remember ho old he was.

"You mean, his wife is having a baby?" Mother said when we told her. We'd all gathered with Earlie and her boyfriend, Arnold, who had come to the picnic with her that summer, and Sydney. "Lightfoot is too old to be making babies."

We all laughed. Earlie said, "Mother you are so crazy."

"What daddy gonna do with a baby?" Sydney said, then she teased me.

"Well, Janie, looks like you ain't the ba-a-by anymore." "I don't care, I have my own babies now."

Sydney, Earlie, and I made plans for Daddy to come out for the Thanksgiving weekend.

"Since I am paying their train fare out, I get to keep them the longest," Earlie said.

We decided we would take turns with them. The first night, they would stay with Earlie. On Thanksgiving, Earlie would drive them to my house. The third night they would spend at Sydney's house. I couldn't wait.

The time crept by slowly.

When they finally arrived at Thanksgiving, I ran out to greet my daddy I hugged him as if I were still his little girl.

Earlie and Sydney teased me. Daddy and I were both crying. He introduced us to his new wife, Louise. His wife was a young pretty woman holding a fat, beautiful baby girl.

"What's her name?" I asked.

"Our little girl is named Lorrie Ann," Daddy said beaming with pride.

"She looks like Earlie with her big dark eyes," I said.

"How old are you now?" Earlie asked, never one to be shy.

"Fifty-nine," he announced. "God blessed me to have another wife and a baby at 59."

"Wow, Daddy, you are old now," Sydney said.

"Naw, baby, I am actually younger with Louise by my side."
Louise blushed. We all laughed.

Li'l David touched his face and accidentally knocked off my
father's hat. Li'l David picked it up and reached to put it back. He
touched Daddy's head, then began to rub. He burst out laughing.

"What is he laughing about, baby?" Daddy asked, not sure what
to make of Li'l David.

"Your bald head," I said. "He's never felt a bald head before."
Li'l David was so tickled. His jovial laughter was infectious until
everyone laughed with him. I was shocked to see my dad was bald.
His black wavy hair was gone. Daddy laughed and hugged me again.
I could smell his Old Spice aftershave cologne. Surprisingly, we all
liked his wife, Louise. She had a cute Texas drawl. She told us she had
been in Raisin City, Calif., for a long time.

Louise explained how she met Daddy at the hospital. He came
to pray for the sick as a visiting minister from Los Angeles. He prayed
for her. After she recuperated, he visited her at church. Daddy told
her he was going to marry her. They dated only a short while. She
discovered she was expecting shortly after their marriage. A young
widow, she had three adult children, Ola and Stella who were married
and close to my age, and Christopher, a freshman at California State
University, Fresno. We had a lovely time. Mother and Henry, Daddy
and Louise were talking like old friends. Mother talked casually to
Louise. She fit right in. Earlie and Sydney acted civilized in front of
our father. Li'l David touched Daddy's square jaw line. He smiled.
He seemed to know through instinct Daddy belonged to us. Daddy
prayed for healing over Li'l David. We all cried tears of joy. It was
so good to see him again. Our neighbors and friends were curiously
amazed at how well our parents got along. All the hurts and regrets
had floated away with time.

Before Daddy left, we promised to drive down to visit them in
Raisin City. We did, too, several times. Three years later, Daddy and
Louise had another child, a little boy named Emmanuel. He looked
just like Daddy. Daddy was 61 when he was born. What a blessing.
Daddy seemed to grow younger and more youthful with time. We
were so happy for them.

David constantly teased my Daddy.

"So you're one of those preachers stealing in the name of the Lord."

"No, son-in-law, I serve the Lord and his son, Christ Jesus," he said seriously, not willing to take David's teasing about God. "I save souls, for that reasons God keeps blessing me. I don't steal nothing."

David laughed as Daddy hugged him.

"God Bless you, son-in-law." Daddy smiled with pride as he looked at his family.

CHAPTER THIRTY-ONE

I knew it was too good to be true. Before the year was up, David received orders for Korea. He was to report to Kunsan Air Base in April 1968.

About two weeks before David was due to leave, he found me an apartment at 2738 Chestnut St. in Berkeley. The rent was kind of steep for us. We had grown accustomed to living on base and the civilian economy was too expensive for our military salary.

I went on a job search because we had three children now and only one income. With him going overseas, our expenses would be split; that would not suffice.

I heard they were hiring at Pacific Bell. I drove to Oakland to take the test for the operator position. One of my old school mates happened to be an employee in the personnel department. I am sure she gave me good references. The interview went smoothly. I couldn't shake the thought that when I was fresh out of high school, I applied for the same position. There was no affirmative action back then. I was puzzled because even though I passed the test, I was told I was too short. I was 4 feet 9 inches tall and hadn't grown an inch since. I felt more confident this time. For the interview, Earlie did magic with my hair and make-up. She fixed it in a high-fashion style. I wore one of her smart outfits with a pair of matching high heels. Thanks be to God. I got hired that very same day.

I was swept up in the excitement. I wasn't accustomed to driving in the Bay Area. Rush hour traffic was backed up. On my way home from the interview, I sideswiped a car. This was my first accident.

By the time that I got home, I forgot to tell David about my new job.

Instead, I gave him the bad news.

"I got in a wreck with this crazy lady. She had me boxed in. When I tried to go around her, she sped up and turned into me." I sobbed through the whole story.

It was only after he calmed down that I gave him my other news.

"Oh, I almost forgot. I got the job at the telephone company. I start work at Pacific Bell next week." He let out a loud yell of relief.

"Good! You need a job so you can pay the deductible after the car is repaired." Believe me, that's exactly what I did with my first paycheck.

The car was fixed just in time to take him to the airport. He left one day before I reported to work.

Time went by fast while David was in Korea. I was so busy with my new career and taking care of three children: Li'l was 8, Terri was going on 4 and Tony was almost 2.

I was very excited about my new job at Pacific Bell. There was so much to learn on the first day at work. I felt so blessed because I didn't have to worry about a baby-sitter. My mother looked after the children.

"You might as well bring them over here, too," she said. "I'm already watchin' your friends' chil'ren. And I have Sydney's kids here already. They can play together. Earlie works late at the beauty shop so her kids are always over here. too."

I just couldn't picture all those children in one house all at one time. There were at least 10 of them.

"Mother, are you sure? That may be too much for you." "They my grandchildren and I'm home anyway."

"What do you think, Daddy?" I said, turning to face Daddy Henry sitting quietly at the dining room table.

Henry's lips poked out; he put on a pretentious pout.

"I don't care what Johnnie does," he said, standing up from the table and then pushing in his chair. "Just as long as you pay her.

"Now, let it be known that if they don't mind, then I will paddle they behinds myself.

"We ain't gonna' kill 'em now," he added. "But if you don't want us to spank them, well then, you had better take them with you."

He made his way out the front door to work on his truck, then yelled back as an afterthought, "Y'all ain't going to kill my wife neither. So you come get them right after work. And I mean before 10 o'clock at night."

He smiled as he closed the front door behind him. My mouth was wide open. Wonder what got into him? I guess that meant I had his approval.

Henry really loved our children very much. He always appeared tough but he never spanked the children. His bark was worse than his bite.

I lived only about two miles from their house so it worked out perfectly. Besides, I didn't have to worry about Li'l David being mistreated by strangers. He could play with his own cousins. They knew and understood him.

My mother and stepfather lived on Addison Street in Berkeley. It was usually quiet on the weekends but on weekdays during business hours, it became a thoroughfare for trucks and cars alike. University Avenue is the main drag in Berkeley, a straight path leading right up to the University of California. It is always filled with traffic. There are blocks and blocks of businesses but only a limited amount of parking places. Most of the employees park one block back. Unfortunately, this happened to be right on Addison Street where my mother lived.

My first day on the job, everything went crazy. Wouldn't you know it? The union called a strike. We ended up walking with our supervisors to a nearby hotel for a meeting. We were advised to join the union or we would have no protection for walking off the job. I didn't know any better, we were told to follow our supervisor's orders. I couldn't wait to get home to tell Mother. I exited the freeway at University Avenue, then turned on to Sacramento Street, drove one block, then made a quick left on to Addison St. I drove up in front of my mother's house, searching fruitlessly for a parking place. That's when I spotted Li'l David running aimlessly.

All of the children, including my nieces and nephews, were running away from him.

My heart sank. I actually felt his frustration as he squealed, groping, feeling his way blindly around in a futile attempt to find someone, anyone at all. No one would come to him! They were laughing at him as he bumped into several cars trying to find his way. He was disoriented and was apparently flustered. He was trying so hard to find someone to touch. He needed assurance that he wasn't all alone. The other children were running, looking back over their shoulders to make sure he didn't find them. They were laughing at him. They seemed to be enjoying it. They found delight in tagging him them running from him before he could touch him. With each and every tag he felt, he would let out a loud shrill of protest and reach for them. I knew he was trying to communicate to them that he was tired of playing this game. He cried out, reaching his arms out, beckoning for them to come to him, to just give him a reassuring touch. Instead they kept tagging him with their hands before running off. They giggled gleefully as they watched him groping around trying to find them. His cousins would take turns. One would touch him, then as he reached out almost touching them, they would dart away.

Without a second thought I simply double-parked across the street from my mother's house. I sat in my car for a few seconds in total shock, crying for my son. I thought his little cousins would play with him, not endanger his life. Terri always adored her big brother. Now I saw her tag him and run. Poor thing. I knew that she was merely imitating the older children.

Then he headed toward the street. People drove down this street like a bat out of Hell. I knew David was terrified of being alone. I had to get to him. He couldn't see the cars coming. I had to get to my baby before it was too late.

I quickly jumped from the car, leaving the door wide open with my keys in the ignition and the motor running. My son's safety was at stake. I loved my nieces and nephews with all my heart. I had so painstakingly cared for all of them. I couldn't believe they could be so cruel, so mean to my little boy. Tears were just streaming down my face as I rushed across that busy street.

I didn't see the large speeding truck.

It narrowly missed me. My red flare skirt whipped up against my legs from the strong breeze as the truck driver sped past, blaring his loud horn at me. I heard a loud swishing sound from the engine as the irate driver accelerated past. I didn't care. My mind was on reaching my poor baby who was now desperately crying for help. I continued across the street. I grabbed Li'l David up and held him close to me, wiping his eyes and rubbing his back. I let him feel my face. He soon calmed down once he recognized me.

Don't they understand? This hurts me to see my sisters' children running from him like he was an animal. He was upset because they would tap him only to run away as he reached for them!

I couldn't stand it any longer. I practically leaped on the oldest nephew, Alex. I grabbed him by the neck of his shirt and practically lifted him off the ground as I carried him inside the house.

"I'm ashamed of you. How could you treat Li'l David like this? He can't hear or see you guys. It hurts me to see you all mistreating him. Why? I changed all of your diapers and took you to the park, bought you nice things. You spent weekends at our house and I always buy you candy and that's how you repay me? This is my son! It hurts me to see you treating him like this!"

"Aunt Janie, we were only playing hide and seek with him." My nephew, a usually quiet kid, spoke up in their defense. He tried to explain. I wasn't listening.

"He could have been hit by a car," I said. "When I was parking, I saw him running out in the street."

Another nephew, George, tried to explain, "He 's not afraid, auntie. He knows that we are playing. He was having fun."

"He could have been hit by a speeding car. You call that fun?" Alex put his head down in shame.

"I'm telling Mother on you guys." Tears were flying as I wiped my eyes.

More tears fell as I ran inside.

"I've got to talk to Mother," I said as I opened the screen door. "She's got to stop this."

My nieces and nephews all followed me as I ran up the stairs. All the kids trailed behind me. When I reached for the screen door, I slammed it shut in their faces just as they tried to enter. I was so hurt my heart throbbed with pain. Mother was preparing dinner. She came out of the kitchen when she heard all the commotion.

"Mother, all these kids were teasing David. He was screaming and trying to find somebody to play with him. He almost got hit by a car because they were so busy running away from him."

All of his cousins were inside now, talking at once, trying to defend themselves.

"You see, Mother, we were just playing with David. Janie just thought we were running from him," said Trena, the oldest niece. "He was having fun, Janie."

"Fun?" I let out a sinister laugh. "You call that fun?" I looked around at my little nephews and nieces and my little daughter, Terri. She was only 3 ½, she didn't know any better.

They all looked so scared then.

"Look at my baby girl," I yelled. "You are teaching her to be mean to her big brother.

"How would you like it if you couldn't see or hear? Just try to imagine how he feels. It is so dark and there's no sound. Nothing but darkness. Try to imagine it. It's a lonely world. How would you like it if nobody touched you and they ran from you? His hands is his only way to see. What if that was the only way that you could talk to somebody?"

All eyes were on me now. Their mouths were wide open. Those poor kids looked at me in astonishment. I very seldom scolded them. I was the one who spoiled them and took them everywhere with me. Their big innocent eyes showed remorse as they stood staring at me. I slumped down in Mother's living room sofa crying my eyes out.

"I'm sorry, Janie." "I'm sorry, Auntie." One by one, they all came over bent down and hugged me.

Mother didn't say anything until I finished ranting and raving. She knew I needed to get it out.

"Don't worry, Janie. I'm going to show those wol's. Just wait."

She started belching again, the same familiar, loud ones whenever she was upset or unhappy.

I hugged her.

"It's okay, Mother. Don't worry, I just needed to get it out," I said as I gathered up my three children and all their belongings. I drove off with my children sitting quietly in the back seat. I didn't know what to do about David's cousins. They were so close to me. It felt bad for yelling at them. But they had to be taught a lesson. I didn't know how, but they couldn't keep treating Li'l David like that.

The next day, I dropped my kids off at Mother's as usual. I didn't mention anything about the incident the night before.

I drove home from work that evening, dreading the encounter I had my nephews and nieces. I was able to park the car in front this time. I stepped from the car, looked around. It was awful quiet. Then I saw all of the children, all of my nieces and nephews, with bandanas tied over their eyes. They were bumping into cars and holding hands with Li'l David. He was leading them around and laughing with glee. He thought they were playing a game with him. He was the only one having fun.

Mother came to the door, laughing at me.

"Girl, close your mouth. I'm teaching them a lesson. These wol's are going to know how it feels to be blind and deaf. I put cotton in their ears and used every scarf and bandana I could find. I tied them on myself and dared them to take them off. David has to show them around. They've had them on practically all day. They had to eat with them on, go to the bathroom, everything. Now they can see how it feels."

I laughed until my stomach hurt. I stayed for dinner. Just before I left for home that night she made them come to me and explain how it felt to be blind.

Mother let out a loud belch. She apologized, then said,

"I really showed those wol's, didn't I?" She reared her head back and laughed so hard tears came from her eyes.

"Yes, Mother, you sure did." I broke out into laughter, too.

From that day forward, they always respected Li'l David.

When school started Li'l David rode the bus to the California School for the Blind. We lived close now and he didn't have to live there. He was back in his home environment and I loved it. He would come home every night and show us what he learned at school that day. Under their guidance, he excelled.

He came home one evening with this tiny red book that fit perfectly into his little hands. Inside it was a stiff, shiny paper with little raised dots on every page. I could hardly wait until the next morning to find out what that little red book with the shiny stiff paper with dots in the funny shapes. I called his teacher Martha.

"I'm sorry but I feel so stupid," I said. "Where did David get that little red book? David pointed to these dots with his hands felt them with his fingers. He arranged his fingers into different shapes. I don't know what he's doing but I think that he's trying to tell me something."

Martha chuckled first then explained.

"Well, you remember when I called you yesterday after work?"

"Yes."

"I asked you what were his favorite foods and snacks, right?"

"Yes, I remember, but I thought you were asking so he could have his favorite foods for lunch."

"No, no. I wanted to know what he liked to eat because I had to figure a way to get the message across to him. I was trying to coax him into learning the Braille alphabet."

"But how would food help him to learn Braille? I don't understand."

"After you told me the story about him smelling his way home when he was lost at your Aunt Flo's house, I knew the way to his heart. You told me his cousins nicknamed him Hungry."

"And what did that have to do with it?"

"I found out the way to David's mind is through his stomach."

"Well, you were sure right about that."

"When you told me he loved peanut butter and jelly, candy, crackers, cookies and gum, this idea went off in my head."

"Where did he get that little book and what do those the little dots in that book mean?"

"That's Braille. He is learning Braille and that's the alphabet."

"Oh," I said, while scratching my head. But her excitement was infectious.

"Little David is so bright. We call him a walking computer here."

"Really? What happened, Martha?"

"Just wait until tomorrow. He'll be bringing something else to show you. He is a fast learner. He learned those Braille letters in one day."

I gushed with pride.

"Oh, thank you, Martha," I said. "God truly sent you to David. I thank the Lord for you."

"Oh, I think that He sent David to me. Anyway, I made the book myself. I was so proud of my little book. I put his favorite foods in the small plastic bags. On one page is a letter of the alphabet in Braille and on the opposite side in the bag are small squares of peanut butter and jelly sandwiches. He can only take one at a time. After he feels the Braille and fingerspells what it says back to me, then he may have another snack. On every page is a snack bag and the Braille letters opposite it. He can only have a snack if he signs the correct letter of the alphabet. That's what we're working on right now."

"Oh, when can I come to the school to watch him?"

"Oh, I don't want you there right now. It may distract him. Just give me a week. Please? He should have it down pat by then. He can show off for you then. Okay?"

"Well, okay," I said reluctantly.

"Just wait until tomorrow. David will have another surprise for you."

After I hung up the phone, I stood there looking out my large window. The bright sunshine beamed at me. I knew God was looking down on my son. This was the first time that I had heard good news about David since we left Washington state.

Li'l David was so excited when he came home that evening. He ran throughout our small two-bedroom apartment touching everything then forming his little fat fingers into different shapes. I didn't know what he was trying to tell me but I figured out he was using sign language. He then took the fingers of my right hand and formed them into the same shape. He touched the object then nodded his head showing approval. He ran me all over the house touching the dinner plates and the forks, the spoons, and forcing my fingers into letters. I didn't know what he was saying but I finally connected he was spelling the names of the items as he touched them. I was so excited. I reminded me of the Helen Keller story. I knew how her parents felt now.

After dinner, we sat on the couch and he opened up his little red book.

Inside on the first page was Braille.

The second page had a bag glued on it. The peanut butter and jelly sandwich was cut into four squares.

Li'l David arranged his fingers on his right hand into different shapes as he used his left index fingers to trail the raised dots on the opposite page. I then figured out that he was reading Braille and fingerspelling the word peanut butter.

I was so excited. Li'l David was learning how to communicate with me.

CHAPTER THIRTY-TWO

D avid came home from overseas in May 1969. We had orders
to go to Florida. David tried to change his orders. I was
excited about going to Florida until I found out how far
the blind school was from the base. First, I prayed, then I went back
to the Navy hospital where Li'l David had his eye surgery. I told his
doctor our problem, then filled out tons of paperwork requesting a
special disposition to stay in California.

At first, the Air Force denied our request to relocate to Hamilton
Air Force Base because there were two school facilities for the deaf
in Florida Li'l David was eligible to attend. But the nearest school
in Florida was about 200 miles away from the base. David then
took this information to the military but we didn't hear anything for
about two months. David requested an extension on his leave. We
were biding time, anxiously waiting for an answer.

I called Mother one evening and she took me to see Mother
Piggis. She prayed with me and for my whole family. After reading
Scripture from the Bible, she told me God doesn't make mistakes.

"You've got to trust God, He knows what he's doing," she said.

"Ooh, thank you, thank you, Jesus," she exclaimed loudly as she
closed her eyes. She clapped her hands, joyfully praising God's name.

"What is it, Mother Piggis?" I asked.

"God is showing me you have to have faith." She read a Scripture
from the open Bible. "God said he would never forsake you, nor ever
leave you." She was clapping her hands together, smiling joyfully.

With her eyes still closed and her head lifted up toward the heavens, she said, "Ooh, thank you, Jesus, thank you, Lord. God is showing me that you are going somewhere but it is by car. I don't see you going far. The Lord is showing me that Li'l David is at the same school and it ain't far, neither.

"I don't see you at the same base but I do see you at another base somewhere. It looks like a lot of farmland there. You will be working there, too. You got a good job and you and David will be happy. Just keep God in your life. Just remember to give it to God and just believe."

We prayed hard that night. It was just Mother P, my mother and me.

God did answer and it didn't take long either. Within 30 days after the request was denied and David had sent an appeal to headquarters, we got a new assignment. We were to report to Castle Air Force Base in Merced, Calif., in June. It was in the Central Valley about 125 miles from the San Francisco Bay Area. I put in for a transfer at Pac Bell and got it!

God is so Good!

I had to report to work in Merced on the same day we moved. David found a nice two-bedroom house in Atwater for rent, a one-story cottage located about two miles from the base, but we only stayed there one month. Soon we were able to move on Castle Air Force Base where our rent was subsidized according to David's rank

Our first Christmas in Merced, we were more excited than the children. We got all three children out of bed before 6 a.m. Christmas morning. Tony was happy with his new guitar because he loved to walk around the court strumming the strings, serenading the neighbors every morning. Terri got her first bike without any training wheels. She was so excited. She couldn't wait to ride it. Li'l David wasn't so happy with his gifts. There wasn't much of a selection in the toy department in the stores for a deaf-blind boy. We got several more Playskool puzzles for his age group and mostly clothes for Christmas.

He liked Terri's bike better and demonstrated by signs he wanted to ride it. We finally convinced Terri to let him ride on the back of the bike with her guiding it. She wasn't happy about this because she only had room on the front of the seat and David sat right behind her holding on to her waist for support. She wobbled while trying to get her balance while pedaling. David hugged her tightly with one arm around her waist. He kept his right hand free and signed repeatedly, "My bike, not Terri's." It was obvious he was very unhappy. He wanted his own bike. Terri was obviously not pleased with sharing her bike either. She complained and whined about the awkward seating arrangement.

It was my idea to let Li'l David ride on the back with Terri. I ignored David as he warned me of the dangers of riding double.

"Look at Little David!" he said, pointing at the children. "His legs are too long and are dangling off the back wheels. That the bike is wobbling. It is unsafe to have two children on it."

"Don't worry," I said. "I'll run along beside them. It will be okay." "It's Terri's bike and she should be able to ride it alone." "Oh, David, they will be just fine."

"If they get hurt, I am holding you responsible, Janie." He went inside, slamming the screen door while mumbling and complaining under his breath. I gave a sigh of relief, thinking the problem was solved about the bicycle. A few minutes later, I grew tired of trying to keep up Terri, who rode the bike very fast.

"Terri, you just ride to the end of the second block and come back, you hear?" I said, standing there with my hands on my hips trying to catch my breath. I turned around to head back to the house. I heard Terri's loud shrill.

"Mama, Mama, help me!"

David heard her, too. He ran outside. Terri was about one block away hanging onto the handlebars for her life.

"Help, mommy, David took the bike from me." I took out running, trying to catch them before they got hurt. David had hold of the handlebars. He pedaled as fast as his little legs could carry him. He giggled with glee. Poor Terri hung on to the one handlebar with both hands. Her rear end was hanging on the edge of the front part of the seat. David was smiling as he blindly pedaled down our street, wiggling and wobbling, miraculously missing every parked car on the road. When I finally caught up with them two blocks later, I grabbed hold of the handlebars and lead them back home. Terri tried to explain through her tears.

"David took the bike from me. He thinks it's his."

I hugged her and tried to reassure her he'd never do that again. We would have to work out something else. We did too. We bought him a brand new Schwinn Twin tandem bike. It was very expensive but we sacrificed so he could have his own bike. Terri, David and I took turns riding with David on the new yellow bike for two. David had so much fun pedaling on his own pedals and holding onto his own handlebars.

We always drove to the Bay Area after work Friday to pick up Li'l David at the school for the blind. Most of the time, we stayed the weekends in the Bay Area. We would spend one night with Earlie and Arnold and maybe the next night with David's brother and sister-in-law, Johnny and Marian. Other times, we would spend the night with our parents. We had a blast for a while. We got to spend every weekend at home with our families. Pretty soon, we grew tired of driving those 250 miles round trip every weekend. That's when we found out from Evelyn about a bus that picked up deaf children and took them to California School for the Deaf. We jumped at the opportunity. Not only would we save us money but it would save wear and tear on our bodies and on our car.

Once Li'l David started taking the bus, he wasted no time in making friends with the deaf children. Initially, I was worried about how he would be treated. The children at the school for the deaf usually didn't socialize with the children at the school for the blind In fact, they had very little contact. I was told by an instructor that, as ironic as it may seem, the blind felt sympathetic for the deaf but the deaf didn't feel sorry for the blind. I kept quiet but I secretly worried how those deaf children would treat my son. David could be somewhat annoying to others, especially to a person who doesn't know why he started to touch them. David could tax our patience sometimes. Whenever we were driving or doing something important, he would make conversation by impetuously grabbing your hands and would start finger spelling to you.

I thought the bus driver would tell me Li'l David wouldn't sit still on the bus and he was annoying the other students by feeling on their faces. I pictured in my mind the children being mean to him when he was alone. He was the only one with the double handicap. Every time we'd pick him up from the bus stop area, my heart would beat uncontrollably.

God has a way of changing things for the best. Once Li'l David identified someone with his fingers, he would fingerspell their name back to them. David only knew how to fingerspell while all the deaf students used American Sign Language. But by the end of the school year, David was signing right along with the rest of the children on that bus.

I requested that someone at the blind school formally teach David American Sign Language but the staff felt like it would be too difficult for him to grasp. I told he had learned how to communicate using signs while riding back and forward from Merced on the bus every weekend. I think they thought that I was exaggerating. They were just underestimating Li'l David, again.

I received a letter from the Neurology Center located in South San Francisco asking that Li'l David report there within a week for a neurological evaluation. One or both parents had to be there and be prepared for a full five-days stay. I was instructed to bring a suitcase, fully packed. They would provide room and board for the time spent there. The neurological center mailed me a map a few days in advance, and written directions to the Stones town Shopping Center in South San Francisco.

I asked for time off from my job for the whole week. David had to stay home with Terri and Tony. We made plans for them to go to the baby-sitter during his duty hours. He would be home in the evenings with the smaller children.

I was very nervous. I had never driven through San Francisco alone. David always drove me and the kids and I just went for the ride. I ended up getting lost and we arrived 30 minutes late, flustered and embarrassed.

When I walked into the large conference room, who caught my eye was a black woman who taught Li'l David during his first year, before Martha. She had given him such a hard time when she was his teacher and there she stood at the far side of the conference table. She glanced up from her papers and started at me belligerently. Nervously wringing my hands, I managed to smile at her. She gave me a dirty look.

I swallowed but the hard lump in throat made me cough out loud. Strange faces turned to glare at me. My eyes skimmed the room, looking for a familiar face or at least someone friendly. I noticed several of Li'l David's classmates sitting with school staff but few of their parents were there. I was relieved when I spotted Martha waving her hand in the air as Evelyn pointed me toward an empty seat next to them.

I cringed when I thought about that teacher. When she was Li'l David's instructor, he was always jerking nervously with a twitch. I couldn't figure out why until one of the dorm counselors told my husband she had slapped my son's face because he didn't sit still. I knew something was wrong because he came home with a bruise on his forehead and scratches on his arms and face. There was always unexplained scars but when I inquired about it, I was given some weak excuse about he was running and ran into a wall or he got into a fight with a student or something. David knew his way around that school like he could see, so I doubted it but I had no proof.

When we confronted this teacher about it, she denied it. I knew she was lying. She couldn't look me in my eyes. I threatened her, but David kept me from keeping my promise. It took every bone in my body to keep from slapping her face. I sat there boiling inside while David held me firmly in my seat. I left out that dean's office so angry

I could spit. I had not seen her since Li'l David was removed from her classroom.

Now here at the neurology conference center, I listened to this same teacher discussing a student and the problems she had with him.

"I tried to teach this 7-year-old how to communicate using signs but he was unable to comprehend. Therefore, I recommended my student, David Bess Jr., go to Sonoma State Hospital. I felt he needed more individual attention."

Oh, my God, she was talking about my child. I wanted to yell, "She is lying." Obviously, I moved or something because Martha placed her hand on my arm to stop me.

"Just wait, I got it," she said.

I waited impatiently as she continued to speak and the doctors in their white coats wrote on their notepads.

"The staff feels it doesn't have the facilities or staff to work with a hyperactive deaf-blind child. I feel he is unable to grasp the communication skills needed for his education. After working extensively with David Jr. his first year at school, I found it difficult to teach him due to his inability to grasp the concept of fingerspelling or sign language. He is unable to sit still for no more than 30 minutes at a time."

One doctor asked what she based her findings on.

"From working with him for his first nine months at school." She wouldn't look at me. "From working with other blind children at the school I am able to discern David's capabilities."

She was telling them Li'l David was mentally incompetent.

I wondered why Martha wasn't telling them about how she had taught Li'l David fingerspelling. I wanted to yell, "His vocabulary expanded so much I couldn't keep up with him since Martha was his teacher."

Then Evelyn stood up and introduced herself.

"I am the superintendent of the deaf-blind department. David was one of my students when he was only 4 ½ years old. He had congenital cataracts at birth. He lost his sight to glaucoma at 5 ½. When his mother brought him back to school that fall he was unable to see. It was quite a traumatic time for Li'l David. His world was always without sounds but when he had sight, he could relate to everything. His sight was his only way to communicate. Now he is completely cut off from the world. That is one of the reasons he runs around touching everything, he is nervous and anxious to feel things. His hands have become his lifeline to the world. You see, if you are blind and can hear you can still be in tune with your environment. If you can see and cannot hear, you can use your vision to stay in tune with the environment. But if you are both deaf and blind, you are shut off from the world. It's dark with no sounds. You are in a dark, lonely world. I wonder how the average person would manage if he had no eyes to see with and ears to hear."

She then turned to Martha.

"This school year Martha has been working with David, not only as his dorm counselor but as his teacher. She can tell you more about David Bess Jr."

Martha cleared her throat, then spoke confidently.

"Davis was my first student. I went to school just to learn how to teach him. I'd heard other teachers complaining about his hyperactivity. I was his dorm counselor before I decided to teach him. It started with a dare from one of the teachers on staff. I have to admit he is a live wire. He has problems sitting for more than five minutes. Well, I took her up on the dare. I took classes in the day for sign language and auditory training at San Francisco State University. I still worked at the dorm at night. David was already assigned to me. I watched him, amazed at his agility and balance. Most deaf children have trouble walking steady. They sometimes lose their equilibrium. David's motor skills are very good. His hand to mouth coordination is exceptional for a deaf-blind person. I have no way to measure his IQ but we all call him the walking computer. He runs down the halls, into his classroom and to his dorm without bumping into things. He knows where his classmates' rooms are and where the dining room is located. The problem we have is trying to slow him down.

"I remember one day I watched him as he stood on the back of a chair and hung his coat and slacks on a hanger without falling. But I thought it was dangerous so after he'd gone to sleep I took the chair and hid it in a closet nearby. A couple of nights later, he found where the chair was. I followed him back to his room where he stood up on the back of the chair rearranging his clothes on the rack again. I had to laugh. I eventually took the chair down to the basement and his mother brought in a stool for his use."

She continued talking about all of David's accomplishments, then looked around as if waiting for a response. She took a deep breath and said,

"I ask that David have the same chance as other seeing students. He only needs someone to teach him how to communicate with fingerspelling. I believe that one day he will be able to live a semi-independent life if he is allowed to remain a residential student at California School for the Blind."

Tears filled my eyes. I just wanted to run up and hug her, I was so grateful.

I looked around. The doctors were still writing notes.

The other teacher, David's nemesis, looked perturbed as she stuffed papers into her briefcase. She made rude sighs as Martha continued speaking but Martha ignored her.

"I attribute David's good skills to his parents. They believed in him and gave David the proper training he so needed. David is living proof of their excellent training." She then went on to describe how she started to teach David new words.

"I was able to open his closed, dark mind," she said as she held up the red book she'd made for David. She passed it around and described how she used his favorite foods to bait him into learning new words. "Once I put those baggies inside the pages with his favorite snacks inside, he caught on so fast.

He learned how to read Braille and fingerspell at the same time. He could only have a bit if he spelled out the words written in Braille. He grasped the concept so fast until I couldn't keep up. He was now hungrier for new words in his books than the food. I increased his vocabulary at a faster pace because he was a fast learner. He became bored easily. I had to fingerspell new words faster as he ran around the room touching everything. His world was a new, happier place

277

now. Everything had a name. And he wanted to know everything, all of the names for them."

Martha would have gone on longer but one of the doctors interrupted her, telling her it was time for lunch. I welcomed the break because I'd left our bags outside the door of the conference room in my haste that morning. Thankfully, one of the young doctors led us to the rooms where we were going to stay the week for the testing.

"Would you mind if I asked you a few questions after lunch," he asked as I started to unpack. I took out the sandwiches I'd brought for our lunch.

"Oh, they've prepared lunch for you and David in the dining room," he said. "Come and I'll take you there."

The doctor ate with us, asking me a lot of questions about David.

"I'm going to be observing David while he stays this week so please try to understand I have to ask these questions in order to make a fair evaluation," he said. I nodded that I understand.

That afternoon sped by as the doctors discussed the cases of other students. I took Li'l David to our room before dinner for a rest. I knew he was tired and I needed time to myself. But just as I reached the top of the stairs, the same doctor came running after us.

"Excuse me, Mrs. Bess," he said. "Is it possible for me to watch Li'l David now?"

"Well, I was going to let him lie down. He's tired."

"This will only take a minute," he said. Reluctantly, I let him in. He sat on one of the twin beds in the room and began to ask questions while watching Li'l David change his clothes. David ran his bath water He thought it was late because he had felt both beds. He patted the bed closest to the door and touched his chest afterward.

"What is he doing with his hands," the doctor asked. "Is he talking to you now?"

"Yes, he told me that bed was his."

"Is that sign language?"

"That is his home sign for the word mine."

"Does he identify his possessions the same way?"

Then David leaned over the tub and put the tip of his bent elbow into the tub of warm water. He nodded his head.

"That means the water is fine," I told the inquisitive doctor.

"How did he learn to run his bath water?"

David climbed into the tub. He picked up his washcloth and began to rub the soap all over it until suds appears. Then he scrubbed his face, arms and legs.

"He watches everything and imitates me and his daddy, too."

"He can't see but you said he watches…"

"I always say watch because I remember when he could see. Now he uses his fingers like his eyes to see."

"Oh?"

"Yes, his hands are supersensitive now. He feels everything I do. He knows what I'm doing and he can almost imitate everything I do. I think he remembers when he could see."

I was getting sleepy so I politely led the doctor to the door. "We'll skip dinner. I still have those sandwiches," I told him. David soon finished his bath and climbed into bed. He quickly fell asleep. I did, too.

The next morning the doctor came up to me.

"You can leave now," he said.

"Who? David and I?"

"No, ma'am. Martha and Evelyn will stay with David. He'll stay here for more testing. We weren't aware he was so independent. Most deaf-blind people can't feel themselves unassisted but David is quite capable of taking care of himself."

They sent me home. Li'l David continued attending the blind school, with Martha as his teacher.

CHAPTER THIRTY-THREE

U nfortunately for David, Martha was soon promoted and assigned a new class. She was going to teach new students who required individualized lessons. They were developmentally disabled as well as legally blind and profoundly deaf.

She confided in me how she really missed Li'l David.

"He is very bright and so energetic. David is totally deaf and blind yet he catches on faster. I spend a whole week teaching them whereas David picks it up in one day. His comprehension skills are great. His memory is phenomenal. Whenever I demonstrate something new to David, he is able to perform it on the first try. He imitates my movements like a sighted person. It is hard to believe he is blind and profoundly deaf."

David always nodded his head for clarification before imitating the movements exactly as demonstrated to him. It still amazes me to watch him as he signs to others. He is a perfectionist. Whenever anyone signs to him, before they finishes a sentence, he completes it for them. If they make a mistake in spelling, or while signing, he corrects them. He is so intuitive. He touches the hands of the signer ever so lightly and yet he can distinguish the letters or signs. Even though, he is profoundly deaf, he mumbles loudly as though he is speaking to you.

Whenever he signs to an experienced person, his movements are fast. He is a good teacher. When he signs to a beginner, he spends hours teaching finger spelling to anyone who wishes to learn. He starts with the alphabet. He patiently forms their fingers to make the proper letters.

David did get another teacher but he seemed bored in the classroom. This one teacher kept him in the classroom daily. There were no outings. Martha always took David and his classmates to the nicest restaurants where they would dine out. They had to dress up in a suit and tie for this weekly event.

Before she took David out to eat at a restaurant, she sent a note home requesting our permission to take him out with the class. I sensed her nervousness. She called us a week in advance inquiring about his table manners and skills using different utensils.

David assured her Li'l David was neat and definitely knew how to use the proper utensils.

"Li'l David uses his napkins appropriately. He constantly wipes his hands and mouth whenever necessary. Believe me, he eats well with a fork and he can use a steak knife or other utensils efficiently. I taught him good table manners when he was around two and a half."

Martha braved it and took her small class of five children out to eat. I could hardly wait to hear what happened.

That Friday afternoon, as we drove up to the dorm, Martha darted from her office into the hallway.

"I need to talk to you about Li'l David."

"What happened?" I asked.

"What?" David said. "Was Li'l David bad this week?"

"Oh, no, quite the contrary," she said with a chuckle. My heart was in my mouth until she said that. I had grown accustomed to hearing complaints from some of the staff who worked in the dorms. I had become defensive about my son.

"Actually, I wanted to complement you on your son's good table manners. I should say excellent manners."

David and I both stammered out, "Thank You." We looked at each other and smiled.

"Let me tell you about David at the restaurant. I was constantly wiping up spills from the other students places. There was food all over the place. But David, he chews with his mouth closed. He picked up his napkin and wiped his mouth between bites and he cautiously felt for his glass with his little short fingers. He picked it up carefully balancing the glass with both hands."

Martha shook her head showing total amazement.

"Not a spill was made. David is the only student that is totally deaf and blind. He has far more obstacles. Yet, he was the only one who ate his food with his mouth closed. When he had to cough or sneeze, he covered his mouth. I couldn't believe my eyes when he picked up the correct fork for his salad. Not a drop of lettuce was left on the table or on his plate. He used the large fork for his main dish. He constantly wiped his mouth to insure no food was on it."

She continued raving on about David.

"What really surprised me was when he reached for his glass and brought it to his mouth as though he could see it. Not a spill either!"

"Janie used to get mad at me for spanking him when he would repeatedly knock over his glass of milk," David said. "He soon mastered handling the glass and he has perfect balance. He knew that he had to use caution when reaching for it."

"Really? He gets spankings for that? I never knew that," she said.

"Why? Do you think I'm being too strict with my son, too?" David asked.

"No, it's just unusual to hear that coming from a parent of a multi-handicapped child. It's just that parents of handicapped children usually spoil them and never insist on them using anything but a spoon when eating. It is considered acceptable for them to shovel the food into their mouth, even to chew with their mouths open. The parents usually spoon-feed them. The poor children never experience independent eating habits. In fact, they are usually overprotective of them and tend to try to shelter them from the public eye. They rarely take them out in public because they don't want people staring at their children."

"Well, when Li'l David could still see, his father was strict," I said. "At first, I felt he was too strict. We would argue about his disciplining David at the table every night. Dinnertime became a nightmare to us. I knew David meant well by forcing my baby to eat his meat with a fork. He would demonstrate to Li'l David how to properly cut his meat and show him how to hold his cup with two hands instead of one.

"When Li'l David was stubborn and didn't obey his father, he would have to sit in his little Mexican chair in a corner with his back to us. I would feel sorry for Li'l David. Poor little guy would use his little hands to beg for me to rescue him.

"Martha, to tell you the truth, I really thought David was a fanatic!"

Martha laughed, then said, "Who taught him how to cut his meat with a knife and a fork? He only used his spoon for dessert."

"I did, of course," David said.

He was so proud of Li'l David. At that moment, I saw all the love and pride he had for his son all in his face.

Li'l David used more and more signs now. He was so advanced we couldn't keep up with him anymore. His vocabulary had grown immensely. He read Braille books constantly. He was like a walking encyclopedia.

We'd grown to love it at Castle Air Base. David and I decided to buy a home by Merced college. I was making a good paycheck at Pacific Bell. We were financially stable. We put a deposit on a new home custom built to our specifications. It was close to the mall and the local college. We picked out our carpet, kitchen cabinets, bathroom fixtures, everything. Everything was supposed to be ready in six months.

Then David got orders for Japan, an accompanied tour which meant we could go with him. I stared at the papers with the orders in total bewilderment. This was a three-year assignment and we had six months to get there. We had some serious decisions to make. We needed to decide whether I should stay in Merced because of Li'l David's schooling. We'd just signed a contract for the new house. And I would have to give up my job. There was no Pacific Bell in Misawa, Japan. In fact, there were no jobs for American dependents at all.

Lord, Lord, help me to make the right decision, I prayed. I didn't want to be selfish but I did want to see the world. Yet I couldn't take my son David from Berkeley. He had made insurmountable progress academically and he felt at home at his residential school.

Lord, I need you to help us make some decisions, the right ones, soon.

We told our folks about it. David's parents were happy for us but expressed regrets that the grandchildren were leaving them.

My mother and my step dad were excited for us. My sisters had mixed emotions. Sydney encouraged me to go with David.

"You need to go with your husband," she said.

But Earlie gave me a warning. "If David takes you overseas, and he starts acting up, how are you going to get home?"

"Oh, Earlie, stop being so pessimistic. I can come home anytime I want to. Anyway, David is not going to mistreat me."

"Oh, yeah? What if he changes? I heard about how the GIs go crazy over those Japanese ladies and then they change toward their wives."

I just shook my head in disgust.

"That's a long way to run. You can't tread water to get back here."

I was so disgusted with her. I refused to talk to her about it again. We worried about Li'l David's education. I had decided to go after all. David had talked me into it. Once David received his official orders to we sat down and talked.

"This may be our only chance to see the world, Janie. I always wanted to take you overseas and I don't know if I'll get another chance. Let's take him with us. Find out if you can give home schooling to Li'l David. We can ask them at the blind school if they will send his lessons to you. I know you have the patience to work with him and we can teach him ourselves."

We went to talk to the dean at the school that same week. It was hard for us but we had to break the news to his favorite teacher, Martha, and Evelyn, his guardian angel.

Both of them were very sad.

"I'll do some research to see if there are any educational facilities over there that maybe David can attend," Evelyn said. "I know there are schools overseas in Europe for the deaf but I am not sure for the blind."

Evelyn called me a few days later.

"In Japan, there is no school there for Americans. That is, unless, he is to learn Japanese sign language." We all laughed. Evelyn always had a way to see the funny side of a dilemma.

The answer came at David's annual school evaluation.

"How would do you feel about letting David stay as a residential student," Evelyn asked us. "What I mean is, Martha and I talked to the superintendent and it has been approved. We just need your written endorsement."

David and I looked at each other and without a single word being spoken, we knew each other's thoughts. I had been praying for an answer and here was Evelyn with an offer we couldn't refuse.

"Janie, you and David Sr. can go to Japan and let David Jr. stay here. He can fly over to Japan during summer vacation and also at Christmas. The government will pay for it. We have several students whose parents are in the military. They are stationed in other states and countries as well. That's why I know all the procedures and laws regarding handicapped children residing in special educational facilities. Their children are left in our care. The military has a program called Children have a Potential. I have paperwork for you to sign. It just gives us power of attorney in case of medical emergencies, etc."

"We had a long talk with my mother to see if Li'l David could stay with her and attend the blind school," I told them. "She insisted he live with her. She volunteered to drive him to school every day. My mother is very kind-hearted and wouldn't refuse to help us. But she is concerned about lacking skills to communicate with David. My parents cannot fingerspell. They merely use home signs to communicate with David Jr."

"David can come over to my house and spend the weekend with my family sometimes," Martha said. "My children love Li'l David. They have learned how to sign and fingerspell with him. He spends a lot of spare time at my house anyway. Instead of sending him to the school cafeteria, I take him home with me for lunch. He has spent the whole day with my children and me. They love David. He taught them fingerspelling so they think that he is a genius. So, David feels comfortable at my house. It's his second home."

David and I agreed this would be a nice change of pace for David. He would have somewhere to go on weekends. We knew he would become bored just staying in the dorm. This would also allow my Mother and Daddy Henry time to themselves.

We readily agreed for Li'l David to become a residential student. David assured me I could take a military hops to come home to see him between his summer visits.

We went back over to my mother's house and told them what plan Evelyn had proposed. Mother felt it would be a good idea.

"I can pick Li'l David up and bring him home with me on the weekends.

Daddy and I can take care of Li'l David. That boy pretty much takes care of himself. I just can't understand what he's saying with his hands and I don't know how to answer him. I can't learn that finger spelling."

"That boy don't have to say nothing," Daddy Henry said. "He's got more sense than the rest of these kids, if you ask me. He wipes off the table after he eats. He puts his dirty plate in the sink and makes sure that he washes the dishes. I seen him wash the dishes and don't none of them have a speck of dirt on them."

"I know. And when he has finished washing the dishes, he dries them and he puts them up the dishes neatly and then he goes to take out the garbage."

"We don't have to tell him nothing," Daddy said.

"He folds the clothes from the laundry without nobody telling him to. When he finishes folding them, they look like they came straight from a laundry."

"I watched that boy fold sheets, towels, shirts and pants. Time and time again, I saw with my own eyes how he just kept smoothing the wrinkles out the clothing. I mean there was not one wrinkle left. In fact, they look like they ironed."

"And he vacuums like he can see, when he finishes, there ain't one speck of dirt on that floor. He gets down and feels with his hands to make sure that there's no dirt on the floor."

"Yes, Mother," I said, almost laughing. "I know David will be a big help to you." That was our sign. God had worked it out.

CHAPTER THIRTY-FOUR

Before I knew it, September was here. David left for Misawa, Japan. He went in advance to secure base housing for me and the children. I made David promise to fly back home to accompany me and the kids overseas. I was petrified over the mere thought of traveling alone to a strange country with two small children. Terri was 8 and Tony was 6; they were quite small at the time. David did come back and we left for the airport in the wee hours of the morning. David warned me he would have to catch a military hop; that is, on a space available basis, so he didn't know for sure if we'd be on the same plane. We could hear the announcement, "Flight 940 going to Elmendorf, Alaska, Yokota, Japan, Misawa, Japan, please prepare to board as your names are called." My heart leapt into my stomach as they called my name but did not call David's name.

I started crying because I didn't want to go if he wasn't going to be with us. We were walking up the ramp through the corridors. I kept looking back, desperately praying they had made a mistake. Well, they didn't. The airline attendant led us up the ramp to the large 747 waiting nearby.

Big drops of water fell from my eyes. I must have looked just like I felt:

Frantic!

David tried to reassure me as I reached back to grab his hand through the ropes that divided us. Families and friends were yelling last minute instructions. David then placed a white paper in my hand.

It had a ragged edge. It had been torn from an envelope in haste. There was a name and a telephone number scribbled on the white piece of paper. I couldn't see anything for the tears. David yelled over the loud murmurs of the crowd, "Don't lose that paper, Janie! Do you hear me? It's important. Call my friend Sgt. Bill Simmons when you get there. He will take care of you."

I could only nod through the tears as I put the small torn paper into a black bag I carried.

Everybody was waving and throwing kisses in the air to their loved ones. "Don't worry, I'll probably be there before you." "David, I'm coming out of here."

"No, Janie, don't worry. Just stay there."

"No," I yelled back. "I'm not going without you."

I looked like a little baby crying. I didn't care. I wanted him with me. I was frightened. I tried to turn around, tried to push my way out by squeezing my way through the crowd. I positioned myself in the center so I could keep my children close to me. They had their little back packs on filled to the max and couldn't move fast enough. I held my children's hands tightly as I tried to get out of the slow-moving line leading to the onramp. Families with their children kept pushing forward. I tried to squeeze my way out of the line. My tiny frame was overpowered by all those big military men with their families pushing forward toward the ramp leading to the aircraft entrance. The airline steward looked agitated as I tried to pull my children out of the line.

"Forward, please! Keep moving forward, please!"

Believe me, I tried my best to get out but no such luck. David threw a kiss at me, then said, "Don't cry, baby, please. Stay there. I'll meet you back there at Misawa." He looked so helpless I tried to dry my eyes at the last. I realized how selfish I was being, putting my family through all this drama.

I tried to compose myself. I wanted to reassure David that I was going to be fine. He stood there hands in his front pockets, sadly watching his little family trudge up the ramp to the plane. I tried to conceal my anguish; to show him I was okay, by smiling and waving, but hot tears were dropping fast. Painstakingly, I had applied my eyeliner and eye shadow that morning. Vanity set in so while waiting on the slow line to move, I took out my small compact and peered into mirror. I was now engrossed with wiping the smeared mascara away with my tear-stained handkerchief. That's when I lost sight of David. I looked around, trying to see over the crowd.

"David! Are you still there?"

I could only hear his voice.

"Yes, I'm here, baby! Love you!"

"Love you, too!" I answered back, tearfully. The crowd pushed us slowly forward into the big jet airliner. The engines roared loudly. The noise was deafening. I was frightened. I remembered Earlie saying, "That's a lot of water to tread." What if we crashed? I would I never see my husband again.

Once we were on the plane, I inched along the narrow corridor behind the other families trying to find seats. I held my children's hands with a death-defying grip.

Tony looked up at me. His big inquisitive eyes sparkled.

"Why isn't Daddy coming with us, Mama?"

"They won't let him on the flight because he already was in Japan. When he came back to get us, he was put on space A. He got bumped."

I started crying again.

Terri was surprisingly calm.

"What does space A mean, Mom?"

"It means space available." I tried to remain calm while my insides lurched violently.

"Oh. I know. There was space available for him. They called his name first, didn't they?"

"No, Terri, they didn't call his name. I wish to God that they had." I tried to explain between tears, "Terri, somebody else came along with reservations and he was bumped off."

"Oh, what does bump him off mean?" Tony asked.

"I don't want to talk about it now. Please? Ok?"

"Okay, Mama."

Terri tried to comfort me, to reassure me.

"Don't worry, Mama. Daddy said he will meet us later."

I managed to smile. "I know, Terri. This is our first time overseas. I wanted us to be together. I just miss him, that's all."

Because I was seated between Terri and Tony, I was able to reach over and give them both a hug.

They watched me with desolation. The tears dropped continuously. I dried my eyes again. The stewardess was very kind and compassionate. She handed me tissues every time she walked by. My children yelled, "Excuse me! My mother needs more tissues, please."

I told myself, You have got to stop this childishness. As the plane ascended to a higher altitude, Tony yelled over the loud engine, "Mama, my ears are hurting!" I searched fruitlessly in my pockets and purse for the Spearmint gum I purchased at the Travis air terminal.

Just then, the pilot announced, "We are now at 35,000 feet and there is a lot of turbulence. I must ask you to remain seated with seatbelts on until the lighted sign goes off."

While he spoke, Tony cried, "My ears! They're popping, Mama!" I remembered David had the packs of gum in his pocket! My thoughts shifted from self-pity to my son who was now screaming. As soon as the seatbelt lights went off, I went looking for our stewardess. Lucky for me, she had several packs and not only handed it to me but to several families with the same problem. Soon, Terri and Tony sat quietly with their headsets watching the movie "Cabaret." starring Liza Minnelli. It was the most boring and longest movie I ever watched. The gum helped Tony's ear problems. Terri leaned over, headset still on, and said loudly, "I remember flying before, didn't I, Mama?"

I just smiled and nodded an affirmation. I did not want to bust her bubble. The only time she had flown was when we flew home from Seattle because David was going to Vietnam. She was 2 ½ months old and I held her in my arms the whole time.

I must have cried myself to sleep because they next thing I heard was the pilot announcing our arrival at Elmendorf AFB, Alaska. I could see nothing but white, white snow all around us for miles and miles. When we departed the plane to transfer to another plane, we saw this huge polar bear standing up on her hind legs right inside the airport terminal. Talk about scared, that was me until I learned it was stuffed.

We had a short layover before boarding another flight to Yokota Air Force Base, Japan.

This was only my second time flying. The first time was from Washington, and now to Japan. I was so scared. We had flown about five hours already. The pilot announced the time and the altitude we were flying. I didn't want to know how high we were up in the air. I was frightened enough without knowing how far we were. All I saw was a wide array of blue sky or water with the white clouds floating nearby. I couldn't distinguish whether it was blue sky or water. Mother Piggis was right. She described this scene to me in 1959 when I was 17.

We had just finished praying. Her arms were in the air, her palms stretched out facing up toward the heavens. Her long neck was extended all the way out. Her face glowed radiantly.

"God is showing me that you will be traveling, Janie. It looks like you are traveling over blue water. I see blue skies and I see these white clouds floating all around. I can't decipher if you are on a ship or a plane. I do see blue all around you."

This must have been what she envisioned because it looked exactly like she said it would.

"Oh, thank you, God, for preparing me for this," I said. I relaxed then, feeling His presence as my mind went back to that special day. I can still remember being in that prayer room, for the first time with Mother P. I was so nervous, so scared and thinking this old woman must be out of her mind, telling me I was gong to marry a GI. I began smiling, then laughing. Thinking about how I felt, how life had given me some bad turns but now realizing God was revealing to me how he had been with me carrying me through all of my trials and tribulations.

I felt better now. I marveled at the beautiful things God had created. The scenery below was magnificent. If there was ever any doubt about how Great God is, it was removed forever from my thoughts. Only He could have created all of these beautiful things.

I never knew there was so much water. We were surrounded by it. I knew God had prepared me for this.

Dusk slowly crept in. I didn't rest well. I kept nodding in and out of sleep. It was dark out now and I could see the stars. I felt like I could just reach out and touch them. Only the glass pane separated us from the moon and the stars. We were seated by the wings of the plane and I could see the flickering red and blue lights underneath the wings. I finally fell asleep from the whirring of the engine. I think that it hypnotized me.

It was 10 hours before the pilot announced, "We are now flying over Mount Fuji. It is now close to your arrival time. If you will look to your extreme right, you will see Tokyo down below. It is a large metropolitan city.

It is westernized in some areas and has the same climate as San Francisco. Everyone please put on their seatbelts and remain seated until after we land before getting out of your seats."

As we circled over Yokota Air base, I spotted hundreds of Japanese protestors standing right outside the base gate waving these white flags and holding signs that read: U.S.! GO HOME!

I was frightened out of my wits. Lord, I'm ready to go back home, these people hate us. Why can't I just have a normal time for a change. Why me, Lord?

After exiting the plane, I strained my neck trying to peer over the huge crowd in the terminal. A stranger eventually steered me to the information counter where I got a map of the base. I had trouble understanding the diagram so I merely followed the family members that traveled on the same flight with us. I felt like I was the only wife traveling without her husband. All of the other wives were holding onto their husband's arms as he carried their luggage and held on to their smaller children's hands. The older children helped carry their luggage.

Somebody helped me when they saw me struggling with the heavy pieces. My little children were having a hard time. It was mostly out of frustration I found myself yelling at them.

"Terri! You get the big bag from Tony. Let go! Give it to Terri, now!"

"But Mommy, I have it." At 6, Tony was still so tiny he looked like he was only 2. The bag he was trying to carry was twice his size. Tony insisted as he stumbled and fell over it.

"I can carry it, Mommy," he said.

"I said give it to Terri. Now!" After the long lines to get to customs, we had to unpack and repack all 10 bags of luggage. I was hot, angry and frustrated. I found a locker nearby and left all but our carry-on luggage. We went to find the base hotel.

After we checked in, we went upstairs to rest. Soon, though, the children and I got hungry so we left the hotel to find some place to eat. The hotel clerk recommended a cafeteria several blocks away. It was very dark when we left. We were trudging through unfamiliar territory as we made our way to this cafeteria. We could hear dogs barking loudly as we walked along this long narrow pathway. Then a pack of stray barking dogs ran straight toward us. I started screaming. My children did, too.

"Run," I yelled frantically. I ran, pushing the children ahead of me. These wild dogs were chasing us. We were their prey now. I had to think fast. I knew we couldn't outrun them. That's when I said, "Terri, stop, take hold of Tony's hand." Terri's dark eyes were big as saucers. She looked to me for help. She had Tony by the hand now, shaking.

"Just keep walking slowly, ahead of me," I said. "Hurry!"

There was nobody in sight but us. These mad dogs were snarling at us. Their eyes had an iridescent greenish glow and they foamed at the mouth. Their tails were down and their big ugly teeth were bared. They slowly approached us, shoulders hunched as if ready to attack.

I knew I had to act fast!

I yelled to my children again, "Don't run!"

"But, Mommy, they're going to bite us," Tony said.

Terri's voice trembled as she spoke, "Mama, can we throw some rocks? My teacher told me one time that if dogs come after you, pretend like you're picking up rocks to throw at them."

"Good idea," I said. "Stop and look down for some rocks. Quick! If you can't find any just pretend you're picking them up." Tony just stood there wide-eyed looking at me, scared to death. He was frozen in his tracks.

"Go! Do it now!" I said.

Terri had already bent down. Tony bent down, too, pretending to pick up rocks. So did I.

Terri said, "I found some rocks, Mommy." Tony said, "Me, too, Mommy." "Then throw them at the dogs!"

Terri and Tony started throwing rocks hard and fast.

I scooped up a handful of rocks I discovered in the hard dirt below. I threw rocks at one dog that appeared to be the leader of the pack. I heard a hard thump as the rock hit him in the left rear hip. He yelped, then scurried away. All of the other dogs turned heel and followed him.

I laughed nervously with relief.

"Terri, Tony, pick up some more rocks. Keep them rocks in your pockets. Looks like we will be needing them while we are here in Japan. Keep some rocks in your pockets. Those dogs might be waiting on us when we return. We have to be ready, just in case."

"How long do we keep these rocks, Mommy?"

"Until I tell you to get rid of them, you are to keep them in your pockets! Understand?"

Tony looked up at me with his big brown eyes and said," Yes, Mommy."

"Okay. Let's go eat. I'm hungry now. I know you are, too. You must have worked up an appetite throwing those rocks."

Terri and Tony nervous giggles soon turned into loud laughter. We were all laughing with relief as we spotted the bright neon sign that read Yokota Air Terminal Cafeteria. After eating their favorite hamburgers and French fries, we headed back to the hotel.

We ended up staying three days at Yokota Air Base before flying into Misawa Air Base. I prayed hard. *Please, Lord, let David be there in the terminal waiting for us.*

When we got off the plane at the base, I was very disappointed. David was nowhere to be found at the small airfield.

After leaving the terminal, a short, thin black man approached me as I stood looking helplessly around. I needed a large metal basket for all our luggage.

"Are you Mrs. Bess?" I was startled when I heard his deep heavy baritone voice.

Quickly answering, "Yes, yes, I'm Mrs. Bess." I assumed he was bringing me a message from my husband. But instead, he said, "I'm Tech Sgt. Bill Simmons and your husband told me to look out for you."

"When did you last hear from David," I asked. "Where is he? Do you know?"

"Yes, he called last night. He told me he got bumped off the plane at Travis. He's stuck in Korea, now waiting on a Space A. He should be back soon. As soon as he can get a hop back here, that's what he told me.

"I am going to take you to Base Billeting so you and the kids can get situated," Bill added as he quickly helped us with all 10 pieces of luggage. He led me to a little blue Toyota.

"This is David's car," he said. "He calls it his little bluebird. He let me drive it while he's gone. My daughter, Stacey, calls it the Little Bump Bump car." We all laughed.

Bill drove on in silence.

Terri and Tony started begging as usual.

"Mama, I'm hungry," Tony said. "When are we going to eat?"

"I want a McDonald's hamburger."

"There is no McDonald's here, baby," I said, laughing. Bill started chuckling, too.

"When we first arrived here, that was the first thing my girls asked for, too." Then he looked at me and smiled.

"My wife, Kelly, has cooked dinner and requests your presence." Before I could politely decline, he said, "She said she will kill me if I come home without you."

Tony started jumping up in the back seat.

"Yes, Mama. Say yes!"

I turned around to see Terri's face.

"Well, Terri?" I said.

Terri smiled and bashfully nodded her consent.

"I guess I'm outnumbered."

I directed my gaze at Bill smiling happily.

"We still need to go to Base Billeting to get a room. And we need to shower and rest for awhile. I'm still tired after the 18-hour flight from the States."

He looked over at me and nodded his acknowledgment.

"Oh, I can still remember. I arrived just one month ago myself, so believe me, I know."

I looked over at him and said, "What time is dinner?"

"How about 4 p.m.?"

I agreed and Bill said he'd pick us up at 4 p.m.

After Bill left, I tried to call to Osan, Korea, to reach David. We were practically out of money. It was payday and he had to come home to get his mail. I didn't have the foggiest idea where the post office was or anything.

I was nervous and scared, too. I didn't know these people. What if his wife didn't like me?

It was 4 p.m. on the nose when Bill showed up at our room. As we drove out of the driveway, I noticed we were riding on the wrong side of the street. Bill noticed my apparent nervousness and said, "We drive on the opposite side of the street over here." As we rode through the base gate it was if we were entering into another world. The strange writing on the signs and billboards looked weird. It was all written in Japanese. I was thoroughly confused as we drove outside the main gate, I read a large, white sign with big bold letters flashing out in English: WELCOME TO MISAWA! That was the last thing I read that I could decipher.

The people were all small like me. This was the first time I'd seen people shorter than me. They shuffled their feet as they went along the narrow walkways in their colorful kimonos. The foul smell in the air made me nauseous. It smelled like someone had died and came back to life. As we rode by in the Little Bluebird car, I could see all of the open marketplaces loaded with fresh fruits and vegetables displayed on open stands on the narrow sidewalks. Raw fish hung from the rafters. Lobster tails were tremendously huge They were arranged neatly in rows on an old wooden display shelf right in front of the market place. Octopus and eel meat were also displayed and God knows what else. It all looked repulsive to me. As I rode along the bumpy narrow streets, I stared through the windowpane of the car in awe at the older men and women as they strolled in and out of the market places dressed in their traditional silk kimonos. Most of the teens and the baby boomers were dressed in Western style garments. Amazing! Over 6,000 miles apart yet I see the same fashions, same hairdos on the younger set. They carried the same big boom boxes so popular in the U.S. with the same music by Michael Jackson, Stevie Wonder and Marvin Gaye blasting from the loud speakers. If it weren't for the black hair, the tight slanted eyes and the pale yellow skin, I would have mistaken them for any teenagers in the U.S.

A few of the pretty young teenage girls wore long straight skirts with a front split exposing their legs to the knee. The gorgeous platform shoes they wore caused them to lean forward as they shuffled along. Of course, their small leather bags matched or coordinated with their ensemble. It was very cold so they wore matching Angora sweaters underneath a long flowing overcoat. Most of the young men wore the fashionable bellbottom pants that were so popular. I was amazed to see a lot of the young Japanese men not only wearing bell bottom pants with their stylish platform shoes; but some of them actually had the large curly Afro hairdos. I couldn't believe my eyes. I could understand this happening in Tokyo, but not in a small village called Misawa-Shi where it snowed nine months out of the year.

Bill saw the surprised look on my face.

"The Winter Olympics were held here in Misawa City in 1972. That's how they became Westernized. They have become familiar with the American way of life. They love our music and the American fashions."

The drive was only a short one. They lived about three miles from the base. We traveled down several small roads and through alleys before Bill slowed up and turned into a dead-end street. The little Japanese cottage sat back off the street between several other small houses. All the Japanese homes in that small village were cute and tiny! I detected the sweet aroma of an Italian sauce cooking. Someone's cooking spaghetti! The aroma of freshly sautéed onions and garlic floated into the car and lingered there as we pulled up into a graveled driveway. Bill stepped on his brakes a few feet away from a small one-story Japanese cottage.

I wondered what his wife had cooked for dinner. My stomach growled just then. I was hungry for sure.

I still worried if his wife would like me. Bill got out of the car and came around opening the door for my children and me. Terri and Tony were wide-eyed and couldn't shield their excitement. We walked up a narrow walkway surrounded by colorful flowers on both sides before reaching the front porch. On the right were the most exquisite green plants I had ever seen. They were small with the limbs and branches twisted and arranged in an unusual patterns. On the left was a small vegetable garden with tomatoes, corn and carrots, and several tall beanstalks. There were actually rows of collard greens.

A short white woman came out from behind a sliding paneled door. It had several white paper panes with black trimming on it. I knew she was his wife. She came rushing out to meet us.

"Hi," she said. "My name is Kelly." She extended her hand. I returned the handshake with a big smile. I looked into her big brown eyes. They sparkled with such genuine warmth. When she smiled I noticed her small dimpled chin. Kelly's complexion wasn't a pale chalky white like most English people I knew yet she spoke with a British accent. Her fair complexion contrasted against her brown curly hair. Her face was perfectly round. I noticed right away Kelly was as short as me. Well, almost as short. She was about two inches taller. Bill stopped and removed his shoes at the small foyer before entering into their house. I followed suit. I just looked back at Terri and Tony to give them a cue but they were already taking their boots off. As I entered the house, Kelly said to Bill, "Oh, look, Puppy, I am taller than she is."

We giggled like two schoolgirls. I understood her excitement.

"I would be happy, too, if I found someone shorter than I." I said and then introduced Terri and Tony.

"Hello, my name is Kelly and these are our two daughters, Lisa, and Stacy," Kelly said to Terri and Tony. Lisa was the oldest. Her perfectly round Afro adorned her small delicate features. Lisa's complexion was like a vanilla latte. Stacy was very petite with soft curly hair was divided into Afro puffs. Her big brown eyes spelled mischief. Kelly handed us soft fluffy slippers just before as we proceeded to step over a threshold leading to the living room. She was so cute. I could tell we were going to be great friends. I felt right at home with her. While we sat and talked, we found out we had a lot in common.

Lisa and Stacy were practically the same age as my two. Bill and David were in the same squadron at Misawa. They had arrived at the same time. Kelly arrived only one month ahead of me.

Over dinner, I discovered that they, too, were stationed at McChord Air Force Base.

She served a large lasagna with French garlic bread and a large tossed salad. As we sat at the kitchen table, we laughed and talked as though we had know each other for years.

"Where did you get that British accent from," I asked.

"I am from British side of Canada." I was surprised when she offered me a hot cup of tea served with milk. I politely drank it. To my surprise, I liked it. Later I explained I had never had tea with milk. I generally drank it with lemon. Whenever I visited her, I drank my tea with milk.

The night went by fast. Bill took us back to Base Billeting so we could rest.

"Bill will be by to pick you up after work and bring you back over for dinner," she said as we left. I was grateful. I didn't tell them but I was running out of funds.

The next morning, I woke up, mentally prepared to contact the Red Cross to ask them for help. I needed to contact David as soon as possible. If they couldn't help me find him, then I would request a loan until David returned. I had to swallow my pride. Just then, the phone rang at billeting. It was David calling to tell me he would be home tomorrow and that he'd contacted the Red Cross and they would give me emergency funds until he arrived. God is so good. The Red Cross sent a representative to pick us up and they gave us a check to tide me over.

Soon after David arrived, he checked the base housing list. We were on the top of the list. Within one month, we were able to move into our house.

CHAPTER THIRTY-FIVE

Several weeks after we got settled in Japan, I had a horrible nightmare. My stepfather Henry, my Aunt Flo, Sydney, Earlie and I were riding in a carriage around Lake Merritt in Oakland. My mother wasn't there. Henry fell into the clear lake. We couldn't find Daddy Henry. My Aunt Flo fell into a lake looking down in it for my Daddy Henry. As soon as Sydney and Earlie jumped in to save them, the water turned murky. Nobody came out of the water. I dived in to save my family. The water turned black. After searching the bottom of the lake, I came up for air, then dove back under frantically searching around for them. Flo appeared above water, then Sydney, then Earlie.

"Where is Daddy?" I asked them. Nobody knew. I looked at our dresses. We were all dressed in black. I woke up screaming and crying and my body was cold. I shivered with chills. I looked around. I was in my bed. I touched my face, there were real tears in my eyes. I rolled over in the bed and felt for David. I needed him to comfort me, to tell me it was only a dream. His side of the bed was cold and empty, with the sheet carelessly turned back where he'd slept. David had left for work already. I sat up in the bed. I covered my mouth. I felt so lonely.

David came home early from work that day. He insisted I sit down. He led me to a comfortable armchair and handed me a miniature china cup filled with hot sake.

"I got a telegram this morning when I went to work, Janie."

"What happened, David?"

David, well, he was trying to hold back tears but they came from his eyes as he attempted to fight them back. I knew then something was wrong.

"Is it Li'l David?"

"No, Janie, just drink the sake, OK?"

"No, David. You tell me what is wrong, now!"

David handed me the telegram after insisting I take a large swallow of sake.

"I'm sorry. I didn't know how to tell you this," David said as I read the yellow piece of paper.

"Daddy had a massive heart attack. He passed, Feb. 29, 1973," it said.

I shook as chills ran through me.

"Oh, no," I said. When we left, he looked so healthy."

"I know," David said.

"David, he told me something before I left. I'll never forget it. He said, 'After you go to Japan, I probably won't see you again.' I said, 'Yes, you will. Daddy. You can come and see us. You and Mother can fly over and spend time with us just like when we lived in Washington state and everywhere else.'

"Daddy Henry said, 'No, Janie, y'all won't see me over there. Uh uh. No-sir-ree. I wouldn't get on nobody's plane. If I can't drive or take a train or bus, well, I ain't going there. Them things keep falling out the sky. I ain't wanting to leave here like that.'

"'Oh, daddy, you'll come over, you're just saying that,' I said.

"'Your mother can go to Japan. I'll send her but I ain't going over all that water. Nope. You probably won't see me anymore.'

"I didn't take him serious. He knew, David, he knew he was going away." I broke down in tears. "I didn't take him serious."

I didn't feel like talking about it. It was too painful. Without thinking, I went to my room and began packing.

David stood in the doorway watching me. "He was my buddy. He was my best friend in the world, man."

David had to borrow money from the Red Cross so I could fly home for the funeral. Terri and Tony flew home with me. David couldn't go because he had no leave time left. The Air Force sent us Space A First priority so we wouldn't get bumped off the flight.

When I arrived at Travis Air Base, Earlie and Arnold were waiting to drive me home. It was a long, quiet ride home. Everyone was so sad at home. Mother was numb, just going through the motions. Her sad eyes met mine as

I walked through the door.

"He died from a heart attack. He was sitting in that chair." She pointed at his brown leather chair. I could picture him still sitting there with his feet up watching TV.

"He had trouble breathing. By the time the ambulance arrived, it was too late. They tried to revive him but they said, 'I'm sorry, ma'am, but there is nothing we can do.'"

I hugged Mother but I couldn't find anything to say. I knew God could only give her the comfort she so needed. It was the first time I helped Mother with funeral arrangements. The funeral went as well as could be expected. Daddy Henry was loved by all. Mother put him away as he requested.

I stayed home with her for two weeks. We got all of his legal papers finalized and most of all the loose ends together. I took Mother to the county courthouse to file the death certificate. I never knew there was that much official business involved with death. I was so thankful Daddy Henry had insisted on me looking at his insurance policy, the deed to their house and other things. Mother was in no condition to handle it alone.

Death is so final. It emotionally drained Mother. That was the first time a member of our immediate family had a funeral. He was the first living relative to die since my grandparents. I was relieved when everyone went home. Mother looked so tired and drained. Dark circles under her eyes were from sleepless nights. Daddy had been with Mother for more than 13 years. They were so happy together, traveling all over. He spoiled her with nice cars, mink coats and diamond rings. I had not slept well myself. I missed Daddy, too. I longed for David to be here with me. We talked on the phone every night. Eventually, I would have to return home. It sounded strange calling Japan our home, but it was going to be home for the next three and half years.

It took us two weeks of waiting before we were able to catch a flight to Japan. We were traveling Space A but going home, we were now traveling on a lower priority. Therefore, we kept getting bumped. We got exhausted from traveling up and down the freeway every night. The first week, Mother drove us there faithfully. I knew she was tired, so the second week I insisted she stay home. I had decided to stay in guest housing until we caught a flight out.

Mother knew I was afraid of sleeping in a strange place with the children, so she asked Earlie and Arnold to go with me. I was able to get a large four-bedroom house on base with a full kitchen with all of the dishes and appliances we needed. I was able to save a lot of money because we cooked our meals. My funds were short and I needed to conserve my cash for the long trip back.

We woke up at 5 a.m. and rushed to the air terminal. They were calling names as we entered the building.

Earlie, Arnold, Terri, Tony and I held hands right there in the terminal and said a prayer to God. I kept repeating the verses from the 23rd Psalm to myself afterward.

They called so many names but not ours. I was so frustrated and ready to give up when I heard my name over the intercom, "Janie Bess!"

I was so excited. We could go home now.

Earlie started clapping right there in the middle of the terminal floor where we were standing. She was as excited as I was.

"Yay," she said. "I'm so happy. Now you can go to Japan!"

People stared at her because it was so early in the morning.

"Shh, Earlie," I teased her. "People will think you are glad to get rid of me. They'll think I was an unwanted house guest or something."

Terri and Tony were jumping up and down squealing with delight. You would think we won the lottery or something.

Arnold hugged me then playfully swung me up in the air in his big strong arms. His tall thin frame hovered over the crowd as he stood there laughing.

"You and Earlie brought us luck," I told him.

We quickly boarded the plane happy to be headed back home. It was a long tiresome journey but this time I knew what to expect. Strange as it may seem, Japan was my home now. I had made lots of friends. I couldn't wait to get there.

We arrived back in Misawa exactly 30 days after we left. We really needed extra money. I went to the Base Exchange to apply for a job. My neighbors warned me I wouldn't be able to get a job there because the only civil servant positions open were for people transferring from other bases. But I was stubborn so I turned in an application anyway. Praise the Lord, I got the job.

I started work not knowing how I was going to speak to the Japanese workers. They kept going on strike repeatedly, for no good reason. They went on strike four times in my first three months there. The U.S. government got tired of it and fired all the workers who refused to work. The base commander ordered all military and government installations in Misawa to hire American civilian workers and dependent wives.

I was a salesgirl at first, then got promoted to cashier in the third month. The pay was so low most American wives didn't want to work. I swallowed my pride and did the job. I needed the money. Li'l David was due to fly over and spend the whole summer. We needed money to help buy school clothes and help finance his flight back to the States. David was now a staff sergeant but he still didn't make enough for everything we needed.

I had a Japanese maid who was worried to death she would have to learn how to fingerspell for Li'l David. I tried to reassure her.

"Suzie, Terri and Tony will fingerspell and translate for you."

"I sorry, Bess-san, I cannot speak English very well. I cannot do. Please, you forgive me?"

When David came home from work, we talked late into the night about how to resolve this issue. David suggested I take a three-month leave to stay home with Li'l David. I knew I had no other choice. But I also knew what my Japanese manager, Maruyama-san, would think—that I was crazy to even have the audacity to request three months off. I had to be, to ask him something like that. I'd only worked there a few months.

I couldn't find the courage to just go up and ask him. I filled out a request form for leave without pay. I came in 30 minutes early just to put the form on his desk. Soon I heard my name over the intercom.

"Bess-san, please report to office, please."

I walked quickly to his office, my hands shaking. He was seated at his large mahogany desk in his matching leather chair. As I stepped into his office, I followed through in true Japanese tradition. I bowed my head to show respect. Licking my lips nervously, I stood directly in front of his desk.

He spoke English but had a thick Japanese accent so it was difficult to understand him. Maruyama-san took pains to speak slowly, enunciating each word carefully.

With his arms extended, he held my request away from his chest as though it was diseased.

"Bess-san, I don't know what to tell you. I see here, you ask for whole summer off?"

"Yes, sir, you see, my oldest son, who is 13, is coming. He goes to a special residential school." I swallowed hard, trying to fight back tears. My chest ached and I felt hot inside.

"Daijobi, go ahead, Bess-san. I'm listening."

"My son, David, is deaf-blind. He is due to come over for his summer vacation. I need to take off because nobody will be able to communicate with him."

Maruyama shook his head in disbelief.

"I know this is an unusual request, Maruyama-san, but my son, he attends a special school in California that is closed in the summer. My Japanese maid cannot talk with him or communicate with him so it's important I stay home, you understand me, sir?"

I paused to see his response. He said nothing. I continued, trying not to talk too quickly.

"I'm asking for time to help him adjust to Japan life. My husband can't take any more leave right now. He has no more leave time this year. You understand."

Maruyama shook his head again.

"I have employees who have worked here for 10 even 20 years but they cannot have a three-month vacation. I hope you understand me, Bess-san." He leaned forward over his desk as he stared directly into my eyes.

"I can give you three months off but I don't know if I can promise you a job when you return."

With that, he set the paper down with resolution.

"You see, I have to find someone to take your place."

He had this insidious look on his face but his dark, small eyes danced with laughter. He gave me a big smile, baring his large white teeth as he looked up over his glasses at me. I wasn't sure if his smile was out of sheer politeness or if he was trying not to laugh in my face.

"I'm sorry, Bess-san, I must find someone take your place, I cannot promise you job back. I hope you understand me. I like you, Bess-san. You good worker but I have to fill position. You understand?"

He continued to look me directly in my eyes. He turned his head slightly to the side as though he expected an acknowledgment from me. I merely nodded my head, not making a sound for fear of crying.

"I sorry. I cannot give you three months. Too long for leave time. You understand?"

I lost my composure completely. My heart was thumping out of control and I felt hot. I had to go before I broke down completely. Without another thought, I took off running away from that mean, uncompassionate man. I could hear Maruyama-san calling my name. "Bess-san, Bess-san, please come back here, please." But I kept running.

My high heels sounded like tap shoes as I ran from his office, down through the hallway of the now empty store. I ran fast, quickly zigzagging between all the pretty garments hanging in the aisles. Thank God the store wasn't open or I would have died from embarrassment.

I heard someone calling out in a loud whispering tone.

"Hey, hey, stop!"

I stopped and listened. The voice was coming from behind a stack of large cardboard boxes stacked high near the customer service counter. I spotted the head of a brown-skinned black woman with big brown eyes peeking out from behind rows of stacked boxes. I noticed her intricate hairdo as she came from behind the boxes, smiling with her hand extended for a friendly handshake. I grabbed her right hand and shook it heartily.

"Hi, I'm Mozella Knight, who are you?" She looked me over thoroughly in a matter of seconds.

"Janie Bess," I said, my voice quivering a bit.

"It's nice to meet you, Janie," she said and I responded with the same.

"Well, I'm not going to beat around the bush," Mozella said. "I want to know why you're crying." She looked me straight in the eye. "Just what did Maruyama-san say to you?"

"Nothing, really," I said as I wiped my tears away.

"You're lying. I know you weren't crying for nothing. You gonna tell me what happened?"

I broke down and she started handing me tissues from the service counter nearby. After a good cry, I blew my nose really hard as if this would expel all the hurt, anger, frustration and sorrow I'd been experiencing in the past few months. I started telling her about my family, my flight over without my husband and the anxiety I felt arriving in Japan alone with two children. Before I knew it, I was spilling out everything about my father's funeral, the situation with Li'l David. Mozella hugged me and tried to comfort me but I'd had enough, everything just expelled from me without stopping.

"I need to be home with him this summer but I need this job," I said. "We are in a financial bind because we had a lot of extra expenses since we came overseas."

"Now exactly what does that have to do with Maruyama-san," Mozella said. "What happened in there?"

"He said he would have to find someone to take my place."

Well, Mozella would have none of that. She was outraged. She told me how she had to go to the Equal Opportunity Treatment office to file a complaint because she felt she'd been discriminated against by Mr. Maruyama.

"Maruyama-san's going to let you have time off," she said fiercely. "Your son is handicapped and he can't fire you, not if I have anything to do with it. I'll take you to EOT to talk with the counselor."

"Oh, no, that's all right," I said. "I know I was wrong. I know I have nerve to ask for time off when I've only worked just a few months."

Mozella grabbed my hand and dragged me back toward the office.

"Come on, we're going to have a little talk with Mr. Maruyama-san." She was still fussing as she led me back to the manager's office. Maruyama-san was surprised to see Mozella standing there with me in tow. She towered over Maruyama-san, and me, for that matter.

"What's this about you finding someone to take her place," she asked. "You can't do that. I'm getting ready to take her to EOT."

Maruyama-san spoke up quickly.

"No, Bess-san, she misunderstood. I no say she fired, I say I find someone to take her place."

"That's the same as saying she's fired."

"No, no, Bess-san misunderstand me. I say I find someone to take her place for the summer until she come back to work."

Mozella stared contemptuously at him as I looked on in surprise.

"You mean you will find someone to take my place for three months until I return to work," I asked, disbelieving.

Maruyama smiled at me as he nodded his head.

"Oh, I thought you said you couldn't keep my job for me, that you would have to hire someone to take my place. But you meant I could take leave and after my son goes back to the States, I can come back to work?"

"Hai, daijobi." he said, asking if it was OK.

"Hai, daijobi," I said, agreeing in Japanese.

Mozella then shook his outstretched hand and I followed suit. Maruyama bowed to us and we both bowed back before we left the office.

That was one of the happier days of my life. Mozella and I found out that not only were we coworkers, we also lived in the same housing complex on base. We became the best of friends.

Time flew fast. Summer and Li'l David came and passed and he returned to school, happy and healthy. Soon, it was Thanksgiving day. It would be Christmas and we were planning to send for Li'l David. David and I had saved some money and we were going to see if his mother or mine would accompany Li'l David on the plane.

But it didn't happen. His teacher wrote us telling us that in less than two weeks, David was scheduled to have cosmetic surgery to have his pupils removed because the glaucoma had caused deformities on the pupil of his eyes. He concealed his eyes with sunglasses because they weren't nice to look at.

David and I talked well into the night. We decided I should be the only one to return home but because of the holiday traffic, it would be unadvisable to drag the children home on another long flight. They were still tired from the last trip. They would stay with David. We didn't have much money but we went ahead with our plans.

Two days before I was due to leave, we were invited to a party. We tried to back out of the invitation, but our Masonic lodge insisted we come for a traditional sayonara party for some of our friends who were leaving for stateside duty.

After they called the couples who were leaving up to the podium, they were given beautiful plagues of recognition and beautiful gifts of teakwood or brass. We were clapping for them and casually enjoying the festivities.

All of a sudden, I heard my name being called.

"Sister Janie Bess and Brother David Bess, please come up to the podium."

Puzzled, we stared at each other. It startled us both when we heard our names. Hesitantly, we made our way there. I stumbled up the stairs leading to the front of the ballroom stage. There stood our worthy patron holding up an envelope. His wife, the worthy matron, stood by his side, smiling happily at us.

She whispered to me, "You are so little." She pinched me on my plump right cheek with such gentle affection as she gave me a big smile. Nervously, I returned the smile.

David looked at me. I could see the questions in his dark brown eyes as he fidgeted nervously in front of all the people.

"Brother Bess, Sister Bess, we've watched you these past few months during your trials and tribulations. You never complained or seemed worried when you had to leave for the states to attend your stepfather's funeral just six weeks after you had arrived here in Japan. We know how hard it was for you emotionally and financially.

"Janie, we heard how you and your children got bumped off several flights several times on your way back to Misawa traveling with your two small children. Yet you two never complained. You kept right on smiling.

"Then Brother Bess, you had to take several hops, too. First, you left shortly after you were assigned here to return to bring your family back. You got bumped. Your family was here without you for over two weeks. You had to stay in base billeting, which is guest housing for more than 30 days while you waited for base housing. Finally, you got on base and had just packed when your wife got the notice her father had passed. You didn't complain. You sent your family home without grumbling or complaining; you were still smiling through all of this. Then only two months later, you had to take a hop to return to the states again to pick up your son and bring him over for the summer. We are sure that this caused quite a financial strain on your budget.

"After summer vacation, you had to take your son back on a space A flight. You were still smiling.

"Now after only 2 ½ months, we found out your wife Janie has to return home to the states to see about your son, David. We understand he is going to have surgery on his eyes within the next few days.

"We know this is not much but we want to give you a little token of our love for you, Brother and Sister Bess. Here is a little something from all of your brothers and sisters at Old Misawa Lodge No. 54 and Rising Sun Chapter No. 29." The worthy patron handed me an envelope. In it was more than $500. My mouth flew open with a loud gasp. David swallowed hard and just shook his head in disbelief. He was trying hard to hold back his tears. I was wiping away tears myself that just kept coming back. No matter how many times I wiped them away, just that much more would reappear on my cheeks.

We were both speechless. Standing up there, I felt awkward yet I was so happy. We gratefully hugged both of the officers and then all of the members who came forward to hug us. David spoke in his usual soft poised manner.

"Man, I don't know what to say. Well, I thank each and every one of you. I didn't expect this and I am just in shock. Nobody's ever done anything like this before and I don't know what to say except thank you very much."

"Thank you all for your thoughtfulness," I managed to ramble out before I started tearing up again.

Ironically, before we left for the party, we had sat down, did our budget and figured out that after our bills were paid, I would have only $200 to travel on and to live off for two weeks. Now we were able to have money for my travel expenses.

I was happy to find out I had been put on emergency leave status so I couldn't be bumped on the flight to the states. My flight was due to leave the next morning. I woke up early because I had to run a few errands before leaving. While rushing around in the Base Exchange, I heard Mr. Maruyama's voice over the intercom, "Mrs. Bess, Bess-san, Bess-san, please come to the office."

I reluctantly went into the office. The last time I'd taken leave, I got called into the office and Maruyama-san put me to work during inventory time. I was trying to avoid him but one of the co-workers spotted me trying to discreetly leave out the front door after making a purchase.

"Aha, I caught you!" she said as she led into the office despite my loud objections.

Maruyama-san sat at his desk with his big smile. "Bess-san, we hear about your son. He have surgery. Is he sick?"

"Yes, sir. He is having surgery but it isn't because he's sick. I am going home because the eye doctors are going to perform cosmetic surgery on my son." I noticed an air of anticipation as all the Japanese workers stood there smiling at me. It was hard for me to talk because I didn't know how to explain about his surgery. I didn't want any sympathy and I knew I would start crying when I talked about David's condition. David is going to have a new pair of prosthetic eyes to wear. The glaucoma had caused such an unattractive distortion of his pupils it was unsightly. The teachers and staff insisted he wear sunglasses so as not to frighten others. I looked around at all the workers. I wanted to get going but I waited politely for Mr. Maruyama to speak to me. I could tell that it was hard for him because he was actually a very shy person.

Clearing his throat seemed to energize Maruyama as he gave an encouraging speech.

"Well, all of the workers, Americans and Japanese alike wanted to do something for you. So we had a meeting and took up a collection for you. I hope that you won't be offended." Mr. Maruyama looked me directly in my eyes. I dropped my head. "It is the only way we know to show you we really care about you. We heard you were going home because your son is sick. I know this must be difficult time for you and your family because Christmas coming soon. We understand how this might cause a financial hardship for you. All of the employees collected this small token of appreciation for your hard work, It is not very much but they wanted to help in some way." He handed me a long business size envelope bulging with green bills in different denominations. Mr. Maruyama faced me as he beamed in proud dignity. "We collected $350 to help you with your expenses."

I was so happy. All I could say was, "Oh, thank you very much."

Mozella was standing right next to me with her right arm resting lightly on my left shoulder. She looked down at me inquisitively while I stood there immobile, unable to speak. Tears flowed freely. Suddenly, I felt a wave of heat rush through my body. Without a second thought, I rapidly fanned my face for relief.

"Girl, are you hot or something?" she teased me. "Look at you. Give this girl a fan or something."

It broke the long silence and everyone present exploded in laughter. I was just filled up with so much emotion. I felt like I would just explode from knowing so many people loved us and cared about us. I never knew such kindness in my life.

On my way out, I hugged each and every worker and thanked them over and over again. Blinded by my own tears. I slowly made my way out of the front door of the exchange. I couldn't wait to get home and tell David the good news.

CHAPTER THIRTY-SIX

When I arrived in the States I found out Li'l David was already in the hospital, at the Oak Knoll Naval medical facility. Martha was able to talk the doctors into letting her stay in the operating room during David's surgery so she could interpret to him and keep him calm. They did the surgery the morning I arrived.

I was so disappointed. I had let Li'l David down not being there before his surgery.

When I got to the hospital, the first person I saw was Martha as she came out of David's room.

"He is just fine," she said as she rushed to me to give me a hug. "Don't worry, he didn't feel a thing. I talked to him before he went out. The doctors told me to have him sign up to five. David only signed up to two, then he was snoring loud."

We bought laughed. I could hear an inner voice say, "*It was meant to be this way. Don't worry. God sent her.*"

I relaxed and enjoyed her company as we sat waiting for Li'l David to wake up. I was hugging a stuffed dog that was really a radio. He would be able to feel the vibration from the sounds as they came from the hidden speakers.

I laid it in his bed beside him. I stayed until he woke up. He ate a big lunch and went right back to sleep. After lunch, Martha went home to be with her family. I stayed to play with Li'l David until late into the night. I fell asleep with him playing with his new toy, the stuffed radio dog.

It was after midnight when I arrived at Mother's. I climbed into bed exhausted. Early the next morning, I went back to the hospital to stay with David. When I got there, his little radio was missing and he was crying for it. I was angry because we never did find another one. It was a birthday present to him.

I was so upset.

"I could never find another toy like that. How could someone be so cruel and take my son's toy?" The head nurse acted so indifferent; she just hunched her shoulders up. I went to the nurse's station and inquired about it. I walked all over the pediatrics ward. Someone had taken it between midnight and 7 a.m. Only someone who'd been on duty those hours could have taken it because no children were awake and no visitors were allowed. I was just broken hearted because I knew that they were exclusively made in Japan.

"Mother, the day David had eye surgery, it was his birthday. I bought that especially for him because he could feel the vibration from the radio when the music is playing. I hope whoever took it has bad luck for this. How could someone be so cruel and steal from a blind-deaf child? What can I do about David's toy? I won't be able to find it again."

Mother sat there belching loud, a sign that she was sick about it, too.

"Uggh! Don't worry about it. Uggh! Just give it to God. They must have needed it more than you did!"

"I never took anything from nobody. I hate them for doing this."

"Uggh! Don't hate nobody. God wants us to love our enemies and to pray for them so that they may prosper."

"I don't want a thief of the blind to prosper. Damn it! I hope they rot in Hell!"

"Uggh! Don't you get upset now. It ain't helping Li'l David."

"He was feeling all over the bed and crying for it. I had to tell him that someone took it."

We never did find the stuffed animal but the following week, David's doctors fitted him with the most beautiful brown eyes. They fit perfectly and looked very natural. I fingerspelled to David, "You look very handsome. I love your beautiful brown eyes."

That made up for the missing stuffed dog.

I stayed home with Mother for two weeks. Time flew by so fast. I visited David every day. David's Aunt Thelma drove me to the hospital to see Li'l David every day. She was such an inspiration to me. She cared for her husband who was a stroke victim for 35 years. I revered in her strength. Later, we sat at Mother's table eating Southern fried chicken and Collard greens with hot water corn bread.

"How are the Japanese people over there," Aunt Thelma asked. "Are you the only black family there?"

I laughed. "No, matter of fact, there are thousands of Americans there. They are of different ethnicities. There are so many multi-cultural marriages in the military. Very few of us are really race-conscious."

I explained the Japanese culture. I spoke a few conversational words in Japanese. They were so impressed.

"The people in Misawa, Japan, are very friendly," I said. "Some of them dress and act Westernized like us and others dress in the traditional silk kimonos." I told them the long story about my job and Mozella, and the wonderful American and Japanese people taking up collections to help us out.

Aunt Thelma left after dinner to take care of her husband. She had a friend stay with him until she returned home.

After she left, Mother said, "I always prayed you would be happy in Japan. And you are. Didn't Mother Piggis tell you that you would be blessed, that you would travel overseas with your husband? Didn't she?"

"Yes, she did," I admitted. "So far, mostly everything that she's told me has happened just as God told her."

Mother embraced me. "You look good, Janie, you look so happy!" "I am, Mother," I said. "I am really very happy."

With perfect timing, I asked, "When are you coming to come to Japan? Daddy always said you could come visit us." On the dining table in an oriental vase were white long stemmed roses arranged neatly. I had sent Mother the hand blown vase from the Hirosaki Glass factory.

"You should come this summer," I said coyly. I tried to appear casual just to see what her reaction would be.

"I think I will," she said, making up her mind.

"Oh, Mother, that would be so great. You will have a good time. You can have your clothes made for almost nothing. I have a maid named Suzie. She will spoil you rotten. She cooks all my meals, cleans my house and takes care of my children while David and I are at work."

"Oh, really?" Mother's ears perked up. Her eyes twinkled when I mentioned my maid Suzie. "Yes, Mother, come on! Daddy said he wanted you to come before he..."

I stopped in the middle of my sentence, I saw her smile disappear and her eyes water. I remembered too late. Daddy Henry's death was still too fresh on her mind. I wish I could have shoved those words back down my throat.

She took a deep breath then answered, "Oh. yes, I got my get-away card from United Airlines. I can come to Ja-pan and bring Li'l David with me." Mother sounded so funny when she pronounced Japan. It sounded like it was two words. She put a heavy accent on the letter A. It sounded like Jay-pan instead of Japan. I knew better than to correct her. It would only make things worse.

"Oh, good, David and I planned to ask you to come over and spend the whole summer with us. He had already asked Mom Bess but Mr. Bess isn't doing very well so she wouldn't leave him. I'm gonna call David tonight and tell him."

While home, I visited my sisters Sydney and Earlie. We all got together and drove down to Raisin City to spend some time with our Daddy Calvin Lightfoot and our stepmother, Louise. Mother and Louise talked like old friends while we played with the kids. Our little sister Lorrie Ann was so cute. She was so talented. She looked like Earlie with her big dark almond-shaped eyes. We soon discovered she could play the piano and she sang in church just like we did. Everyone thought our 2-year-old brother Emmanuel looked a lot like Sydney and me. He had big sad-looking eyes. The pupils of his eyes were black just like Daddy's. He was so serious-looking for a toddler yet so cuddly and cute. We took turns hugging him. I joined Lorrie Ann on the piano and we played one of Daddy's old favorites, "The Old Ship of Zion." Everyone joined in singing. It was like old times. We marveled at the fact my father was still making babies. Lorrie was born just before his 57th birthday. She was 11 months younger than my son Tony. Now there was my 2-year-old brother, Emmanuel, born just before Daddy turned 60. He was a younger version of my Daddy. When I was a little girl, I remember Daddy praying way into the night, "Please, Lord, let me live to see my chil'ren and my chil'ren's chil'ren, too."

I don't remember him asking God for more chil'ren but He blessed him with two more anyway. We were amazed because Louise had three adult children also. Her oldest girl, Ola, was about my age, her second oldest daughter, Stella, was two years younger. Both were married with children the same age as mine, too. Then when her youngest son, Christopher, finished college, he went into the Air Force as a commissioned officer. She was a very young woman but she and Daddy seemed like equals. My daddy looked and acted like a young man in his 30s. I grew tired just watching him with his unbound energy. He raced my nieces and nephews down the country roads passing them up like the road runner. I could see nothing but dust behind him as he sped past them. He surely lived up to his surname Lightfoot. The neighbors all cheered him on.

Louise then told us a story about the time he went for a walk and returned with a raccoon for their dinner.

"Rev chased that raccoon on foot until he was close enough to touch him," she said. "He aimed his homemade slingshot at the creature before shooting it right between the eyes with a smooth rock. He was so proud of his catch. It reminded him of his younger days when he was just a boy hunting back in the Mississippi woods."

I also visited with my in-laws, John and Lessie Bess, for a few days. Daddy Bess taught me how to cook his favorite Chili recipe from his hometown in El Paso, Texas.

Shortly after Li'l David's surgery, a letter from my husband arrived in the mail. When I opened the envelope, something fell out.

I reached down to pick it up. I couldn't believe my eyes! It was a cashier's check for $1,600. I showed it to Mother. She sat attentively listening as I read the letter out loud. My hands trembled while my eyes scanned over the words.

"Hi, Baby,

"I know that you are surprised to see that check. You won't believe this but as I was walking through the chow hall today when the base chaplain approached me. I don't know how he knew me. I always smile, you know. This officer smiled back at me. I saluted him immediately. Looking at my name tag on my uniform, he said, 'Excuse me, Tech. Sgt. Bess?'

"'Yes, sir, I'm Tech. Sgt. Bess.'

"I was nervous, thinking what did I do now?

"'Will you come to my office after lunch today?'

"I said, 'Yes, sir.'

"Janie, I have to admit I was worried. I couldn't figure out why he wanted to see me. I rushed to his office. Soon as I walked in, he handed me a long business envelope. I stared at it as I looked at him for an answer.

"'Open it, Sgt. Bess. Please.'

"I opened it slowly. I didn't know what to expect. I pulled out a check. Hold your breath because you won't believe this. I know I don't go to church and I love to drink liquor. I am always cussing and raising Hell, so I couldn't even imagine what it could be.

"Baby, it was a check inside for $10,000! I started thanking God right there in front of him. So with that cashiers check I sent, buy a commercial ticket home at the airport. Have a Merry Christmas. Buy presents for the family. You can stay until after New Year's Day, if you like or if you want to, come home. I hope you will be here for New Year's Eve. But you don't have to rush back, take your time and enjoy yourself. I truly thank God for this wonderful blessing. When I asked the chaplain where did all the money come from, he told me anonymous donors gave it to us.

"So enjoy your self. Don't worry about Terri and Tony. They are doing fine. Our friends are helping me with the kids. My boss gave me time off, too. Baby, spend that money as you see fit. We have enough to pay up all our bills and money in our savings account, too.

"Love, your husband,

"David."

I could only say, "Thank you, Lord! Thank you, Jesus!" I ran all over Mother's house shouting for joy. Mother stared at me momentarily then walked away shaking her head.

"That gal done lost her mind," she said.

I grabbed my coat and headed for the door.

"I'm going to the Oakland Army Base and purchase my airplane ticket back to Misawa." Mother casually picked up her keys to her blue '72 Mercury Monterey and held them out for me. Without saying another word, I zipped out the front door to handle my business.

Li'l David was released from the hospital two weeks later. I expected him to come home but his teacher Martha insisted he stay with her. After what she had done for Li'l David, I couldn't refuse her.

On Dec. 28, I left from the San Francisco Airport. My flight was only 12 hours. I sat in first class next to a nice couple traveling back to Japan. I lost them when I went through customs. I had to hurry to catch a train. I had so much luggage, filled with Christmas presents. A Japanese redcap actually felt sorry for me and carried it to the waiting train. It was the longest ride with no one to talk to. I missed my children. This was the first time I'd traveled alone. I couldn't wait to get home. I had on a suede coat with an ermine fox collar. I was so hot and sweaty. The stylish wig I wore felt like a hat on my head. I was only minutes from pulling it off my head when the conductor called out the stops in Japanese. I didn't know where I was. I got off the train to stretch my legs and look for someone who spoke English. An American couple stood about 25 feet away waving at me. I waved back thinking they might be from Misawa. I knew a lot of people from the base exchange where I worked. A young man and his wife introduced themselves.

"Why were you riding on the cattle car train," he asked.

"What's a cattle car," I asked.

"That's the poor man's train," his wife quipped. "It's not clean and you have to fight for a seat."

"I did, too," I said, laughing ruefully. "I stood holding on to an overhead rail for at least an hour before someone got off the train."

The man said, "Let me see your ticket." He paused. "You're supposed to be on the same car with us. Your seat is right behind us."

"No wonder the conductor looked at me strange."

The young man grabbed my luggage and we started walking to the other end of the train, to a sleek passenger car. I laughed thinking how that ticket agent cheated me out of my first class seat. I described my long ride on that cattle car.

"I was so nervous on that train," I said. "The heater blasted from underneath my seat. It was so hot. It burned my legs through my leather boots."

They laughed with me.

"There was this poor dirty peasant lying in the aisle sleeping on an old dirty cloth sack."

"That's why it's called a cattle car."

"I pushed my baggage under my feet and clutched my purse close while I fought off sleep."

"We were so glad to see an American. We were the only ones standing here waiting for a train."

"Me, too," I said. "I was so relieved to see you guys. If I hadn't found you two, I would have probably caught the wrong train heading to who knows where."

I learned a valuable lesson that day. No matter what color you are, black, white or whatever, Americans have a natural bond while living in a foreign country. We were laughing and talking together like old friends. We found our seats nearby and continued conversing. I found out they were from a small town in Pennsylvania. I told them where I was from. They had heard of Berkeley because of the Vietnam protests at Peoples Park near the university.

Before long, we pulled into Misawa-shi. The small town in the northern Honshu mountains was covered in snow. It was so thick and white.

Their ride home pulled up first. They offered me a ride. I called home. Suzie said, "David-san he leave already." They insisted on waiting with me until David showed up.

We exchanged addresses and phone numbers. Funny thing, when I look back, I realized we never met again. God just loaned them to me on that particular night.

In the spring, David And I made plans to send for Li'l David. We asked my mother if she would like to have a paid trip to Japan as a chaperone. Mother wanted to come to Japan. She was excited yet nervous about the long flight. Twice, she tried to back out of it. Earlie almost convinced her to stay home. I had to really plead with her to bring Li'l David over.

Big David was competing in the Air Force Talent Contest at Misawa soon. If David won the finals, he would travel to other bases entertaining troops worldwide.

The big day finally arrived. The kids were excited about "Grandmother" coming over. Not many black parents traveled overseas. A couple of our friends' parents had made the daring flight to Misawa Air Base earlier that year. My friend Ernestine's mother came and left a few months before my mother arrived. After Mother arrived, another friend's mother flew in, too. Everybody really applauded them, saying "You were so brave to fly over here."

I will never forget the day Mother arrived. She stood in front of the train station waiting with Li'l David as we pulled up. We were late because we got lost. David rushed out of our '68 orange Firebird.

"Hurry, Janie, we're in a loading zone," he said.

I looked at him like he was crazy. "You always act like I'm a child. David, I know it's a loading zone."

We were both tired from the long, confusing drive to the town of Aomori. We had gone to the glass factory in Aamori just the week before so I thought he would remember how to get there but apparently he didn't. When I told him he had made the wrong turn five miles back, he yelled, "Why did you wait so long to tell me the turnoff?"

"I told you to turn at the stop sign but you were speeding and missed the turn."

We had a hollering match after that. So we were not in the best of spirits when we pulled up. That is, until I saw Mother. I was shocked to see my mother using sign language with Li'l David. The last time I went home, Mother told me, "I don't know how to talk to him. I can't do those funny things with my hands." I tried to teach her finger spelling before I left, but I confused her.

"Mother, when did you learn to fingerspell?"

"David sat on my lap and I couldn't move," she chuckled lightly. "He forced my fingers into these different shapes until I did each letter perfectly. I know the alphabet now."

Tears of joy streamed down my face.

Just then, David showed up with their luggage, he exclaimed, "What are you crying about now?"

I laughed between tears as I explained, "When I saw Mother fingerspelling with Li'l David I just burst into tears. I-I'm just so happy."

David shook his head.

I looked up to the heavens. "Thank you, God," I said repeatedly.

David said, "God has enough to deal with so quit bothering him."

"God is never too busy," Mother responded. "He is everywhere."

David grumbled under his breath before changing the subject.

"Mrs. Prather, I hope you are planning to stay awhile."

He gave Mother a great big hug. She looked so happy.

Without waiting for an answer, David grabbed Li'l David in a playful hug before they went though their "routine." First, they gave each other "Five" before they performed some fancy moves with their elbows and hands. This went on for at least two minutes. We all cracked up. It amazed me how Li'l David recognized each person by merely touching them. He had a made up a signature handshake for everybody he knew.

"I feel so complete with my family here," I said drying my eyes.

David rolled his, then picked up their luggage, and headed for the car.

"I'm planning to stay at least two months," Mother said as she walked, trying to keep up with David. "Is that okay?"

"Okay? That's wonderful. You can keep Janie company. I am singing in 'The Sounds in Blue' Show. If I win, my group and I will travel all over the Far East entertaining all over Japan, Thailand and the Philippines. Janie won't be lonesome while I am gone."

"Are you trying to stay away while I am here?" Mother looked so youthful for her 60 years. I was so proud to be her daughter.

"I hope you are not too tired because we are invited to a party tonight," David said. "And you are the honored guest."

"Dress your best because everyone dresses up for the parties here in Misawa."

A big smile appeared on Mother's face.

"Good," she said. "I brought all my nice clothes with me. I got the perfect outfit for the party tonight."

"We want you to get out and enjoy yourself while you're here," David said.

Her dark eyes shined brightly. "I didn't come over here to sit in the house, you know."

"I know everyone must be hungry," David said without waiting for an answer. He drove down the crowded, narrow streets searching for a restaurant. Mother grabbed her chest when she realized we were driving on the opposite side of the street. She lost her composure. It was so funny to see her like that.

"We are on the wrong side of the street," she yelled.

My mother always seemed cool and calm. This was one of the few times I saw her excited. After parking on the side of a narrow street, we walked past many businesses, dress shops and open marketplaces until we came to a quaint little Japanese restaurant.

Old Miyako Café flashed from a neon sign on the big glass windowpane. On display in the store windows were plastic models that looked like authentic cooked meals on fancy dishes. Each dish was numbered to match the menu taped on the restaurant door. David explained to Mother while I read the menu. I was a pro at matching numbers with the printed menu. I already knew what Mother would like and what she wouldn't eat by the look on her face. Ever since the Winter Olympics were held in Misawa-shi, they took up the practice of displaying the different meals. The Japanese people could read English but were shy about speaking the language.

We sat on beautiful giant silk cushions. The oriental cushions accented the red and black lacquer dishes and tablecloth on a low table. Being we were all short, it was actually quite comfortable for us to sit low.

First they brought out red and black lacquered trays with large bowls of clear hot soup followed by steaming hot tempura vegetables. The tempura shrimp came, next the sweet and sour pork, oyster beef with green beans followed. She brought out steaming hot Gyozas (we call them Pot stickers in the U.S). The food just kept coming! A large bowl of Osoba was placed right under our noses. It was filled generously with rice noodles, meat and assorted fresh vegetables in a hot clear liquid. We couldn't wait to try it. We didn't expect to have such large servings. Japanese food had a distinctive flavor. There was a distinct difference from the stateside Chinese foods I was accustomed to.

We had a blast teaching Mother to use chopsticks. She kept dropping hers back into the plate. I noticed Li'l David was doing very well with his. There was a noticeable improvement since his last visit. Now Terri and Tony had mastered it like the natives. David had a natural knack for using them. He spoke Japanese to the waitress and the hostess. Terri, Tony and I bowed every time they came to the table with a new dish. They thanked the waitress, "Domo Ara Gato nay," they said. David beamed with pride when they spoke Japanese.

I persisted on using the chopsticks even after I continuously dropped my food. I figured if Li'l David, Terri and Tony could do it, I could do it too. Afterward, I helped myself to a white Japanese spoon and gave Mother one, too. It looked like a miniature scoop. Mother picked it up with a puzzled look on her face.

"Where is the spoons and forks around here?" We busted up.

They served a large banquet to us. Between bites of sweet and sour pork, Mother told us what a wonderful time she had traveling with Li'l David.

"Everybody was so nice to me. They really helped me with Little David. When we went to the reservations counter at United, the ticket agent, she was Japanese, too. Well, I told her I was flying to Ja-pan with my grandson and…"

David interrupted,. "It's pronounced Japan, Mrs. Prather, not Ja-pan."

Mother simply continued her story, "I told her Li'l David can't see or hear, but he is so smart. He travels everywhere. I told her he flew back and forth to Ja-pan on the plane last year." The agent told me, "I'm going to put you on a non-stop 10-hour flight to Ja-pan."

David hunched me. I knew it was a signal to correct Mother's enunciation.

I knew better. I just let her talk.

"Mother," I said, "I know you and Li'l David are very tired. When we get home, I want you to take a nap. It's nighttime in the States now."

"Ooh, wee, I am tired," she said. "Sitting those long hours on that plane and then racing with the attendant to catch that train from Tokyo to Aamori was hard on me. I didn't know I could run so fast. Li'l David was laughing so hard. He held on to me tight and ran right 'side me, too. He must've thought we were playin' or somethin'. That train don't wait neither. I asked that Japanese conductor, 'Why you no wait on me?' He told me, 'I am very sorry, we cannot be late. We never late.'"

Mother shook her head. "I see why they never late. Half the people missed that train. They don't care. Those doors on that train close so fast! We just did get our luggage thrown on by the nice agent who helped me carry it."

"I am glad the agent suggested the train to Misawa," I said. "The fog from the mountains was so bad the planes are delayed from landing in Misawa for hours, sometimes for two to three days."

"I was so proud as I watched Li'l David," Mother said. "He was so neat and polite on the flight here. Every time he finished eating, he neatly placed the soiled fork and spoon back into the plastic wrap and closed up the container. It looked like he hadn't touched his food. The stewardess said he didn't eat anything but I opened it and showed her his empty dish. She was impressed with him. She was very nice to me, too."

My mind wandered off. Terri and Tony were having their own private conversation. Li'l David was fingerspelling to his daddy.

I lifted the small bowl with the hot clear soup and sipped it. Mother eyes spelled out her disapproval. She looked surprised when I assured her it was proper to lift your rice or soup bowl to your lips while eating in Japan.

"Just don't lift your plate." With reluctance, Mother followed my lead.

We laughed when she told us the agent looked at her passport and couldn't believe she was 60.

"Well, you will have to celebrate your 61st birthday here," David said.

"We are keeping you here for your birthday in August," I added. "We will give a big party for you, Mother."

"Yeah, just as long as you don't tell my age," she responded.

We promised to keep it a secret.

At the party that night, everyone treated Mother like a celebrity. They all commended her on her bravery. Just the idea of her flying over 6,000 miles of water was a courageous act. Most our friends stationed at Misawa were born and raised in the South so they were surprised Mother was born there, too. Most everyone knew David and I were from California but they seemed surprised my mother was black. Before Mother arrived, I was asked on more than one occasion what my nationality was. I always answered black or African-American. I never knew why they looked at me with disbelief. One of the reasons was David would make remarks such as, "Janie doesn't know what she is." I always objected, but it made no difference. That is, until they met my mother with her dark café complexion. I was just a lighter version of my mother. When she spoke, they picked up her Mississippi accent.

It was on after that. She was the life of the party. Mother was never shy about expressing her true feelings. She really warmed things up when she complained about the cold cuts being served with hard liquor. It was customary for the military to have plenty of liquor at any event big or small.

There were high-ranking officers in all professions imaginable attending the party. I had requested only punch or coffee for my Mother. Someone managed to slip Mother a goblet filled with red Chablis. After one sip, she started, "Why did these people serve cold cuts with all this alcohol?" Someone snickered. Some looked around to see who was speaking.

David prodded me toward her. "Go get your mother. She is about to turn this party out."

I tried to pull Mother away from the crowd gathering around her.

"I'm sorry, we have to go now, Mother." Meanwhile, other guests swarmed around her in a circle agreeing with her. They laughed when she said, "You gotsta' serve greasy hot food when they are drinking hard liquor."

I tried to pull her away again to quiet her down but I was too late. I spotted the near-empty glass in her hand. She tipped it up finishing off the last drop of wine.

"Who gave her this wine? I asked.

Everyone standing near her feigned innocence. They hunched their shoulders or replied, "I don't know" or 'I didn't."

I knew the effect the liquor had on her but when I discovered she drank one whole glassful, it was already too late. Before I could do anything, someone egged her on, "Mrs. Prather, why don't you serve cold cuts with liquor?"

"When you serve cold food, people get drunk and they tear up your shit," Mother said. My mother never cussed unless she was very angry or upset. I tried to lead her outside, but one of our friends hugged her and wouldn't let us leave. That led fuel to the fire.

"She is refusing to come with me." I whispered to David. He huffed off. I watched him as he tried fruitlessly to convince her to leave. It didn't work. The more he insisted Mother come with us, the more she gravitated toward our friends. And she got louder.

"I'm grown, I came to Ja-pan with my grandson all by myself. When I get ready to leave, I know how to catch a taxi back to yo' house."

"Let her stay," someone said. "We'll watch her. Y'all can go on home."

David didn't want to leave her but we had no choice. The hostess handed us our coats and boots while we stood helplessly in the foyer looking back at Mother. She looked right at home laughing and talking with our friends. Nothing I did or said could make her to leave David fussed at me all the way home.

"You should have forced her to come with us, Janie."

"Oh, David, Mother will be all right. She's having so much fun for the first time in a long time."

"Yeah, but she cussed and she's loud and obnoxious. Did you give her something to drink?"

"No, before I could get her a glass of punch, someone had given her a goblet filled with something red in it. I assumed it was punch until I smelled it."

He just about blew a fuse then. He called back over to his friends party.

"Be careful, my mother-in-law will turn the party out," he said. I could hear the hostess over the loud music talking into the receiver.

"Oh, no, we are enjoying her so much. She is fo' real! She is the hit of this party. Ya'll go on to sleep. Bye."

Defeated, David held the receiver to his ear still.

Just then, the host spoke into the receiver, "Don't worry, Brother Bess, we'll bring her home safe. We'll take care of her."

David couldn't sleep worrying about Mother. In the morning, he insisted, "Call over to their house because your mother didn't come home yet."

Just as I reached for the phone, it rang.

"Hey, Sister Bess, your mother spent the night with me and my husband."

"I was worried. Is she all right?" Mother's indisguisable laughter roared through the receiver.

"Yes, she's just fine. We are having a ball!' "Oh," I said. "That's good."

David took the phone. "We'll come and pick her up right now, if you like. We are sorry for the inconvenience."

I put my ear close to the phone so I could hear. "What inconvenience? Your mother-in-law is cool!."

David stammered, "No, I'm talking about what she said last night. I apologize."

"She was right. You don't feed people cold sandwiches and give them alcohol. We had the finest of liquors at the party. Girl, she told the hostess off, too."

"Oh, no," I said out loud.

"Where's Sister Bess," she asked. "Is she there? Let me speak to her, please." David handed me the receiver.

"We're fixing Mother some breakfast now so don't look for her then we are taking her sightseeing. So relax, she is my mama, too, now."

All I could do was say, "Okay."

My friend didn't bring Mother home until late that night.

She came in laughing and talking with my friends as if they had known each other for at least 10 years.

"We have adopted your mother. I hope you don't mind."

I have to admit I was happy for Mother but I felt left out. She had only been in Misawa for less than 48 hours and already she was having a blast without the family.

Oh, well, at least Mother is happy.

From that day forward, she was invited to my children's classrooms where my friends taught school. My co-workers at the Base Exchange took her out to dinner and everywhere. I very seldom spent any quality time with her.

Finally, I sat her down and told her, "Mother, I want to spend some time alone with you. My friends keep taking you places but I want to show you around, too."

Mother listened quietly before answering.

"I was trying to give you some time alone with David before he left. I can go with you after he leaves on tour."

"That's a deal, Mother," I said hugging her.

At the base competition David sang solo and won the singles competition hands up. Then his group Black Satin won the group competition also. Naturally, Mother was right again. David was leaving and we would have quality time together.

He soon left for Yokota Air Base, Japan. If they won there, they will go on a special singing tour to Thailand and then on to the Philippines, South Korea, etc.

The day after David left, Tony was competing in Hirosaki in a Judo tournament. We had to wake up before 5 a.m. to meet his teacher at the base gym.

Mother insisted on cooking fried chicken for our lunch. Even after, I told her they always served good Japanese food at these events.

Everybody on the bus was turning around looking toward us as we rode along.

"Mother, I smell that good old fried chicken," someone said. "Don't be holdin' out on us. now."

Mother busted out laughing.

"I hope you brought enough for everybody."

"You think I didn't," Mother quipped back. "I cooked three chickens this morning. It is hot and ready. I wrapped it up and put it in this cooler so it'll stay hot."

I must admit my mouth watered just thinking about her golden brown chicken. She described how she used her special seasonings without giving away her family secret. I couldn't take it anymore.

"Give me the breast, Mother, please," I whispered. Mother laughed. "I told Janie she was going to be hungry."

Tony was only competing in the yellow belt competition. His tournament didn't start until the late afternoon. They stopped for lunch. The Japanese people were providing lunch to the attendees and their families. It was impolite to refuse their food. It was considered an insult. Well, when they served steamed clams and oysters with a bowl of hot steaming rice in the cafeteria, well, almost all the Americans backed out. Only a few brave ones managed to get the clams and oysters down. There sat Mother with her new cronies, eating fried chicken in the back of the cafeteria. I was glad I ate my breast meat earlier on the bus. There was none left. All the Americans, regardless of ethnicity or cultures, enjoyed Mother's Fried Chicken while laughing and teasing with her.

Before the week was up, most the people at the judo tournament ended up at our house for dinner. After the tournament, Mother announced, "This

Saturday night if everybody will bring some seafood, chicken or rice to my daughter's house, I will make you guys all the Creole Gumbo you can eat."

Boy, everybody started cheering, That Saturday, our little housing was packed. People were coming and going. They brought everything, rice, crab legs, hot links, chicken, shrimp, prawns, oysters, and scallops to put in the pot. Some placed their take-out orders, others hung around to socialize. We had a blast.

David was still on a singing tour. I was hoping he would be back but he was now in Thailand singing in a show.

CHAPTER THIRTY-SEVEN

As much as I hated it, the time passed too fast.

"I've got to get home and check on my house," Mother said one day. "Them wol's may have torn it down by now. Looks like David planned this —so he wouldn't be here with me." We laughed. "Li'l David has to get back to school soon."

Because of the thick fog that time of the year, the planes had trouble taking off and landing at Misawa. There were numerous delays this time. I decided I had better get an early start with their orders.

I found out that before David left on tour, he took care of everything.

David had done his research and made certain all the paperwork was in order.

I took a taxi over to the base comptroller's office to turn the paperwork in.

The captain read the orders.

"Ma'am, David Bess Jr. has permission to travel on a military flight. But there is a problem. Your mother is not a military dependent."

"I know but she is his grandmother and she is authorized to travel with him as his interpreter-guide."

"Mrs. Bess," he said, shaking his head. "Due to the military regulations, your mother cannot fly on a military flight to the states."

"Then how is my son getting home? He has to get back in time for school."

Pointing to a paragraph in the orders, I said to the captain, "It states right here my son is authorized a chaperone. My mother came with him because she is the only one who knows how to communicate with my son. He needs someone who knows him and also in competent in tactile signs. He cannot travel 6,000 miles alone. He is 13 years old but he cannot see or hear. He cannot travel with a stranger."

I was so angry. This young captain was not budging. "Ma'am, calm down, we will make sure he has an interpreter."

"My son is not traveling with anybody," I said, folding my arms in front of my chest. "They have to know how to guide him in strange places and fingerspell into his hands. He cannot see or hear. I will not send my baby with anybody. My mother came over with him and she is not leaving without him. My husband paid her way so she could travel with him."

"Why doesn't your husband travel with him Space A?"

"My husband is on temporary duty. He is somewhere in Asia, singing with the 'Sounds in Blue' show."

"Well, I'm sorry, ma'am, but as I stated before, your mother cannot travel on a military flight because of the insurance clause. You must understand my position."

"No, I understand what you're saying but I don't understand why my mother can't go with my son. I am not sending my child with just anybody just because you said he can do signs with my blind son."

The captain walked off, returning with another officer. He, too, tried to convince me my mother wouldn't be able to travel with my son.

I stalked out of there, not knowing what to do. I called one of David's friends for advice. He told me to wait at home until he called. I paced and paced until the phone rang.

"Janie, come back here and bring Li'l David," he said, adding that I was to talk with a colonel about my problem.

"Why should I bring Li'l David?"

"Sister Bess, just do as I say."

I returned to the office with Li'l David. I fingerspelled to Little David, "Sit here, I have to talk to these people about some business. Relax. Read your book. I will be right back." He nodded his head and I started to leave. I looked back making sure he would be okay out in the waiting room. He took his Braille book out his backpack and began to read. He had a smile of contentment on his face.

I was so proud of my son. I marveled at his independence. I remembered how once upon a time, I couldn't even leave him to use the bathroom. He would be terrified to be alone. Now he was such a fine handsome young man. Everyone loved him and he reflected love back.

I entered the room where this colonel sat at a large desk. I don't remember exactly what he said but I know it was basically the same story they told me before. My mother wasn't approved to fly with Little David. I didn't know what to do.

"Oh, Lord, help me," I cried. They looked at me as if I'd lost my mind. Because they ushered me out a different exit, I didn't realize until I got home I had left Little David in the lobby.

"Janie, where's Li'l David," Mother asked when I got home.

"Oh my God," I said. "I left Li'l David in the lobby reading his book."

"What's the matter wit' you? You done lost your mind!"

"I don't know," I said, lying. I didn't have the heart to tell her they refused to let her fly home with Li'l David. I didn't have any extra money.

"You better go get him before they call the police on you, gal." Before I could call another taxi, my phone rang,

"Mrs. Bess, this is the comptroller's office. We have a young man here sitting in the lobby with a Braille book. We cannot communicate with him."

"Oh, I'm sorry, I was so upset, I forgot my son. I went out another exit so I forgot he was with me. I'll be right there. I'm waiting on a taxi now. Thanks."

Just then the taxi pulled up so I hung the phone up and ran out to get my son. He must be frantic and worried by now.

"Oh God, forgive me, how could I forget my son?"

Before the taxi could come to a full stop, I leaped out the door and ran into the comptroller's office building. But Li'l David wasn't in the lobby. The receptionist peeked out of a room.

"Mrs. Bess?"

"Yes, I'm Mrs. Bess, where's my son?'

"Oh, he's in the office with the squadron commander. He had just returned from lunch and saw the young man sitting there."

David was sitting in the commander's chair. He had a big bag of candy in his hands but he was munching on some chocolate chip cookies. He was laughing and having fun feeling the commander's brass bars on the shoulder of his uniform. I reached over and spelled to Li'l David.

"Hi, Mom," he spelled. "I am having so much fun." He felt the engraved letters of the colonel's name on a carved teakwood desk plaque. He spelled each letter out in his hands holding it up for the colonel to see.

"What is he doing," the colonel asked.

"He is showing you how to spell your name."

He looked so awkward as he tried to imitate David's hand shapes. He bit his bottom lip as he tried to grasp the concept of talking with his hands. He followed David's lead.

Li'l David chuckled with glee.

"That's good," I said. "You're doing it."

"I am?"

"Yes, he is nodding," I said with pride. "Li'l David, he is signing yes, good job." I was excited for the colonel. He reminded me of a proud little boy then. He had forgotten all about Li'l David's disabilities. Instead he was the student now and Li'l David was the teacher. By the time we left the office to go home, Li'l David had taught the whole staff at the comptroller's office their names in sign language and a different signature handshake for each of the men. After talking to the ladies, he hugged the female employees. Laughing gleefully, we left the office with the signed papers for my mother to fly home with Li'l David on a commercial airliner instead of the military plane, all paid by the military.

David made it home just a couple of days before they left for the States.

"David, I think you planned this trip so you wouldn't be here with me," Mother said. "Did you?"

"Yes, I knew I was going to win the talent show. I planned it that way." "You did, huh," I teased.

Mother looked shocked. I could tell she wasn't expecting that answer.

David hugged her.

"Mrs. Prather, what I meant is, I wanted you to enjoy yourself, to be here with Janie. I knew she would need your company while I was gone."

"Mother was no company," I said. "All the teachers and my friends took her shopping and sightseeing almost every day for the six weeks. She has only been home with me for only the last two weeks."

"I really enjoyed Ja-pan," Mother said, thanking David. "Everybody has been so nice to me. I felt right at home."

She smiled. A sincere look of gratitude was on her face. David actually blushed. He hugged Mother.

"I love you Mrs. Prather. I thank you for taking care of Li'l David. He looks so good."

Mother teased David, "Yeah, but I'm not going to forget you got here just in time to see us off. You gonna pay for this later."

David cracked up.

I drove Mother to the airport. The fog had lifted and she was ready to go. Li'l David sat between Terri and Tony signing with them. They were laughing and having a good time.

Li'l David was ecstatic about leaving. He kept verbally saying his favorite and only words. "Bye-Bye" Then he would sign it to me. I felt a wave of sadness come over me. I was going to miss my son. I didn't want him to go. I wanted my mother to stay, too.

I knew it was time to mentally let go of my son. I had done it enough since David was a baby lying in the preemie ward and during all the eye surgeries, too.

The ticket agent explained to Mother she would have to stay overnight in Tokyo. She would have to rent a hotel room. The cost was $80.

"Eighty dollars," Mother said. "I'll sleep in the terminal with Li'l David 'fore I pay that much money for a room."

"Mother, stop being so tight. you have enough money. Your flight is free, so stop being so petty."

I kissed them good bye

She laughed at me then took Li'l David by the hand. She led him into the plane. We watched the jet airliner take off before heading back to the base.

It was early in the morning when the phone rang waking us from a deep sleep. A man's voice with a strong Japanese accent spoke, "Mushy, Mushy? Bess-san? We have your mother, Mrs. Plather here."

Oh, Lord, what has Mother done now? "Mushy, Mushy, Hai, this is Mrs. Bess."

"Hai, this is the representative from the International Airport in Tokyo, we have your mother and her blind grandson here in the office."

"What happened? Is my mother and son okay?" My hand shook as I turned on the light. I glanced over at the alarm clock. It was 2 a.m.

"Your mother say she no have money to stay in hotel. She say she no have $80. Nay? Can you please pay the charge for her and her grandson?"

"My mother has money. May I speak to her, please?" As soon as she said hello I started yelling.

"You have plenty of cash and I gave you over $200 in yen." I took a deep breath to keep from screaming. "Why don't you pay the money. They're gonna put you in jail for vagrancy, if you don't stop it."

"I ain't paying $80 for no room, I only have about five hours to go. Humph! Me and Li'l David will just sleep in the airport on some chairs."

"Mother stop being so stubborn. Pay the $80 in yen. I can't get to you. Your flight leaves at 7 a.m. You are over 500 miles away. So I can't help you."

I was so angry. I was ready to really bawl her out, but those foreign phones were unpredictable. The line went out. There was no dial tone. I called the airport back but none of the employees understood English. Then all I heard was a dial tone. I slammed the phone down. I kept David awake talking about it because I tossed and turned until the morning waiting for a return call that never came.

I just started praying. I kept calling every chance I got. I pictured my mother and son in a Japanese jail. They put you in a nasty pen and fed their prisoners rice. Two days later, I finally got through to the states.

"Janie? Is that you?"

"Mother, when did you get home? Why didn't you call me back. I was so worried about you and Li'l David."

"Oh, shoot, we made it home two days ago. It was fun. Those Japanese people were so nice to me. That hotel they tried to get me to stay in was about two miles away. That was too far from the airport. It would have cost me a fortune to catch a taxi back. I tol' them I wasn't paying all that money for a room." Mother was giggling like a teenager. "They paid for our room at another hotel, right across the street from the airport. Wasn't that nice?"

"Yes, Mother," I said with relief. I could just picture her arguing with that airline representative.

"They came that morning, woke us up and carried all our luggage for us. They picked us up in a limousine. I felt like I was the president. They drove us right to the airport and then they changed our longer flight to a non-stop flight. Wasn't that nice?"

"Yes, Mother, that was nice."

"Remember, the commander gave you a return ticket for an 18-hour flight. Well, the nice Japanese man changed it into an 8-hour flight. They were so nice to me and Li'l David." She reminded me of a kindergartner on the first day of school.

"They really like Li'l David, too. He was fingerspelling their names and everything. I asked them their names, I'm not sure I spelled it right but they were so happy when David started teaching them how to spell their names."

When David came home from work, I told him what happened.

"Your mother turned Japan out. They're going to lock her out the country and throw away the key.'

"But she said they were really nice to her."

"Yeah," David teased. "They changed her flight to get her out their country sooner."

"You stop talking about my mother," I said as I jabbed him in the side with my elbow.

"Ow, that hurts, you know," he said, laughing. We both drifted back to sleep.

CHAPTER THIRTY-EIGHT

In September 1974, we got our return orders. David had put in a humanitarian request to return to Northern California so we could be closer to Li'l David's school and be a complete family again. He put on his wish list three choices: Castle, Travis or Hamilton. I wanted Castle Air Force Base so I could get my job back at the phone company. We were scheduled to leave in June 1975.

But when we saw our orders, we weren't happy. The military sent us to New Mexico, saying there was a residential school for the blind in Alamogordo, N.M. We tried to explain David was blind and deaf, not just blind but they still refused to give us an assignment. His deaf-blind counselor wrote a compelling letter to attach to our request. But the military still refused, insisting New Mexico had a school to accommodate our son.

We arrived home on the 4th of July in time for a family reunion in Oakland. We had a blast.

David had to report to duty at Kirtland AFB in Albuquerque, N.M., by July 18. We left on July 8 to get all three children set up. School started in early August in New Mexico. I tried to be optimistic about our new assignment but David was adamant about us returning to California.

"Janie, get busy," he said. "Research the area for schools."

While we were waiting for base housing, in a hotel room. I did just that. I searched the Yellow Pages. When I found the school, I called the number immediately. It was summer so I was prepared to leave a message on the recorder. I stuttered and stammered at first then introduced myself. He told me he was the dean at the school. I confessed to him I was totally unprepared to speak to a real live person. His Spanish accent ringed over the phone as he laughed at me. I apologized for calling so early in the morning.

"Oh, It's okay, I was just in preparing my office for school," he said. "It starts in two weeks."

Through our lengthy conversation, I discovered the school was in Alamogordo, near Cannon Air Force Base. It was a school for the blind only. They had no deaf students there. It was about a two-hour drive from Albuquerque.

I told him our plight. During the conversation, I bragged about my son's achievements and how he had overcome so many obstacles in his short lifetime. The dean was so impressed he asked to meet Li'l David that day. I convinced him to come the following afternoon instead.

He showed up the next day on time. We sat in the hotel dining room eating. He watched in amazement as my two smaller children interacted with their big brother in sign. I discovered he didn't really know sign language. I interpreted for him to Li'l David. He thought David would be a great asset to the blind school. He would be the first deaf-blind student. He said there was teacher who taught sign language. He felt Li'l David would be able to communicate with her.

"Because there are no other deaf students attending this school, there is a strong possibility she could work with him one on one," he said. I was excited about the new school. David was more subdued. He wanted to see the school first, but he was more concerned about us finding a place to live.

David was a technical sergeant with more than 11 years service so we qualified right away for base housing.

Within two weeks, we moved into a lovely four-bedroom house at Kirtland Air Force Base. After our household goods arrived, we took time to unpack them. Li'l David helped us. He flexed his muscles.

"I am strong," he signed to me.

"Yes, you are," I signed back.

"And I am smart, too," he said.

Big David signed.

"We're going to have to do something to break down this giant ego problem."

"Oh, leave him alone," I said.

"He has to learn not to brag so much."

"For a long time, he thought he wasn't so smart or strong. His teachers used positive reinforcement on him as a teaching tool. It worked."

David gave me one of his that's-a-bunch-of-bull looks.

After we settled into our new house, we enrolled Terri and Tony in school.

After they started school, Li'l David protested.

"I am the big brother. My little sister and brother go to school. I'm supposed to be first."

"David, you will have to wait," I explained. "We're trying to decide where to send you to school."

"I want to see the dean, Mr. Hernandez," he signed. He closed my hand into a fist and held it close with his left hand until he finished. I hated that. He made sure he had my full attention. It's like having someone cover your mouth when you try to speak. He made sure he finished his sentence with no interruptions.

"I want to go to the new school here in New Mexico. Then later, I'll go back to California School for the Blind." He signed fast while squeezing my right hand closed. "I could teach them sign language."

I was frustrated because he had found a way to talk without any argument from me. He won that bout. When he finally freed my hand, I was too outdone to argue with him. I knew it was fruitless to try to convince him to wait.

I gave in. When he finally let me talk, I signed, "Maybe, you're right. Let me talk to Daddy about this. Okay?"

Emphatically, he signed "Yes" several times.

In amazement, I shook my head.

I told David, "Li'l David needs to go to school while we are waiting on your reassignment results."

After much thought, he said, "Okay, let's go check out this school."

I was so excited for Li'l David. He would have something to do. He was bored. I have to confess, my hands cramped from fingerspelling eight to 12 hours every day. Li'l David loved to talk.

That night, after the children were tucked away in their beds, David and I sat close together relishing the quiet time alone.

"Baby, we need to make a plan of attack," he said.

"What do you mean, David?"

"Baby, I don't want you to get too excited. We're merely going to visit. I don't feel this school is going to fit David's educational needs." He held me at arms length, his deep set eyes penetrating through me. I swear he could read my mind.

"So I want you to be prepared. We already know they only have one teacher who knows sign language. I know you have your hopes up but I am not so sure this is the best school for David. He knows the teachers at CSB. We know they love and care for him. These people don't know our son. He may regress if his brain is not stimulated. David is very bright. So we need to remember, his education is first. I am going to fight for that reassignment to California."

I knew better than to argue with him.

Secretly, I enjoyed living in New Mexico. I had found a job at American Furniture Store in downtown Albuquerque. David had no idea I'd been hired. He was set on leaving. I liked the friendly neighbors. I had made friends with a couple across the street, a master sergeant and his German wife. They had three children. We hit it off. He worked nights so while he slept I would take her shopping because she couldn't drive. Our children played together nicely. Li'l David enjoyed teaching them sign.

I tried to talk with him while we packed our bags for the overnight trip to see the school.

"David, try to be optimistic. It may be a blessing. God may have sent Li'l David here."

"Stop messing with God," David said. "He has more important things to do. That's why he gave us common sense." He sat on the bed next to me. "I already know we have a good case, Janie. California School for the Blind doesn't start classes until September so we have time to fight this, and get Li'l David back in time for school."

I started to say something about staying in Albuquerque. I knew to leave it alone. David had made up his mind.

"I'll ask for time off. We will spend the night at Cannon AFB in guest housing. It's near Alamogordo. That way we will be rested up."

I was excited about going to Alamogordo.

"I love to travel and eat out," I said. "I don't have to cook or clean for one whole day."

"Yeah, I know," David said. "You're spoiled after living in Japan." He looked up then took a deep breath. "You've had over three years of freedom. Suzie cooked, cleaned and baby-sat for you." His sideways smile appeared across his mouth. "You ain't worth two dead flies now."

When he laughed, I punched him on his shoulder.

"Hey, that hurts!"

I hugged him close.

"Oh, that didn't hurt you. I'm just playing and you know it." I planted a big kiss on his left cheek. It left a red imprint and I wiped it away.

It was a beautiful day when we drove to Alamogordo to the blind school. I saw the petrified forest and other famous sites on our drive there. The next morning after a counselor took us on a tour, we went to the dean's office. We let him know we were skeptical about the school's curriculum for the deaf.

"You see, we are not worried about David's mobility skills. He gets around well, like he can see," David explained with pride.

"He needs to be able to communicate with the staff and the students," I added.

At lunch we discussed the school. It didn't sound as advanced as the California program. When we first arrived, we met the teacher who was supposed to teach David. We were told she was proficient in American sign language. Well, that wasn't true. When she eagerly arrived on the scene, I was talking to Li'l David in his left hand. Big David was conversing with him in his other hand at the same time. David answered us back fingerspelling interspersing conversation between the two of us. This was a regular occurrence whenever David and I talked to Li'l David. He loved it because we always included him in our conversations.

This teacher watched us in awe. Our hands moved fast in rhythmic movements.

Little David's hands answered even faster in response to our questions. I sensed her intimidation.

"Ooh, can he understand what you are saying," she asked. "You two are talking in fingerspelling and signs at the same time. Does he really understand when both of you talk to him at the same time. It seems so confusing to me."

"Oh, yes, we are having a family discussion," I said, smiling at her. "My husband and I are having a friendly debate about something and we asked Li'l David's opinion."

Big David laughed.

"He is trying to stay neutral but it is hard if the issue is not in his favor."

"Oh," she said, her eyes flitted back and forth watching us.

David called Li'l David a knucklehead. Little David burst out laughing so loud, his heavy voice vibrated throughout the lobby. I placed my finger over his mouth, then signed quiet, please. He kept snickering.

"He asked me, 'Who's here? Is there a lady here?'" I said it out loud so the teacher could hear what he said.

"Yes, it is a teacher standing here."

"How does he know," she asked.

I interpreted to Li'l David what she said. He signed back.

"I smell her perfume. It is Chanel No. 5, the same one Mrs. Greenleaf wears."

A look of disbelief appeared on her face. I was just as shocked. I never knew he could tell the difference between perfumes.

"He never fails to amaze me," David said.

"Li'l David taught his whole family fingerspelling," I told the teacher. "We are still learning sign language. His sister and brother knows more than we do."

We introduced Li'l David to her. He spelled her name back to us to insure the spelling was correct. Then he took her hand and spelled it back to her.

"He talks fast in sign language," she said. "He is an advanced signer."

I bragged then, "He also knows Grade II Braille."

She was shocked. "How did they teach him when he can't hear?"

"Little David is very fast," David said proudly. "He picks up things very quickly. Li'l David is intuitive. His senses are very strong."

She asked us so many questions. We knew right then and there this school was not for our son.

"I have never met a blind child as advanced as David."

"Yes, he is quite brilliant. He is called a walking computer in Berkeley by his colleagues," David bragged.

"Well, your son will be able to teach me to sign faster," she said. "I have to admit I've grown rusty because we have no deaf children here."

During the afternoon break, we went to the dorms, They were quite impressive, but we knew we had to tell them the bad news. They seemed so excited about David coming on board.

We returned to the dean's office after the break. We broke the news to the staff. They seemed so disappointed. The dean sat us down with a nice cup of coffee.

"Well, what do you think. We know your son is more advanced than we anticipated. You should have warned us," he chuckled nervously.

David and I just sat listening. There was an uneasy silence.

"I talked to the sign language instructor," he continued. "She admitted he was quite advanced in signing. We had never seen anyone talk to two people at the same time as if in a verbal conversation." His inquisitive eyes twinkled in amazement. "How did he learn to do that?"

"The dean of the deaf-blind, Mrs. Greenleaf, and his teacher, Martha Jackson, at CSB talked to him like that all the time," I said. "I thought all deaf children knew this method."

"Oh, I see." He cleared his throat. "She admits she is a little rusty but thinks Li'l David can teach her sign language and help her learn to fingerspell faster."

"Oh," David said. Our eyes met. I swear, we could read each others' minds. I knew just what he was thinking.

"We feel he would be a great asset to this school," the dean said.

David and I responded at the same time.

"That's well and good, but who's going to teach Li'l David while he's teaching her?"

David and I looked at one another and burst into laughter. We guffawed. Embarrassed, I said, "Oh, we're sorry."

"Speak for your self," David said. "I'm not sorry. We have to think of our son's future."

The dean blushed. He was speechless.

"We need to get David back to CSB before someone takes his place. The dean is holding a slot open for him but we need to hurry."

"I understand," the dean said, slowly nodding his head. "We appreciate you bringing David to our campus. The staff and all the children really enjoyed him."

We thanked him for his time. We stood up ready to leave.

"Is there anything we can do for you before you go," the dean asked. "I'd be happy to help you any way I can."

"Matter of fact, you can. We need you an official letter to take to my commander showing there is no a school here conducive with my son's educational needs."

Without hesitating, he typed a letter stating Li'l David was too advanced and they didn't provide sign language classes. Their school specialized in training for the blind exclusively, he said.

David took the paperwork to his assignment section the next week. Without waiting for the official orders to California, David sent Li'l David back to Berkeley in time for the fall semester. My mother was happy he was back home again, too.

"I still kept Li'l David's bedroom ready for him. I knew he'd be back."

I went to work on my new job as a cashier the same day David flew home with our son. I worked there five months. I received several raises because I could work PBX, cashier, accounts receivable and sales. I was all over the store working in different departments. I had gained some weight so David began to call me Squeaky. He said, every time I walked, I squeaked.

One day, he came into the office to see me, he forgot and said, "May I speak to Squeaky?"

"Squeaky," the receptionist asked.

"Oops, I'm sorry, I mean Janie."

From that day forward, my little secret was exposed. Everyone there called me Squeaky.

It was so much fun meeting new faces, selling furniture and linens, too. But one month later, David received orders to report to Travis Air Force Base in California. He was ecstatic.

"It is only 35 miles from the California School for the Blind in Berkeley," he said.

I grew sad. I didn't want to leave. I did miss my son and my family, though. My mother and sister visited us just before we left to go home. They came for Thanksgiving. I took them to the historic Old Town to the unique quaint shops on cobblestone sidewalks and streets. They bought a lot of the Southwest jewelry and art pieces. Mother bought me a beautiful necklace and earring set in real silver. I was so happy. I had another set my co-workers gave me on my last day with a silver jewelry box. The kids and I flew home with Mother and Earlie a few days later. David still had to clear base. He drove our '65 Firebird back home to California.

While David was on his leave, we celebrated Christmas and New years at home with our families.

After the holidays, at Travis Air Force Base, we finally got base housing after a three-month waiting period. As soon as we were unpacked, we started spending the weekends visiting our families in the East Bay.

Earlie fixed my hair at her beauty shop every weekend. I helped clean the shop in exchange.

One day she said, "Janie, you should go to beauty school and get your license."

"I was trying to get hired back at the telephone company." "You can come work with me."

She had leased an old defunct Laundromat on San Pablo one month after we returned home. She and her new husband started to work remodeling right away.

351

I had so much fun helping her decorate. I helped her select her paint, wallpaper, lightings, and all accessories. I decided to do as she suggested and get my beautician's license. It would take me over nine months.

"It's like having a baby, it only takes nine months," Earlie said. "There's no diapers, milk, crying, though, just good hard-earned money."

While David was on leave, he drove us down every day. We helped break down a hollow wall. Behind it was the most beautiful curved staircase leading up to a second floor room. She decided to make it into a boutique.

We help paint, lay linoleum and carpet. It was such fun being home with my family.

The only thing that dampened my spirits was when I discovered my oldest sister, Sydney, was sick. She had a nervous breakdown. I visited her in the hospital. She was so despondent and reserved, not like the spunky outspoken sister I knew. My heart was heavy.

Unexplained tears flooded my eyes one day for no apparent reason. I began reminiscing about all the fun we had together. Sydney picked me and my children up and took us to picnics. When David was gone, she always visited me. I had to laugh as I thought about the time she brought all the children over one morning without warning. She blew her horn outside my apartment building and started yelling upstairs.

"I've got to go to work," she said. "I don't have anybody to watch my kids today."

She let her kids out of the car and they came running up the stairs, bamming on my front door while another rang my bell. They woke up Terri, who was a baby at the time. One by one they entered the apartment. I was flabbergasted. The oldest boy, Alex, announced, "I have the chickenpox, George has the measles, Marty has the mumps and Denise has the flu."

They stood there wide-eyed and excited. I couldn't do anything. I yelled at Sydney to come back as her little Volkswagen sped off. They were covered with bumps, faces swollen. I had to play nurse for the whole week. They were quarantined at my house for two weeks.

By the end of the week, Li'l David inherited the chicken pox, Terri had the measles and I had the flu.

I couldn't help but love her even though she tricked me that time.

She eventually came home but she still wasn't the same. I took off every day while they ate lunch to go to her house to sit and talk with her.

After a few visits, I saw her smile return.

"I want to see Li'l David," she said one day. I brought him over to visit her. I didn't tell him she was sick.

David was uncanny. Somehow, he sensed it.

"Why is Sydney different now?" Before I could answer, he said, "She is sick?"

I nodded a sign for yes.

I asked Mother about it that evening.

"Did you tell Li'l David Sydney was sick?"

"No," she said, adding. "That boy is blind, but God gave him more sense than most people have in their big heads."

As soon as we were settled in our new place, I went to beauty school. I really enjoyed the school. I had so much fun creating new hairdos, learning how to perform chemical services, and talking to the clients and fellow students. By the time Earlie's business was established, I was almost ready to graduate from beauty school.

Meanwhile, we drove down faithfully every weekend to pick up Li'l David from the dorm at CSB. Sometimes, on the weekends, we stayed the night with Earlie and her new husband, Arnold. Our husbands became very close. Our children played together nicely. Li'l David was so happy to see his big cousin Trena on Fridays. She was very kind and patient. She spent a lot of time talking in sign with him. They went to the park nearby and she introduced him to her many friends. Li'l David had fun teaching her friends how to fingerspell.

I had David into buying us a new car. The Firebird had broken down on me so much one day, I refused to go another day being pushed from the busy streets where we lived. One night after he had to pick me up, I made him promise to take me car shopping. We ended up in Sacramento buying a new white Ford Granada. I swore I wouldn't be late for school anymore because of the car trouble.

I was so happy. Soon, I would be able to work with my sister and make lots of money to help David with our expenses. It was expensive driving back and forth to pick Li'l David up every weekend.

I was counting down the days before I graduated from school.

"Two to go," I yelled out at 6 a.m. one Friday morning as I prepared to leave for school. David and the kids barely stirred in their beds. They were due to get up soon. I felt giddy and nervous. Then an unexplained sadness overcame me. I shook it off. Under my breath, I said. "Ah, it's nothing." I went about fixing David's lunch, ironing the children's clothes for school. I prepared a big breakfast for everybody.

I was so excited, I couldn't stop yapping. I could tell my family was not in the mood. Finally, it was time to go.

I went about working on my clients when the student receptionist yelled over the intercom, "Janie Bess, you have an emergency call." We were only allowed to take emergency calls so I knew it really had to be an emergency. My nervous stomach jumped as I made my way through the floor to the office. Every eye was on me. I hunched my shoulders trying to appear calm. My mind raced.

I hope Mother is okay. She's been complaining of chest pains lately.

Trena spoke to me when I answered the phone. She was down in Berkeley where David lived during the week with my mother. The owner of the school sat at her desk eavesdropping.

Trena slowly began telling me the story.

"Janie, I don't want you to get upset. Li'l David's okay but he came home from school this afternoon and..."

"And what, Trena," I screamed into the phone.

"He found a gun."

"A gun? Oh, no." My heart was in my mouth now. I could hardly breathe. I wiped sweat from my face with my hands. "It was taped under his bedroom dresser."

"How did it get there," I asked, my voice trembling. I practically whispered when I asked, "Where is David now?"

"He is okay, Janie. We just got back from the hospital. I found the tip of his finger on the floor and held it onto his finger with an ice pack until we got to the emergency room. The doctors sewed it back on. Li'l David's here. Don't worry, he's doing okay now."

"I'm coming," I said. "Let me call Big David. He should be getting off work soon. We'll be down as soon as possible."

The owner knew from the conversation I needed to leave. She just said, "Go, we'll clock you out." I ran out of the school and rushed home to pick up my family. We seemed to crawl with the rush hour traffic. When we arrived at Mother's house, I jumped out before David could park the car.

I found out my nephew had sneaked the revolver into the house and taped it under the dresser. Li'l David is very structured. He does not like for anything to be out of place. So when he discovered his dresser drawers wouldn't close, he tried to fix it. He pulled the drawer out and discovered the gun taped underneath. He mistook it for a toy gun. His cousin, Denise was lying in the same bedroom taking a nap when he came home.

"He put the gun to his right finger and pulled the trigger," Denise said. "I heard this loud boom and Li'l David fell back on the bed screaming in pain. He held his hand up and one finger on his right hand was bleeding." I hugged Li'l David close to me as she and Trena tried to explain what happened. I couldn't sign to Li'l David.

I realized it was his right hand and it was the finger he needed to type on the Brailler. He did everything with his right hand.

"That bullet is lodged in the wall right above the bed. It just missed me," Denise said.

"Li'l David showed me how he found the gun, he demonstrated how he put the gun to his finger and pulled the trigger," Trena said, falling back on the bed demonstrating. "Then he fell back on the bed screaming, acting out the whole thing for me."

Grinning, she searched my eyes for a true reaction to this near tragedy. David came in with the kids and she explained everything again. David wanted to see the gun. Mother had it.

Mother explained it was hers. She hadn't registered it because she had been ill. Well, she hadn't lied about that.

Surprisingly, the police released it to her. Mother brought it to David.

"That's a snub-nosed 38," he said. "David could've blown his head and Denise's head off, too."

My nephew came in from the garage. He was shaking.

"I'm s-s-sorry." He always stuttered whenever he was nervous. "I ain't never going to t-t-touch a g-g-gun again. I-I-I c-c-could've k-k-killed my s-sis sister and Li-li i'l Da-da-v-vid, too." His eyes were clouded with tears.

I hugged him to me.

"I hope you learned your lesson," I said, relieved. I took a deep breath. "I really expected the worse."

My son came so close to death. I kept thinking, What if he had decided to put it to his head instead and what if he pulled the trigger?

I sank down on his bed.

"Oh, my God, Thank you, Lord." Suddenly tears of relief gushed from my eyes. David hugged me. He spoke soft comforting words to me. We embraced one another.

Li'l David patted me on my back. Then he signed with his left hand. "I am fine," he said. "Don't worry, Mama." I cried tears of joy.

The doctors told us it could be months before we would find out if David's reattached finger would ever work. He wore a bandage for months. We didn't know what was going to happen.

When we returned Lil David to school on Monday morning, the teachers were waiting for him. I had warned them what happened.

"Oh, no," Martha said. "He was doing so good on the Brailler. Now he can't communicate or type anymore. That right finger is crucial for him to use on the Brailler."

After she saw the look of despair on my face, she said in a reassuring voice, "We've weathered more storms than this, so we will work through this one, too."

A few days later, she called me at home to give me a progress report. "David is learning to use the Brailler with his left hand now. He is a miracle", she exclaimed.

I laughed with relief.

"Oh, thank you, God, you did it again," I said.

She said, "Yes," she added. "Thank you, God."

CHAPTER THIRTY-NINE

After a year living on base, we bought a cute little cottage home in Suisun City in old town. I loved my little house. I decorated it with an Oriental collection I acquired from Japan. Terri and Tony were teenagers then with lots of new responsibilities. I felt guilty because I had to leave them at home while David and I were at work.

In the summer, they had to watch their big brother. There was a school a block away from our house. All the children in our neighborhood went swimming at the pool there.

Terri asked me one day before I left for work, "Can we go swimming?"

"Yes, just make sure nobody hurts Li'l David." He swam like a fish. When we were in Japan, he taught his siblings as well as a lot of children how to swim. He was an outstanding swimmer. He loved the water.

That afternoon, Terri took Tony and Li'l David to the pool. When I returned home that evening, she said, "That lifeguard wouldn't let Li'l David swim."

"He refused to let him in," Tony said. "He said Li'l David had to sit on the side lines. And someone would have to watch him."

"I tried to explain," Terri said. "I told him Li'l David taught us both how to swim."

I was livid. My daughter looked so sad.

"I'm going over there to talk to the lifeguard," I said. "That's discrimination. Just cause he's blind? David can swim better than most adults."

"Don't worry, Mom, Terri said. "I sneaked past him when he wasn't looking and led David over to the high dive. Before he could stop us, Li'l David jumped into the pool and I followed him. He stayed down for a long time. That life guard was mad at me. But Li'l David emerged out of the pool laughing so loud, his voice echoed all over the place. All the kids started joining in around him. They begged the lifeguard to let him stay in. Tony led him in between the other kids. They encircled him to keep him so then, the lifeguard finally gave in."

"Oh, Terri, I am so proud of you." She smiled with relief. My children were the first black family in the neighborhood. I feared they would run into trouble with bigotry. I never thought about them running into trouble about Lil David's disabilities. I knew Terri knew how to handle this situation. But I worried about Tony.

One day Terri had gone to a tournament with her softball team. Tony was home alone with David. Tony ran into the town bullies one day while he was walking through the park with Li'l David. These big boys towered over them. They stood in front of Tony staring him down. He didn't falter. He kept on signing to Li'l David as if they weren't there.

One of the boys asked, "What you doing? What's wrong with him?"

Before Tony could answer, another asked, "Why he's making those funny noises?"

"You mean, you never seen a deaf-blind boy before?" Tony said. He shook his head in disgust. "I 'm doing sign language with my big brother, David."

"What's sign language," one asked.

"You have to be smart to do sign language."

"Why you have to do sign language?"

"Because David talks with his hands. You want to try it?"

One of the braver ones said, "Yeah, I'll try it."

By the time I arrived home that Saturday afternoon from work, there was a group of children lined up at the door waiting to learn how to fingerspell their names. Tony stood casually there interpreting for Li'l David.

My children were the most popular children on the block after that.

I went to work feeling better now that I knew they could handle most anything after that.

I needed a church home badly. That was the only thing I felt missing in my life. My father made me promise to stay in church.

"Promise me," he said years ago. "Wherever you go, find a church home and sing in the choir, Baby, sing for the Lord."

I finally found a church I liked. I found it one day while reading the Daily Republic newspaper. I read the ad, "The Mount Calvary Baptist Church in Suisun City. A Bible-preaching, Bible-teaching church filled with the gospel of Jesus Christ."

I've got to go there, it sounds like a black church, I thought.

It was a tiny church with a small congregation. The people were so friendly. The Rev. Claybon Lea Sr. was truly a man of God. I felt the spirit there and knew this would be my new church home.

I always attended the 11 a.m. service. I took all my children with me. Li'l David would get antsy during the service. He couldn't see the preacher nor hear the sermon. I had trouble trying to interpret the words of the sermon. I felt so helpless when the music played. I clapped my hands together so he could know when the choir was singing. My fingerspelling was great but my sign language was atrocious. I stumbled through the sermons not fully able to enjoy them. David would become restless and sign to me, "Who is the preacher? What is his name? What is he saying? What is he doing?"

I would try my best to explain but before I could spell it into his hands, I would lose the text.

He wanted to know who was sitting by us, what they were wearing, their names, addresses, and all the statistics. I tried to quell his unbounded energy long enough to enjoy the sermon. It was to no avail.

I kept praying, "Lord, please, I want David to learn the Bible. When he is at my mother's house a gentleman comes and picks him up. He takes him to the Jehovah's Witness meetings. He has given him a Bible in Braille. I am happy he is learning about You, but, I rather he is taught the same Biblical teachings I learned through my faith.

Li'l David brought his Braille Bible to church the next Sunday. I thought this would alleviate the problem and keep him busy. Well, it didn't. Li'l David still asked me questions during the sermon, "Who is God? Who is Jesus?"

I didn't know how to explain this in fingerspelling. Still, I brought him whenever I could. I tried a new method. I wrote down the Scriptures and tried to spell it to him later. This didn't work, either.

In frustration, I prayed, "Please Lord, show me how to teach my son about God, I don't know how to explain it and I want him to know You just like my other children."

I trusted God because he'd always answered my prayers before. I just didn't know how He was going to do it.

We would get out around 1:30 p.m. I would have to rush home to cook dinner after church, then we would make a mad dash to Interstate 80 to drive Li'l David back to school in Berkeley.

God blessed me with a new beauty salon around that time. I was very proud and worked hard to keep it neat and clean. My children were hired as my janitors.

After opening the salon, I found it difficult to attend the 11 a.m. service because we had to rush home after church, change clothes, and clean the shop before we drove Little David back to his residential school.

Someone suggested I attend the 8 a.m. worship service. So I decided to try it. The next Sunday, I left my children at home. I decided to give the morning service a try.

I sat up near the front row because the Rev. Lea always encouraged us to move forward in the pews. As I took my seat, I noticed a petite light skinned lady standing at the front of the congregation. She was just about my height. She was interpreting the pastor's sermon in sign language to a group of deaf students sitting in the front pew!

I had visited other churches in Berkeley that had interpreters for the deaf. I always wondered why there were no interpreters at the black churches I attended. This was the first time I had seen this in a black church. I was so excited. I didn't remember what the sermon was about. I was enthralled with watching the lady's smooth flowing hand movements as she interpreted in sign language. I was so happy to see a black female interpreter. Her hands moved smoothly as she made each sign. It was so beautiful to watch. The expressions on her face mirrored her words of love and faith. I had an insatiable desire to talk to her.

Maybe she can help me teach my son about God.

Silently, I prayed as I waited impatiently in the foyer for her.

People stopped her as she made her way out the door. Wringing my hands, I slowly made my way through the small crowd gathering outside.

"Excuse me, ma'am," I stammered. "I was wondering if you could help me?"

Her warm smile melted away my fears. "Yes, what can I do for you?"

I swallowed hard to hold back my tears of sorrow as I struggled through explaining my son's multiple disabilities. I could see her struggling to imagine a blind-deaf child and trying to figure out what happened to him.

"What? You mean he's deaf and blind, too?"

I could only nod my head in order to hold back the tears I had shed for the first years of sorrow.

Then she asked, "How does he use sign language if he can't see?" Pride replaced self pity.

"You see, Li'l David is very smart." She looked at me in disbelief as everyone did before meeting him. "He is called a walking computer by his teachers at the school for the blind."

"But I thought you said he was deaf."

"He is deaf and blind, too."

"Does he see at all?"

"No, but he has a photographic memory." My eyes shined brightly as I described my son's miraculous feats. "He does everything. He walks around as if he could see."

Before she could ask me anything else, I blurted out, "Li'l David is 14 ½. When I bring him to church next Sunday, you can meet him." She had this look of skepticism written all over her face. "You will see just how smart he is."

She walked with her seven deaf students, whose arms were locked together, to a large blue passenger van with the words "Jesus Saves" in big bold white letters on the back spare tire.

"Is your son at school now," she asked.

"No, matter of fact, he's home now."

"What other problems does he have?"

"He doesn't have any other problems."

"That's it?"

"Yes, that's it."

She didn't miss a beat as she loaded her students into the big van.

"The reason I ask is because most children who are both deaf and blind usually have autism or some type of mental retardation or something," she said.

"Oh, no, David is smart. He knows how to communicate in both American and tactile sign language. The problem is, his family only knows how to fingerspell."

"Can I meet him today?"

"Sure."

As an afterthought, she turned back around, "Oh, what is your name?"

"Janie Bess and my son's name is David Bess Jr. We call him Li'l David."

"Oh, yes, I forgot to ask where you live and I need directions. By the way, my name is Lula."

After giving her directions and exchanging phone numbers, I sailed home.

This was one of the happier days of my life. I burst through the door.

"David," I yelled, searching around for my husband. I found him in the back yard barbecuing on his Weber grill while basking in the bright afternoon sun.

I was so excited I talked too fast.

"Hold up! Slow down," David said.

I took a deep breath.

"Now who is this lady?"

"Her name is Lula," I said.

"I don't want any strange people coming to my house," he grumbled.

Ignoring his last statement, I rambled on about how I met her and how she may be able to teach Li'l David about God.

"When is she coming?"

"In an hour," I yelled as I ran inside to change into something comfortable.

Before I knew it, the doorbell rang. I ran to the door to find the same lady with a female companion standing there. She looked so different from when I saw her in church. She had pink rollers in her hair now and was wearing a pair of blue jeans. It was quite a contrast from the smartly dressed woman I met earlier.

I invited her in and introduced her to my family. She introduced her friend as well.

Li'l David was going through his rhetoric. He was asking me way too many questions. "What is her name? Is she married? When is her birthday?"

I couldn't answer fast enough for him. He felt her face. "She is very pretty," he spelled. Lula asked, "How does he know?"

"Believe me, his hands are very sensitive," I said. "He doesn't say that about everybody."

We were all laughing and talking like old friends when she got up to leave for her dinner date. But Li'l David wouldn't let her go after discovering she could sign with him. It was on!

After much coddling, I finally persuaded him she had to leave. David had to practically pry Li'l David's hands from Lula's.

She politely chuckled. "It's okay."

Turning to me, she stared warmly into my eyes. "Little David is much more than I expected. He is very intelligent, and quite a character, too."

We stood outside saying our good-byes. Out of the blue, Lula said, "I was wondering if Li'l David would like to come to dinner with me and my friends."

I was surprised. I thought she was anxious to leave him because Li'l David could be pesky sometimes. He hadn't learned how to let go. He was feeling on her face again and all over her head. He touched the big pink foam rollers placed precariously on top of her head.

He laughed out loud. His hearty laugh turned into a snicker.

I quickly pulled his hands away. I signed, "Would you like to go to dinner with Lula this evening?" I expected the usual hand sign for yes. Instead he fingerspelled into my hands, "If Lula takes those rollers out of her head, then I will go to dinner with her." I spelled each letter out loudly as he fingerspelled to me. Lula knew exactly what he spelled. She howled with laughter.

I stood there stunned. Li'l David had never done that before. David said, "Did he say that?'

Grabbing his hands from mine, David spelled into his hands again, "Do you want to go to dinner with Lula?"

Li'l David spelled, "Tell her to take those rollers out of her head first."

David burst into a hearty laugh. Li'l David joined in laughing, too.

Lula said, "You think he can hear us or something?"

"Sometimes, I think he can," I said. "He always laughs at the right time as though he hears what we're saying."

Still chuckling, Lula signed back to him, "Okay I will take the rollers out. I promise. And then I will pick you up at 5:30 p.m."

Little David signed "O.K."

David said, "I see you two will get along just fine."

By the time Li'l David arrived back home, Lula announced she would switch her classes for the deaf to the 11 a.m. worship so she could teach David at the early morning service.

Every Sunday morning, Lula would meet David in the church vestibule. Together, they sat while she patiently interpreted the signs for the devotion, hymns and the sermon. She diligently worked to teach him about God and the

Word.

When Christmas rolled around, Lula made an announcement in Sunday school.

"David Bess Jr. will be on our Christmas program tonight. Everyone will have to come out tonight for a royal treat."

David wasn't much of a churchgoer but when his children are on program, he makes sure he's there.

When Lula led Li'l David up to the front of the church that night, she put on a tape. "Oh Holy Night" blared from the speakers. Li'l David signed to the music. It was amazing to see him do the signs to the words right on time. Everyone stood and gave him a standing ovation. The Holy Spirit hit some of the mothers of the church. They shouted praises to God above.

I cried tears of joy. My husband beamed with pride.

Shortly after this happened, Lula accompanied me to Berkeley for a meeting with his teachers and counselors. The conversation went to the time Li'l David shot the tip off his finger. The teachers commended my niece Trena for her quick thinking, saying it saved David's finger. Still, in the months after David quickly learned to fingerspell and read Braille with his left finger. Six months later, after a lot of therapy, David was put to the test. When they removed his bandages and brace, he could move his right index finger, still sign with it and could still use it to read Braille. I know God showed us another miracle through our son.

Lula told the story to the Rev. Lea. The following Sunday, he asked me to bring Li'l David forward. David stood up as the pastor told the congregation the story of God's miracle. Li'l David placed the Rev. Lea's hands in his and showed him how to spell his name with his right hand. Praise Be to God!

The Rev. Lea presented Li'l David with a wallet he had made from a pair of Italian leather boots. It had David's name engraved in it. Twenty years have passed and the Rev. Lea has passed on but Li'l David still has that wallet. He reminds me, by signing, "Rev. Lea had it made specially for me."

In the late 1970s, Lula introduced Li'l David to Johnny Mathis. He had a special affection for the blind. Lula told Johnny Mathis what Li'l David had accomplished and how smart he was. Johnny Mathis hired him to translate his music into Braille for blind music students. Li'l David loved his new part-time job. He was proficient using the Perkins Brailler. Lula wrote an article about this featuring Li'l David in "Jet" magazine.

CHAPTER FORTY

Our marriage had some challenges thrown at us. My husband spent one year on volunteer assignment for Korea. The children and I remained in California near Travis Air Force Base. We had our own home and our children were in high school as well. My salon business kept me very busy. Terri and Tony were very active in school sports at the time. Terri played basketball and volleyball, and ran track. Tony was on the track and wrestling teams. Li'l David lived in Berkeley with my mother. After graduating from the school for the blind, he went to work at the Lions Blind Center in Oakland. He still came home on the weekends to visit us. His counselors and staff at the Lions Blind Center sent recommendations for Li'l David to attend Helen Keller School for the Blind in Sands Point, N.Y.

We refused to let our son go. We both felt that was just too far away.

In 1983, I sold my beauty shop to travel with my husband. I was excited about our assignment to Hickam Air Base, Hawaii.

After I sold my shop, at the last minute, they changed our orders to Clark Air Base in the Philippines. I was leery about going there. It was known as the Divorce Capitol of the World. I had friends who were stationed there before. Most of them returned home early with their children. They appeared shell-shocked as if they had been in a war zone. They left the States feeling confident and happy but returned without heir husbands and they were never the same. They had given up families, jobs and security to be with their husbands.

Then most their husbands would leave them for Filipino women there. I learned a lot about that country through my diverse clientele. While I cut and permed hair, my many clients warned me about the Bar girls in the P.I.

"Some of them bar girls will take your husband from you, just for a ticket to the States," they said.

I went to the Philippines anyway, believing my marriage would survive the odds. Miraculously, it did, but not without me putting up strong solid defenses. I asked the Lord to stay by my side at all times. I know he was there because I took some foolish risks and did some foolish things. Once I saw my car at a bar. These girls were sitting on the hood of the car. Using my keys, I quickly jumped in and started the car. I stepped on the gas and sped off. You should have seen how fast they jumped off the hood of my car. The word passed fast on the strip. Nobody bothered my car or my husband after that. I was known as Bess' crazy wife.

Before we left the States, my husband assured me there were jobs and social activities for Li'l David in the Philippines. Soon after we arrived, I discovered there was nothing for Li'l David to do. He sat home all day bored. At night, his father took him out to the local bars. Li'l David was about 23 at the time.

"Li'l David needs a life," David said. "He needs to have fun and meet real women. He needs a sex life, too."

I felt sorry for my son because in the States, he went to camp every summer. He skied in the winter at Lake Tahoe. He went to parties with his deaf friends and he had a good social life. I knew his father meant well but I didn't trust these women. I have to admit he never had a serious relationship before. Yet he needed a companion or something. I prayed for him to find a decent woman who would be able to understand him and love him for what he was.

I knew there were lots of young Filipino women looking for an American whether he was healthy or not. Some would marry anybody. They could be deaf and blind, crippled, mentally retarded or whatever. Some of the women were just that desperate. They were anxious to leave their poor homeland for the States at any cost.

When we first arrived at Clark Air Force Base, we stayed at the Maharaja Hotel right outside the main gate. This hotel was right outside Friendship Gate. One week after we arrived, David's boss came over to pick him up for work. He brought a young Filipino girl with him. She stood in his shadows. He pushed her gently from behind him to the front.

"I'd like you to meet a good friend. Her name is Beng,

She extended her hand. I shook it and introduced myself and my family.

"She really needs a job right away," he said. Before we could say anything, he added, "You can trust her. She worked for my friends for three years. She never took anything. She is a good house girl."

I tried to explain I didn't need a maid. I looked up at David who gave me that look. He warned me the first day we arrived in the Philippines. "Don't get a house girl until we are settled, okay, Janie?" I had assured him I would wait.

As I spoke to her, a big smile appeared on her face. It really touched my heart. When I looked into her dark eyes, I found it hard to refuse. Li'l David stood beside me. Reaching out in front, he felt her arm. He asked, "Who is this girl?"

Li'l David moved fast. Before I could stop him, he touched her face gently. The usual response from most people was to shirk away from him when he touched them. His bass voice made loud, unintelligible sounds, which was intimidating to strangers. She just stood there. She let him take her hand. She seemed relaxed. When Li'l David touched her face, she didn't even flinch. Instead she smiled. I learned a lot about people by how they reacted to my son. I knew she was very kind and understanding.

"This is my son, David Bess Jr.," I said. Looking at him, she said, "Hello, David Jr."

Because his prostheses looked so natural, she didn't suspect he was blind.

She looked directly into his eyes.

"We call him Li'l David."

She said, "Hi David."

"He can't hear you, nor can he see you. He is blind and deaf. He uses his hands to communicate with us. We use fingerspelling and signs to talk to him."

I spelled her name into his hand.

"If you can learn the fingerspelling, then, I will hire you. Okay?"

"Okay, I'll try to learn it."

"Can she stay for awhile so she can get acquainted with you guys," David's boss said. "I'll pick her up after work."

"That will be fine," I said, but added, "I can't pay you now. I don't have any money."

She didn't budge. She simply smiled, then said, "That's okay." Reluctantly, David left for work, complaining to his boss as he walked away. By the time David returned home, Beng was talking rapidly using fingerspelling. With Tony translating, David taught Beng to fingerspell. Tony and Beng took turns talking to him. That gave me a free moment to handle business at the base.

From that day forward, Beng was at my hotel room every day.

Before we rented a house, I was the only hotel guest who had a personal maid coming to the hotel. When we moved off base to a five-bedroom house, Beng was right there helping us unpack. She was one of the family now.

That summer, Evelyn Greenleaf, Li'l David's former counselor, came to visit us. She was working in Guam teaching the schools how to integrate sign language into their school's curriculum. She sent me a ticket to visit her. I flew to Guam and stayed a week with her. It was fun!

Guam was just like the Philippines except everyone there were more Americanized.

Soon, she returned the visit. When we picked her up at the airport, Li'l David, by touching her face, recognized her right away. He was so excited to see her. While Evelyn was there, Terri, who was working in the States, came over on vacation. She and Tony became very close with Beng in a short time.

"I have a sister now," Terri said. Beng and Terri looked so happy. I found out later she couldn't find her family. Her father died a few years back, but her mother and siblings were alive. She didn't know how to find them. I promised her I would try to help her to find them. I had no idea how difficult that would be. There were so many islands and the natives moved several times a year.

Evelyn asked Beng to take her out in the country.

"I want to watch the Caribou," she said. "I want to take pictures of those Filipino buffalos to send home to my family."

"We have to take a tri-cycle," Beng said.

Evelyn looked puzzled. "A tricycle? That's too little and too slow."

We laughed. Chuckling, Beng said, "You'll see."

Evelyn followed her outside to the front gate.

Beng called out, "Hey, Padigo." A young man on a motor bike pulled up in front of our gate. Beng and Evelyn slid into the side car attached to the side of the bike. They rode off with on a "tri-cycle."

I felt this was the perfect time to have private time with my daughter, Terri, before she returned to the States. I walked the streets of Angeles City with my daughter beside me. I explained to her the cultural differences and about how to stay out of trouble over there. We browsed through many different little shops lining the street just outside Friendship Gate at Clark Air Base.

"Terri, things are much different here than in Japan or in the states. You are considered an adult when you are over 16."

"Really?"

"Yes, you can go to the bars and nightclubs on the strips but I just warn you don't get in any tangles with the people over here. You are 19 now, so I want you to be careful. Okay?"

"Mom, I know. I'm not going to do anything wrong."

"Okay, good."

She shrugged her shoulders.

I said, "My first two weeks here, I was a mess."

"Why?"

"They openly flirted with your daddy, Tony, and even Li'l David, too. I couldn't get used to the bold, flirtatious ways of the women. They ignored me completely. I found out later the islanders were encouraged to acknowledge the male members of the family. Most the men were in the Air Force. They only hired a few Americans civilians over here. It was quite an adjustment to us dependents wives. Women were taught to be submissive toward men."

"Mom, I don't care. I just came to visit you guys."

We browsed through several novelty Rattan shops, and furniture stores that made custom-made pieces of furniture. The Sari-Sari stores served fresh lumpia and barbecue chicken on a stick. There was banana lumpia, vegetable lumpia, pork lumpia and chicken lumpia. I finally persuaded Terri to eat a banana lumpia and taste my coconut milk drink.

People stared at her as we walked.

"She is so beautiful," someone said.

"She looks a lot like Janet Jackson," they whispered loud enough for us to hear.

"I wish I had Janet's income," Terri responded. We cracked up.

I didn't see it. They said Tony looked like Michael Jackson. I didn't think so, but it wasn't important to them. Michael and Janet Jackson set the fashion scene at that time.

I took her to Mary Lou's beauty & boutique where I worked. The boss, Mila, told the stylists to give us "the works." They gave us a full body massage, facials, manicures and pedicures. We had a fun-filled day of pampering.

My seamstress showed up at 8 a.m. the next day.

"Make my daughter whatever she wants, please," I told her. "She is only here for a few days. She has to go back to work in the States soon."

My seamstress whipped up a new wardrobe for her in a day.

Whenever we walked the streets with Li'l David, the ladies sitting out front on bar stools would run over and say hello. They fingerspelled their names to him. I was shocked.

I soon found out why every bar girl knew my son's name and could fingerspell.

"You guys know how to sign with Li'l David," I asked.

"Yes, we met David and his father. They taught us fingerspelling."

They thought I was one of the Filipino maids.

"You work for Sgt. David," they asked me. "You Filipino? You speak Tagalog?"

"No. I'm American and I am Li'l David's mother." We looked so different I could tell they didn't believe me. I found out from them David had hooked our son up to a young, pretty girl. Later, I discovered she was one of the working girls.

When I confronted Big David, he said, "She wants to marry David."

"Why," I asked. "We haven't been here but a few weeks and already she wants to get married? Yeah, I bet she does." I told him about our encounter with an elderly Filipino man earlier that day. He offered up his daughter to Tony.

"I have a beautiful daughter," he said. She looked all of 16. "You want to get married? Are you stationed at Clark? She will marry you. Okay?"

I pulled Tony away as fast as I could. Tony was only 16 himself and looked 14. I remember when the man asked Tony about his daughter, Tony chuckled lightly. I could tell he was embarrassed. When I pulled him away, I noticed he had inherited his father's sideways smile. I just shook my head.

I quickly brought Li'l David's relationship with the bar girl to a halt. My husband was furious. He swore this girl really loved my son. I wasn't convinced.

I went to base headquarters to see the base commander. I complained about the lack of services for a young deaf-blind dependent overseas. Before the day was over, I had orders cut for my son to return home. I took him back to the States a few days later.

Before I returned to the Philippines, I made sure Li'l David had his old job back at the Lions Blind Center in Oakland. My mother was so happy to have him home.

"I missed Li'l David," she said. "All the other wol's are always in the streets. Li'l David always kept me company. I'm glad he's back home. He washes the dishes and takes out the garbage without me saying anything."

I returned to the Philippines and went back to work at the salon there. The owner had hired me first off, coming to my hotel room to offer me a job days after I first arrived.

"Oh, I heard some of the ladies talking in the manicure area," she told me when she offered me the job. "They said you were the best hairdresser. They wouldn't let none of the women touch their hair, just massage, manicure and pedicure. Two of them are in the Air Force. They said they were on the same flight with you. Did you tell them you would do their hair in the Philippines?"

"Yes, I told them, if I found a job."

"You have one then. I will pay you good money. These ladies are waiting on Janie Bess to start work. They told me you stayed at the Maharajah. So I came searching for you. The front desk clerk told me where you stay."

I was flattered.

I felt good having my own money again. My hair and nails were done free.

I could buy what I wanted now.

Tony attended Wagner High School on base. With my children gone and David at work, I was bored. To offset boredom, I joined an exercise group at the base gym. I also joined the Gospel Choir at the base chapel. We traveled all over performing at different churches and communities. I also became active in Women's Aglow ministry. I needed to keep Jesus in my life more than ever.

The Philippines is a beautiful tropical island. The people there are very friendly and hospitable. They loved to entertain. I had lots of fun but I was sad. So many American dependent wives walked around like they were shell-shocked. Most the wives had a weary sadness about them. They always seemed to be unhappy even though they had maids, gardeners and a personal seamstress. You very seldom saw their husbands at home. I knew why. I felt there were spiritual warfare going on. The island was a devil's workshop.

My theory was confirmed when I went to a briefing with my husband when we first arrived on the island. The commander who spoke that morning said, "For those who don't know, the P.I., as it is called, is the Divorce Capitol of the World." There was a hush as everyone took that in.

He talked about the bar girls in the local clubs downtown and of the high rate for sexually transmitted diseases. He warned the military members about the traps they would fall into. He commended the few dependents wives who were brave enough to attend the briefing with their military husbands.

"When I looked over the sign-in sheets, He said, I noted there were over 300 active duty members present, but only a handful of dependent wives accompanied them."

When the colonel asked the married service men to stand and raise their hands, 3/4 of them were married with children.

"Out of all the men here, only 25 percent of you will return stateside still married and accompanied by your wives and children. The rest of you will leave here divorced or remarried by the time your tours are up."

Loud voices rumbled throughout the auditorium.

He raised his hand to quell the audience.

"And almost all the single men here will leave here married to one of the bar girls."

I was shocked. I knew I had my job cut out for me. I was glad I came, though. I knew I had to keep praying to survive over there.

During break time, my husband said, "See, Janie, you shouldn't have come here. There's hardly any wives here. This is men's talk."

"I don't care," I shot back. "I read the bulletin in the base newspaper. It said: Dependent wives are encouraged to come. They are welcome. I am learning what to look out for over here."

To stay busy, I became active in the Enlisted Spouses Club. Before the year was up, I was elected correspondence secretary. I bowled on two leagues. I attended church regularly. I enjoyed singing with the Voices of Clark Gospel Choir. Yet, I took time to fly home every six months. I flew home so much everyone thought I still lived in the States. I had to check on my other two children, Terri and Li'l David.

The next year I was voted president of the Enlisted Spouses Club. That's when things changed for the wives over there. Things got better after I invited the NCO Club manager to one of our luncheons for a discussion. He was surprised when all the frustrated female dependents started blasting him for letting young native teen girls dance on the lunch tables clad in nothing but bikinis during lunch time.

"We bring our children in here. They should not have to look at near-naked women in front of them dancing while we're eating lunch." By the time he left our meeting and returned for the next one, he had a plan. No more women dancing until after 5 p.m. They even started a ladies' night. We played games and had raffles so we could win prizes. The prizes were beautiful capiz shell lamps, and all sorts of unique things such as the Double Papasan chair. We had a blast. Our husbands started coming back to the base to party with their wives instead of hanging out at the bars with the bar girls.

After working off base for two years, I opened my own beauty shop in my kitchen. I had so much fun fixing the wives hair and makeup. We laughed, had prayer meetings and Beng made us meat and banana lumpia or barbecue.

Three and a half years flew by fast. Right before we were set to return to the States, Mother called.

"I'm ready to come to the Philippines," she said. I was so excited. David called his mother to see if she would accompany my mother. My mother already had her passport so she didn't have to go through as much red tape as David's mother. Li'l David was away at camp for two months. So Mother decided that was the perfect time for her vacation, too.

She arrived just in time for the Enlisted Spouses Installation banquet that weekend. All the ladies came dressed in their finest. It was a beautiful occasion. After I sat down from passing my torch to the new president, she said, "I am so proud of you, Janie." I blushed.

I took her shopping all over the place. I took her out in the country to let her see my surprise. A master carver was hand-carving The Lord's Supper into my mahogany dining room table. We went to Manila to shop in a jitney.

Mother went home loaded with souvenirs. We had to ship her stuff later because she had too much weight to carry on the plane.

We had planned for Mrs. Bess to be there at the same time with Mother. We wanted them to have a good time together. But she had to get a medical release to travel overseas because she had gone through a triple bypass so she came one week after Mother left.

She stayed for one month also. Big David had three more months of extended time over there. I was ready to go home. Tony had graduated from Wagner High School. College would be starting soon. We had survived the unrest that removed Ferdinand Marcos from the presidency of the Philippines and protesters blocking the gates at all the bases. My son and his friends all had T-shirts that read, "P.O.W. Clark Air Force Base." The letters stood for Prisoners of Wagner High.

Tony was just as anxious as I was to return home. He planned to start junior college that fall. David made arrangements for us to fly back to the States with Mrs. Bess on a commercial flight.

The day the movers were packing our household goods, Mrs. Bess complained about her stomach hurting. I figured she was uptight because the move was a little too much. David and I were used to moving. We were emotionally involved in making sure everything was packed correctly by the movers and that our jewelry and other valuables were packed safely away. Our house was in an uproar as we ran about instructing the movers where to pack things. It was an emotionally charged day. David and I screamed back and forth at each other and at Tony and poor Beng with last minute instructions.

We had to rush Mrs. Bess to the hospital that afternoon. We were due to leave the next morning. They said they had to keep her overnight and then she would be fine. Later that night, they called us to tell us she had a stroke.

She never did recover. I asked to have her sent home on a medi-vac plane but they refused. It was the same story about insurance regulations and so on. We were scheduled to leave in July but after Mom Bess fell ill, it was mid-August before we could go home. I had to call the Assembly member in her hometown to get a release for her to travel on the government plane home. I raised so much sand with all the officials, finally, they got permission after a $2,500 bond was put up for her insurance. David, Tony and I rode on the medi-vac with her.

An ambulance was waiting for us when we landed at Travis Air Force base. I could have kissed the ground. The paramedics rushed Mrs. Bess to a hospital in Oakland. The next day she was transferred to a convalescent hospital near her home. After a few months of rehabilitation, Mrs. Bess went home. Mr. Bess had died suddenly in 1978 so David's brother Johnny hired a live-in home care provider and they split the cost. She spent alternative weekends with Johnny and his family or with us.

Mrs. Bess turned 74 on Feb. 6, 1990. We gave her a big party and we all attended. We knew it was only a matter of time. The same night, she was rushed to the hospital. Two days later we learned she'd suffered a massive heart attack and was in a coma. It was hard to see her like that with all the tubes and wires attached all over her body. She passed Feb. 8, 1990, in her sleep. There was a large funeral with friends and family attending. It was difficult for David, Johnny and Freddy and the rest of the family, especially Johnny, who always called his mother Shorty.

"Well, Shorty, we hung tight until the end," he said at the funeral. "I am going to miss you but I know I will see you again."

CHAPTER FORTY-ONE

Li'l David showed signs of restlessness and boredom at his job now. People at the Lions Blind Center were complaining because when he finished his work, he would interrupt his co-workers by trying to sign to them. He worked fast so he had his work finished way ahead of the rest. One of the staff members asked me if we had thought about letting him live independently. Li'l David had told them he wanted his own apartment. I didn't feel that was wise.

"David can't see or hear," I told them. "I know he has been taught to live in an apartment when he lived at CSB but I still have my doubts about him managing his own cooking. I know he was taught how to type his own notes to take to the local grocery near the campus and he knows how to use his cane for mobility but I don't trust him living by himself. How will he know when someone calls or visits?"

David was more concerned about Li'l David having a social life.

"When is Li'l David going to have some fun? Does he go to dances? Does he have a girlfriend or something?" David asked the staff. "My son needs a social life besides attending the Lighthouse for the Blind camp once a year."

"David goes skiing with the blind skiers to Lake Tahoe every winter," the staff member told us.

"What?" I said, interrupting them both. "You put my baby on skis? How does he do it? He might run into a tree or something."

"Oh, no, they have special equipment and the opticon that helps them get around. It defines shapes and everything."

"Yeah, I know, they used it in an experiment with David when he was only a young boy," I said. "He ran all over the Greater East Bay Mall with it. They used him because he has no fear of anything."

"So what else does he do," David asked.

"Well, he attends lots of parties with the deaf staff here. David is a good dancer."

"I know, his cousin, Trena taught him how to dance."

"Does he have a girlfriend or any close dates," David persisted. "I want my son to have a real life with women, sex, everything. How is he really doing?" David's right eyebrow went up as he smiled sideways at the staff member.

"I think he is doing fine," the staff member said.

"No, I mean does he have regular sex like most young men." David was nothing if not precise.

"Oh, yes, David has several girlfriends."

"I want Li'l David to have a real life."

"Oh, believe me, he does," the counselor said.

"Have you thought about sending him to Helen Keller in New York," the counselor asked. "He would have a real chance to grow independent. The counselors have come out here several times. They ask for David Bess every time."

"Really? Why?"

"They want him to attend their school. It is an advanced school. It is a rare privilege. They only accept the advanced deaf-blind. David is exceptional, so they would like him to attend."

"I was thinking about something closer to home," I said. "I don't want to send David that far from us."

"Well, just think about it. They have a regional district manager who has really taken a liking to David. They will teach him independent living skills. He will learn how to travel alone, count his money, balance his checkbook, do his own laundry, shop, cook his meals and everything. Everyone does not get this opportunity."

"David already knows how to do his laundry," I responded, laughing a bit. "I taught him those things when he was small. He washes dishes better than my seeing children. He folds clothes so neat they never need ironing. He smooths the wrinkles out with his hands while they are still warm. He can cook in the microwave with the Braille dots on it. He can sew on his own buttons and hem his own pants. He was taught at CSB how to walk the streets of Berkeley and how to shop, too. He knows how to use a Brailler and everything and he knows how to use the special tele-brailler to talk on the phone so what else can they teach him?"

"Just think about it, Mr. and Mrs. Bess," he said.

David and I just brushed it off. We wanted him close to home. We were thinking more about him living in Berkeley and working on a job near my mother's house. That way he would be closer to the family and they could help us keep an eye out for him.

David's teachers kept after us. They kept trying to persuade us to send Li'l David to New York to the Helen Keller Center for the Deaf-Blind. I was nervous about sending him so far away. David stood firm on his decision to keep Li'l David near home until the Lions Blind Center called us. The staff members told us Li'l David was becoming a menace at work. They suggested that he move on to another job in Los Angeles. The worker went with us to see the area in central Los Angeles. The job wasn't challenging at all. He would just fold envelopes all day. The apartment complex he would live in was with only elderly blind people.

No, that wasn't for Li'l David. He wouldn't have a real life there. We brought him back home to look for an apartment closer to home and his job at the Lions Blind Center. Someone called us from the Helen Keller Center. They asked us to please send David for a trial stay. I told them we would hash it out for a few days and get back to them. Evelyn called us that night. She encouraged us to give it a try. We always trusted her judgment and we knew she had visited the Helen Keller center many times before. We finally agreed to let him go for a short stay.

I flew to New York with Li'l David. He made me so proud to travel with him. This was my first flight there. I was nervous. Li'l David couldn't sleep the night before because he was too excited. We heard him getting in and out of bed all night long. He drove us crazy with his loud boisterous laughter. I knew it was because he was anxious to go.

David drove us to the airport, giving me last minute instructions on what to check for at the school. I realized he was more nervous than I was about Li'l David going out of state this time.

My mind soared as the plane took off. I marveled at the way things were turning out for my son. Never in a million years would I have thought David would be attending an advanced school. Attending Helen Keller was like attending a university for the deaf and blind.

The strangest thing, I never worried as much about David's loss of sight as I did about his deafness. To me, if he could hear or speak, he would be like Ray Charles. But without communication skills, he would have been lost. David was talking to me as we took off. He laughed so loud some of the passengers looked over annoyed. I didn't care. I was so happy for my son.

After arriving in New York, again I read my instructions from Helen Keller. They said to call them when we arrived at the airport. I looked at my watch, it was already after 9 p.m. I looked for a pay phone so I could call the staff. Someone answered the phone in a sleepy, tired tone. I was instructed to take a taxi there. The taxi driver pulled up as soon as I stepped outside the terminal. I gave him instructions.

"I am going to the Helen Keller Center in Sands Point, please."

He didn't say a word. He took off so fast David and I lurched forward then backward in the back seat. I felt like I was going to rouse up my old whiplash injuries. The driver peered at us through his rearview mirror.

"Where you from, ma'am?"

"California," I said proudly.

He didn't say another word to me after that.

We rode past tall city buildings that went so high I stretched my neck trying to see the top of them. We rode along with me trying my best to sign to Li'l David. He wanted to know what the driver's name was. I knew this guy wasn't much for talking so I just made up a name.

I signed, "His name is Bud."

David wasn't going to let me off that easy.

"What is his last name? Is he black like me or is he white, Mexican, Chinese or Filipino?"

"David, he is a hefty middle-aged white man. Are you happy now?" I asked.

David snickered. He knew how to get my goat. If I ever had to go on a police line-up to identify someone, I was trained by David to watch for everything, I would be an expert witness. I would be able to give a perfect description about a suspect because David wanted to know their ethnicity, race, hair and eye color, and what clothing they wore. I had to keep my hands on him otherwise he would try to feel for himself.

"What do you see?" David signed to me.

"David, I see tall buildings and lots of traffic and large buses and trucks, too."

"Try to rest," I finally said. "I'm tired of talking." David took out his Braille Readers Digest and began to trail his fingers along the shiny vanilla colored pages with the raised dots. He chuckled when he read something funny. I was relieved he had something to do besides talk. My fingers were stiff from the long hours of signing on the flight.

I closed my eyes and tried to rest. I woke up from my catnap. David was asleep with his book still open, his fingers resting on the last words he read before he dozed off. It was dark out. There were no more city lights now. We sped past giant fir trees and big boulders. If I didn't know any better, I would have thought I was back in Washington State. Gone were the bright lights, the bridges, snarling traffic, blaring horns. It was practically black outside. The beaming headlights on the taxi led us through a dark, deep forest. I began to worry. I knew there were some weirdoes in New York. I tried to strike up a conversation to see if I could feel him out, to ease my mind.

"So, how much farther is it from here, sir?" I asked.

He didn't say anything at first. He just looked at me in the rearview mirror.

"Just relax, ma'am, it's quite a ways yet," he said.

We swerved and curved as his brakes squealed out in protest. I gripped my purse and held on tight to the armrest. It seemed like we had been riding forever on those long winding roads before we arrived at the school. It was a beautiful tall gray concrete building. The landscaped grounds were just magnificent to see. This wasn't what I'd pictured at all. It was so nice. My eyes took in all the acres surrounding the school. He drove us around and around until we came to a sign pointing us to the reception area. It was so peaceful and serene. When we stepped out of the taxi, I could hear the crickets and the other night creatures. An owl hooted a greeting as the taxi driver unloaded our baggage. I only had one small piece of luggage. David had brought his house with him. I spun around, trying to take in everything. I couldn't wait until the morning to explore the campus.

After paying the taxi driver a huge amount of money, we went inside and introduced ourselves. A nice young woman led us to our rooms. David's room was just across from mine.

"You will sleep here tonight and in the morning we will take you to your assigned rooms," she said. "It's after 12 p.m. so everyone is asleep.

"We don't usually get guests in this late," she added. "We expected you sooner."

"I'm sorry," I said. "We arrived at 8 p.m. but it was such a long way from the airport."

"Oh, no, it is only 30 minutes away."

Surprised, I said, "Well, it took us well over two hours to get here."

"Yes, those taxi drivers know when you are from out of town. They take you the long way."

"Oh, so that's what he was doing," I said. "I asked him how far, and he just said, 'It's quite a ways yet ma'am.' I paid him $100 to get here."

"What a shame. We should have warned you about those drivers. Usually we pick up our guests, but that is before 9 p.m."

I was too tired to talk anymore. She sensed my fatigue.

"There's a shower. Here are fresh towels and for you and David. I will take him across to the room next to you." She signed her name to David as she spoke to me. He signed her name back for confirmation.

"Yes, my name is Molly," she said. "David, nice to meet you." She signed to him she was going to take him to his room next door to mine. It was only a guest room until in the morning, then he would go to his assigned room. We had traveled to the first floor to our room on some slate gray flooring. I was really impressed already. After I showered, I fell into a deep comforting sleep in a nice queen-sized bed.

The next morning, after breakfast, they assigned David to another room. I stayed in the same guest room. I was only going to be there for a couple of days if everything went well. If not, I was taking my son back home.

After lunch, they took us on a tour of the whole campus. It was exhilarating to walk around the campus with its beautiful bloom of azaleas, begonias and tulips. The landscaping took my breath away. The aroma from the flowers seemed to have a hypnotic effect on David. He kneeled down right in front of the flower bed to capture the different scents from all the flowers. I noticed how mature he was now. I knew he was going to ask for the names of the different flowers. He conversed freely in sign with all the staff members. There was one on each side of him carrying on a three-way conversation. For the first time in my life, I felt left out. David felt right at home. Someone was always there by his side interpreting everything. This was the first time I had seen this. I mean everything we said to each other was interpreted to him in signs and then to me verbally. No one was left out of the conversation.

Even when David's nervous tick caused him to jerk, they didn't seem bothered. David was informed of everything in sign language. At home, we sometimes rushed through our conversations with David; the long hours of fingerspelling literally cramped my fingers. They used all signs and even name signs for everybody.

The staff and students made up signature signs for each person's name. David was so happy. He chuckled constantly. He was so content. He was not as restless now.

David was in his own special world. I couldn't wipe that big smile off his face if I tried. This was truly going to be the thrill of a lifetime for him. I was happy for him yet I felt I had lost my baby. I always thought he would be with me the rest of his life. But now, I knew God was preparing him for this all along. This explained his stubborn ways and his strong will to survive. His inquisitiveness and determination with unlimited fear was all there because God knew he would need it and use it for his own good one day. I knew this was God's purpose. I thought about Mother Piggis when I was just a young girl of 19. She told me these things would happen. I doubted it then but I thanked God for sending her to me or I would have given in a long time ago. Sometimes when I felt like giving in, I would hear her voice saying, "God has job for you and your child and I ain't going to take it back." That's what kept me striving and fighting for Li'l David.

After the afternoon tour was over, I went to my room to take a nap. I was still tired from the trip. I told Li'l David I would come to his room later. He waved a casual bye-bye as he followed his new friends. I would meet him at his room before we went to the dining hall for dinner. I had walked so much I was exhausted. The campus was much larger than I imagined. I flopped down on my bed. I fluffed my pillows before placing them underneath my head to prop my head up slightly. Folding my arms behind my head I slowly inhaled and exhaled to relax my tired, aching body. The bright afternoon sun beamed in through my window blinding me. I rolled over on the bed to pull the blinds closed.

I heard Li'l David's loud laughter. I peeked outside. I spotted him as he bent down to touch a bright violet tulip. He then touched the yellow, fuchsia and violet begonias.

He then picked the same tulip. Li'l David had an uncanny sense of color. He could distinguish different colors. When he folded our laundry, he would fold it by size and by ownership and would sign the correct color of the item. David was the first to discover this unknown gift. He observed him one day when we lived in New Mexico as he checked on Li'l David in his room folding clothing. He held three tube socks in his hands. There were two identical socks with a green stripe and one with a red stripe. Li'l David felt all the socks in his hands. He dropped the red striped one and folded the matching pair. He nodded then chuckled.

When David told me about it, I didn't believe it so I gave him different color T-shirts and asked him the colors. He got it right 99 percent of the time. Not only did he tell me the correct color, he identified who the item belonged to. Terri was about my size by the time she was 10 years old. We even had mother-daughter look-alike outfits. David knew our clothing apart.

He very seldom got our clothing confused. He smelled everything just like a hound dog and he got it right almost every time. He had a keen sense of smell.

Li'l David had gotten down on one knee to get closer to the begonias. He leaned his head down to smell the colorful array of flowers. He shook his head in approval. I knew I was eavesdropping but I couldn't help myself. He grabbed the interpreter's hands.

I knew he would spell each color out to the interpreter as he touched each flower. I could tell the interpreter was impressed because he asked him again which color was what. I watched from my window how the interpreter reacted to David's correct response.

He gave David a high five handshake. David laughed.

David fingered a yellow begonia again before picking it from the garden. I grabbed my Polaroid camera from my night stand. He was close enough for me to catch that Kodak moment. I ran out the door and snapped the picture. I stood in the doorway watching as male the interpreter signed to David. His loud laughter echoed all over the campus.

I returned to my room to lay back down. I knew everything was going to be just fine.

When I woke up from my nap, it was 3:30 p.m. I hurried to meet David in his room before dinner.

When I arrived to his room, he signed to me, "Mama, I picked this purple tulip and yellow begonia for you." He handed me the two flowers. My eyes watered with love and gratitude. I was so grateful for my first flowers from my oldest son.

It didn't take much for him to leave me, but it took everything for me to leave him. Strong March winds practically blew me over so I stood near the open window of his bedroom watching him unpack. Shivering, I folded my arms to ward off the cold. The thought of him living here alone in Sands Point made me shudder even more. It marked the first time he would be far away from family.

I made a mental note to tell the teachers and staff about Li'l David's nervous tic. He jerked involuntarily whenever he was upset or in unfamiliar surroundings. I had warned the staff during the morning orientation David "talks" by making loud incoherent noises.

I witnessed the bright red sun descend before disappearing from sight.

The loud rumblings in my stomach reminded me we hadn't eaten since morning. I looked at the large clock on the wall. Yep, it's almost time for dinner. In San Francisco, it was merely noontime.

I tried to be patient as I waited for him to empty the first piece of luggage. Li'l David meticulously removed neatly folded garments from his matching luggage and placed them neatly in the dresser drawers of the large oak armoire that stood catty-corner in the large room.

Inside the double doors of this exquisite antique was a large shiny mirror reflecting my tear-stained face. I wiped tears away with my hands grateful for once he could not see me. I quickly turned away from my sad mirrored image.

Grabbing his hands, I finger-spelled, "David, we have to hurry to the dining hall. It's almost 5:30."

After he placed the last pair of socks into the drawer, I signed into his hands again, "Okay, let's go. Time to eat."

He signed back, "Okay, I am ready to eat now."

I lead him down the stairs through a string of hallways.

"I smell fried chicken," he said. "I am very hungry."

Forgetting to sign, I answered back, "Me, too." Sometimes I would forget he was deaf. I giggled to myself. Embarrassed, I looked around. He chuckled too as if responding.

Sometimes, I wondered—how does he sense so much?

As we turned the corner, we walked right into a wide entrance leading to the main dining room. David paused and then spoke to me with his hands.

"Mom, I think I'm going to like it here."

"Why, just because they have fried chicken," I joked back, too moved to be serious.

"No, it's because I am so happy and proud. Out of all my deaf-blind friends, I was the only one picked to come here."

I didn't dare tell him that Helen Keller Institute selected him five years earlier, but his dad and I didn't feel he was ready. His counselor had teased us, "It's not David who isn't ready but you two who are having a hard time letting him go."

I felt nobody knew or understood my son as I did. David was so trusting. He loved everybody. He believed everybody loved him, too. Who would protect him? He always lived close to his family. My mother only lived 10 miles from his job. He is 3,000 miles from home now. I heard people from New York were cold and uncaring. I watched the news and read stories about a crowd witnessing a rape or an attack on an innocent bystander. No one even bothered to call the police or lift a finger to help.

It seemed like just yesterday I almost beat up some teenage boys I caught stuffing daisies into Lil David's mouth as others held him down and hit him. It just seemed like a few days ago when he almost got hit running across the street, or his cousins had to defend him.

Mother Piggis always reminded me, "God ain't going to let nothing happen to Lil David. God has work for him to do. Out of all your children, he's the one you shouldn't worry about."

I wasn't going to worry about David any more.

We were invited to an arts festival in Long Island. After touring the large campus for three long days, I was drained mentally. I welcomed the change. We left early on a subway train. Li'l David and I had a great time tasting authentic New York Steak sandwiches and jumbo pretzels. He was excited about the carnival. Li'l David really enjoyed the clowns walking around on stilts. Their bright, elaborate costumes were comical. Lucky for me, there were interpreters there for the Deaf-Blind to explain everything. He cracked up when he felt their long wooden legs.

Most the people in the small town of Sands Point seemed accustomed to living close to the deaf-blind students. Nobody stared or gawked. Everyone was very cordial and friendly. I really liked the quaint little town in upstate New York. It wasn't at all like I imagined. It was a definite contrast to New York City. It was a beautiful suburban community with Cape Cod houses and neatly manicured lawns. I touched the gladiolas that stood tall over the custom landscaped garden. Li'l David bent down and smelled the gladiolas.

"I like the purple gladiolas the best," he signed to me.

"That's because purple stands for royalty," I signed back.

He laughed out loud.

I could tell David was very happy and content at Helen Keller. He recognized some of his old classmates from long ago. When he felt their faces, he burst out in loud laughter. He took their hands and spelled their names.

One of the guys said, "Oh, no, David Bess is here."

It was old home week for him. He soon mastered the campus. He traveled independently to his classes. I stayed behind and talked to his counselors and the dean. When it was time to eat, he walked ahead of me. He knew where all trays and utensils were kept. He memorized all the staff members' names by touch. I found out from one of his dorm counselors, he made quite a hit with the girls. In my eyes, he was the best dressed and handsome man on campus. Both teachers and counselors complimented me on raising such a fine young man. I spent the last day there making certain everything was in order before packing my things for my trip home.

I watched Lil David move his bed and dresser until he was satisfied. He had spent half the day hanging family snapshots on the cork bulleting board in his room. If I didn't know any better, I would've thought he could see the faces in the photos.

Everyone communicated in sign language even when the teachers were talking among themselves, they still used sign language as well as speech. I felt like a foreigner in a strange land. I only knew a few signs.

I called home that night and filled David in on everything.

"Li'l David's running the school now," I teased. David chuckled.

"I'll be home tomorrow," I said. I missed my husband and the rest of the family. It would be a long, lonely flight home.

CHAPTER FORTY-TWO

All our children were gone now. It felt strange with just David and me. I was just getting used to it when I got a call from my mother.

"Flo's grandchildren are in a foster home. Why don't you and David take them?"

I asked David.

"Let me think about it," he said.

Meanwhile, I went to see them myself after work one day.

"They are so cute," I told David. "They need to be with their family."

"Let me think about it.'

Then the time came when we had to let their workers know if we would take them or not.

"Let me see them first," David said. "I'm not ready for this, but you know, I have a weakness when it comes to children."

When they brought those three brothers into the waiting area, they went right to David. Before it was over with, he was just as excited.

About two months later, they came home with us. It was a big adjustment. Tony was 22 and Terri was 24. Both had joined the Army. Li'l David was still in Sands Point. And how we had three little boys. Six months later, Dominiq, Terri's son, came to live with us, too. He'd been living with his father in Texas.

We now had four little boys in the house. There was now Darrell, 5, Darnell, 3, and Avory, 2. Dominiq, our grandson, was 2, also. They kept us busy. Four hyperactive boys were a little much for us. I signed them up for dance lessons and guitar lessons, everything to keep them busy. Pretty soon, we were traveling all over the Bay Area as they performed in talent shows and festivals.

Li'l David stayed in New York more than two years. When he returned home, he insisted on staying in Berkeley in his own place. Mother and my niece and nephews all lived near him. But he had become used to living on his own. He loved his apartment in Berkeley.

Then my mother became very ill. She had a kidney failure and was put on dialysis. I soon found out mother wasn't getting to her dialysis appointments regularly. She was unable to drive because she was sick. I insisted on taking her to her appointments which were every other day. She refused. I still came to take here. I was spending a lot of time in traffic after work at the beauty shop running back and forth on Interstate 80 to help Mother.

David was worried about her, too.

"Don't worry, you stay with your mother," he said. "I got the boys."

I was very worried about Mother. Her skin was now ashen and she was tired. She wouldn't eat. Finally, one day, she called the hospital because she was in a lot of pain. The doctor started running tests on her.

My sister, Earlie, wasn't herself. She didn't seem to remember Mother was sick. I told her husband, Arnold, to take her to the doctor because now she acted like a child sometimes.

Later, Arnold called me.

"Janie, Earlie has Alzheimer's."

"I thought that only happened when you get old."

"No, little children can have it, too." I was so sad. All my close family members were sick now. Sydney was already sick. Now Earlie was sick, too. On top of it, Mother wasn't doing so well anymore. She was always tired and listless. She was forgetting a lot, too. I was so worried and very lonely. I missed my sisters' laughter and even their teasing. I felt so alone.

I talked Mother into spending the weekends at my house. I found out she could have her dialysis done near my house or wherever

393

she traveled. David and I insisted she stay with us. I took her out to eat. She went to the bowling alley to watch us bowl. When we took the boys out of town to compete in talent shows, she went right along with us. She was laughing and enjoying herself again. One day, after she returned home to Berkeley, she called us.

"Janie," she said, "I was thinking, we ought to do like the Filipino families and buy a bigger house together. Since I've been sick, the grandkids don't come around like they used to." She tried to mask her disappointment by laughing. "Them wol's just seem to be too busy."

"Mother, that sounds good to me. I'm on my way to work but you can talk to David. See what he thinks." I handed the phone to David who had a puzzled look on his face. When I left, David was still on the phone talking to Mother. It sounded like for once in a long time, they were agreeing on something.

"Start looking for a new house," David said. "Mother-in-law is moving in with us soon."

"What? You're serious?" I couldn't believe my ears.

"Yes, we're going to need a bigger house now. She said she will help us buy a house."

"You're sure," I asked again. "You and Mother never could stay in the same room very long together, you know."

"Oh, we'll be fine. Mother-in-law is cool with me," he said.

"Okay, I don't want to hear any mess from you two. I am staying neutral."

"Yeah, so get us a real estate agent right away. Tell her we are looking for at least a four-bedroom, maybe five, with a lot of space."

I thanked God, then I went to work right away calling around for a real estate person. I finally found a woman who was sincerely interested in helping us.

We found several houses we liked but it was contingent on Mother selling her house for the down payment. Mother's house wasn't selling for the price she wanted. She had been harboring all kinds of junk for years and wouldn't let it go.

"Mother, you have got to get rid of this junk," I told her one day at her home while trying to sell her house. "This is a choice neighborhood and you have an open plan but you need to haul away your old junk." Mother wouldn't give in.

Then one day while she was at the hospital, they discovered a growth on her colon; it was malignant. A few days later, she was wheeled into surgery. They removed her colon and she seemed to improve with time. She did look a lot better.

"We got it all," the doctor told us. "Just continue going to go to dialysis, Mrs. Prather. But we want you to think about a kidney transplant. You only have the one left. It shows here in your records, your left kidney was removed in 1965."

"I know, but when it is time for me to go, I'll just go."

Mother could be so stubborn at times. We talked to her about a kidney transplant. I tried to talk her into signing up on the donor list but she refused to do it. I was determined to keep after her. Mother was stubborn, never relenting.

"When it's my time to go, I'll go," she said, "But until the good Lord calls me, I am going to be okay. I lived good with one kidney for over 25 years."

I convinced her to stay with us until she recuperated. So she did.

While she was at dialysis, I sneaked down to her house in Berkeley and paid her brother, Earl, to haul away her old newspapers, bottles and other collectibles. I asked my nephews George and Alex to come over and rearrange her furniture so her house would show as the real estate saleswoman instructed.

Mother had a fit until she started getting bids for her house. I know it was hard for her to let go. So many good memories were in that house from marrying Henry Prather to my son's birth to raising her grandchildren there. She had mixed feelings and it showed.

Meanwhile, we had lost a few houses we bid on with the contingency to sell clause. They found buyers who had the down payment already. We had to wait for Mother's house to sell before we'd have the down payment. We had all agreed Mother would pay the down payment for the house and we would make all the house payments. She wouldn't have to pay anything else.

We all agreed when God sent us the right house, we would know it.

Then we saw a four-bedroom, three-bath tri-level house with more than 2,700 square feet, a wraparound deck and a kidney shaped swimming pool. We knew. It was the one.

From day one, David had planned to rent out our old house for income. But real estate agent took us on a tour of this house in an exclusive neighborhood, I could tell David had second thoughts.

We went with the real estate agent on my lunch hour thinking I would be back in time for work. I had to cancel my afternoon appointments because I couldn't get David out of that house.

"This house is more than you qualify for, unless you want to sell your house, too," the agent said. "With a larger down payment, you can qualify."

"Oh, I'll sell my house for this one!"

I was shocked. Mother was at dialysis. I couldn't wait to pick her up and tell her the good news. I took her by to see it again later that same day.

"Oh, yes, this is it." Right away, she claimed the downstairs bedroom and bath which were right next to the kitchen.

Before I even told Mother, David and I had already signed a contract to sell our house.

Within two weeks, Mother's house sold, then ours. We moved in that summer right after school was out. The boys spent the whole summer in the swimming pool. Mother bought new furniture for her bedroom. David and I didn't have to buy anything. The custom-made Oriental furniture we shipped home from Asia was the perfect decor for our new home. I knew God had special ordered this house for us.

❧

Li'l David seemed happy in his new home in Berkeley. I'd found a rehabilitation worker to assist him. He had a room mate from the job program he worked in. But pretty soon, he and his roommate began to clash over the bathroom and other issues. So his room mate moved out. David was alone until we picked him up on the weekend. He caught the bus to and from his new job.

One day, my nephew George was on a hauling job and spotted these police officers conducting a drug bust. Guess who was walking through it? Li'l David. He had gone to the laundry mat on Sacramento Street and was headed home unaware of what was happening. The officers had their guns drawn and were handcuffing the suspects as David ambled through with his white cane and his laundry bag thrown over his shoulder.

George rushed out of his truck and hustled Li'l David inside. He drove him home.

Then Li'l David took out his garbage and forget his door key. He was locked out. He was able to tell somebody. I don't know how he explained it but he did. The neighbors helped him get in. Then one night we stopped by to see how he was doing. We were told he was downstairs at a party. He had a beer in his right hand. I watched him in awe as he carefully sat it down to teach a young lady how to fingerspell. We cracked up. David was going to be fine. I knew God had him covered.

We relaxed after that. My mother would pick him up on the weekends when we couldn't make it down so we knew he was going to be fine. Tony returned home from the Army. He met a young lady, soon they were engaged. Terri was in the Army, too, but she was stationed in Germany. We got a letter from her announcing she was going to Iraq. She was in the military police. She one of the first females to fight in Iraq. She helped rescue the Kurds from Kuwait.

We were worried for her. When we got news she was back safe in Germany at the Army post, we shouted for joy.

Tony got married that November. We got a letter from Terri telling us she had married to a young man in the Army. She sent us a video. She looked so happy in the video. I cried because I couldn't be there with my daughter. Her husband was very handsome.

She called us, "I am headed to Kentucky to an Army post there with my husband." Her son, Dominiq, was one of our boys, but as soon as she was settled, she asked me to fly with him to Kentucky so he could be with her and his stepfather. I needed a break. I gladly accepted.

The boys were getting big now and very hyperactive. I was taking plenty of vitamins; to improve my stamina. I couldn't resist the thought of having a vacation. Besides, I never had enough quality time alone with my grandson.

Working full time, helping my mother and raising a new family with four wild little boys all under 10 was enough to keep me occupied.

By this time, David had retired from the military and started a new job as a life insurance salesman. I had opened a new salon with my friends. Business was flourishing. The children were doing well in school. Mother, in between her dialysis appointments, went everywhere with me, David and the boys. On

Sundays, after church service, we went everywhere together. Then we'd drive down to the East Bay to visit our family.

We were one busy but happy family.

My little sister, Lorrie Ann, came to live with us along with her two little children. She was going through a divorce and needed a place to stay.

After she moved into her own place, she would come over to our house to help us with Mother. After she took Mother to the doctor one day, she called me at work.

"Janie, there is something wrong," Lorrie said, "When I went in to pick up Mother, I overheard the doctor say something about seven months.

"I asked Mother, 'What did the doctor mean? I heard him say something about you having only seven months?'"

"Mother said, 'That doctor doesn't know nothin'. Anyway, what you doin' listenin' to my conversation?'"

"I told Mother, 'I heard him say seven months or something.' Do you need surgery then?'

Mother told Lorrie, "Naw, gal, you stay out my bizness."

That's when Lorrie decided she had better tell me. She looked deep into my eyes.

"Janie, you go with her next time. She has another appointment in three weeks. You be sure and take off that day. I have to work or else I'd go."

Mother insisted on driving herself but she was too weak. She didn't look so good. She was having trouble dressing. Mother prided herself on being independent. She still washed her own laundry, took her own showers and everything. She still cooked meals for the family. She was always home when the kids came home from school.

Mother made it clear she didn't want me to go with her to her next appointment. I went anyway.

"Mother, you can't drive," I said. I had no idea what would happen. I expected, maybe, she needed different medications for her illness but nothing else. I entered the examination room after the doctor called me in.

"Mrs. Prather wants me to tell you our findings from the last lab and X-ray results," the doctor told me.

"Yes?" I felt like I had swallowed my tongue. I trembled for no apparent reason. My nervous stomach started dancing a jig.

"I'm sorry," he said. "I told your mother, Mrs. Prather, her liver wasn't working properly. After a full examination and x-rays, our fears were confirmed."

He looked at Mother with such compassion. I knew then something was terribly wrong.

"I told Mrs. Prather she cannot function without her liver. I persuaded her to tell you but it was too hard for her so I asked her if, with her permission, of course, I could tell you."

"Mrs. Prather has cancer."

I stammered. "But her doctor in Oakland said he got it all!"

"That was colon cancer four years ago. Now she has liver cancer."

"Can she have surgery to remove it?"

"No, ma'am. You see, it is already to far gone. There's nothing more we can do."

I shook my head.

"No, no. Oh, Mother." I started sobbing. I tried to stop when I saw the helpless look on my mother's face. "It's okay, Mother. I will take care of you." I said, wiping tears away. I took a deep breath to compose myself.

"Mrs. Prather, I will have to warn you, you will be in a lot of pain," the doctor said. "We can give you morphine."

Mother frowned. She said firmly, "I ain't gonna feel no pain."

"I have to warn you, you will be in immense pain near the end," he persisted.

"I told you, I ain't gonna be in pain."

Mother stood tall staring him down. Her eyes reflected no fear at all. Her voice was strong. Her determination to refuse defeat against this horrible disease was evident. Mother's faith in God was unwavering.

"What can I do, doctor," I asked. Mother answered me.

"You pray for strength, Janie, pray hard. God is not going to let me suffer."

"Please, Lord, help us," I cried.

"I won't feel no pain," she repeated.

I knew she believed it. I felt her inner strength and drew from Mother as she turned to me.

"C'mon, Janie. Let's go." We walked out hugged together.

That day Mother taught me something more valuable than life itself:

Humility, pride, love and strength in our Father above.

Mother still went to dialysis on schedule. The head nurse told me, "Mrs. Prather can come as long as she likes but I have to be honest with you. This is only to keep her morale up.

"Besides," she added, "we enjoy her. She is somethin' else. She keeps us laughing."

They held monthly support meetings every third Sunday.

At one meeting soon after we learned of the cancer, Mother bragged about our boys.

"You see my great-grandsons? They're called Triple D.A. They sing and dance like Michael Jackson. They auditioned for Star

Search twice. You should see them. They be kicking their legs up high and spinning around. That oldest one, he does double flips and somersaults. Ooh wee! He is good."

Everyone's eyes were on Mother, listening intently as she described their moves.

"They perform at different shows. I go with them everywhere they go, too."

She told the nursing staff at dialysis how they won first place in several statewide talent contests. When I took the boys in to pick up Mother, the staff asked them to perform at their annual picnic in July at Lake Solano. They said it would be in honor of my mother that day. They called it Johnnie Prather's Day. The whole family came. My sisters Sydney and Earlie, Lorrie Ann, and all the grandchildren and great-grandchildren were all there. My daughter, Terri, had just resigned from the Army so she came home to be with her grandmother, too.

Mother was at her best that day. She was so proud of her family. The boys did a dance and they sang "My Girl" by the Temptations to Mother. There wasn't a dry eye in the park afterward. We all had a beautiful time. There were plenty of food and entertainment. They gave Mother presents and said Mother had made such a difference at the dialysis clinic.

"We love you, Mother, and we know that you will always be remembered," they said.

Mother could just say, "Thank you."

I looked at Mother in a different light. The woman who once kept care of me was now needing her family to be there for her. She looked so tiny now and weak. Her sturdy frame was now frail and thin. She wore a wool knit cap to ward off the cold even though it was hot outside. She never stopped smiling. We wheeled her to the car at the end of the day.

"This was one of the happiest days of my life."

Mother was in the bathroom getting ready for dialysis. I found her sitting in the bathroom on the closed toilet.

With frustration, she complained about being late for dialysis. She was fumbling with her colostomy bag. She had always prided herself in being able to keep it clean. She always took her showers, did her personal hygiene, and dressed unassisted for her appointments. That was the first time I saw defeat in her eyes.

Mother still refused to let me help her dress. Even though she was late for dialysis, she insisted on going. We had to go out of town to her clinic. I was flying down the freeway trying to get her there when I heard a loud pop!

I pulled over on the side of the freeway.

I had a blowout. I called my roadside service. They sent me someone out to fix it. It was a long wait. By the time I got her there, it was too late. They let her stay anyway because she insisted.

Within a few days, Mother couldn't get out of bed at all. She was too weak to even move. She became visibly worse. She had to be helped to and from the bathroom.

Our family strained from all the sleepless nights and little relief from caring for her. Terri, David and I took turns caring for her in between our work schedules. Terri's husband, Everett, came from his hometown, Georgia, to be here with her, too. He stayed three months, then he returned home to attend school. Terri was working and decided to stay on here and help us. I thank God for my daughter. Tony was in Iraq working on a government job.

Hospice came in to help us. Li'l David came home around the same time. We moved him back home from Berkeley. With Mother being so sick, we needed him near us. I didn't want to worry about getting to him in an emergency. He didn't understand why mother couldn't get up. He wanted to fingerspell with her. Even though I explained Mother was very sick he didn't seem to accept it. He was persistent. She still tried to talk to Li'l David.

She was withering away but still, she didn't complain.

Sydney's son, George, came out to our house in an ultra-stretch limousine with his brothers, sisters and nieces and nephews. He rented it to take Mother on a trip with her family.

"Mother Rawness, where do you want to go," he asked.

Mother smiled at him. I felt such relief. She managed to say, "Janie knows. I want to go to Suisun City by the water."

So that's what we did. George confided in me, "I was going to take her to Reno like I did before. I rented a limousine and took my girlfriend's mother and Mother Rawness to Reno. They had a ball. I rented a suite for them. I gave them both $200 to play the slots but Mother Rawness, shoot, she kept her money. She said, 'I ain't giving no machines my money.' She saved it." We cracked up.

When we got down to the Suisun Marina, Mother asked if she could get out to pray by the water. I remembered the late Mother Piggis had told me water was spiritual. When we lived in Suisun near the marina, Mother and I always took walks down by the slough together.

Time went quickly after that trip. Mother wasn't breathing well. She had a temperature. She had a faraway look as if she was looking toward the heavens. I knew the time was nearing. I hastily called the ambulance. I didn't know what else to do. They drove her to the hospital. I followed in my car. The doctor kept her there for only a few hours but Mother refused to take the morphine. The doctor gave me a prescription for morphine. I was instructed to insert the depository into her colostomy opening.

"There is nothing we could do," the doctor said. "We know, from past experience, cancer patients would rather be home with their families when they go. It makes it easier on them. She will feel better if she is with you. She will merely waste away here without the love and attention from her family."

I handed him the right-to-die papers she'd signed seven months before.

"I ain't going on that machine," she'd said then. "When God calls me, I'm ready. I saw Mrs. Bess, my brother Earl and my sister Carrie on that machine. It didn't do nothing but delay their time. Anyway, that's a waste of our tax money."

I called the family to warn them she was preparing to leave us soon. The vacant look in her eyes and the will to complain or talk was gone. She no longer seemed to hear my voice. Friends and relatives came by to see her but she showed no response to their many flowers and gifts. During her last days, her eyes stayed closed. She very seldom opened them. I sat on the side of her bed and talked to her anyway for I knew she could hear me. She never stirred. She refused to eat anymore. Mother just lay lifeless waiting for her time to leave.

That's when I began to call our family members.

"Mother is dying, please come see her soon." They kept saying they'd come by tomorrow. "Tomorrow she may not be here. I can feel it."

Everyone, with the exception of my immediate family, seemed to be in denial.

I stared at those morphine depositories the doctor had given me to insert into her colostomy. I couldn't bring myself to do it.

When George showed up, it was just before dusk. Mother tried to raise up speak to him but the words were unintelligible. He seemed to know what she was trying to tell him.

"I know, Mother Rawness, I know. You don't have to talk. You can go ahead now if you want."

He brought his girlfriend. I told her about the morphine I was supposed to insert. She was attending nursing school. She told me she could insert the morphine. We hugged after she did so. I was so relieved.

"Mother, you won't hurt no more, just like you said." I kissed her. She didn't move. Her lips were cold. Her body was stiff.

George's friend felt her pulse.

"She's not asleep, she's gone," she said.

"Oh, my God, Mother said she wasn't going to hurt."

I felt so cold myself. I remember talking to Mother. Her eyes were closed. She looked like she was sleeping but I knew Mother had gone on home. George, Alex and the other nephews were out on the back deck by the pool. I broke down crying. A long loud wailing sound escaped my lips. They must have heard me from the open window. They came running in.

"Oh, Lord, no," someone said. "I didn't get to tell her good-bye. She just left us."

George kissed her and told her good-bye again. Terri had just came home from work. She pulled me from the room. I don't know how I did it but I called and made arrangements.

I was feeling numb by the time everyone arrived. They showed up all times of night. I remember calling the funeral home, then the doctor arrived. He pronounced her dead.

When they came to take her away, I don't remember what I did. But one of my closest friends said later, "Somebody called me and told me that you, Janie, had tried to run out to the hearse to go with your mother. I know you didn't do that, did you?"

"I don't remember." I confessed.

"Oh no, Janie, your mother taught you to be strong. Your mother wants you to be strong to carry on her legacy. She left here not complaining or crying. She told me, 'I don't have to worry about Janie. She was my baby but she turned out to be the rock of my family. I can depend on her to keep the family together.'"

I knew then I had to do what Mother wanted me to do. Be strong.

Mother wanted her funeral at the same church we grew up in. It was beautiful.

The officiating minister warned everybody there was a three-minute limit on all acknowledgments. The highlight of the whole funeral was the speech my father gave. He stood up and walked up in front of the pulpit.

"I am Rev. Calvin Lightfoot. Sister Johnnie Ree Lightfoot Prather was my first wife. I loved her very much. I didn't quit her, she quit me! You see, we were married for almost 20 years. But she didn't want a preacher for a husband.

"I loved my wife and always will, but God blessed me with a new wife, Evangelist Louise Lightfoot. I have nine children, with my stepchildren." He raised his arms up as if directing a choir. "Stand up, Sister Lightfoot, that's my wife, Sister Louise Lightfoot. There's my children. Stand up, Sydney." Sydney stood up. When he called Earlie's name, she said, "Tell that crazy man to shut up."

We all snickered in spite of ourselves. We all knew Earlie was in her later stages of Alzheimer.

"Stand up, Janie, that's my baby," he said beaming with pride.

I stood up but only to get Daddy's attention. I signaled with my hands and lips for him to sit down. He ignored me. He called Lorrie, Immanuel, then his stepchildren, Ola, Stella and Chris, to stand up. We all obeyed.

"My oldest son died, too, I just found it out the other day. Umph, umph, umph." Daddy wiped his eyes. Before he could speak again, the officiating minister said, "Rev. Lightfoot, we are so sorry but time has run out. Thank you."

"Yes, thank you, sir," Daddy said as he slowly sank down into a chair in the pulpit area. I was so relieved. Everyone was trying to hold their laughter.

"Whew," I said under my breath.

There was not a frown or sadness in that place after Daddy sat down. Everyone's eyes were down but you couldn't erase the grins off their faces. I believe God sent Daddy to make everybody laugh.

I could just hear Mother saying, "Lightfoot, there you go flapping your lips. Shut up and sit down, man."

CHAPTER FORTY-THREE

I f there is a discount or a sale going on at some store or event, you will likely find me there. My frugality always seemed to draw me to the strangest places.

Every year in October, Marine World celebrates Deaf Awareness Day. They offered discount tickets to the deaf community and their families and friends. Of course, I bought advance tickets for my family and for some of my church members, also.

David was very excited about going there.

"I will see a lot of my old classmates there," he said. He chuckled softly and continued signing. "It will be like a class reunion for me." He was very excited. It was hard to keep him calm. Our small boys were excited, too. They could hardly wait to ride on the elephant's back.

"I am so excited because the park has hired interpreters who will communicate with me and my deaf-blind friends, too." He kept repeating himself. "Most of my old friends from Berkeley will be there."

"David," I signed back rapidly into his hands, "you already told me that. OK?"

David laughed loudly. He loved to get my goat and I do not know why I let him know. It did him all the good in the world to get me riled up. To hear him laugh was music to my ears. I loved to hear his boisterous laughter.

Until David was about 12, he never smiled much. He did not even know what true laughter was. His teacher Martha had taught him how to laugh and how to have fun. His whole personality seemed to change whenever he smiled.

David had trained Li'l David to walk behind always holding on to the shoulders of his guide with both hands whenever he was traveling in a large crowd. So this is what we were doing as we made our way to the gate. I would look back over my shoulder to see if he was keeping his hands to himself. He had his mischievous smile on now as we made our way through the crowd. He held his head up high. You wouldn't know he was blind unless we told you because of his perfectly fitted prostheses. They looked amazingly like his own eyes. His brown eyes complemented his dark coffee-bean complexion. David had trimmed his thick coarse beard and goatee into a nice Van Dyke. He always took pride in his appearance. He looked so handsome. His barber had cut his coarse black hair into a nice clean Flattop with a high fade on the sides. It was a very a neat style. He had insisted on going to the barbershop just a few days before the event. He walked with his head so high up in the sky, giving others the impression that he was stuck-up. The only give away was the big smile on his face. I had not seen him this happy in a long time.

After standing in a long line, the ticket master handed us our reserved passes.

"There are volunteer interpreters working here today," he said.

"I know, my son David has been telling me about it for over a week now."

"You can spot them easily. They are wearing bright orange vests."

My eyes scanned the crowd for a bright orange vest. I was frustrated because I couldn't see over the crowd. This was the one time that I hated being so short. I strained my neck, searching to see. I hoped I could just spot one orange vest. I didn't see any interpreters anywhere. The children were growing restless.

"I thought that you said that there were going to be some interpreters here for Li'l David," Darnell said. I just looked at him and rolled my eyes. "Where are they, anyway?"

"I don't know."

"Mama, do you know where the interpreter is," Avory said. "Can we just go and find them?"

My grandson, Dominiq perked up with, "Grandma, can we find a seat now?"

I put my hands on my hips and cocked my head to the side.

"If I knew where the interpreter was, then I would not be standing here looking around for him." I rolled my eyes upward. "One question at a time. Please."

It was next to impossible to control four hyperactive boys. They were pushing and shoving one another, then having a tug of war to see who was going to be first in line. Li'l David was no joke either. He kept trying to fingerspell with me while we stood in the middle of the slow-moving crowd.

"Who is here?" he asked. Frustrated because I couldn't find an interpreter, I fussed at my four little ones. I wanted them to calm down. They were still pushing each other around in the line. I felt like a helpless child myself.

Finally, I found a row of seats for us at the dolphin show. They rushed down and quickly claimed their seats. Then I saw an interpreter standing by the front entrance. David and I hurried over to walked over.

"Can you sign with him," I asked. "My son needs a deaf-blind interpreter. I can't move my hands fast enough to keep up with him."

"We only have one deaf-blind interpreter here and she's standing at the front gate," he responded. He could only interpret for deaf people.

"You mean out of all the people here, you only have one who can interpret for the deaf-blind?"

"Yes, ma'am. There are very few who can sign to the deaf-blind. It requires tactile signing. It is has to be one-on-one with the deaf-blind."

"I know, sir. Believe me, I know."

He explained anyway. "Very few are trained to do this. We are just volunteers who came out to help."

"Well, where is she then," I asked.

"She's a tall, slender, blond woman. You had better grab her up before someone else does."

Without waiting to hear the rest of the story, I grabbed Li'l David by the hand and started running toward the front gate. I retraced my steps as we hastily made our way back to find that interpreter. I didn't want to leave my little boys too long with my friends because they were quite mischievous. Quickly I made my way practically dragging Li'l David behind me as he attempted to pullback to fingerspell to me. David and I needed to stop and stand in one place in order for me to use fingerspelling. I'm not very good with sign language and he spells so fast sometimes, I can't keep up anymore. Just as I stepped inside the metal turnstile with Li'l David in tow, I felt a sharp tug on my arm.

I felt Little David pulling back.

Without looking, I impatiently pulled his arm. I felt another sharp tug.

Someone was pulling Li'l David in the opposite direction.

On the opposite side of the turnstile was a petite woman of Asian descent.

She held David's hands and was signing with him.

To get her attention, I touched her on her shoulder. She paused, then looked up and smiled.

"Are you the deaf-blind interpreter," I asked.

She signed back quickly, speaking out loud.

"No, I am a friend of David's."

"Oh, well, we are looking for an interpreter," I said. Then I looked at her with a gleam in my eye. "Would you like to interpret for him today?"

"Oh, I can't. I am with my group and I will get lost."

"Well, you had better go. I see a bunch of people waiting for you. And I have to hurry to catch a deaf-blind interpreter."

"Wait," she quickly signed. "I need to ask you a favor. I knew David for a long time. We both worked at the Lions Blind Center."

"Oh, that's nice." My eyes searched around for the orange vest on a blond lady.

David was busy trying to introduce me as we held up a long line of impatient people waiting on both sides of the dull silver turnstile just inside the main entrance. They were loudly voicing their objections as David continued to talk. It was as if there were no other people in the world there but them.

I hated to interrupt but I had to before the people in line became hostile. I wanted to remain polite but I needed to get going.

Grabbing David's hands, I quickly signed into his big brown hands, "What is her name?" David eagerly fingerspelled her name. His fingers spelled out each letter: S-H-I-R-L-E-Y.

I fingerspelled her name back to him, carefully forming each letter into his hands as he held his right hand up in front of my face while holding my right hand with his left.

He made certain I fingerspelled the letters correctly back to him. Afterward, he touched her chest. He then turned to Shirley and signed "This is Mom, her name is J-A-N-I-E B-E-S-S." He touched my chest. He placed my hand inside of Shirley's. We shook hands.

A man in line behind her snapped, "Look, lady, we don't have all day. We are trying to see the show."

Then someone behind me in the line yelled, "And we are trying to leave!" I apologized.

A third party said, "Yeah, well, then break it up, will you?" I stammered another apology to an angry woman peering over my shoulder.

I signed fast to Shirley.

"Sorry but we have to go find an interpreter for David."

"Okay," she signed. But then Shirley went under the turnstile over to our side to continue talking. She signed to David and spoke to me at the same time. Holding out her hand, she said, "Hello, my name is Shirley."

"Hello Shirley, glad to meet you," I signed back to her.

I became annoyed. David and Shirley continued signing. I gave up. This must be an important conversation, I told myself. I'll just relax. Besides, I was tired after all the excitement.

She signed to David, "I want you to marry me."

I wasn't very sign literate but I knew the sign for "marry me."

Oh, Lord, this girl can't be asking David to marry her. This cannot be for real. Two weeks ago David and I had stood in my kitchen. I prayed with Li'l David because he signed, "I want to get married."

"I want a wife," he told me then.

"David, you need a girlfriend first and you have to love her," I responded.

"My sister and my brother are married. I am the oldest and I am not married yet."

I didn't know how to answer that one.

"Okay, we'll pray. We'll ask God to send you somebody who will love you and you will love her, too."

We had stood right there in the middle of the kitchen floor. I had grasped his hands. Closing my eyes, I begin to pray combining fingerspelling and sign language to the best of my ability. I wanted Li'l David to know what I said to God.

"Lord, I come to you. I am asking a special favor. Lord, you said that whatever I ask of you, you would give it to me. Father, this prayer is not about me, but for my son, David. Lord, he has suffered so much and he very seldom asks for anything. My heart cries out him. Lord, you sent him overseas to Japan and to the Philippines, then to New York to Helen Keller Center. He lived all alone in Berkeley for almost two years by drug dealers and addicts and only You, Lord, knows what else. You made the drug dealers his friends and his protectors. They looked after him, they learned how to communicate with him too, and no harm ever came to him. Lord, you allowed him to visit his friends in other cities traveling alone on buses, trains and airplanes. You helped me to find him an apartment in Sacramento.

"Since I lost my mother, I'm afraid to let him go. Now, Father, he's looking for a wife. Lord, I am asking that you help us. I am asking for someone who will love him for who he is, someone who can communicate with him. And someone who is not ugly because his father will have a fit. Just let her be pretty.

"The main thing is, I want someone who can see. Someone who will be able to travel with him and be a companion. Someone who will laugh with him and tease him sometimes with love. I don't care if she is black, white, Asian, Polynesian or whatever. Lord, I ask this, please, in Jesus' name. Amen."

Now there we stood in the middle of Marine World and a young, attractive woman had asked David to marry her. I could hardly believe it. I asked for one who had vision but was deaf. I mentally pictured David with a young black woman. I didn't expect to see an Asian woman with my son.

She signed, "I love you." Not only did she propose to him right there standing inside a metal turnstile, she signed to me while speaking.

"I will see you later. I have to give you my phone number. David can call me on his TTY phone." How did she know he had a TTY unit? My mouth stood wide open as I watched these two conversing.

He signed back, "Yes, I love you, too," He nodded. "Yes, I will marry you."

Lord, Have mercy, please. I hope this is right. Tears of joy fell from my eyes. I didn't wipe them away. This was the first time I cried happy tears in a long time!

God, I know that I asked you but I didn't think that it would be this soon.

"I'll return and give you my address and phone number before I leave," Shirley said.

"Where do you live?"

"In Sacramento!"

"Really? David has an apartment in Sacramento already but he is still living with me for a little while." I explained, "You see, my mother died from cancer a few weeks ago and I just couldn't let him go."

Shirley ran off to meet her friends. The people who grumbled in the line earlier were smiling at us now. I heard someone say, "That Japanese lady just proposed to that black deaf man."

With Li'l David still holding on to my right shoulder, I rushed on to find an interpreter. We finally did. After the water-skiing show was over, his interpreter left us. I was tired of chasing hyperactive little boys all over the amusement park. My fingers ached from signing and fingerspelling with Li'l David. He was still overly excited. I couldn't shut him up. For the last two hours, David kept signing, "Where is Shirley? I want to see Shirley!" Impatient, I signed back roughly into his hands, "David! I don't know and I don't care! We're going home now!"

413

His nervous tick started up. His body tightened up and his face changed. One corner of his mouth turned into an ugly snarl. He was breathing so hard he was hyperventilating. He sounded like a horse after it raced in a dead heat.

Annoyed and in a menopausal state. I snapped, "Calm down." My hot flashes began to rise from the bottom of my feet to my head. Embarrassed, I wiped away the sweat from my forehead with my hanky. Signing back to David, I said, "David! Relax! I don't know where she is!"

He stomped his feet in protest.

"Cool it," I yelled to my boys running wild. They had purchased giant water guns in bright neon colors and were squirting each other. If someone happened to get in their way, they got wet, too.

"Okay, that's it! Let's go!"

They slowly made their way toward me.

Darnell complained. "Mama, I'm not ready to go yet. We're having so much fun."

Darrell cut in with, "Yeah, Mama. Why we have to leave now?"

Avory cried out, "I didn't get any cotton candy. Mama, you promised me."

"OK, OK, here!" I handed Darrell $20. "Darrell, take this money and get Avory some cotton candy. You guys can have a treat, too."

They screamed in delight. "No ice cream," I warned them. "I don't want it melting in my car."

I sat down on a nearby bench right near the front gate. I started digging into my large straw purse. I couldn't find my keys! I shook the bag hard. I didn't hear the familiar jingle. Frantically, I dumped my purse onto the bench besides me. Nothing.

Darrell, Darnell, Dominiq' and Avory slowly returned, smiling happily with their treats in their hands and, of course, no change. I announced, "I've lost my keys."

My eyes watered up. I sent the boys scrambling to the Lost and Found. They came running back. Dominiq arrived first with the other three boys following.

"Grand-mommy, they said they didn't find any keys and no one's turned any in."

"Here," I said, patting the concrete bench. "Sit here with Li'l David while I walk back to the front gate to check. I may have laid them down on the counter top when I picked up our tickets."

But they weren't there. The nice lady at the ticket booth suggested I look in my car.

"I doubt they're there but I'll go check," I said.

I walked briskly to my car. The parking lot seemed so big. Lots of people had left. The parking lot was practically empty. It was getting dark. I glanced at my watch. It was almost 6:30 p.m. We had to get home. I spotted the car. Yep, that's it, all right. There it was. The worn seats was evidence we had small children.

I ran as fast as I could across the parking lot. *Please, Lord, let me find my keys.*

I peeked into the window on the driver's side and there they were dangling from my key chain still in the ignition!

I rushed back to the bench to get my kids. There was that girl again signing to David. I wasn't going to be so patient with her this time. I needed to find a metal coat hanger. I just had to get my car door open. My friends in Oakland had taught me a trick with the hanger.

Shirley was signing to David and he was saying, "Yes." My poor son. He will agree to anything.

I smiled as I signed an apology. "We have got to go now." I signed fast to her.

Shirley was speaking to me. And she was not signing now. She said, "David says he wants to come visit me. Here is my address. I live in a group home. In Sacramento."

"Really," I said. "David has an apartment there as I told you earlier. Give me your address. He visited his blind friend Joe this past summer and fell in love with Sacramento. He will be moving there soon." Shirley scribbled her telephone number on a torn piece of white paper.

"Tell David to call me on his TTY unit. I can help him get a job and he can work with me washing dishes at Red Lion Inn right there in Sacramento."

I signed back, "Okay. That's a very good idea. See you later."

I signed into David's hands what she told me.

"I'll make sure that he calls you." David was chuckling as we started walking toward the main gate. "It was nice meeting you," I signed to her as we walked away.

"I am proud of you, Mom. You were very good signing with Shirley," David said.

David then signed, "I am going to move next week to Sacramento. I need to work as a dishwasher with Shirley so that we can get married soon."

And that is what he did too.

David and Shirley are engaged now. They are on a cruise to Barbados as I write this. God is Good! He does answers prayer. This was truly a vision from God.

Earlie

Sydney and Earlie with their children

Mother

Sidney and Earlie, Janie and David in Japan, Avory, Darnell, Darrell & Dominiq, Linda Herring and Me at Eastern Star Function(1974), David singing in Misawa A.B. in Japan, Mother in Japan and John Bess Sr., Lessie, Henry and Mother (1962)

David and Janie,
little David and Terri

My father,
Rev. Lightfoot

Lula at David's
Baptism

Louise,
Immanuel &
Lorrie,

David with Grandma Johnnie

David Swimming

Left & Right: David with his instructors

David learning to use the cane

David skiing

At Hellen Keller National Center for the Blind & Deaf

David (age 21) Enjoys a day at the park

Front Row left to right: David Sr., me, David
Back Row: Terri and Tony

David at age 17

David being interviewed at his job in Fairfield,
Ca. for an article that was published in a local
newspaper. (The Daily Republic News. 1992).
Here he is using the telebrailler.

Little David all grown up and how he looks today

Terri Bess today

Me and my daughter Terri (2003)

Front row left to right: Grandson Lamar, Shirley, Tony Jr., me,
and Grandson Lamont. Middle row: David, Sr. Tony, and Leea,
Lamar, Lamont and Tony Jr. (2004)

David and Shirley when they
first started dating

Tony, Lea, TJ, Lamar, Lamont

CPSIA information can be obtained
at www.ICGtesting.com
Printed in the USA
FSHW02n0048241018
53234FS